Beneath the Fiction

Studies on Cervantes and His Times

Eduardo Urbina
General Editor

Vol. 7

This series is published with the financial support of the Department
of Modern & Classical Languages, Texas A&M University, and
the Centro de Estudios Cervantinos, Alcalá de Henares (Spain).

PETER LANG
New York • Washington, D.C./Baltimore • Boston
Bern • Frankfurt am Main • Berlin • Vienna • Paris

William H. Clamurro

Beneath the Fiction

The Contrary Worlds
of Cervantes's *Novelas ejemplares*

PETER LANG
New York • Washington, D.C./Baltimore • Boston
Bern • Frankfurt am Main • Berlin • Vienna • Paris

Library of Congress Cataloging-in-Publication Data

Clamurro, William H.
Beneath the fiction: the contrary worlds of Cervantes's Novelas ejemplares /
William H. Clamurro.
p. cm. — (Studies on Cervantes and his times; 7)
Includes bibliographical references and index.
1. Cervantes Saavedra, Miguel de, 1547–1616. Novelas ejemplares.
I. Title. II. Series: Studies on Cervantes and his times; vol. 7.
PQ6324.Z5C53   863'.3—dc21   97-11704
ISBN 0-8204-3820-0
ISSN 1054-1403

Die Deutsche Bibliothek-CIP-Einheitsaufnahme

Clamurro, William H.:
Beneath the fiction: the contrary worlds of Cervantes's Novelas ejemplares /
William H. Clamurro. –New York; Washington, D.C./Baltimore; Boston; Bern;
Frankfurt am Main; Berlin; Vienna; Paris: Lang.
(Studies on Cervantes and his times; Vol. 7)
ISBN 0-8204-3820-0 Gb.

Front cover illustration: Julius Komjati, "Sleeping Shepherd," etching, 1926.
Denison University Gallery, Gift of Mrs. George Martin.

The paper in this book meets the guidelines for permanence and durability
of the Committee on Production Guidelines for Book Longevity
of the Council of Library Resources.

Printed in the United States of America.

For Ryan D. Shafer
student and friend

and

In memory of
Ruth El Saffar
and
Philip Clamurro
teachers

Acknowledgments

Chapters One and Eight previously appeared, respectively, in *The Journal of Hispanic Philology* and *Cervantes*, and I would like to thank the editors for permission to reprint these studies in their revised form. Likewise I want to thank the Denison University Art Gallery for permission to reproduce the etching, the "Sleeping Shepherd" by Julius Komjati, used for the cover design; this picture captures the spirit of the complex relationship between reality, reading, and the world of dreams with which the *Novelas ejemplares* will end. A sabbatical leave and the award of an R. C. Good Fellowship from Denison University helped support research for this project during the 1992-93 academic year. Finally, generous support for the publication of this book has been provided by the Centro de Estudios Cervantinos in Alcalá de Henares, Spain, and by the Cervantes Project at Texas A & M University. I wish to express my sincere gratitude to all of these journals and institutions.

Contents

Preface

All books have their subject matter, the main point under discussion; but they also have their external, extra-textual stories. This book is no different. What it announces and attempts to present is an analysis of Cervantes's *Novelas ejemplares*. The chapters that follow take as their basic starting point the notion that each of the *novelas* embodies a vision of the interlocking problems of individual identity and social order. What is explored in each case is unique to the given story and yet coherent with a larger Cervantine vision. The contradictory, problematic nature of the social order as portrayed is often intentionally depicted by Cervantes. But at other times it emerges indirectly, unintentionally revealed, as it were, through the cracks and fissures of language and detail. Our awareness of this complex, double message prompts the application of what I define in the introduction as a picaresque approach to reading.

The ostensible themes and critical concerns, along with the particular analytic perspective employed here, are mainly an attempt at a unified reading. They do not pretend to argue for the deeper, hidden unity of the *Novelas ejemplares* as a work, if such a unifying principle in fact exists. One of the most durable convictions that I bring to my own attempts at reading Cervantes's *Novelas* is the sense that they cannot be reduced into a unifying framework, especially if such unity requires turning a deaf ear to the diversity of these texts or to the lingering ironies within all of them.

To acknowledge this slightly paradoxical and vexing challenge—to find or impute artistic unity while nonetheless granting each text the necessary license to define its own character—brings me to the second or external dimension of this project. As opposed to a previous book, one in which my struggle to make sense out of the style and ideological implications of Quevedo's prose was a solitary and arduous task, this present study is the product of intense and extensive interaction with others. Or to put it another way, if my task with Quevedo's texts was the product of reclusive reading, this commentary on Cervantes's *Novelas* owes as much to dialogue, to the necessary human interactions that define one's life as a teacher or as a scholar who engages his or her colleagues through conferences, exchanges of letters, conversation. The story behind this book, then, is one that owes much more to the teachers, students, and colleagues who have helped, inspired, and challenged me along the way.

I remember and here acknowledge with gratitude certain key moments and important people. My interest in the *Novelas ejemplares* was renewed in early 1977, after reading Ruth El Saffar's *Novel to Romance*. Shortly thereafter I was visiting my former teacher, Juan Bautista Avalle-Arce, and as we walked through the fields on his farm in North Carolina, I mentioned how impressed I was with El Saffar's book but also how I felt it to be ultimately inadequate to the whole of the work. Avalle-Arce remarked that, yes, something always seems to elude our attempts to pull them together, to find the key. Later that same year, I met El Saffar when we found ourselves on the same panel at the MLA Convention in Chicago, thus beginning what was for me a long and inspiring friendship, lasting until her untimely death in 1994. Much of what I would later discover, write about, and try to teach to various groups of students would owe a great deal to Ruth, as much or more to her larger creative approach to reading as to the specifics of her book.

My experiences with my students, meanwhile, have been equally essential to what I finally came to write down. I remember a most excellent, improbable seminar on the *Novelas* that I conducted at St. Mary's College of Maryland; the seven students in that group helped me to see many crucial elements in these texts. Later, another St. Mary's student, Michelle Shewbridge, taught me a lot—and gave me several ideas and much material for my own later researches—with a fascinating paper on "Fainting in the *Novelas ejemplares*." Later, at Denison University, I was fortunate enough to get to teach courses involving Cervantes's works (both the *Quijote* and some of the *Novelas*), and also to direct Senior Honors research projects on Cervantes, from all of which I benefitted a great deal. I would like to thank all of them, and especially acknowledge Elizabeth Papelian, Matthew Clemente, Michael Millar, Laura Blaha, and Adam

Woodruff. Their own Cervantine research strengthened and inspired mine.

I would also like to thank the twenty members of my autumn 1995 Peninsular Literature course. These students patiently and with good humor endured my Quixotic if not neurotic state during what was the most painful and intense final stage of research and writing. They also aided me in bibliographic searches and allowed me to try their patience with my commentaries on the *Novelas*. So, I herewith publicly thank M. Alger, S. Baxter, C. Byrne, S. Chai, S. Chalmers, L. Comparato, A. Crimmins, C. Crummey, M. Doty, L. Gray, B. Hotchkiss, P. R. Lockhart, J. Orzech, L. Rysko, M. Samuel, R. Stinchcomb, D. Swank, S. Trukenbrod, A. Tuyn, and J. Ward.

Many friends and colleagues, at Denison University and elsewhere, have read parts of this book at various stages of its writing and have also made immensely valuable comments on my arguments as well as offering useful suggestions on critical and historical documentation. Among my good friends at Denison, I would like to thank David Goldblatt (Philosophy) and Michael Gordon (History) for their astute comments and references. In the Department of Modern Languages, I owe a debt of gratitude that I can never repay. I thank in particular Judy Cochran, Susan Paun de García, and Eduardo Jaramillo. Above all, I owe a special debt of gratitude to Gary L. Baker, whose patient and level-headed reading of the entire text helped me both conceptually and aesthetically to bring a little order out of chaos. I must also thank most effusively the brilliant, good-natured, and patient help of my colleague in the Denison Academic Computing Center, Charles Reitsma, without whose numerous and timely rescues, I could never have finished the formatting of the text—and might well have gone totally insane. Special thanks are also due to Dr. Jill K. Welch (of the Ohio State Univ.) for her superb proofreading and excellent comments on style and clarity, as this text was nearing completion. For a final proofing and a careful check of all textual citations, I am most grateful to my student Edward S. Knotek, II (Denison 2000), whose eagle eye and cheerful patience helped make this final phase not only tolerable, but even a bit enjoyable.

Beyond Denison's idyllic borders, meanwhile, many other friends and colleagues have most generously given advice, read early drafts, and generally encouraged me, often when I was close to losing heart. In particular, I would like to acknowledge with sincerest gratitude the help and interest of Joan Cammarata and Diana de Armas Wilson. A very special debt of gratitude is owed to Theresa Sears, whose reading of an earlier draft and whose penetrating comments on it greatly helped my thinking. Above all, I would like to thank Eduardo Urbina; his encouragement over many years, his intense interest in this project, and the exemplary readings and editorial comments have been immensely valuable. Finally, I would like to express special thanks to my friend and colleague Henry M. Sayre (Oregon State University), who has encouraged me and greatly influenced my critical development over the course of twenty-five years. Although principally involved in Art History and criticism, and justly recognized for his work in those fields, Henry has helped me through more trials and tribulations of critical aporia and writer's block than I care to recall. Without his decisive help, I doubt that I ever could have pulled this bizarre crazy-quilt of critical commentary together.

Certain names are singled out on the dedication page, and several more are mentioned above. But I owe much gratitude to many others—teachers, students, and friends too numerous to list here. Suffice it to say that this study is dedicated with gratitude to all my teachers, students, and colleagues. Given the depth of my affection and appreciation toward all of them, I fear that this offering is inadequate and unworthy. But I trust that they will all accept the sincerity of my effort and my profound thanks.

Granville, Ohio
May 1997

Introduction: The Contrary Worlds of the *Novelas ejemplares*

Cervantes's *Novelas ejemplares* rival *Don Quijote* for their artistic merit and significance in World Literature. Yet unlike the *Quijote*, the *Persiles y Sigismunda*, or the *Galatea*, the *Novelas* are not a single unified text.[1] The "work" is several works, narratives whose textual diversity engages and ultimately troubles the reader. The superficial simplicity of these stories masks numerous levels of self-critiquing narrative irony and socio-cultural inequity and instability. Given their diversity of action, theme, and form, each individual text challenges the reader in its own way. At the same time, the sequential movement through the entire collection produces a subtle and surprisingly modern—or postmodern—lesson in reading, as we shall learn from a pair of critical dogs. Any one of the twelve (or eleven, depending upon whether one considers the *Casamiento* and the *Coloquio* two *novelas* or only one) is sufficiently rich to merit critical attention in its own right.[2] Ultimately, however, the collection demands to be dealt with as a totality, as a whole. Cervantes himself prompted this urge in the famous passage of the "Prólogo" that teasingly mentions "el sabroso y honesto fruto que se podría sacar, así de todas juntas, como de cada una de por sí" (I, 52).[3] Following from this hint, many critics have sought to find a unified vision or pattern of development in the *Novelas*.[4] But even in the more

---

[1] The *Quijote* can, of course, be dealt with as two separate and distinct texts, as Ruth El Saffar has done in *Beyond Fiction*, see especially the first chapter, 1-15; see also the recent study by Henry W. Sullivan, *Grotesque Purgatory: A Study of Cervantes's* Don Quixote, *Part II*.

[2] A prime example of this would be Alban K. Forcione's *Cervantes and the Mystery of Lawlessness*, a substantial book devoted almost solely to the *Casamiento/Coloquio*. As Forcione's study suggests, meanwhile, the amount of critical attention devoted to the *Novelas* is revealingly uneven, privileging some of the texts over others.

[3] The edition of the *Novelas ejemplares* to which I refer in this study, unless otherwise indicated, is that of Harry Sieber, and all quotations are identified by volume and page number in the text.

[4] See for example J. Casalduero, *Sentido y forma de las* Novelas ejemplares; J.

significant and comprehensive studies of the *Novelas* something always slips away. The formal diversity of the individual *novelas*, and more pointedly the troubling ironies, loose ends, and inequities determined by social rank and cultural inclusion, or exclusion, undermine the validity of the conceptual framework that many critics have imposed.[5] These ironies and counter-messages both challenge and privilege the reader because they determine what I call the doubleness of the narrative rhetoric and the plurality of the complex, self-revealing social worlds of Cervantes's texts.[6] Yet, while some of the major critical works on the *Novelas ejemplares* implicitly recognize this inherent contrariness in the texts,[7] there is, I believe, an ultimate inadequacy in these readings.

The reading demanded by the *novelas* themselves is one built upon a realization of the doubleness and irony produced by the juxtaposition of the illustrative story to the dense, subtle texture of detail and cultural codes of the text. The essential mode of reading that I propose—and that has guided my encounters with the *Novelas ejemplares* for the last fifteen years—considers the story and the implicit or explicit *ejemplo* advanced by Cervantes. But my method

Rodríguez-Luis, *Novedad y ejemplo de las* Novelas *de Cervantes*; El Saffar, *Novel to Romance*; A. Forcione, *Cervantes and the Humanist Vision*.

[5] For instance, the set of categories and the symmetries that Casalduero finds in the published order of the *novelas* has always struck me as ingenious, suspiciously neat, and ultimately unconvincing. See *Sentido y forma de las* Novelas ejemplares, especially 20-28.

[6] I use the terms "doubleness" and "plurality" to refer to quite distinct issues. "Doubleness" refers to the effect of a narrative rhetoric that, as in the picaresque (discussed below), reveals a message distinctly counter to the narrator's ostensible intention; "plurality," by contrast, refers to the codes of connotation, kinds of discourse, cultural detail, locations, and so on, that reveal the inherent ironies of the message. Clearly the latter concept (plurality) contributes to the final effect of the former.

[7] See for example Forcione's suggestion that Cervantes's diversity and creative freedom ought to guide our critical approach: "To the extent that the *Novelas ejemplares* are composed in this deceptive, demanding discourse, their ultimate message may well lie in the freedom with which they dignify their reader and in the example of the creative use of freedom set by their author" (*Cervantes and the Humanist Vision* 29).

entails a reading beneath and beyond the ostensible plot. In effect, it attends to the multiple codes of the language and the peculiarities of a narrative rhetoric that both advances and yet works against the message putatively dramatized by the central action. In this, I am partially in accord with the approach taken by Roland Barthes, especially in his notorious reading of Balzac's *Sarrasine*.[8] While I do not follow his method to the same detailed extent, I believe that Barthes's notion of the classical, "readerly" text applies emphatically to Cervantes's *novelas*—and in fact more appropriately to the *Novelas ejemplares* than to the *Quijote*. As Barthes suggests,

> To interpret a text is not to give it a (more or less justified, more or less free) meaning, but on the contrary to appreciate what *plural* constitutes it. . . . In this ideal text, the networks are many and interact, without any one of them being able to surpass the rest; this text is a galaxy of signifiers, not a structure of signifieds; . . . (5; italics in the original).[9]

Barthes is, of course, writing about the classical, readerly text as exemplified by nineteenth-century realism. But what he says about the nature of that kind of literature is really more pertinently understood as the subtle anatomy of the mode of reading that many seemingly accessible, "transparent" texts determine and require of their readers.

My approach to reading, or decoding, the connotations of Cervantes's "readerly texts" and my focus on the essential plurality

---

[8] *S/Z*; see especially 3-21.

[9] Further on, in comments on his notion of "connotation," Barthes argues that "Functionally, connotation, releasing the double meaning on principle, corrupts the purity of communication: it is a deliberate 'static,' painstakingly elaborated, introduced into the fictive dialogue between author and reader, in short, a countercommunication (Literature is an intentional cacography)" (9). In remarks about ancient prose narratives that are, not surprisingly, most pertinent to the diversity and inner contrariness of the Cervantine *novela*, M. A. Doody notes that "In order to understand the ancient novels we need to know both what happens in them, and how those happenings can be expected to be interpreted by the reader. 'The sufferings of love' is a generalizing phrase, but novels are never abstract, they deal always with particulars, and must aim to get the reader engrossed in specific characters, incidents, descriptions and observations" (*The True Story of the Novel*, 33).

of their language and the doubleness of their narrative rhetoric brings me to an unexpected place: the dynamics of the picaresque narrative and one's approach to reading such texts.[10] The Barthesean sensitivity to connotation, to textual plurality, and to a complex, countercommunicative interweaving of cultural codes is indisputably pertinent to the indirections and contrary motives—the tensions between narrator and author, between overt self-defense and inescapable self-incrimination—that are fundamental to the best-known picaresque texts.[11] The relevance of this connection is well articulated by Friedman:

> As in the exaggerated version of the theme in *Don Quijote*, *Lazarillo de Tormes* illustrates the interdependence of process and product. The reader is privy to Lázaro creating himself, *haciéndose*, both on the page and in conformance with the image he would like to convey. By exposing its seams, so to speak, the text elevates the writer's task, while at the same time it underscores the peculiar rhetoric of the narrator. ("Trials of Discourse" 189)

The contentious and necessarily duplicitous relationship between the known and unknown historical authors and their fictional, "self-confessing" narrators determines a genre that, however multiform it has come to be, is immediately recognizable. It is also a genre that Cervantes himself never chose to explore in the conventional way, by writing a picaresque novel.[12] In none of his texts does Cervantes

---

[10] In this admittedly curious detour from the orthodoxies of Cervantine, *Novelas ejemplares* studies, I am much influenced by the studies collected in the recent book *The Picaresque: Tradition and Displacement*, and also by E. H. Friedman's highly insightful book, *The Antiheroine's Voice: Narrative Discourse and Transformations of the Picaresque*.

[11] In this regard, see Johnson, "Defining the Picaresque," *The Picaresque* (159-82), and Friedman, "Trials of Discourse: Narrative Space in Quevedo's *Buscón*," *The Picaresque* (183-225).

[12] On the complex issue of Cervantes and the picaresque, or the picaresque in Cervantes's fiction, there is a vast bibliography; I mention some of the more pertinent studies in those chapters in which the *novela* in question incorporates or plays with picaresque elements. On Cervantes and the picaresque, see M. Durán, "Picaresque Elements in Cervantes's Works," *The Picaresque* (226-47).

create a picaresque narrator, nor does he follow the pattern of plot suggested by the *Lazarillo* or the *Guzmán de Alfarache*. Rather, the complexity of the fictional worlds rendered in the *Novelas ejemplares*—the tension between a simple story and a counter communication of codes, often woven in as ostensibly subordinate details—subtly turns us into picaresque readers. Thus we are prompted to read with an ear tuned to the contradictions and dissonances that issue forth from the interaction of dramatized example and surrounding social and cultural conflicts.

Largely for this reason—the essentially picaresque doubleness of narrative rhetoric, of narration undermined by the complexity of its own story and by the troublingly ironic details of the *Novelas ejemplares*—the chapters that follow focus on the closely related issues of identity and social order. In fact, in nearly all of the *Novelas ejemplares*, the resolution of problems of lost and found identities and the overcoming of conflicts created by "disturbances" in a given social order form the major thematic component. While the *Novelas ejemplares* are diverse in tone and kind, they nonetheless project a consistent, if complex, view of social order and identity. Cervantes's notion of identity must be understood in both individual and collective terms. What begins as a tension between inner reality or a conception of oneself, on the one hand, and one's social identity (rank, relation to others within a social system, ethnic and cultural inclusion or exclusion, etc.), on the other, often forms the core problem of the story. The conceptions of identity and ideal social order embodied in these stories reflect Cervantes's sense of the validity of inner virtue, even when virtue seems to clash with the socially driven norms of *honra* and *opinión*. At the same time, Cervantes's notion of social order accords with the belief that the hierarchies of social rank reflect not only an ascending order of privilege, but of virtue as well.[13] His view of society and moral-

---

[13] The all but automatic linkage of virtue and beauty with members of the nobility (and in at least one case with the upper levels of the merchant class) prevails,

ity—the essence of the *ejemplos* that his tales dramatize—is conservative and orderly. Clear from the actions of the *novelas* and the many authorial intrusions into the texts, this view is Cervantes's conscious, exemplary message. The totality of the text, however, contains and reveals more. For in each *novela*, the details of action, character, and cultural context uncover the ironies, inequalities, and inconsistencies of the same order that the author affirms.

At this point, the relevance of these two themes to the core question of the language of the *Novelas* should be apparent. Clearly, language is the stuff of fiction. Yet the problem of language—its particular structures and manipulations, the tactics of narrative rhetoric—in the *Novelas ejemplares* is more complex. As in the best-known texts of the picaresque, where language is the key to the problems of identity and social order that prompt the ostensible picaresque confession, the Cervantine *novela* is also based on a narrative rhetoric of doubleness and self-critique. My examination of Cervantes's *Novelas* will show that questions of identity and social order lead us to the core problem of reading, the subject that forms the subtly latent but most crucial concern of the *Casamiento* and *Coloquio*. In questioning and confronting the problems of identity and social order, we perforce question the essential fabric that creates identity and largely regulates social order: language. Language is the material that bridges the gap between the individual (identity) and the group (social order). Our journey through the whole collection will show that the "negative validity" of language consists in its necessity, however deceptive and inadequate it might be as a medium.[14] This is the real miracle, and the real point, of giving

---

especially in those stories of the romance genre or where a "happy marriage" is the evident goal of love and struggle. There are, however, many cases in which the presumed virtue of the (usually male) aristocrat is anything but uncontaminated. Marriage in itself is not a socially hierarchical-dependent institution, but it does reflect the notion of stability and patriarchy that lineage implies and requires, as Sears (*A Marriage of Convenience*) has argued.

[14] Concerning Cervantes's sense of the "negative validity" of language, El Saffar has stated that "Although Cervantes certainly felt intimately drawn to the written word, he appears to have discovered in it finally only a negative validity. That is, that the

language to the dogs in the final text, the *Coloquio de los perros*. By giving them the power to connect to each other and to us, as well as by revealing the irony and the price paid in the always incomplete search for the connectivity of art, the concluding text represents not only Cervantes's most penetrating look at a world of social conflict and corruption, but is also his most subtle and pertinent lesson in reading, his most fascinating illustration of the self-exposing doubleness of narrative.

In the subtitle of this Introduction, I deliberately use the plural—worlds—to emphasize the diversity of these texts. With the use of this term, I also wish to underline the socio-cultural dimension of the *Novelas ejemplares*.[15] The late twentieth-century reader approaches a study of Cervantes's *novelas* with some trepidation. As with any seventeenth-century Spanish text, there is an immense amount of cultural and social context that needs to be part of one's critical equipment. Yet, while we may never understand these texts exactly as Cervantes's first readers did, our distanced cultural and historical perspective provides an ironic advantage. It allows us to see certain ideological and socio-cultural concepts with greater clarity than many of the readers of the Cervantine social and cultural world could have. The paradox of advantage and disadvantage in this sort of reading situation has been well stated by Wolfgang Iser. As Iser suggests,

> The field of action in a literary work tends to be on or just beyond the fringes of the particular thought system prevalent at the time. Literature

---

written word is necessarily that which is not, but it is at the same time the only means by which one can discover that which is. It is surely this final intuition which leads Cervantes, in his later fiction, back into tales of more fantastic content—tales which stretch the concept of verisimilitude to its extreme" (*Novel to Romance*, note 14, 8).

[15] There is also a very real sense in which Cervantes's "worlds" reflect, in several of the *novelas*, a diversity of places and cultures, a geography of identity, and the importance of travel—and travail—in the process of creating, recovering, or losing identity and one's place in the proper social order. On the issue of movement in Cervantes, see especially S. Hutchinson's *Cervantine Journeys*, which has influenced my approach to the *Novelas*.

endeavors to counter the problems produced by the system, and so the literary historian should be able not only to gauge which system was in force at the time of the work's creation but also reconstruct the weaknesses and the historical, human impact of that system and its claims to universal validity. If we wanted to apply Collingwood's question-and-answer logic, we might say that literature answers the questions arising out of the system. Through it, we can reconstruct whatever was concealed or ignored by the philosophy or ideology of the day, precisely because these neutralized or negated aspects of reality form the focal point of the literary work. (*The Act of Reading* 73)[16]

Thus, despite (and in effect aided by) our distanced, limited, and discontemporaneous position, we are able to perceive the structures of ideology and the socio-cultural ideals or values inevitably materialized in the Cervantine text. Read in this light, the *Novelas* are not only exemplary of the values and virtues purportedly championed by Cervantes, the orderly and respectfully conservative beliefs of his time. They also reveal the complex, slightly grim, and perhaps melancholy structures and social prejudices of a most repressed and repressive culture.

But another sort of exemplarity is offered in the prologue. Despite Cervantes's intriguing, and possibly misleading, assertion mentioned previously—concerning the "sabroso y honesto fruto que se podría sacar, así de todas juntas, como de cada una de por sí"—the notion that the text is a free and liberating offering is also clear.[17] The reader's autonomy, the play of imagination and creative engagement are openly invited and inscribed into the work:

Mi intento ha sido poner en la plaza de nuestra república una mesa de trucos, donde cada uno pueda llegar a entretenerse, sin daño de barras;

---

[16] My critical approach is much indebted to Iser's *The Act of Reading: A Theory of Aesthetic Response*. In addition, my more general critical presupposition, i.e., that a text reveals unintended socio-critical elements as well as the intended aesthetic and didactic message, is consistent with my ideological readings of the prose of Quevedo; see *Language and Ideology in the Prose of Quevedo*, especially 154-80, "Quevedo's World as Political Language: Reading *La hora de todos*."
[17] On the rich implications of play and illusion in the *Novelas ejemplares*, see Wardropper, "La eutrapelia en las *Novelas ejemplares*."

> digo sin daño del alma ni del cuerpo, porque los ejercicios honestos y
> agradables, antes aprovechan que dañan. (I, 52)

This metaphor subtly shifts the emphasis from clear, didactic instruction to the meta-ethical sphere, or spheres, of the neutral, morally disinterested, orderly yet unpredictable billiard table. The suggestion that the reader comes to this "table," cue in hand, to try his or her skill, moreover, defines the reader's role as active, autonomous, and creatively implicated.

The *novelas* are instructive—*ejemplares*—but they are also the vehicle or imaginative space of entertainment and, as Cervantes clearly states in a most resonant image, of recreation. In the short paragraph that follows the previous passage, we move from a billiard table to the more ample and amenable space of the garden:

> Sí, que no siempre se está en los templos; no siempre se ocupan los
> oratorios; no siempre se asiste a los negocios, por calificados que sean.
> Horas hay de recreación, donde el afligido espíritu descanse. (I, 52)

Cervantes here gently separates the imaginative ambit of his texts from the more conventional places of the religious and spiritual ("los templos"; "los oratorios") as well as from the necessary distractions of one's livelihood ("los negocios"). The garden is a created space—nature modified—that delights but that has no rigid, morally instructive mission. Recreation here should, I think, be taken to mean the healthful, rejuvenating play to which Cervantes's images of the garden and the billiard table allude. But I would argue that we are also dealing with "re-creation," an act of imaginative remaking. Which is to say, it characterizes our own, necessary activity as readers.

Cervantes does not, however, leave us here, in the possible, pleasant garden of rest, recreation, and relatively autonomous freeplay. Picking up on the possibilities of exemplarity, unity, and ulterior meaning or purpose, the penultimate paragraph saddles the reader with perhaps the most disquieting challenge, or tease, in all of the Cervantine *obra*: "Sólo esto quiero que consideres, que pues yo he tenido osadía de dirigir estas novelas al gran Conde de Lemos, algún misterio tienen escondido que las levanta" (I, 53). The blunt assertion that the *novelas* have some hidden mystery elevating them to a level worthy of the Dedicatee (the Conde de Lemos) puts us in the uncomfortable position of having to decide if this is a true statement, or if it merely represents a gesture of flattery toward the Conde. What would this mystery be? The mystery of a subtly dramatized Christian humanism juxtaposed to visions of lawlessness (that Forcione finds most graphically enacted in the *Coloquio*)?[18] The mystery of a spiritual journey from alienation to acceptance and integration (as El Saffar would have it)?[19] Or perhaps the more mundane, secular mystery of the ultimate rightness and triumph of the consecrated, patriarchal social order (as Sears would argue)?[20]

It strikes me that some of the "mysterious" coherence and unity of the *Novelas ejemplares* is, essentially, Cervantes's belief in the ultimate rightness of the given social order and the orthodox Christian beliefs and values of his epoch. This is openly affirmed in those *novelas* that seem to end happily and is reflexively supported by the cautionary examples of those texts in which a character ends

---

[18] Again, see *Cervantes and the Humanist Vision* and *Cervantes and the Mystery of Lawlessness*.

[19] As El Saffar states, "The development traced in this study is one which reflects Cervantes's emergence beyond despair and alienation in his own life to acceptance of an integrating totality the ultimate truth and perfection of which, though impossible to grasp in human terms, serves to obliterate the distinctions in this life which make such questions as individual vs. society, and truth vs. fiction appear relevant. The larger dialectic in which the later works engage involves man's struggle not with other men or with perceived reality, but with his own salvation" (xiii). *Novel to Romance*, while firmly fixed on the implications of the *Novelas ejemplares*, represents a major effort in the increased appreciation of the "romance" genre and its manifestations in the Cervantine oeuvre. The difficulty with El Saffar's approach is two-fold: first, her theory insists upon the fact that certain texts *had to have been* written before or after others, rather than simply accepting the possibility of periodic alternations between one tendency (realist) and another (idealist). The second problem is more ideological. El Saffar was seeking to find the critical and philosophical bases that would argue for a particular spiritual progression that Cervantes experienced and that, in the life and critical work of El Saffar herself, took on ever greater importance.

[20] See Sears, *A Marriage of Convenience*.

up alone, failed, or ambiguously alienated. But there is nothing especially mysterious about the assertion of a basically conservative, affirmative world view. What is mysterious is the diversity of narrative form and of the worlds represented across the *novelas*, as well as the complexity and irony within each text that express with subtle but troubling efficacy the complex, anti-ideal social and cultural realities in and beyond the text. Cervantes tells us his story and makes his (not always explicit) exemplary point. But in the course of telling the exemplary tale, each *novela* unfolds and opens onto areas often strangely tangential to the main story. In so doing, each *novela* creates or uncovers a world whose details and seemingly minor elements, persons, and actions all work to cast a critical light upon the positive, dominant values of the social order that Cervantes portrays and ostensibly celebrates.

The *novelas* dramatize their respective examples or moral lessons. At the same time they evoke a larger world, with its necessary but often unruly details, the smaller truths of human reality. Our reading of the *Novelas ejemplares*, however, is not only a search for an understanding of what is, or might be, contained in lesson and text. It is also an interaction, an imaginative dialogue. With a slight translation of terms, some of what Adam Phillips has said about psychoanalysis seems apposite to my own conception of the *Novelas ejemplares* and the act of reading:

> Psychoanalysis is a story—and a way of telling stories—that makes some people feel better. But there are, and have been, many stories in the culture and in other cultures through which people examine, and do other things to, their lives. Psychoanalysis—as a form of conversation—is worth having only if it makes our lives more interesting, or funnier, or sadder, or more tormented, or whatever it is about ourselves that we value and want to promote; and especially if it helps us find new things about ourselves that we didn't know we could value.[21]

---

[21] *On Kissing, Tickling, and Being Bored* (4); Phillips's entire "Introduction" is most appropriate to the kind of imaginative literary analysis that will be employed in the chapters to follow.

While Cervantes's *novelas* do not necessarily demand a psychoanalytic perspective, they are nonetheless stories that delight and disturb and to which we return repeatedly with a sense of wonder and curiosity, perplexity, discomfort, or anticipated pleasure. Although in the chapters that follow, my principal interest centers on the problems of identity and social order, certain chapters will confront other issues—madness, the erotic, the question of fiction and metafiction—as demanded by the text in question. I believe that each *novela* instructs us in the subtle shifts that our critical approach must make, and I have tried to respond to the character of each text with that in mind.

The cultural and geographic diversity of the *Novelas ejemplares* is in itself quite striking and, I believe, suggestive. From Spain to the islands of the eastern Mediterranean, from Carrizales's Peru to the England of Ricaredo's family, Cervantes's tales encompass a rich and conflictive human landscape. Quite as much as in the *Quijote* itself, the composite effect of all twelve *novelas* is a dramatization of Spain itself as a cultural community and as an imperial nation. Cervantes's stories repeatedly assert the triumph and rightness of the society's reigning values, even as the presence of, and interaction with, different nationalities and dissident, marginalized social and ethnic groups uncovers the anxiety latent in the efforts of the dominant cultural and social order to prevail. Seen from this perspective, the *Novelas* represent Cervantes's most comprehensive vision of Spain within a larger cultural context.

Finally, I would suggest that my readings of the *Novelas ejemplares* are more the product of creative criticism, or perhaps idiosyncratic textual analysis, than they are works of erudition. Although various historical and critical sources have been consulted, I am more interested in the process and adventure of the act of reading. Clearly, following the traces of the historical and the socio-cultural within the texts, or conversely, studying the historical and cultural contexts surrounding and determining these same texts, is a worthwhile task. For my present purposes, however, I have chosen to focus on the texts themselves, their language, narrative form, and in particular the tensions and contrasts projected by the ironic juxtaposition of an ideal virtue, on one side, and the disorder of the fictional world in which the story unfolds, on the other. Not unlike the unique adventure of reading *Don Quijote*, our encounter with the *Novelas ejemplares* is initially one of intellectual curiosity; we learn about these complexly rendered social and cultural worlds, the contrary worlds of Cervantes's stories. But ultimately this encounter is also a process in which strong, thematically rich, and resistant texts change us, make of us the necessary, adequate readers of these same texts. The adventure of our encounters with, and picaresque readings through, these dissonant worlds, is our own exemplary education.

Chapter One
Value and Identity
La gitanilla

La gitanilla, while perhaps not the most prismatic of all the *Novelas ejemplares*, is one of the most deceptively ironic and, in some ways, troubling of the group.[1] Although the richly developed character of the female protagonist, the *novela*'s happy ending, and the prominent role of poetry within the novelistic frame, all have prompted many critics to read the work as a highly idealized tale or romance, such readings, however plausible and convincingly argued, often simplify this markedly heterogeneous text.[2] Beyond the inevitable narrowings of focus that any act of interpretation requires,[3]

---

[1] In addition to the critical works cited in my subsequent notes, studies that have contributed to my thinking on this text include Juan Bautista Avalle-Arce, "*La gitanilla*," *Cervantes* 1.1 & 2 (1981): 9-17; Ruth S. El Saffar, *Novel to Romance*, 86-108. Among the numerous other studies on the *Novelas ejemplares* in general and on *La gitanilla*, in particular, see especially Peter N. Dunn's "Las *Novelas ejemplares*," in *Suma cervantina*, 81-118, and Julio Rodríguez-Luis, *Novedad y ejemplo de las novelas de Cervantes*, vol. I, 107-41. A recent and suggestive study of *La gitanilla*, emphasizing the sharply ironic implications of the historical situation of the gypsies is found in J. V. Ricapito's *Cervantes's* Novelas Ejemplares: *Between History and Creativity*, 11-37.

[2] The best known exposition of this concept is, of course, given by Northrop Frye in his *Anatomy of Criticism*, especially 33-37; see also Frye's *The Secular Scripture*, especially "The Word and the World of Man," 3-31. Ruth El Saffar (*Novel to Romance*) was one of the first to apply the term to certain of the *Novelas ejemplares*, and since then, the concept has been used broadly, if divergently and critically (e.g., by Forcione, as noted below, and others), in discussions of "La gitanilla."

[3] Along with the very sensitive reading proposed by Alban K. Forcione in his *Cervantes and the Humanist Vision*, which for the most part is of the idealizing sort, see S. F. Boyd, "The Mystery of Cervantes' *La gitanilla*," *Forum for Modern Language Studies* 17.4: 312-21; Balbino Marcos, "Un exponente ideal de exaltación femenina: *La gitanilla*," *Letras de Deusto* 1985, 15.33: 95-111; Joseph B. Spieker, "Preciosa y poesía (Sobre el concepto cervantino de la Poesía y la estructura de *La gitanilla*)," *Explicación de Textos Literarios* 4.2: 213-20; and Karl-Ludwig Selig, "Concerning the Structure of Cervantes' *La gitanilla*," in *Die Romanische Novelle*, 214-19. For perhaps the most ingenious reading of this *novela* and its title character, see G. Camamis, "The Concept of Venus-*Humanitas* in Cervantes and Botticelli," *Cervantes* 8.2 (1988): 183-223.

I would suggest that, despite the notable critical consensus that tends to see this *novela* as approaching the romance, *La gitanilla* is precisely interesting for the ways in which it subverts many of the romance genre's expectations. Most readings informed by an interest in the romance genre choose to ignore these dissonant elements and, instead, fix on the obvious problem of the trial and purification of love—a classic romance theme. Given such a perspective, all too much of the "untidy detail" of the story is passed over in haste. But, as E. Michael Gerli has pointed out, this *novela* includes numerous seemingly digressive or secondary episodes, problems, and issues that complicate and ironically undermine the pure idealism supposedly embodied by the main characters, an idealism that is often presented as the dominant feature of the text.[4] In fact, it is the anti-ideal that infuses and gives a special quality to this *novela*. Moreover, as I will show, the presence of these dissonances and subversions in the text makes *La gitanilla* especially revealing of the harsh, this-worldly social structures and values that lie at the heart of this deceptively complex text.[5]

---

[4] See E. Michael Gerli, "Idealism and Irony in *La Gitanilla*," *Cervantes* 6.1 (1986): 29-38. Gerli later develops this critical perspective further in "A Novel Rewriting: Romance and Irony in *La gitanilla*," *Refiguring Authority: Reading, Writing, and Rewriting in Cervantes*, concluding in part that "In *La gitanilla* the plots, characters, landscape, and motifs of romance are ironically interlaced and subverted through contrast with a subtly crafted vision of a cynical world presided over by the type of petty passion, abuse of privilege, and prosaic venality we associate with the indeterminate universe of the novel. . . . It is, in fact, a complex work of 'pluriregional' narrative art—to use Martínez Bonati's valuable notion—built upon the interaction of irony and idealism, of reality and fantasy, of novel and romance" (38-39). On the ironies and somehow accepted implausibilities of this *novela*, see also R. M. Price, "Cervantes and the topic of the 'lost child found' in the *Novelas ejemplares*," *Anales Cervantinos* 27 (1989): 203-14, especially 206-09. A most thorough and ingenious reading of the complex and sometimes evidently contradictory implications of this text is to be found in R. ter Horst, "Une Saison en enfer: *La gitanilla*," *Cervantes* 5.1 (1985): 87-127.

[5] On this issue of thematic and ideological complexity, see A. Weber, "Pentimento: The Parodic Text of 'La gitanilla'," *HR* 62.1 (1994): 59-75; as Weber suggests, "While it is undeniable that humanist treatises such as these [e.g., Fray Luis de León's *La perfecta casada*] constitute significant intertexts for 'La gitanilla,' it does not

The central argument of this chapter could be summed up as follows: in the *Novelas ejemplares* Cervantes defends and affirms an orderly world grounded upon essentially humanistic yet aristocratic values. At the same time, however, the complex and heterogeneous text that endeavors to represent this idealized world continually and inevitably reveals its own contradictions—contradictions that are, in turn, the contingent products of the dissonances within the social reality of Cervantes's time.[6] Viewed from this sociocritical perspective, *La gitanilla* is an especially telling case in which to explore the fundamental questions of personal identity and social order that are crucial throughout the *Novelas*. To illustrate this conception of the *Novelas*, the first thematic element to be considered is Cervantes's use of money and exchanges. The choice of these elements reflects my belief that, in the interactions of personal identity and social order, not only in *La gitanilla* but in many of the *Novelas ejemplares*, money frequently serves as a language that speaks about identity and social order, usually connecting the two.[7] But while money takes on a linguistic function in this *novela*, language itself and the peculiar interplay of kinds and levels of language are also central to the exploration of identity and order. Thus, focussing on an instance of the inclusion of poetry, I consider the role of language—or languages—within the text and how the interplay of discourses contributes to the exploration of the questions of order and identity. Finally, combining these observations on the function of money and

necessarily follow that Cervantes reproduced uncritically the doctrinal content and didactic aim of these works. On the contrary, 'La gitanilla' evinces a conflict of discourses—one irreverent and parodic, the other reverential and exemplary—that reflects Cervantes' ambivalent response to the humanist ideology embodied in female conduct books" (60).

[6] This critical approach is much indebted to the conceptions of novelistic discourse proposed by Mikhail M. Bakhtin; see especially Bakhtin's "Discourse in the Novel," *The Dialogic Imagination*, 259-422.

[7] In addition to the provocative though brief treatment of this aspect of the *Novelas ejemplares* in Sieber's introductions, two excellent studies of the question are Javier Herrero's "Emerging Realism: Love and Cash in *La ilustre fregona*," *From Dante to García Márquez*, 47-59; and Carroll B. Johnson's "*La española inglesa* and the Practice of Literary Production," *Viator* 19 (1988): 377-416.

on the uses of language, I suggest a reconsideration of Preciosa, one that takes into account the subtle and not-so-subtle inconsistencies and dissonances of what she says and does, as well as what is said and done to her in the *novela*.

I. Value and Identity

Along with the various romanticized symbolic values imputed to her, Preciosa and her story combine the ironically fortunate resolution of her problem (ironic in that her return to her proper place requires the apparent loss of her autonomy and free spirit), with the subtly destabilizing effects of money, wherein money is presented both as an object desired in and for itself and also as a symbol of exchange.[8] Consider, for example, the specific attention given to money and how this emphasis affects the narrative structure of the *novela*. Before don Juan de Cárcamo/Andrés Caballero (the necessary other half of the "love interest") even enters the story, nearly a third of the text is devoted to the quest for cash, specifically a series of episodes involving Preciosa and the activities of the gypsies. Throughout the story, moreover, money and other objects of material value appear at moments of narrative importance. In particular, there are two scenes early on in the *novela* in which money enters as a central element. The first instance is Preciosa's brief stop at the house where several idle *caballeros* are gambling. Here, the surplus of money reflects—and underlines—the ambiguous and perceptibly decadent moral nature of this privileged and supposedly honorable aristocratic class. This scene is quickly followed, and sharply contrasted, by Preciosa's visit to the home of a local government official, the *teniente*, ostensibly to read his wife's fortune. In this

---

[8] As Harry Sieber has noted in his introductory notes, money and the details of financial transactions form a kind of *leitmotif* that runs through several of the *Novelas ejemplares*; see his remarks on *La gitanilla* (20-22) and on *La española inglesa* (28-30).

second episode, the embarrassing lack of money both provokes
Preciosa's surprisingly cynical satiric comment on morality in politics
and government, and also places the *teniente* and his wife, doña
Clara, in terms of their clearly identified yet problematic position
within the larger social order. In the fruitless search of the man and
his wife for even the smallest coin with which to pay the gypsies, we
see comically dramatized the irony of the fact that personal virtue
is—at least here—quite unconnected to material wealth and that the
teniente's nominal civil authority has little to do with his real
economic power.[9]

Throughout the *novela*, money has a variety of functions, both as
plot device and as part of a carefully crafted allusive language. As
a determinant of actions, for example, money and the getting of it are
a major motivation for the gypsies. In a subtly contrasting narrative
usage, money is also a device that creates a certain freedom and aids
in the maintenance of disguise. Specifically, the money that don Juan
brings with him allows him, when he becomes Andrés the gypsy, to
placate his new companions by purchasing items that he can then
claim to have stolen. Money thus saves him from having to stain his
noble nature by actually stealing. In this particular instance, don
Juan's money assures and protects of his virtue, while at the same
time it buys for him a necessary part of his, or Andrés's, gypsy
identity: his activity as a thief, something expected and demanded of
him by his new society. Finally, in a very different situation, in
which objects of wealth are used as a plot device, near the end of the
novela, the rejected Juana Carducha plants some of her jewels in
Andrés's bags. This action and the objects involved are crucial to the
dénouement, for the discovery of the jewels provokes the youth's
arrest, which in turn leads to his impulsive killing of the insolent

---

[9] See especially the interaction between Preciosa and the *teniente* (I, 81-82).
Preciosa's sardonic advice—that the official take bribes ("Coheche vuesa merced,
señor tiniente; coheche, y tendrá dineros, y no haga usos nuevos, que morirá de
hambre" [I, 81])—underscores this irony as it also subtly questions a certain aspect
of the social order.

soldier and thus to the necessary crisis and fortunate revelations of the *novela*'s conclusion.

But money is not merely a versatile and convenient narrative device in *La gitanilla*. As in our own (non-fiction) world, money is also a language: both a vocabulary and a vehicle or device of exchange and connection.[10] It is therefore not surprising to find that, in *La gitanilla*, much of the exchanging of money for other things is involved with acts of conversation—though at times in ways that produce ambiguity rather than clarification. Moreover, the main connecting point amid all these concerns—wealth, money, and language—is the female protagonist. With regard to the symbolic function of money and wealth, for no other character of the story are these terms so extensively employed as they are for Preciosa.[11] As her name signals, she is the valuable and valued person (or object). This value is not only attached to her physical beauty, a conventional and necessary element of the romance, but is also linked to her skill as an earner of income for the gypsy band. This latter meaning is clearly projected, particularly in those passages revealing how Preciosa is viewed by her gypsy grandmother. In the opening description of the girl, the narrator states "Y, finalmente, la abuela conoció el tesoro que en la nieta tenía, y así, determinó el águila vieja sacar a volar su aguilucho y enseñarle a vivir por sus uñas" (I, 62)—a rather misleading comment, since Preciosa pointedly does not engage in the normal gypsy activity of stealing. Rather, it is her skill in song and dance that proves profitable; as the narrator puts it: "Porque su taimada abuela echó de ver que tales juguetes y gracias, en los pocos años y en la mucha hermosura de su nieta, habían de ser

---

[10] On the implications of money, and specifically the coins, in *La gitanilla*, see ter Horst, "Une Saison en enfer," especially 117-22.

[11] Concerning the implications of the word (*preciosa*) itself, it is interesting that Covarrubias merely gives "Lo muy estimado; algunas vezes vale tanto como gracioso" (*Tesoro de la lengua castellana o española*, 879). *Autoridades* repeats this central idea—"Excelente, exquisito, y digno de estimación y aprecio" and adds: "Significa tambien chistóso, festívo, decidór, agúdo, agradable y gustoso" (*Diccionario de Autoridades*, Tomo Quinto, 348).

felicísimos atractivos e incentivos para acrecentar su caudal" (I, 62). Above and beyond the obvious point that the *abuela* sees Preciosa's talent and beauty as effective economic tools, the allusion to profitability in these passages reminds us that the young girl is constantly engaged in lively yet wittily ambiguous communication, or commerce, with the social worlds around her.

In *La gitanilla*, money talks. It talks in the sense that, among other things, it functions as a symbolic supplement to the words with which men, especially Clemente (the *paje-poeta*) and don Juan, speak to Preciosa. The actual implications of money can, however, be confusing. The careful reader has probably been struck by a sense that there is something just a bit strange—and perhaps crass—about the *paje-poeta*'s practice of enclosing a gold coin in the folded paper of the poems that he gives to the gypsy girl. After the first such gift, one of the gambling *caballeros* boldly snatches the paper from Preciosa and discovers the coin: "Abrió el caballero el papel y vio que venía dentro dél un escudo de oro"; he then remarks that "En verdad, Preciosa, que trae esta carta el porte dentro: toma este escudo que en el romance viene" (I, 73). To which her witty reply is, in part,

> Pues cierto que es más milagro darme a mí un poeta un escudo que yo recebirle; si con esta añadidura han de venir sus romances, traslade todo el *Romancero general*, y envíemelos uno a uno, que yo les tentaré el pulso, y si vinieren duros, seré yo blanda en recebillos. (I, 73-74)

What is striking about this passage is that, although surprised, Preciosa seems hardly embarrassed by any mercenary overtones that the message might include. Her nonchalant acceptance of the coin, moreover, is surprisingly more in keeping with the values of the gypsy that she is not than with the generous-spirited woman that she dimly senses she is, or the aristocrat that she will turn out to be. The curious inconsistency of this acceptance of the money is emphasized by the fact that, when the *paje-poeta* gives her a second poem-wrapped *escudo*, she immediately returns the coin, thereby prompting us to wonder what her acceptance of the first coin was meant to imply.

Part of the meaning of money in the initial episodes of *La gitanilla* seems to be that Preciosa—in her usual indifference to it—is basically unlike her gypsy brothers and sisters, that she holds to a higher, or perhaps we should say more aristocratic, moral standard. At the same time, with regard to the men giving it, money is both the honorific expression of the high value that they attribute to Preciosa and is also part of an inevitably ambiguous expression of desire. For, while idealization may be the surface tendency of the text, one cannot avoid the contingent and troubling moral ambiguity. Although for the men these generous gestures and the tokens involved (the coins) may be ideally both an intensifier and an objectification of their purer sentiments, the latent suggestion of the devaluing objectification of women and of the "commerce" with them—i.e., prostitution—persists and works to undermine the idealism and simplicity of the message.

An equally significant instance of money as language attends the entrance of don Juan de Cárcamo (renamed Andrés Caballero with his initiation into the gypsy society) into the narrative. Of special importance is don Juan's opening speech, in which he first declares his love for Preciosa and then identifies himself in terms of family background and also in more general terms of social rank and material wealth. Here the uniquely individual and sentimental elements of character are presented as being closely connected with specifically *material* details of social identity. For example, after his opening words ("Yo vengo de manera rendido a la discreción y belleza de Preciosa"), don Juan presents himself in bluntly social and material terms:

> Yo, señoras mías . . . soy caballero . . .; soy hijo de Fulano . . .; soy hijo
> único, y el que espera un razonable mayorazgo. . . . Y con ser de la
> calidad y nobleza que os he referido, y de la que casi se os debe ya de ir
> trasluciendo, con todo eso, quisiera ser un gran señor para levantar a mi
> grandeza la humildad de Preciosa. (I, 83-84)

The youth's introduction then concludes with the following: "Cien escudos traigo aquí en oro para daros en arra y señal de lo que pienso daros; porque no ha de negar la hacienda el que da el alma"

(I, 84). Don Juan is, of course, simply making his case, identifying himself and trying to stress how worthy he is of this beautiful woman who, despite her most improbable social rank, has won his heart. But the materialization of the youth's sentiments and the pointedly material terms given to his unique identity seem a bit superfluous—and thus, paradoxically, even more significant. In this passage, and throughout the *novela*, then, money functions as a significant yet ambiguous element of the expression of both sentiment and identity. Part of what informs its potent ambiguities, moreover, is the inescapable, if at times indirect, reminder of where it comes from and what the getting and having of it says about the social role of its possessor.

Preciosa's reply to this declaration of love and marriage proposal (I, 84-87) includes, among other things, her laying down of the terms and conditions for testing the youth's sincerity. It also allows her to reiterate her tellingly unconventional concept of female autonomy, a concept that the "happy ending" of the *novela* will dramatically reject. But within its narrative moment, and given the idealizing tendencies and narrative exigencies of the story, an improbable and quite romanticized female power is operative. Thus, for the enamored don Juan, Preciosa's word is law. Yet even in the midst of the warm if arbitrary and improbable fantasies of the romance genre, Cervantes's text continues to incorporate the heterogeneous realities of an unromantic and in fact threatening world. For example, with regard to the monetary part of don Juan's proposal—his "earnest money," as it were—Preciosa herself is overruled by her gypsy grandmother when the girl tries to reject the offered gold. The old woman's motives are emphatically practical and they explicitly reveal the social and cultural conflicts that the gypsies encounter in their dealings with mainstream Spanish society. Significantly, the woman's first argument for keeping the money elaborates upon the concept of money as language, introducing another telling metaphor when she states that "la mejor señal que este señor ha dado de estar rendido es haber entregado las armas en señal de rendimiento" (I, 88). The socially charged image of money as weapon is repeated later in one of the several remarks by the *gitana vieja* concerning the usefulness of money as a way of buying favor and clemency from the officers of the law: "Mira, niña, que andamos en oficio muy peligroso y lleno de tropiezos y de ocasiones forzosas, y no hay defensas que más presto nos amparen y socorran como las armas invencibles del gran Filipo . . ." (I, 88). In short, the efficacious signifiers of love and sincerity can very well, as the old woman knows, speak in other contexts and for other ends.

To return to my initial argument, then, money is a subtle, complex, and powerful language in *La gitanilla*. Coins and other objects of material value operate in the text as *signifiers* (tokens of respect, love, social prestige, etc.) and also as *signifieds* (wealth as object, in and for itself). In addition, the various moments of the *novela* when money enters prominently are also usually instances in which there is a problem of identity: either a question of personal identity (e.g., the *paje-poeta*'s, or don Juan's initial effort to document his own, or his misapprehension of Preciosa's true identity), or a deliberate problematizing of social position and rank (as in the case of the gambling gentlemen or that of the *teniente*). As I have argued, moreover, the linguistic function of money in this *novela* is often less to clarify and affirm than it is to add ironic resonance to the ostensible and assumed representation of ideal virtue or conventional social order.

II. Language: The Role of Poetry

What makes the whole question of money and its implications in *La gitanilla* particularly dissonant and thematically important is the complex juxtaposition of money as language to the other, more obvious languages of idealization that surround Preciosa and that take on special force in certain moments of the text. If, as I have noted, money and objects of value may be seen to function as one kind of language in this *novela*, then the more conventional manifestations of language must also be considered.[12] While *La gitanilla* is very much a heterogeneous weaving of various kinds of discourse, one of the most prominent, most idealized, and most problematic languages of the *novela* is the language of poetry.[13] As has been pointed out by K. L. Selig and others, Preciosa is not only a performer, a user of poetry, but in fact can be seen as an embodiment of the art.[14] This is to say that, partly as a result of the special and repeated emphasis given to her physical beauty and to her performative skill, she comes to seem an earthly version of the muse.

The narrative or allusive functions and implications of each specific poetic interlude in the text have been variously commented upon, perhaps most ingeniously by Forcione.[15] But at least two

---

[12] With regard to the numerous levels of ambiguity in the languages of *La gitanilla* and to the consequences of this discursive complexity, see Lesley Lipson, "'La palabra hecha nada': Mendacious Discourse in *La gitanilla*," *Cervantes* 9.1 (1989): 35-53. As Lipson states, "In *La gitanilla* it is the validity of the spoken word that is constantly doubted and questioned and the potential ambiguity in everyday discourse is brought into vivid relief" (48). Concerning the role of poetry in this *novela*, Lipson notes that "The imposing presence of poetry provides another essential layer of ambiguity to confuse the issue of identities, relationships and true meanings. The tale does not, as is implied by Forcione in his *Cervantes, Aristotle and the Persiles*, link poetry, Clemente and the Cervantine artist in general with criminality. It rather divulges a broader principle—that of multivalence and complexity in the disarmingly simple act of speech. While the old gypsy would unflinchingly exchange a yes for a no, controlling this arbitrary use of language and meaning is Preciosa's literary raison d'être" (48). On the role of poetry, see also M. Joly, "En torno a las antologías poéticas de *La gitanilla* y *La ilustre fregona*," *Cervantes* 13.2 (1993): 5-15.

[13] This particular aspect of the *novela*, as both theme and as structural element, has been much studied; see especially Forcione, 215-22; see also Karl-Ludwig Selig, "Concerning the Structure of Cervantes' *La Gitanilla*"; and Georges Güntert, "*La gitanilla* y la poética de Cervantes," *Boletín de la Real Academia Española* 52 (1972): 107-34.

[14] See Karl-Ludwig Selig, "Concerning the Structure of Cervantes' *La gitanilla*"; see also Joseph B. Spieker, "Preciosa y poesía (Sobre el concepto cervantino de la poesía y la estructura de *La gitanilla*)" and Georges Güntert, "*La gitanilla* y la poética de Cervantes."

[15] See *Cervantes and the Humanist Vision*, not only the section entitled "Preciosa and the Theme of Poetry" (215-22), but also the sensitive and enlightening reading of the poem in praise of Margarita of Austria, "Margarita of Austria and the Redemption

features of the direct intercalations of poetry as language into the text strike me as needing special comment in light of the issue of identity: first, the notably static nature of the scenes where the poetry is recited, and second, the peculiar role of the shadowy figure Clemente (the *paje-poeta*) in his relation to the poetry and to Preciosa and don Juan.[16] The several poems included in the *novela* display a variety of forms and thematic intentions, from the allegorical celebration of the royal family, to Preciosa's therapeutic incantation that restores don Juan from a moment of near-fainting brought on by the boy's jealousy. But at least four of the poems concern Preciosa herself: the two poems given to her by Clemente and the poems that make up the musical dialogue in the penultimate section of the *novela*, the interlocking *silvas* of Andrés and Clemente, followed by Preciosa's reply, in *redondillas*.

The scene in which this latter poetic interchange takes place occurs near the end of the *novela* (I, 119-21), and of all the inclusions of verse, this particular moment is the most static, removed from the pace and the other language(s) of the *novela*. Moreover, it evokes—as much by its setting and the disposition of the characters as by the language itself—the mood and expectations of the pastoral tradition more than any other part of this *novela* (or of any of the other *Novelas*

---

of Spain" (208-15).

[16] It is worth noting that he appears and reappears through the story in at least two different guises and that he names and renames himself, explains and reexplains his "story," in ways that profoundly but subtly undermine the reader's sense of truth—the "full disclosure" problem. Consider for example the question of his name: when he first gives any name at all, the night that he is found by the gypsies, he first calls himself Alonso Hurtado (I, 111). But this name is evidently as concocted as his first *historia*, concerning why he was traveling alone and where he was going. Later he calls himself "don Sancho" and finally the gypsies rename him "Clemente" (I, 117). At no point, however, does the text quite establish a convincing sense of credibility concerning this character and what he says; it is as if his main function within the text were a sort of subversion of narrative certainty as such. For a provocative and insightful commentary on the problem of this figure's identity and his narrative function, see L. Lipson, "'La palabra hecha nada': Mendacious Discourse in *La gitanilla*," especially 40-45.

ejemplares, for that matter).[17] As the narrator introduces it, we find an all-too-conventional scene:

> Sucedió, pues, que estando el aduar alojado en un valle cuatro leguas de Murcia, una noche, por entretenerse, sentados los dos, Andrés al pie de un alcornoque, Clemente al de una encina, cada uno con una guitarra, convidados del silencio de la noche, comenzando Andrés y respondiendo Clemente, cantaron estos versos . . . (I, 119)

What follows is a dialogue of alternating *silvas*, ostensibly in praise of the beauty and virtue of Preciosa. But it is also—as one would expect in the language of the pastoral—an implicit celebration of the autonomous beauty of a certain kind of language, of a certain way of seeing and ordering reality. The first of the strophes, sung by Andrés, clearly suggests this more comprehensive idealization:

> Mira, Clemente, el estrellado velo
> con que esta noche fría
> compite con el día,
> de luces bellas adornando el cielo;
> y en esta semejanza,
> si tanto tu divino ingenio alcanza,
> aquel rostro figura
> donde asiste el extremo de hermosura. (I, 119)

Clemente replies, repeating Andrés's final line, by bringing the woman into the now established context of extra-ordinary beauty and value. He does so in part by means of a phrasing that subtly and completely integrates the girl's name, returning it, through the grammar of the passage, to its adjectival essence even as it maintains its nominal sense, thus immediately signaling the woman herself as well:

> Donde asiste el extremo de hermosura
> y adonde la Preciosa
> honestidad hermosa

---

[17] On the pastoral in general, see Thomas G. Rosenmeyer, *The Green Cabinet: Theocritus and the European Pastoral Lyric*, and with special relevance to the pastoral-musical episode of the *La gitanilla*, see chapter 7, "The Music," 145-67.

con todo extremo de bondad se apura, . . . (I, 119)

This dialogue or pastoral duet of the two men effects an enumeration and exaltation of Preciosa's qualities. But it goes beyond the merely physical and adds to her virtues a transcendent level of power and influence. The woman becomes the bringer of harmonies in a higher sense, as Clemente's lines indicate:

cuando el son de su nombre allá se oyera,
y en la tierra causara,
por donde el dulce nombre resonara,
música en los oídos
paz en las almas, gloria en los sentidos. (I, 120)

Finally, Preciosa is rendered by this poetic dialogue the embodiment of an ideal, as the concluding strophe (interestingly enough, sung by Clemente) makes clear in its summation of her qualities—which is to say, her meaning:

Corona del donaire, honor del brío
eres, bella gitana,
frescor de la mañana,
céfiro blando en el ardiente estío;
rayo con que Amor ciego
convierte el pecho más de nieve en fuego;
fuerza que ansí la hace,
que blandamente mata y satisface. (I, 120)

If we focus primarily upon the woman being praised, what this passage creates is the not unexpected reiteration of the idealization that, in several different contexts and languages, has already occurred. But also noteworthy in regard to the two men singing this highly conventional encomium, is the suggestion that here as elsewhere we encounter a subtle attenuation of the distinction between the two young men. In the act of poetry, and perhaps through the power of poetry, the mysterious Clemente and the temporary gypsy Andrés become a single voice, almost a fusion of the two characters. This, in turn, suggests another possible reading of the function of this shadowy figure, given that Clemente and his true sentiments toward Preciosa are never explained satisfactorily.

When he first appears in the story, he seems to be in love with her. Later, when he reappears, in disguise, at the gypsy camp, he confesses that he in fact never was in love, and rather than seeking the girl, he is fleeing a problem with the legal authorities. Finally Clemente simply and unceremoniously disappears from the story.

What the interaction of don Juan and Clemente—and in fact of all three, including Preciosa—suggests is that the *paje-poeta* is less a rival or significant separate character than he is a source of lyricism and an amplification of the male protagonist, don Juan. Considered from this more poetic perspective, Clemente provides a complementary aspect of don Juan himself. Such an interpretation is supported by the effect of this peculiar pastoral moment, the way in which poetry, and especially this sort of poetry, redefines the locus and verisimilitude of sentiments, from the fictive and personal to a more penetrating but more transpersonal level. Finally, this reading of Clemente accords with his progressive diminishment as a separate person, his subtle integration into the *persona* of don Juan. This poetic solution to Clemente's identity problem (concerning his representational and narrative functions) does not fully answer the question, of course. As is so prevalent throughout the *Novelas ejemplares*, an identity like Clemente's remains symbolic of subtly irresolvable questions. We are reminded that identity in general often eludes easy comprehension.

Preciosa's reply to the song of Andrés and Clemente, however, tends to break the spell, not only in its formal and stylistic shifts to *redondillas* and to a more material, less conventional or idealizing register of language, but also in its return to the theme with which Preciosa has previously established her concept of herself: the idea that her virtue and integrity are more important to her than beauty, wealth, or position. Her insistence that "por mayor ventura tengo / ser honesta que hermosa," while quite conventional and in fact praiseworthy, seems also, in its directness and simplicity, to reject a certain excess of the idealism that the foregoing pastoral discourse implicitly affirms. The imagery of her third strophe, meanwhile, not only dramatizes by its concreteness the statement about sincerity and humility that Preciosa's poem is trying to make, but also evokes once again the complex suggestive possibilities of coins, money, and the ironic fact that this woman will prove to be not who or what she seems:

> En este mi bajo cobre,
> siendo honestidad su esmalte,
> no hay buen deseo que falte
> ni riqueza que no sobre. (I, 121)

Preciosa's argument for primacy of inner worth and for the fact that chastity and virtue ("honestidad") are sufficient to ennoble a humble subject (the "bajo cobre") is very much a moral commonplace. But it is ironically significant within the larger thematic context of *La gitanilla*, given the central fact that she will turn out to be anything but "bajo cobre." The suggestion of *cobre*, moreover, which immediately evokes the notion of a coin of lowest value, contrasts with the gold *escudos* that earlier in the *novela* were given to Preciosa and also with the "cadenas de oro" (I, 133)—a conventional symbol of marriage and also an emblem of noble rank—that will adorn the ending of the story. The effect of these allusions is in part a subtle reminder of the ironies of her identity (and by extension, the identities of the others), as well as of the harsh and conflictive social and material realities found in the world through which the gypsies, Preciosa, and don Juan variously navigate.

Preciosa's song repeats and suggestively echoes her earlier arguments concerning the importance of virtue, the power or prerogatives of inner and outer beauty, and the inherent equality of each and every person, where the purity and worth of the soul are concerned. Her presentation of these concepts is not unfamiliar, given the possibilities of the pastoral world. But the particular phrasing of the arguments is tellingly provisional and incomplete, as we find in the final strophes:

> Quiero ver si la belleza
> tiene tal prer[r]ogativa,
> que me encumbre tan arriba,
> que aspire a mayor alteza.

> Si las almas son iguales,
> podrá la de un labrador
> igualarse por valor
> con las que son imperiales.
> De la mía lo que siento
> me sube al grado mayor,
> porque majestad y amor
> no tienen un mismo asiento. (I, 121)

Throughout Preciosa's poem we hear echoes of other Cervantine texts, and in particular we are reminded of Dorotea's pleading to don Fernando in Chapter XXXVI of *Don Quijote*, Part I.[18] The arguments—e.g., on the primacy of true inner virtue, on the essential equality of souls, and so on—are, and are meant to be, convincing in their own right. But although Preciosa is to an extent correct that "majestad y amor / no tienen un mismo asiento," she in fact does not fully know herself, for the "mayor alteza" to which she questions the possibility of rising is something that she already possesses.

The function of poetry, then, in *La gitanilla* (while it works toward a variety of ends) involves the evident intention to create idealizing digressions and expansions. In this light, and especially in its most elegant manifestations, it seems quite disharmonious with the more realistic and sometimes satiric registers of language used by Preciosa herself and by others in the earlier sections of the *novela*. Similarly, the poetic interludes, considered in the context of the narrative flow of the action or in light of the hypothetical exigencies of characterization, seem relatively static, largely decorative, and non-essential. Yet, seen from another perspective, the performance of poetry is a vital

---

[18] In Dorotea's rather long speech to don Fernando, she confronts the "class distinction" problem—which in fact does exist, Dorotea being no lost or disguised noblewoman but rather the daughter of a wealthy farmer—with the following argument: "Y si te parece que has de aniquilar tu sangre por mezclarla con la mía, considera que pocas o ninguna nobleza hay en el mundo que no haya corrido por este camino, y que la que se toma de las mujeres no es la que hace al caso en las ilustres decendencias; cuanto más, que *la verdadera nobleza consiste en la virtud*, y si ésta a ti te falta negándome lo que tan justamente me debes, yo quedaré con más ventajas de noble que las que tú tienes" (*Don Quijote*, I, 443; emphasis added).

part of what Preciosa is or is made to represent. It is one of her prime talents, and to the extent that the ennobling of the young woman, in the early part of the *novela*, is central to the story, the presence of this ennobled and higher form of language has signifi-cant consequences. Just as Preciosa—with her extraordinary physical beauty, in implicit contrast to that of the other gypsy women as well as to the rest of womankind, and in her distinctly different, non-gypsy moral values and behavior—is set apart from her contingent world, so too does the poetic language that she on occasion com-mands set itself aside from and contrast with the other levels and kinds of discourse—some of them her own—of the text.

III. Identity through Restoration and Loss

The complexities of change and exchange, of money and what it talks about, of the language of poetry and what it ideally affirms as well as what it ironically undermines, all come together in the person and problem of the lost and recovered woman, Preciosa—or more correctly Constanza. It is curious that the *novela*'s happy ending, involving the restoration of the girl to her true family and the resolution of don Juan's problem with the law (his murder of the insolent soldier), produces, or requires, Preciosa's submissive renunciation of her verbal and personal freedom. The conventional and somewhat melodramatic *anagnorisis* (I, 125ff) can be understood as the simple return of the lost child to her true parents and thus as a resolution with a certain thematic and sentimental rightness to it. In this light, the young woman's sudden and uncharacteristic submissiveness is simply a result of her own recognition of identity and her realization of the fact that she now belongs to a new world. At the same time, on a more broadly sociocritical level and in terms of the deeply embedded narrative and structural contrasts of the *novela*, the restoration scene and Preciosa's behavior from this point forward seem to be of a piece with the underlying system of contrasts, subversions, and dissonances that penetrates the text. We

have here in these concluding scenes not only the return of Preciosa
to her proper aristocratic place, but also another intensification of the
clash and contrast between social realms and the ironic inconsistencies of supposedly respectable, aristocratic values.   Preciosa's
aristocratic and mainstream family, as it emerges here, evokes subtle
and problematic contrasts with her temporary, inauthentic, and yet
in some ways more ideal gypsy family. With Preciosa's replacement
into this prior yet final world and with her requisite return to a norm
of subordinate female behavior, we are also made aware of her
catalyst-like quality. She inspires great change and action around
herself, but in the end she returns to a prior state, fundamentally—and from a proto-feminist point of view—disappointingly
silenced and unchanged.[19]

The juxtaposition of Preciosa as gypsy daughter with Constanza
as child of the aristocratic class is consistent with a pattern found
elsewhere in *La gitanilla*. Throughout the *novela* there are a number
of peculiar, rarely noticed, and basically ironic, critical pairings and
contrasts.   For example, the embarrassment of the evidently
"penniless" *teniente* and his wife, suggesting the precariousness of
civil service, is subtly recalled in the scene where the young don Juan
de Cárcamo first enters and declares his love for the gypsy girl. In
the process of giving his family background, don Juan mentions his
father's reason for having come to the Royal Capital (*la corte*) and
does so in a way that reminds the reader of the concrete yet problematic reality of social and economic pressures, even for a nominal
aristocrat.[20]   But one of the most significant pairings, in terms of

---

[19] Concerning the problem of the return to the established, limited order, especially
for the female character, see T. Sears, *A Marriage of Convenience*, in particular chapter
4, "The Dangers of Desire" (127-41).

[20] Even though the youth has made much of his family's wealth and position, he
points out to Preciosa, as a further support of his case but which in another light can
be seen to put his father and his family in general in a more problematical light, that
"Mi padre está aquí en la Corte pretendiendo un cargo, y ya está consultado, y tiene
casi ciertas esperanzas de salir con él" (I, 84). In effect, the senior Cárcamo is
seeking a government post, and while there is no doubt that the two families (the
Cárcamo's and that of the *teniente*) are socially and materially of different levels, it

Preciosa and the question of identity, is that of the two fathers and the two betrothals.

   As we will recall, there are two very different scenes in the *novela* concerning Preciosa and the apparent disposition of her in marriage to don Juan de Cárcamo: first, there is the moment early in the story when, after the brief "initiation" of don Juan/Andrés into the gypsy band, the *gitano viejo* in effect gives her to the youth (I, 100ff). Later, near the end of the *novela* this scene is counterpoised by the moment in which her true father don Fernando de Azevedo, the Corregidor of Murcia, gives his very willing consent and unites his recovered daughter Constanza with the redeemed and, in a different sense, recovered don Juan de Cárcamo (I, 129). If we assume that, on some unconscious but fully consistent level, Preciosa senses that she is not a gypsy, then perhaps her behavior in these two related moments has a certain thematic plausibility. But on a purely logical, narrative level, the difference between her two reactions raises questions. In the first episode, the old gypsy begins his long speech to the newly re-baptized Andrés by apparently giving—or attempting to give— the girl to him:

> Esta muchacha, que es la flor y la nata de toda la hermosura de las gitanas que sabemos que viven en España, te la entregamos, ya por esposa, o ya por amiga; que en esto puedes hacer lo que fuere más de tu gusto, porque la libre y ancha vida nuestra no está sujeta a melindres ni a muchas ceremonias. (I, 100-1)

This rather blunt and unadorned gesture of betrothal comes at the head of what will be a long and fairly detailed speech on the moral values and customs of gypsy life, with particular reference to male-female relations and the troublingly easy disposability of the unfortunate women.[21] But in their obvious purpose, i.e., as prelude

---

is also clear from this that their total social world is continuous and complexly connected.

[21] As the *gitano viejo* bluntly explains it, "Entre nosotros, aunque hay muchos incestos, no hay ningún adulterio; y cuando le hay en la mujer propia, o alguna bellaquería en la amiga, no vamos a la justicia a pedir castigo; nosotros somos los jueces y los verdugos de nuestras esposas o amigas; con la misma facilidad las

to the betrothal, the old gypsy's words establish a crucial thematic and moral context, providing yet another chance for Preciosa to articulate a profoundly discrepant position, not only with regard to the gypsy norm, but also in terms of the general custom of the mainstream Spanish culture of the age. For what one generally remembers from this moment of the *novela* is the woman's definitive rejection of the rules and tendencies of the gypsy code of behavior, especially as they touch on male-female relations.

Preciosa's first words of reply to the old gypsy's extended speech make this willful separation and rejection emphatically clear:

> Puesto que estos señores legisladores han hallado por sus leyes que soy tuya, y que por tuya me han entregado, yo he hallado por la ley de mi voluntad, que es la más fuerte de todas, que no quiero serlo si no es con las condiciones que antes que aquí vinieses entre los dos concertamos. (I, 103)

In context, perhaps the most remarkable thing about Preciosa's reassertion of her personal autonomy and her very different values is the fact that it passes totally uncontested by the *gitano viejo* or by anyone else. Once again, her word is law—at least here. Her restatement of the special rules of her relationship with don Juan, moreover, balances and modifies to a certain extent the apparently anti-conventional, violent, and generally grim social norms and behaviors of the gypsies. Thus, the possible harshness and the full weight of the ostensible immorality of this world (in contrast to mainstream Spanish society)—what Forcione has called its "demonic" quality—seems significantly attenuated by the régime of personal values that Preciosa wills into being.[22] What this particular

---

matamos y las enterramos por las montañas y desiertos como si fueran animales nocivos; . . ." (I, 101).

[22] See Forcione, "The Natural World of the Gypsies" (*Cervantes and the Humanist Vision*, 184ff). In my sense of the text and what actually *happens* and is *said*, Forcione's emphasis on the "demonic" seems excessive; for example he notes that "the Gypsy world, as a demonic order of lawlessness, terror, lust, and incest, forms the traditional lower world of romance in which an imprisoned heroine awaits the coming of a redeemer or a mysterious turn of providence that will restore her to her proper identity" (186). But Preciosa hardly seems "imprisoned" at any point in the

scene, with its deliberately heightened contrast of values between Preciosa and this Cervantine version of gypsy culture, in effect achieves is primarily yet another intensification of the sense that Preciosa stands above this unorthodox and supposedly lawless world. In effect, she has the power of spirit to impose an order and to transform, in frankly startling and improbable ways, the "natural" and evil tendencies of her temporary (gypsy) society and of the most important individuals of the story, in particular don Juan, whose desires and intentions, however sincere and honorable, she seeks to purify and test even further.

But the true significance—and the deeper strangeness—of this early episode only fully surfaces in the complex echoes of its inescapable juxtaposition to the second betrothal, the passage near the conclusion of the *novela* in which Preciosa has been restored and returned to her true family and social place. Significantly, the recovery and recognition of Preciosa occurs as a consequence of the arrest of Andrés/don Juan for his impulsive killing of the insolent soldier. In the face of this crisis and given Preciosa's fear for don Juan's life, plus the emotionally charged discovery of her own true identity, it is not too surprising that the girl's usual self-possession and verbal command would suddenly be replaced by almost total silence. Her silence might also be related, in more complex symbolic ways, to the crucial fact that this highly charged moment of the story (don Juan's arrest) and the re-placing of the young woman into the arms of her authentic parents marks the single instance in the *novela* when the gypsies come into full but fully helpless, vulnerable contact with the mainstream society. Once the larger community's laws and customs intervene, the powers and possibilites of language, high-spirited wit, and the tricks and defenses of this marginal group all

---

story, and while there may be a clear lack of conventional "order," lawlessness is a bit of an overstatement; finally, whatever other tones and suggestions are present or contingent in this text, "terror" (as in many moments of the *Persiles*) is hard to find, at least in this particular gypsy world as rendered by Cervantes.

seem to collapse. Preciosa's sudden docility is as marked a change as is the uncharacteristic immobility of the gypsies.

But with the change in Preciosa's behavior we also have to consider the implication that her previous attitudes and beliefs, what she has both articulated and embodied, are being called into question or at the very least are being severely limited. What we have heretofore encountered throughout the text has been Preciosa as a striking and (however improbable) admirable exemplar of female autonomy, of good judgment and wit, of indomitable free will, and of idealized yet judicious criteria concerning romantic love and Christian marriage. In this light, the transformation of the woman's character, through the restoration of her social identity, seems to recast and revise much of what we have seen and assumed through-out the text. Or to put it another way, we are prompted to consider the irony of the fact that, within the desired and privileged world that Cervantes overtly celebrates, a certain breadth of individual female autonomy will have to be renounced in exchange for another, deeper level of authenticity in one's identity—at least for the woman.[23]

In the resolution, or the part of it that deals with Preciosa's, or Constanza's, sentiments and wishes via-à-vis her suitor don Juan, there emerges a fundamentally different position, a notably distinct set of values on the woman's part. As the text presents it, when asked by her parents what her feelings toward the imprisoned young man are, Preciosa "Respondió que no más de aquella que le obligaba a ser agradecida a quien se había querido humillar a ser gitano por ella; pero que ya no se extendería a más el agradecimiento de aquello que sus señores padres quisiesen" (I, 129). To this totally submissive position, the father replies by imposing his own will, which in this case, given the thematic and sentimental exigencies of the romance

---

[23] Again, as Sears puts it, "The ideal woman, like Costanza, expresses no desire, makes no willful choices. Instead, she is led calmly to her enclosed fate, just as her story proceeds inexorably to its close under the auspices of the marriage plot" (141); while this may seem a bit overstated, given the totality of the text, this is where the woman of La gitanilla ends up: quite reintegrated and submissive.

genre, coincides with the desires of the two lovers; as the father
expresses it, "yo, como tu padre, tomo a cargo el ponerte en estado
que no desdiga de quién eres" (I, 129). Thus the specific words of the
text clearly link the resolution of the tested and long-suffering love
(mainly don Juan's, but also Preciosa's) with the constantly present
but previously unsettled question of identity (primarily Preciosa's,
but by extension don Juan's and certainly Clemente's), as implied by
the phrase "estado que no desdiga *de quién eres*" (emphasis added).

The question of *why* Preciosa's happy restoration coincides with,
or requires, a dramatic silencing of her verbal and personal autonomy and the implications of this radical change have been much
discussed.[24] One might imagine or argue that her initial qualities of
willfulness and independence of spirit will be maintained despite her
return to this radically different social realm. Conversely, one could
state that Cervantes, in "restoring" Preciosa, has subtly rejected and
expelled a dangerous degree of feminine liberty, just as he rejects the
values of the gypsy world. But it is inescapably clear, in the final
crucial scenes, that the previously active, interactive, and independ-

---

[24] On this question, El Saffar (citing Ana María Barrenechea) rationalizes this change
by stating that "Only in the pastoral of gypsy societies, were women given active
roles. . . . [and that] Preciosa, on discovering her noble origins, immediately gives
up her characteristic willfulness and shows the submissive manner expected of girls
of her station" (note 29, 102). But Gerli highlights the irony and complexity of the
situation, noting that "Preciosa's liberty, the very source of her spiritual integrity,
is denied through the resolution, for as soon as she is transformed into the well-
born, well-dressed Doña Costanza, the strong, vigorous and pert little gypsy
becomes a silent, submissive and demure member of society who speaks only when
spoken to" ("Romance and Novel: Idealism and Irony in *La gitanilla*," 37).
Rodríguez-Luis has also noted the contrary implications of this silence: "El que no
brille ahora la discreción de Preciosa saliendo de sus propios labios podría
explicarse en razón de la proximidad del final y el deseo del novelista de concluir
con los pormenores del desenlace, pero esto no basta a justificar la facilidad con que
la gitanilla, pese a las muestras de hallarse aficionada a Andrés que ha dado, está
dispuesta ahora a renunciar a su tan preciada libertad de elección" (138);
Rodríguez-Luis's explanation, however, strikes me as a bit incomplete: "Y es que,
en realidad, Preciosa desaparece ahora para ser sustituida por doña Constanza de
Acevedo, la cual no necesita una voz propia, como sí le ocurría a la gitanilla, cuyo
escenario era el mundo real" (138).

ent woman—once back in the home and in the *possession* of her rightful parents—becomes the passive object, the obedient possession of others, something that she has throughout the text signally refused to be.

Or rather, from the perspective of the woman's return to her proper aristocratic place, the *novela*'s long and curious passage through the anti-society of the gypsies and Preciosa's own—only apparent—freedom, can now be seen, retrospectively, as an extended process of exchanges, a process at the end of which the woman is not so much rendered merely an object, under the circumstances of restoration, but rather in which her initial and final reality as *woman*, woman understood as social object in the Spanish culture and society of Cervantes's time, has never been totally absent. Within this fictional world—where Cervantes has artfully exaggerated certain conventional virtues and the possibility of individual autonomy but has not overtly questioned conventional social order—triumphant love and the comedic restoration of social harmony require that the fantasies of spirit give place to the concrete realities of social definition and limitation. Value, language, and identity in *La gitanilla* are thus linked such that the text's system of conversations and exchanges, of disguise, theft and return, can intimate an idealized world, one in which Erasmian concepts of Christian marriage can be expressed, and yet a world where a given man or woman is never very far from limitations and conformity.[25]

The world of *La gitanilla* is, then, more darkly ironic and conservative than the initial gestures of female autonomy, dramatized in the opening scenes, would suggest. The reader, not unlike many of Preciosa's admiring and bedazzled customers and onlookers, is to be forgiven if he or she falls for the elegant con game, the comforting illusion, that Cervantes, through his most impressive device, Preciosa, perpetrates: a seeming celebration of freedom, autonomy

---

[25] See Forcione, and especially his concluding pages (222-23) in which he acknowledges that "La gitanilla" contains much more than the dramatization of an Erasmian conception of love and marriage.

of will, and free choice in love, that masks a deeper reaffirmation of rigid values and of class-conscious "identity as conformity." In the elaborately ordered—and ultimately orderly—world that Cervantes creates here and throughout the *Novelas ejemplares*, the fortunate recovery of true identity requires that the precious free spirit, Preciosa, be removed from the socially unorthodox and beguilingly subversive gypsy world and be restored as Constanza, the *constant, conforming* woman.

Chapter Two
The Frontiers of Identity
El amante liberal

In comparison with *La gitanilla*, *El amante liberal* has attracted less critical attention. Yet this second *novela* also explores the trials, losses, and recuperations of identity, though in tellingly different ways. Like *La gitanilla* and *La española inglesa*, *El amante liberal* exemplifies the genre that Ruth El Saffar and others have called the Cervantine "romance."[1] With its exotic settings, its melodramatic and highly improbable twists of plot, and the trials and tribulations of love, *El amante* also reminds us of Cervantes's *Persiles*. Similarly, the sea voyages and the juxtaposed cultures and nationalities suggest an affinity with *La española inglesa*, another text notably well grounded in an historically specific moment.[2] But there are certain elements unique to this *novela* that complicate and enrich thematic analysis. In particular, an adequate interpretation requires analysis of the interplay between the love story of Leonisa and Ricardo (along with the problem of Ricardo's tempestuous personality and its putative change at the end) and their encounter with the exotic, foreign, and erotically disturbing world of the Ottoman Turks.[3]

---

[1] See in particular El Saffar, *Novel to Romance*, in which she places *El amante liberal* as, along with *La española inglesa*, one of the "The Last Written Novelas" (139-49).

[2] The business of sea voyages and clashing cultures is, as numerous critics have reiterated, all but indispensable to the romance or *novela bizantina* (or *novela de peregrinaje*); see, for example, de Armas Wilson, *Allegories of Love*, 3-23. On the implications of the voyage, journeys maritime or other, see S. Hutchinson, *Cervantine Journeys*.

[3] Concerning the Turks in general, see P. Coles, *The Ottoman Impact on Europe*; H. Inalcik, *The Ottoman Empire: The Classical Age 1300-1600*; B. Z. Kedar, *Crusade and Mission: European Approaches toward the Muslims*; R. Schwoebel, *The Shadow of the Crescent: The Renaissance Image of the Turk (1453-1517)*; and K. M. Sutton, *Western Hostility to Islam and Prophecies of Turkish Doom*. With regard to the Turk in Spanish literature, see A. Mas, *Les Turcs dans la littérature espagnole du siècle d'or*, especially his section on Cervantes, vol. I, 289-383. Finally, a very useful study is O. Hegyi, *Cervantes and the Turks: Historical Reality versus Literary Fiction in* La Gran Sultana *and* El amante liberal.

Most critical readings of *El amante liberal* give primary attention to the problem of love, the obstacles that must be overcome, and the final resolutions that allow restoration of the ideal social order symbolized by marriage and by a return to one's original society and culture. This approach usually privileges Ricardo, centering on questions of psychology or character development. Ricardo's impulsive, egocentric nature and his obsession with his own quite limited view of things, his self-absorbed love for Leonisa, and his inability to understand her true feelings, create the principal obstacle that must be overcome in the *novela*. From this perspective, the rest of the text becomes a sequence of adventures and sufferings that bring Ricardo to a new level of self-knowledge. Everything builds toward the concluding scene in which Ricardo finally realizes his basic lack of understanding and his inordinate sense of self-importance.[4]

Concerning the theme of identity, the action of the *novela* traces a process by which Ricardo comes to be worthy of Leonisa and also transcends his own egocentrism. One might schematize the process as follows: in the first stage, Ricardo (in the sea-side garden, or picnic, confrontation scene) finds himself "out of his senses," or as we might say, alienated from from an adequate self-awareness. In the second stage, as a captive on Cyprus, he is "out of his culture." In this part of the story he endures captivity, is forced to be patient, and as a result goes through a process of change. The third stage corresponds to Leonisa's and Ricardo's liberation from physical captivity and their return to Sicily. With this return, Ricardo comes full circle, geographically at least, to his point of departure. But the

---

[4] See, for example, El Saffar, *Novel to Romance*: "In *El amante liberal*, the main male character learns a lesson that none of Cervantes's early characters could learn. Ricardo discovers, through a nightmare of bizarre adventures, that union with the other is possible only if claims over the other are renounced. Like other late characters, Ricardo moves from an initial position of absolute alienation to a final position of integration, bringing with him into a final reconciliation not only Leonisa, whom he marries, but the renegades Mahamut, Halima, and her family" (149).

entire process is only completed with the fourth and final stage, the moment in the middle of Ricardo's speech when—after renouncing his suit of Leonisa in favor of Cornelio's pretensions—he realizes that he has no authority over Leonisa. Ricardo's magnanimous gesture of stepping aside and relinquishing his claims to Leonisa, followed by his more enlightened realization that Leonisa is not and never has been within his power to *give* to someone else, thus symbolizes his transformation. He realizes what liberty and liberality, or generosity, really are.

The *novela* can thus be read as an exemplum in which the incomplete state of one person's maturity and awareness is replaced, after a series of trials and tribulations, by a fuller and more integrated sense of self and a more sensitive respect for others. Considering the problem of identity in *El amante liberal* from this perspective, Ricardo's attainment of true liberality (in which the senses of both *generosity* and *freedom* are very much in play) and how this refines his love are the central objectives. This strikes me as a plausible reading of the *novela*. At the same time, I believe that it is incomplete, for such readings tend to relegate the Turkish characters and the eastern Mediterranean setting to the status of aptly threatening plot devices and colorful decor. In fact, a consideration of the peculiar dynamic of the interaction with the world of the Turks, a world in which seduction and fear are afforded a subtle but crucial catalytic role, is indispensable to a reading of this text.[5] I would begin by suggesting that the sufferings and displacements across the cultural frontiers represented by Cyprus and the contested lands of the Mediterranean are what change Ricardo, giving him an awareness of the value of autonomy and free will. As Ricardo discovers, to be worthy of Leonisa's love requires a process of self-discovery

---

[5] As I shall suggest further on, the implications of specific customs of the Turks—particularly with regard to their imperial expansion and their tendency to recruit, capture, and otherwise integrate non-Turks into their world—are crucial. On the Ottoman practices of interaction with foreigners, see especially P. Coles, *The Ottoman Impact on Europe*, 44-71; see also H. Inalcik, *The Ottoman Empire*, 80-85.

and suffering, a process actualized within, and determined by, a world of conflictive, ambiguous frontiers.[6]

The location of the action marks a crucial difference between *El amante liberal* and *La gitanilla*. The identity questions that, in *La gitanilla*, are pursued in the seemingly free but largely marginal socio-cultural spaces of the gypsies within Spain itself, are now explored on the islands and the high seas of the Mediterranean, the contested boundary between Christian Europe and the Ottoman Empire.[7] This second *novela* makes it clear that, for Cervantes, the socio-cultural implications of the setting of the story along cultural frontiers and in places of hostile yet seductive human interactions are fundamental. But what is the significance of these exotic cultures and locales?

First of all, the story's complex interaction of the Christian Europeans and the various Turks, renegades, and other "outsiders" reiterates more deeply the questions of identity and marginality explored in the gypsy world of *La gitanilla*. Once again, we have characters who move, in this case some voluntarily and others not, from a familiar culture to a different, hostile yet exotic one, and who then return, significantly changed, to their point of origin. In this second *novela*, however, there are some important departures from the patterns of the first tale. The element most pertinent to the issues of identity and social order (which here is more a "socio-cultural" order) is the presence of the Ottoman Turks. On one level, the Turks and their culture provide the necessary and conventional threatening

---

[6] The world of *El amante liberal*, with its complex and conflictive Mediterranean center, is very much that described by F. Braudel, in *The Mediterranean and the Mediterranean World in the Age of Philip II*, see especially vol. I, 57ff.

[7] It is worth noting that *El amante liberal* is also the only *novela* in which not even a secondary character is identified as being from Spain itself. Although the Sicilian culture and nationality would imply a close affinity, this distinction or separation of cultural identity displaces the focus into a doubly exotic context, Sicilian and subsequently Turkish. It is also crucial to realize that the island of Cyprus itself was historically considered to be a place of sexual license; see especially, R. C. Jennings, *Christians and Muslims in Ottoman Cyprus and the Mediterranean World, 1571-1640*, 14-39.

force.   The Turkish element also foregrounds the question of language (and "languages"), stressing the subtle limits of communication, given the Turks' own different language, as well as the other intermediate, composite languages mentioned in the story. Most of all, the Ottoman culture introduces radically contrasting values and, less obviously, contains implications of attraction and repulsion, seduction and threat.[8] The less threatening clash of cultures found in *La gitanilla*—the ostensibly majoritarian yet, in fact, aristocratic stratum of Spanish society, represented by don Juan/Andrés, as it opposes and interacts with the distinctly marginal, suspect, yet fluidly coexisting gypsy world—is replaced in *El amante liberal* by much more violent conflict and the more complex interaction between the Christian Europe (Sicily) and the world of the Ottoman Turks. What distinguishes *El amante liberal* from the rest of the *Novelas ejemplares* is precisely this complex encounter with the seductions and threats of the Ottoman culture. We must therefore consider how these geographies and cultural frontiers affect the questions of identity, language, and social order. Cervantes does, of course, explore the theme of the confusions of love. But in *El amante liberal* he also treats the question of the emergence of a more authentic identity in terms not only of individual volition and self knowledge, but also as collective and cultural identifications. Likewise, he deliberately exploits the symbolic implications of both the "other" culture and the suggestions of conflict and attraction that obtain in this contested zone of contact and interaction. By placing this *novela* in culturally intermediate places and in a specific historical moment, Cervantes dramatizes—against a conflictive and highly

---

[8] This aspect of the *novela* and of the real European-Ottoman dynamic takes form most notably in the figure of the *renegado*. The Ottoman practice of attracting and incorporating non-Turks is thus crucial. On this tendency, see Coles, *The Ottoman Impact on Europe*, who notes that "During the reign of Suleiman, it was almost impossible for a free-born Moslem, whatever his qualifications, to reach a position of eminence either in the army or in the bureaucracy" (74); see also 154: "Constantinople . . . attracted and made use of a stream of renegades and refugees from the European states with which it was in conflict."

ambiguous background of cultures and confusing human motives—the problem of identity both in terms of individual self-
knowledge and of collective socio-cultural identification.

I. Euro-Turkish Frontiers of Identity

In *El amante liberal*, identity is considered from both the collective
and the individual perspective. The ostensible main plot and the
focus on the words and actions of Ricardo and Leonisa articulate the
personal dimension. The love interest and the extensive role of
language—or languages—underline the importance of the individual, of interiority, selfconsciousness, and the relationship between
will and action. At the same time, the involvement of the supposedly
secondary characters, the role played by the Turks, and the attention
given to this culture and its people, as they implicitly contrast and
question the European Christian identity, shift our attention to a
more collective conception of identity. This level stresses nationality,
religion, and ethnicity, as these dimensions are represented not only
by Ricardo and Leonisa, but also by Mahamut, Halima, and other
seemingly minor characters. Given this broader conception of
identity, in the socio-cultural as well as the individual spheres, it is
clear that there is a fundamental connection between the ostensible
main plot—the tangled love story of Ricardo and Leonisa—and the
actions or subplots of the secondary characters. The implications
posed by Mahamut, given his status as a renegade, moreover, are of
special importance, as are the vacillating sentiments and cultural
loyalties of Halima, the *cadí*'s wife.

El amante liberal treats the question of identity in a context of
special historical and cultural importance for any Spaniard of the
age—and particularly for Cervantes, the ex-captive and veteran of
Lepanto. The fictional time-frame of this story is as precise as are the
locations of the action: of all Cervantes's *Novelas ejemplares* no other
is situated with such precision in a particular historical moment
(1570, slightly after the conquest of Cyprus by the Turks and thus a

little before the Battle of Lepanto).[9] Moreover, in no other Cervantine *novela* do we find quite as much detailed attention paid to the culture of a distinctly alien people. Cervantes's portrayal of the customs and behavior of the gypsies in *La gitanilla* could be seen as comparable. But I would argue that something quite different is going on in this second *novela*. In *La gitanilla*, Cervantes's presentation of the customs of the gypsies is distorted by an intentional idealizing. By contrast, the treatment of the political and social practices of the Turks in *El amante* seems more objective, even though here too we find a more positive view of a foreign culture than we might have expected.[10] Curiously, however, this aspect of the text—the role and implications of the Turks—has not received very much critical attention.[11] It is my contention that the placement of the action within this European-Turkish zone, within settings that are culturally as well as geographically borderlands, in places of conflict and interchange, of religious and ethnic apostasies or rejections and confusions, endows *El amante* with its peculiar character and, for the modern reader, its elusive ambiguity. The complex, mixed signals that the open, culturally integrative dynamic of the Ottoman Empire sends out—its simultaneous aura of difference and threat, along with its many levels of attraction for the outsider—play a role that is much more than merely decorative in this *novela*. They are in fact the catalyst for the trials that bring transformation.

The exotic aspect of the setting is the first thing that we encounter. Significantly, we are not in the totally removed, enclosed, and hostile environment found in the Algiers of the Captive's Tale in *Don Quijote*, Part I. Rather, we are in a place of both captivity and

---

[9] Concerning the history of this event as well as the customs and hardships of maritime life, see J. Beeching, *The Galleys at Lepanto*.

[10] Once again, on this issue see R. Schwoebel, *The Shadow of the Crescent*; K. M. Setton, *Western Hostility to Islam and Prophecies of Turkish Doom*; and R. W. Southern, *Western Views of Islam in the Middle Ages*.

[11] The notable exceptions include O. Hegyi, *Cervantes and the Turks*, and A. Mas, *Les Turcs dans la littérature espagnole du siècle d'or*; in the latter, see especially "Cervantès et la transposition de la réalité turco-barbaresque," vol. I, 289-383, and also "Le Portrait des Turcs," vol. II, 295-341.

fluidity, an area of conflict and encounter.[12] The first scene and much of the subsequent action of the *novela* take place on Cyprus, an island where the two main antagonistic forces in the Mediterranean (Turks and Europeans) had recently fought and where the social and administrative structures of the Ottoman Empire had been established on Cyprus soon after their conquest of the island in 1570.[13]

The situation of Ricardo and Mahamut, as it is presented in the opening pages (which is, in a further level of deliberate complication, really the middle of the story), is in some ways conventional. Given their status as, respectively, captive and renegade, Ricardo and Mahamut underline those aspects of the Ottoman culture that would seem strange and threatening in the eyes of Christian European society. For the Spaniard of Cervantes's time, as for any European Christian of the Mediterranean region, the Islamic world in general and the Ottoman Empire in particular represented an evil and implacably competitive force.[14] But the true nature of this Euro-Turkish antagonism went beyond the simple notion of unmixed hatred or unremitting desire for total defeat of the opponent. The relationship had dimensions of competition, of two implicitly "imperialist" political and cultural entities clashing over the disputed territories and peoples at their borders. There also was a fairly extensive, structured, and even orderly, system of interaction and contact between the European and Islamic worlds.[15] Thus, in addition to the obvious effects of the cultural and geographical displacement experienced by Ricardo, Mahamut, and Leonisa, the juxtaposition of the Christian and the Muslim in this *novela* explores

---

[12] Concerning the situation of captivity and ransom in the North African context, see especially Ellen G. Friedman, *Spanish Captives in North Africa in the Early Modern Age*.

[13] Again, see Jennings, *Christians and Muslims in Ottoman Cyprus*, especially 40-106.

[14] On this issue, again see R. Schwoebel, *The Shadow of the Crescent*; also B. Z. Kedar, *Crusade and Mission*, especially 199-203, "Crusade and Mission in their Age of Decline," which deals with the relative hardening of antagonistic positions and the European abandonment of missionary efforts from about the fourteenth century onward.

[15] See E. G. Friedman, *Spanish Captives in North Africa in the Early Modern Age*.

the paradoxical situation of a profound antagonism, on one hand, and the intimate interaction of the two cultures, on the other. What this *novela* reveals—and what is distinctive about the practices of the Ottoman Empire—is the range of possibilities for crossing the frontiers of culture and identity. One could be a helpless victim or captive of the Turks, but one could also be a willful convert, or the object of quite understandable attractions and seductions.

A sense of the ambiguity of identity emerges at the very beginning of the narration. The *novela* begins *in medias res*, with an opening speech delivered by a totally unidentified person. This ambiguity is further underlined in other parts of the *novela* by both the language and the structure of the narrative, notable for their indirections and postponements of revelation. The first paragraph is a lament ("—¡Oh lamentables ruinas de la desdichada Nicosia . . .") spoken by the unidentified captive. The allusion to the recent conquest [las ruinas] apenas enjutas de la sangre de vuestros valerosos y mal afortunados defensores"—clearly indicates the historical place and moment, ironically contrasting with the mystery of the speaker's identity. Only with the beginning of the second paragraph are we given a clue about the speaker: "Estas razones decía un cautivo cristiano" (I, 137). But the symbolic effect of the opening paragraph is clear in its comparison of the speaker's state to the ruined and defeated condition of the city. The futile gesture of personification and communication underscores this figurative link: "Si como carecéis de sentido, le tuviérades ahora, en esta soledad donde estamos, pudiéramos lamentar juntas nuestras desgracias" (I, 137). We still do not know—beyond the obvious situation of the man's captivity—what is the other great misfortune to which he alludes. But the rhetoric of this opening speech, as well as the setting and the narrative tactics of indirection, serves to connect closely a personal misfortune (still unexplained) and a larger historical reality, the Turkish conquest of Cyprus.

Immediately after this opening speech, a second character enters, one who will play a very important role in both the narrative and the symbolic dimensions of the *novela*. This other man is described by the external narrator as a Turk: "un turco, mancebo de muy buena disposición y gallardía" (I, 138). Following the now established tactic of incomplete and gradual revelations, this "Turk" identifies the first speaker ("Apostaría yo, Ricardo amigo . . ."), but does not identify himself. It is only later that we learn who he is, and the first clue is somewhat surprising, since we are given the curious information that the two men, captive and Turk, are compatriots. As the Turk puts it,

> Pero dejemos estas cosas, pues no llevan remedio, y vengamos a las tuyas, que quiero ver si le tienen; y así te ruego, por lo que debes a la buena voluntad que te he mostrado y por lo que te obliga *el ser entrambos de una misma patria*, y habernos criado en nuestra niñez juntos. (I, 138-139; emphasis added)

In effect, this Turk isn't really a Turk, at least not by birth. From the outset, then, this peculiar distinction of identity is underscored: Mahamut is really a Christian and a Sicilian. He is originally from a Christian and European, yet also intermediate, island cultural world and now evidently wishes to return to it. Even more curiously, we are never told his real name: throughout the *novela* he is called "Mahamut," and even at the conclusion, with his return to his native land and his reconciliation with the Church, his "Christian" name is not revealed.

Why Cervantes gives us this initial and deliberate mis-identification and why he maintains the ambiguity of the name to the end is never revealed. But implicitly it resonates with the larger thematic issue of the interplay of cultures and how this interplay mirrors the inner confusions of identity that lie at the heart of this text. Mahamut is, in effect, a figure of frontiers and borderlands, as much as he is a man who has simply abandoned one cultural identity for another. Far more than Cornelio, the ostensible antagonist and rival, Mahamut represents the third element of a curious triangle whose other points are Leonisa and Ricardo. The triangle is not the familiar love triangle, but one of identity, or more precisely, of the confusions and clarifications of identity as explored in a movement into and out of the feared and yet beguiling enemy culture. The difference between the conventional love triangle and this triangle of iden-

tity—and the reason why I give particular importance to Mahamut—is that, while Cornelio at first appears to have great importance as the obstacle between Leonisa and Ricardo, Mahamut has
ultimately much greater significance in his role as the all but
indispensible intermediary who facilitates the reunion of the two
lovers and their final liberation. In the adventures of identity and
self-knowledge, there takes place a complex process between the
individual and the various frontiers that exist and that he or she is
forced, in one way or another, to cross. For Ricardo and Mahamut,
captivity and apostasy are destinations, destinies, or detours that
mutually intersect and illuminate each other. The apostate, or *renegado*, offers the means by which the captive can attain liberty.
Reciprocally, the captive provides the apostate with the opportunity
to return to his homeland and religion.

At the same time, from the critical perspective set out above,
Mahamut's identity as a *renegado* has yet another level of significance. Given that Mahamut is a renegade and Ricardo a captive, the
text establishes a parallel relationship of simultaneous resemblance
and difference between these two characters: with the juxtaposition
of *cautivo* and *renegado*, we have the two possibilities (or extremes) of
transition and interchange between the Christian-European and
Muslim-Turkish worlds.[16] Ricardo's situation as captive is understandable in conventional terms: he is a victim, one who has been
brought involuntarily into the Turkish-Muslim world. But the comparable situation of Mahamut might strike us as strange. At least for
the late twentieth-century reader, Mahamut's status as a *renegado*
requires some clarification. The text itself gives us very little help.

---

[16] On the fascinating issue of the *renegado* or Christian conversions to Islam, see E.
G. Friedman, *Spanish Captives*, 46; R. Schwoebel, *The Shadow of the Crescent*, 127ff;
and B. Z. Kedar, *Crusade and Mission*, 103ff. With particular regard to the Turkish
attitude on this phenomenon of conversion and assimilation, H. Inalcik notes that
"The Ottoman Empire, of all Islamic societies, was the one most open to foreign
cultural influences; but from the beginning of the sixteenth century the forces of
religious fanaticism became increasingly powerful" (181-82), suggesting that by
Cervantes's time the question of openness and toleration for the convert to Islam
was becoming more complex.

In contrast to Ricardo's rather extensive narration (I, 142-154), Mahamut only makes a few brief, ambiguous allusions to how and why he came to be a renegade. For example, he refers to his present condition as follows: "quizá para que yo te sirva ha traído la fortuna este rodeo de haberme hecho vestir deste hábito, *que aborrezco*" (I, 139; emphasis added). A bit further on, he refers to the "deseo encendido que tengo de no morir en este estado que parece que profeso, pues cuando más no pueda, tengo de confesar y publicar a voces la fe de Jesucristo, de quien me apartó mi poca edad y menos entendimiento" (I, 139). The last phrase is especially telling. It suggests, if in a slightly round-about way, that the change of religious and national identity—the crossing of a religio-cultural frontier—now lamented by Mahamut, had been a deliberate and voluntary action on his part.

Although Mahamut, in the passages cited above, does not explain in detail why he entered the Ottoman world and converted to Islam, this mentioned but suppressed motivation reminds us of certain phenomena of human interaction and changes of loyalty that were not uncommon in the sixteenth and seventeenth centuries. While there was constant, deliberate, and forced "integration" of non-Muslim and specifically non-Turkish men and women into the Ottoman Empire, Mahamut's words remind us of the instances in which this change of cultural identification was made more voluntarily. The Ottoman Turks, even after they had reached the height of their political power and cultural sophistication as an empire, functioned as a warrior society, always expanding (or trying to expand) their territory and sustaining the empire by means of *razzia* or skirmishes along their borders. They nourished the empire in part by means of tributes exacted from the nations and peoples at the frontiers that found themselves under Ottoman hegemony.[17] But in

---

[17] As Inalcik notes, "The Ottoman Empire was thus to become a true 'Frontier Empire', a cosmopolitan state, treating all creeds and races as one, which was to unite the Orthodox Christian Balkans and Muslim Anatolia in a single state" (*The Ottoman Empire*, 7); see also P. Coles, *The Ottoman Impact on Europe*, especially 44-69. Coles notes that "For all its external pomp and circumstance, . . . the empire of the

addition to the payment of tribute in the form of money and material, the empire routinely demanded donations of men and women, usually children or youths and almost always non-Muslims.[18] As a very intentional policy, the empire preferred to train and educate Christian youths—in general, obtained at about the age of ten—rather than native-born Turks. These recruited and reeducated "Turks" were also, of course, converted to Islam. In one sense, these non-Turkish Turks were slaves, but in another sense they were a privileged group. For example, many of the males among them were trained to become members of the most prestigious military unit: the Janissaries. Other men might become Vizirs or high officials of the civil administration. The women, meanwhile, would often become the favorites of the harems and on occasion might rise to positions of considerable influence, especially if they achieved the status of Sultana. In effect, then, not only in the cases of children brought into the empire by force but also with those older men who voluntarily entered the empire, these ex-Christians often had the distinct possibility of "upward mobility." Given these curious Ottoman customs, for many European Christians the Turkish Empire represented a world with rather strong attractions.

At this point we can return to the case, now perhaps less mysterious, of Mahamut. As the *novela* clearly suggests, this young man is one of the favored and influential slaves, of the kind that the Ottoman empire sought out and cultivated.[19] We can now also

---

Ottoman sultans remained . . . faithful to the purposes of the . . . raiding party . . . [I]t was organized for plundering and it subsisted on plunder" (69)—perhaps an oversimplification of a system that by Cervantes's time had considerable economic contact of other sorts with the Mediterranean world.

[18] See H. Inalcik, *The Ottoman Empire*, especially 69-85, on the recruitment, or incorporation of young non-Muslims and their education and acculturation into the Turkish-Islamic world.

[19] Mahamut alludes to his own privileged condition and status when, in offering his aid to Ricardo, he notes that "No hay en toda esta ciudad quien pueda ni valga más que el cadí, mi amo, ni aun el tuyo, que viene por visorrey della, ha de poder tanto; y siendo esto así, como lo es, yo puedo decir que soy el que más puede en la ciudad, pues puedo con mi patrón todo lo que quiero" (I, 154).

imagine something of Mahamut's unexplained personal motivation and his subsequent sense of remorse: Mahamut is a man who has voluntarily crossed the cultural frontier, in all likelihood initially attracted by the possibilities for personal and material advancement that the Turkish world offered, and perhaps also attracted by the opulence of the Ottoman civilization. We could say that he was, figuratively, seduced by and into this other culture. He was the object—rather than the victim—of a quite understandable socio-cultural seduction. Similarly, although there is even less information given directly in the text, we can imagine the circumstances of the Greek *renegada*, Halima, the *cadí*'s wife, to whom Mahamut will end up being married after their safe return to Sicily. Mahamut and Halima form a sort of parallel to Ricardo and Leonisa. The return and restoration of cultural and religious identity to Mahamut and Halima echoes the resolution of the emotional and psychological turmoils and confusions of the two main characters, especially Ricardo.

Like Mahamut's impulsive apostasy, Ricardo's hot-headed manner reflects a level of immaturity in his understanding of himself and others. He is the captive of his own mistakes of perception and bad judgment, all of which reflects his state of incomplete self-realization. Ricardo's errors and immaturity are comparable to Mahamut's in the latter's hasty abandonment of his religious and cultural identity. The initially incomplete but finally fully realized identity of Ricardo and the lost, then recuperated identity of Mahamut thus draw the basic outlines of a larger picture of the attainment and clarifying of a masculine identity, both in its individual, psychological aspect and in its larger socio-cultural dimensions. As in so many other cases in the *Novelas ejemplares*, and as we have seen in *La gitanilla*, Ricardo and Mahamut are, in a certain sense, not just two distinct characters, but rather represent an amplification of the male protagonist. The two men are complementary; they dramatize, in distinctive ways, the tribulations and final success of the search for authentic identity, one from the direction of the confusions of love and understanding, and the other from the perspective of cultural and religious self-identification.

II. Languages, Borders, and Silence

The role of language, or more correctly languages, in this *novela* is, as always in Cervantes's texts, complex. But language in *El amante liberal* has certain features that are unique in contrast to the rest of the *Novelas ejemplares*. Very much like the setting in the geographical and cultural borderlands, language—in various forms: as narrative discourse, as "foreign" languages and thus systems of communication and non-communication or misunderstandings, and finally as silence, the speaking that is expected but does not (quite) emerge—dramatizes the struggles for identity and liberation. Language and its confusions, moreover, are initially a large part of Ricardo's problem. Subsequently, as the larger story develops, language emerges as the vehicle that helps to establish the authentic personal and cultural identities for which several of the main characters search.

In *El amante liberal* language means several things. It includes the various individual and shared social-class ideolects or discourses implicit in Bakhtin's concept of heteroglossia.[20] At the same time, as we are frequently reminded, the treatment of multiple languages reminds us of the mundane yet symbolically crucial fact that the story involves numerous *foreign* tongues. Ricardo, Leonisa, and others speak Italian; the Turks speak Turkish; the Greek renegades speak Greek and Turkish (one assumes); and many of the characters speak a dialect or *patois* composed of mixtures of several languages.[21]

---

[20] See Bakhtin, *The Dialogic Imagination: Four Essays,*especially 259-422.

[21] Cervantes has his character Leonisa refer directly to this linguistic mixture, when she tells Ricardo "Vete con Dios, que temo no nos haya escuchado Halima, la cual entiende algo de la lengua cristiana, a lo menos de aquella mezcla de lenguas que se usa, con que todos nos entendemos" (I, 174). In context, Leonisa's—or rather, Cervantes's—use of the term "lengua cristiana" is quite unremarkable; but in

In this situation of ambiguous borderlands and motives, of hostility and seductive attraction, languages are not only a necessary, routine part of the picture, but are also yet another dimension that dramatizes the central issue of the loss and recuperation of identity and cultural place.

Language in this *novela*, moreover, has a peculiar function in its simple diegetic role, as narrative discourse. Here one finds more complexity than might be expected, in particular certain problems of credibility. Although *El amante liberal* on first reading strikes one as a fairly straightforward adventure story or "romance," on successive readings one is troubled by the way in which first-person narrative alternates with external, third-person narrations and judgmental intrusions, repetitions, flash-backs, and strategic silences or *non-speech*. In effect, a wide variety of discoursing goes on in this *novela*. But looking retrospectively on the whole effect, mimetic and diegetic, we see that these same discursive moments and devices (e.g., Ricardo as speaker/narrator; Ricardo re-narrating his own harangues; dialogues; moments of enforced silence; Leonisa's curious speech near the middle of the story) not only advance the narrative. They also intensify and enact the core problems of egocentricity and isolation that characterize the ostensible main theme of the *novela*.

Upon considering language as narrative discourse, as both a structural element and a subtle representation of the theme, the reader is struck by the plurality of the narrative discourses, who speaks, what their motives and states of mind are, as well as the sequence in which these narrations occur. The order in which the *novela* presents the story is almost as disturbing as the amount of time and verbal space given to seemingly trivial or secondary issues—e.g., Mahamut's long exposition, near the beginning, explaining in gratuitous detail the civil-service practices of the Ottoman Turks when there is a change of administrator for a

---

addition to helping the story skirt the issue of the Sicilian, rather than Spanish, tongue being spoken, the term also reminds us of the larger religious and cultural frontiers at issue in this story.

territory.[22] As I have noted above, the *novela* begins with a highly rhetorical lament by Ricardo. In fact, Ricardo—who, to put it charitably, is a bit verbose—dominates large stretches of the story. The discourse of this myopic and self-indulgent character provides a necessary portion of the story, the prior action. At the same time, as we find in his own internally embedded reportage of his harangue during the confrontation with Cornelio in the picnic scene, Ricardo's "language" is a large part of his initial problem. He orates, or better put, verbally imposes himself and his own erroneous vision of things by means of this dominating, domineering language. As a result, we are justified in questioning the reliability of his respresentations.

The language of Ricardo's opening lament dramatizes his peculiarly inflated and oratorical discursive tendencies. The very first lines of the *novela* not only locate the story in a specific time and place, but also tell us much about our troublesome hero. They reveal, for example, the poetic yet self-indulgent quality in Ricardo's rhetorical use of Cyprus and the ruins of Nicosia:

> —¡Oh lamentables ruinas de la desdichada Nicosia, apenas enjutas de la sangre de vuestros valerosos y mal afortunadas defensores! Si como carecéis de sentido, le tuviérades ahora, en esta soledad donde estamos, pudiéramos lamentar juntas nuestras desgracias, y quizá el haber hallado compañía en ellas aliviara nuestro tormento. (I, 137)

But in addition to its highly revealing presentation of his mentality, this passage sets for the *novela* a pattern, with Ricardo's balanced, graceful apostrophe initiating a series of interlocking, backward-circling narrations (his own, Mahamut's, Leonisa's).

As if to warn us of Ricardo's tendencies, however, the third-person, external narrator of the *novela* immediately places and undercuts the excesses and the pathetic fallacy of Ricardo's speech ("como si ellas [las murallas] fueran capaces de entenderle; propia

---

[22] These details, of course, fit with the historical reality; as H. Inalcik has noted, with the Ottoman conquest of Cyprus, "Ottoman law was immediately introduced" (*The Ottoman Empire*, 71). See also R. C. Jennings, *Christians and Muslims in Ottoman Cyprus and the Mediterranean World, 1571-1640*.

condición de afligidos que, llevados de sus imaginaciones, hacen y dicen cosas ajenas de toda razón y buen discurso" [I, 137].) With the juxtaposition of Ricardo's first oration and the narrator's ironic correction, this opening scene presents not only Ricardo's physical location (on Cyprus, after his capture and shipwreck, etc.), but also hints at the alienation, inner conflict, and misunderstanding in which he has found himself from the earliest stages of his love for Leonisa. Ricardo is, in much more than the literal sense, a captive, a ship-wreck, and an alien wandering confusedly within a baffling world. This is Ricardo the captive on Cyprus, but it is also Ricardo the confused lover and the man who has not yet found or recognized his true identity. The next significant and highly revealing example of Ricardo's character as embodied in language is the extended narration in which he recapitulates to Mahamut the prior action of the story, from his point of view, up to the moment when he and Leonisa are captured and taken off on separate ships. His narration of the action stops at the point when he watches Leonisa board the other ship. At this point, overcome by emotion (in a most unmanly fashion), our stout hero faints dead away, as does Leonisa (I, 105). Prior to that convenient break, Ricardo recapitulates the scene of the confrontation with Cornelio. The following part of Ricardo's harangue gives a good sense of his problem. He begins by directing his verbal attack at Leonisa:

> Contenta estarás, ¡oh enemiga mortal de mi descanso!, en tener con tanto sosiego delante de tus ojos la causa que hará que los míos vivan en perpetuo y doloroso llanto. Llégate, llégate, cruel, un poco más, y enrede tu yedra a ese inútil tronco que te busca; peina o ensortija aquellos cabellos de ese tu nuevo Ganimedes, que tibiamente te solicita; . . . (I, 144)

Ricardo goes on, at great length and with about the same excess. His words directed at Cornelio reflect a similar lack of moderation: "Y tú, ¡oh mozo!, que tan a tu salvo piensas llevar el premio más debido a mis buenos deseos que a los ociosos tuyos, . . ." (I, 144). Ricardo's speech—and here it must be remembered that this is a situation of discourse-within-a-discourse, reenactment within diegesis—clearly shows not only egocentricity, but also self-indulgent rhetorical excess. The quasi-Petrarchan texture of such locutions as "enemiga mortal de mi descanso" and such images as "enrede tu yedra a ese inútil tronco" combine with the allusion, half erudite and half demeaning (sexually), to "ese tu nuevo Ganimedes." All of which reflects a sensibility quite obsessed with its own desires and projections.

The effect of the entire passage is more informative of the turbulent mental landscape of our protagonist than it is of the reality of either the action within the scene itself or the reactions, sensations, or presence of Leonisa and Cornelio. They too are there, in a sense; but they are invisible, or rather mute, inaudible. The reader is far more aware of Ricardo's aggressive verbosity. As this re-created discourse suggests, for Ricardo the use of language is one of his problems: he doesn't let anyone else get a word in edgewise, as one might say, and his manner of "making his case" undermines his own possible merits, in the eyes and ears of Leonisa—or anyone else who might be in the area. As Ricardo blunders through his off-putting attack, the response from both Cornelio and Leonisa is a startled silence.

With the attack of the *corsarios* and their abduction of Leonisa and Ricardo, the question of language and languages changes from the problem of Ricardo's speechy pathologies and toward the question of otherness, language plurality, incomplete understanding, and the silence that results from one's ignorance of other languages. Ricardo's entry into the uncertain and dangerous sphere of the Muslim pirates heightens his confusion. As he notes at one point in the midst of his long narration, "aunque estuve presente a todo esto, nunca pude entender lo que [Yzuf y Fetala] decían, . . ." (I, 149). This situation of incomplete understanding is interwoven, comically at one point, with yet another hint at Ricardo's verbal excess. Ricardo himself reports that his captor Fetala becomes so fed up with his ranting and lamentations (after Leonisa is carried off on the other ship) that he threatens him with bodily harm if he doesn't keep silent: "mi amo [Fetala], enfadado de oírme, con un grueso palo me amenazó que si no callaba me maltrataría" (I, 150). At this point, the reader might silently applaud.

Toward the middle of the *novela*, Leonisa reappears, saved from drowning after the shipwreck and now about to be sold as a slave to the highest bidder, by the Jewish merchant. From here on, both the narration and the action of the *novela* move forward more or less together, with only minimal flashback or embedded narrative. This section of the text also develops further the issues of language and communication, silence and incompleteness of revelation. The passage most emblematic of these latter questions is the scene in the house of the *cadí*. Ricardo (a.k.a. Mario) has come, summoned by Halima; meanwhile, the *cadí* is busy at the mosque, and Ricardo and Leonisa find themselves alone for a brief time. This is the first direct encounter of the two since their separation (Ricardo had seen Leonisa, from seclusion, when she arrived, brought by the *mercader*; Leonisa still believes that Ricardo is dead). The dominant tonality of this moment is one of stasis and suspended silence, first established by the description of Leonisa and the surroundings:

> Estaba Leonisa del mismo modo y traje que cuando entró en la tienda del Bajá, sentada al pie de una escalera grande de mármol, que a los corredores subía. Tenía la cabeza inclinada sobre la palma de la mano derecha y el brazo sobre las rodillas, . . . (I, 168)[23]

At Ricardo's entry into the scene, the text stresses the visual and the static. As Cervantes presents it, Ricardo literally *sees* the silence: "Así como entró Ricardo, paseó toda la casa con los ojos, y no vio en toda ella sino un mudo y sosegado silencio, hasta que paró la vista donde Leonisa estaba" (I, 168-69). After Leonisa recovers from the shock of seeing alive a man she thought dead, she responds to Ricardo's first words with a gesture requesting silence, in light of their location: "Púsose Leonisa en esto el dedo en la boca, por lo cual entendió Ricardo que era señal de que callase o hablase más quedo"; Leonisa then tells him: "—Habla paso, Mario, que así me parece que

---

[23] On the implications and iconic richness of this moment, see I. Lerner, "Aspectos de la representación en *El amante liberal*," *Filología* 22.1 (1987): 37-47.

te llamas ahora, y no trates de otra cosa de la que yo te tratare" (I, 169). The imposition of constraint on speech here is plausible in the context of plot, but at the same time it is significant for the larger thematic question. It is not yet time for full revelations. From her own position, Leonisa's move to limit the scope and content of their verbal contact here is necessary for other reasons: Leonisa is not yet ready to go public.

This scene also contains Leonisa's first extended speech. While it is more than a little evasive with regard to what she truly feels, it is crucial to the narrative for its account of her side of the adventures. Notable in her narration is the curious fact that, while Leonisa passes through moments of much physical danger, from shipwreck and so on, she states that she was never abused or mistreated by Yzuf or, after he is killed, by the Muslim sailors (in effect, pirates) who bring her ashore and then protect her.[24] Exploitation of the erotic or of the possible threat to her honor is here foregone by Cervantes. This suggests a degree of chivalry or decency that reflects back positively on persons who, as *turcos*, would normally in Cervantes's time be expected to be the embodiments of evil in precisely these areas (i.e., sex and violence). This positive reflection is all the more striking in that it is counter-balanced by the thoroughly unchaste, unchivalrous actions of the *cadí*, Alí Bajá, and Hazán Bajá later on.

The house of the *cadí*—and by extension, the Cyprus that is controlled by the Turks in 1570—is an arena of linguistic and communicative ambiguity and incompleteness. This fact determines the functional and symbolic importance of Mahamut who as a *renegado* is by definition an intermediary, an interpreter. The other renegades, the crewmembers and captive galley slaves, and many others speak, using one language or another, as best they can. Throughout there is a sense that language too is a zone of borderlands. Leonisa's words, referring to Halima's comprehension of various languages, clearly apply more broadly; as she states to

---

[24] As Leonisa relates it in her story, "Ocho días estuvimos en la isla, guardándome los turcos el mismo respecto que si fuera su hermana, y aun más" (I, 171).

Ricardo, "Vete con Dios, que temo no nos haya escuchado Halima, la cual entiende algo de la lengua cristiana, a lo menos de *aquella mezcla de lenguas* que se usa, con que todos nos entendemos" (I, 174; emphasis added).   Cervantes's tactic here is significant: with the conventional "suspension of disbelief" and the simple fact that a story has to be written in *some* coherent language, we read the words of Turks and others in Cervantes's Castilian and merely imagine that they are speaking Turkish, and so on. But Cervantes keeps returning to the fact of plurality, foreignness, and incomplete understanding. We are not allowed to forget this other barrier: we are in zones of cultural juxtaposition and contention where people attempt to understand each other ("con que todos nos entendemos") through strange filters of clashing languages.

III. "una graciosa burla"

One additional symbolically rich element of this *novela*—in part conventional but also closely related to the issues of language and the seductive attractions of a putatively hostile culture—is the role of costume.[25] Throughout the *Novelas ejemplares*, clothes make the person, as it were, and there are numerous highly charged and emblematic scenes in which a woman (or on occasion a man) makes an appearance in stunningly beautiful dress. The purpose, as well as the effect, is usually to intensify the sense of someone's inherent physical or spiritual beauty. But in *El amante liberal* we have not only this conventional aspect but also the implications of costume as part of a culturally signifying system. It is thus a language that can express either difference or belonging, and thus relatedly, the possible confusions between the two.

---

[25] As Marjorie Garber suggests in *Vested Interests: Cross-Dressing and Cultural Anxiety*, there has long been a particularly erotic charge, to the European or Western mind, in the costume and clothing of the Middle East—in her phrase, "the Western fantasy of the transvestic, pan-sexualized Middle East, a place of liminality and change" (337).

The first significant example of this element of dress is the initial entrance of Mahamut. He refers to his clothing as this "hábito que aborrezco"—in other words, as a mark of cultural identification that he wishes to reject and also as a symbol of his entrapment. Later, the function of clothing as identifier is exploited to cause "visual confusions" of a deliberate and telling sort. But perhaps the most important instance of the clothing-as-signifier element in the early part of the *novela* occurs with the reappearance of Leonisa. When she is brought to Cyprus by the Jewish merchant (whose motives, strangely devoid of the erotic, are apparently mercenary), she is decked out as elegantly as possible—in order, we presume, to enhance her sale price or exchange value. Cervantes, as is his wont, takes pleasure in realizing the descriptive potential of the moment. Leonisa enters

> vestida en hábito berberisco, tan bien aderezada y compuesta, que no lo pudiera estar tan bien la más rica mora de Fez ni de Marruecos, que en aderezarse llevan la ventaja a todas las africanas, aunque entren las de Argel con sus perlas tantas. Venía cubierto el rostro con tafetán carmesí; por las gargantas de los pies que se descubrían, parecían dos carcajes, que así se llaman las manillas en arábigo, al parecer de puro oro; y en los brazos, que asimismo por una camisa de cendal delgado se descubrían o traslucían, traía otros carcajes de oro sembrados de muchas perlas; en resolución, en cuanto el traje, ella venía rica y gallardamente aderezada.
> (I, 157)

In the *Novelas ejemplares* women often enter the scene in a kind of brilliant, quasi-enchanted aura created by beautiful clothes and often improbable heaps of jewels, but Leonisa's entrance and what is expressed by her costume are different. First of all, Cervantes presents the *moda berberisca* aspect of the dress in a most positive light: the exotic quality of dress and scene both enhances Leonisa's beauty and also allows suggestions of the inherent, legitimate beauty of the Afro-Arab women—and by extension, the culture as a whole.

Second, the passage craftily presents both Leonisa's intact virtue and virginal character, on the one hand, and her reality as erotic object, on the other. In point of fact, this entrance is not only her most striking visual moment, but is also the one place in the *novela* in which she is most emphatically seen in erotic terms. In many ways, it is a conventional moment. But it is also quite distinct in the broader Cervantine context. That the eroticism is attenuated, indirect, and somewhat static only adds to its significance. Leonisa's face is veiled, as is the Islamic and Hispanic custom, but her ankles are exposed ("las gargantas de los pies que se descubrían"), not only showing off the gold anklets but also provocatively revealing the feet and ankles themselves.[26] Likewise, there is an ambiguous, revealing-concealing, sensuality in the description of her arms, also adorned with gold: "los brazos, que asimismo por una camisa de cendal delgado se descubría o traslucían, . . ." In what is without doubt the most visually sensual moment in the *novela*, the diaphanous cloth allows the flesh itself to shine through, to be dis-covered within its concealment.

The Islamic-Moorish setting and costume give license to the *novela* to indulge in a moment of sensual contemplation, allowable because this world is *not* Leonisa's proper world; she is a captive, a victim. But as was suggested earlier, her sexual victimization here does not go beyond the visual. She is more the object of awe and admiration than the pitiable victim of physical, sexual aggression. At the same time, the sensual, erotic costume and the visualized desire of this scene subtly evoke the opulent, seductive character of the Islamic and, especially, the Turkish world. To put it another way, the *image* of Leonisa as she is clothed or semi-veiled here is not unlike the complex attractiveness of the exotic world that might have been perceived, or imagined, by the young and foolish Mahamut. The Leonisa of this key scene, then, is not only the specific character placed in a kind of moral and physical danger, not only the "woman as object." She is also a subtle embodiment of the confusions and seductions, the reality of the dangerous power of erotic contempla-

---

[26] At this point, one is reminded of another famous scene of what some might call Cervantine foot-fetishism, the first sight of the cross-dressed, disguised Dorotea in *Don Quijote*, I, ch. 28.

tion, that are part of the subtext of the European-Turkish cultural frontier.

The entrance of Leonisa at this point also fulfills its crucial plot function. This vision of beauty and sensuality not only awes the reader and, presumably, Ricardo, who is also looking on. More importantly, it fires the lustful interest of the three Turks, Alí Bajá, Hazán Bajá, and the *cadí*. This three-way conflict of greed and desire sets up the climactic battle at sea in which the evil forces, all intent on obtaining Leonisa, in a sense turn against and consume one another. After this spasm of violence, the previously helpless cap-tives—Ricardo, Leonisa, and the others—as the surviving beneficia-ries of a poetically just outcome, regain their freedom. With Ricardo and the other Christians now in control of the ship, a safe return to Sicily is possible.

At this point, however, in the aftermath of the battle and on the threshold of the desired and triumphant return to Sicily, something odd and seemingly gratuitous happens. Now in control of one of the Turkish ships, with all the banners, clothes, and other trappings of their former captors, Ricardo comes up with a peculiar—and potentially dangerous—idea. He decides that they will sail into the Sicilian harbor all dressed in Turkish disguise: "En este entretanto había Ricardo pedido y suplicado a Leonisa que se adornase y vistiese *de la misma manera que cuando entró en la tienda de los bajaes*, porque quería hacer una graciosa burla a sus padres" (I, 183-184; emphasis added). In effect, Cervantes is, in the guise of Ricardo's whim, echoing the earlier scene of Leonisa's appearance on Cyprus, and although danger and victimization are no longer part of the picture, the sensual indulgence is. Beauty for the purpose of inspiring wonder is clearly part of the motive, as the text indicates:

> Hízolo así, y añadiendo galas a galas, perlas a perlas, y belleza a belleza, que suele acrecentarse con el contento, se vistió de modo que de nuevo *causó admiración y maravilla*. Vistióse asimismo Ricardo a la turquesca, y lo mismo hizo Mahamut y todos los cristianos del remo, que para todos hubo en los vestidos de los turcos muertos. (I, 184; emphasis added)

As the foregoing passage implies, the "wonder and marvel" are the result of a natural beauty further enhanced, or one might say supercharged, with an oriental opulence of clothing, jewels, and other adornments.[27]

But it is also a function of the troubling expressive power and implications of the threatening yet seductive eastern empire from which they have (perhaps not completely) escaped. The ambiguity of this sort of *admiración y maravilla*, the point (one supposes) of Ricardo's *graciosa burla*, is suggested by the more or less anticipated effect that the ship's arrival has upon the Sicilian onlookers. As the ship approaches,

> Estaba toda la gente confusa, esperando llegase el bizarro bajel; pero cuando vieron de cerca que era turquesco, porque se divisaban los blancos turbantes de los que moros parecían, temerosos y con sospecha de algún engaño, tomaron las armas y acudieron al puerto todos los que en la ciudad son de milicia, y la gente de a caballo se tendió por toda la marina;
> ... (I, 184)

Fortunately, no guns go off before the true identity of the ship's passengers is revealed. But it would not be idle to note that Ricardo is, as it were, playing with fire. This would, however, be an almost crassly realistic reading. What is happening here has, I believe, a more metaphorical and non-rational purpose. The ship's arrival and the fabulous, multi-colored ("bizarro") appearance of it and its passengers are a visual but non-literalist symbolic reiteration of the marvel and wonder that is the mixture of the fearful and the beautiful: the European vision of the Ottoman Empire, another phenomenon of these borderlands of warring cultures.

The last pages of the *novela* bring Ricardo and Leonisa back to where they began. They also bring Mahamut and Halima (who will of course end up marrying Mahamut) back to a land, culture, and religion that they have long sought. The adventures and tribulations

---

[27] A most intriguing commentary on this particular scene is offered by G. Díaz-Migoyo, "La ficción cordial de *El amante liberal*," *NRFH* 35.1 (1987): 129-50; see especially 144-45.

of the story thus are redeemed and rewarded by the sense of return and a regaining of that which was lost or renounced. But there still remains an unresolved element to the story of identity, as the final scene reveals. Ricardo makes his magnanimous speech, presenting Leonisa to Cornelio. Then, abruptly, he stops himself, realizing that "no es posible que nadie pueda demostrarse liberal de lo ajeno" and that "no doy a Cornelio nada, pues no puedo." It is now, finally, Leonisa's turn to speak. First, she clears the air, explaining that

> Si algún favor, ¡oh Ricardo!, imaginas que hice a Cornelio en el tiempo que tú andabas de mí enamorado y celoso, imagina que fue tan honesto como guiado por la voluntad y orden de mis padres, que, atentos a que le moviesen a ser mi esposo, permitían que se los diese; . . . (I, 187)

She then states that "Esto digo por darte a entender, Ricardo, que *siempre fui mía*, sin estar sujeta a otro que a mis padres, a quien ahora humildemente, como es razón, suplico que me den licencia y libertad para disponer [de] la que tu mucha valentía y liberalidad me ha dado" (I, 187; emphasis added). Leonisa's brief speech and her resolution of the apparent conflict are a subtle combination of level-headed good sense, the emergence of a willful individuality, and also a conventional submission to familial, patriarchal authority.[28]

Leonisa, as we see, appears to have the last word. What is particularly significant about what she says is that it puts much into perspective. It indicates, if we needed the clarification, how impulsive and misguided Ricardo had been. The speech also marks her expression—pending her parents' permission—of her own will and desires. That her decision falls in favor of Ricardo is not surprising, given the expectations of the romance genre and the needed comedic resolution of apparent conflict. But it is somewhat ironic, in light of Ricardo's vision of the situation obtaining with Leonisa, Cornelio, and himself. We suddenly recall that nearly everything heretofore known about Leonisa has been presented to

---

[28] On this issue, see Sears, *A Marriage of Convenience*, and with special regard to *El amante liberal*, see 138-40.

us mainly by Ricardo or, in the cautious meeting scene in the house of the *cadí*, in a highly guarded and filtered way.

Leonisa can only emerge fully, with the possibility of this partial and in fact incomplete sort of "free speech," after her displacement and period of borderland captivity and danger in the lands and hands of the Turks. Her taking of the word at this point is a crucial turn. It seems more symbolically required by the larger theme than by verisimilitude. Leonisa's voice here is both her emergence and her act of judgment, placing herself and others within the total scheme of the problems of identification and allegiance variously dramatized throughout, but especially reasserting the order symbolized by marriage.[29] The trials of identity through which *all* of the main characters have gone have not only served to aid in enlightening and transforming Ricardo. They have also aided the emergence of Leonisa, of Leonisa's relative autonomy—an "autonomy" both limited and predictable in its conformity to and affirmation of a larger, all-encompassing patriarchal system and set of values.

With Leonisa's concluding and clarifying moment of self-expression, the *novela* rereads itself in our imagination. It becomes not just a tale of adventure and adversity, but also a complex structure in which love is tested, emotions purified, and in which the passage across cultural and geographic borders and threatening seas is both a trial and also a symbolic language for the confusions of identity that lie at the heart of *El amante liberal*. In *El amante liberal* the adventures and dangers experienced in this contested Mediterranean world—as well as the Ottoman world itself, seen as another model of human possibilities, both seductive and repellent—are presented in such a way that they question the concept of identity, putting it in "tela de juicio." Finally, this text dramatizes the necessity of

---

[29] In this regard, I find myself largely in agreement with Sears (*A Marriage of Convenience*) and her argument that, throughout the *Novelas ejemplares* and especially in this one, the patriarchal order wins out and its most pervasive and potent institution—marriage—is the vehicle that both carries out this task and also makes it seem most fortunate and liberating (i.e., the triumph of true love).

challenge and ordeal while it also reveals the subtle and inevitable ambiguity of the cultural and psychological bases of any identity.

Chapter Three
The Carnival of Crime
Rinconete y Cortadillo

The transition from *El amante liberal* to *Rinconete y Cortadillo* provides one of the most drastic contrasts of continuous reading, from one *novela* to the next, within the *Novelas ejemplares*. Not only do we leave the world and conventions of the romance genre, but we also move from a text in which action and conflict share equal importance with the interplay of languages, to one in which discourse takes on primary importance, but in ways quite distinct from the first two *novelas*. In *Rinconete y Cortadillo* there is no central problem or challenge, either for the two young boys of the title or for anyone else encountered in the story. Instead, the *novela* is a series of loosely connected, seemingly minor events. Moreover, in comparison to the other *Novelas ejemplares*, this text foregrounds and complicates the question of genre more acutely than any of the others. *Rinconete y Cortadillo* prompts us to ask whether or not it is a *novela* in any of the ways that the others are.[1] Given the lack of any plot in the usual novelistic sense and the importance of dialogue and verbal play, *Rinconete y Cortadillo* has about it more the character of an *entremés* than a *novela*.[2]

---

[1] On the questions of structure and genre, much has been written about this text; see in particular R. M. Johnston, "Generic Polyphony and the Reader's Exemplary Experience in Cervantes' *Rinconete y Cortadillo*," *Revista Canadiense de Estudios Hispánicos* 16.1 (1991): 73-85; and R. G. Keightley, "The Narrative Structure of *Rinconete y Cortadillo*," in *Essays on Narrative Fiction in the Iberian Peninsula in Honour of Frank Pierce*, 39-54.

[2] Concerning the theatrical element of this text, see D. Ynduráin, "*Rinconete y Cortadillo*: De entremés a novela," *Boletín de la Real Academia Española* 46 (1966): 321-33. See also, M. Nimetz, "Genre and Creativity in *Rinconete y Cortadillo*," *Cervantes* 10.2 (1990): 73-93; H. Reed, "Theatricality in the Picaresque of Cervantes," *Cervantes* 7.2 (1987): 71-84; and F. J. Sánchez, *Lectura y representación: Análisis cultural de las Novelas ejemplares de Cervantes*, especially 107-14.

But other ends are served by this interlude of colorful, grotesque characters, jargon, festivity, and comic incident. In *Rinconete y Cortadillo* languages define the boundaries of individual identity within a specific, marginal social world.[3] After the opening scenes—the meeting of the two boys at the inn, the collaborative cardsharping swindle, and their first adventures upon arriving in Sevilla—the setting shifts to the house of Monipodio where all subsequent action, such as it is, takes place. Here, the story becomes a chain of scenes whose purpose seems to be little more than the comic representation of a picaresque underworld. This colorfully rendered *inframundo*, however, is completely without a picaresque *historia*. What this *novela* lacks, or has deliberately eschewed, is the form and explicatory purpose of the familiar picaresque narrative.[4] What it will elaborate and explore, however, is a vision of society through the lens of the festive, a vision without picaresque alienation but, nonetheless, with a disquieting reminder of the intimate connections between the underworld and the putatively decent society of the reader.

At this point I should confess to my own problem with this text. I have always found *Rinconete y Cortadillo* one of the most accessible and enjoyable of the *Novelas ejemplares*. Yet at the same time, I find it the most vexing to fit into any meaningful pattern pertinent to the rest of the collection. For this reason, I have tended to relegate the *novela* to a lesser status. To pursue the *entremés* analogy a little further, I am tempted to call this text an interlude within the larger context of the *Novelas*. Granted, this contrastive difference is an effective and perhaps intentional break within the collection, a contrast to the norm of the Cervantine *novela*, which usually involves the working out of one or more intricate problems of sentiment or

[3] On this issue, see A. Hermenegildo, "La marginación social de *Rinconete y Cortadillo*," 553-62 in *La Picaresca: Orígenes, textos y estructuras*.
[4] On the question of the picaresque in this *novela*, and in the Cervantine in general, the bibliography is vast; but see in particular Casalduero (*Sentido y forma*), 103-05; and P. Dunn, "Cervantes De/Re-Constructs the Picaresque," *Cervantes* 2.2 (1982): 109-31.

identity, or the detailed rendering of a complex world (as in the *Coloquio*).

But largely because *Rinconete y Cortadillo* lacks the plot, elaboration of character, or other novelistic features present in the other *Novelas ejemplares*, it foregrounds even more acutely the questions of language and social order that, along with identity, are the focus of this present study. No doubt the most noticeable element of the text—and the aspect that has been taken most erroneously, in my opinion—is the question of social order, often reduced to the argument about Cervantes and the picaresque.[5] As I have stated above, this *novela* appears to be a window into the picaresque world. Yet there is no picaresque *historia*, no plot, either biographical or autobiographical, that is projected by, contains, or follows its roguish protagonists. In a manner radically different from the situations of Lazarillo or Pablos of Segovia, Rincón and Cortado are orphans of the imagination, boys without a significant past or future. They are peculiarly and most improbably innocent.

Nonetheless, the issue of social order is central to this *novela*. The brevity of the fictional time that transpires in the story enhances the importance of the synchronic, structural reality of the society presented. The prominence of jargon, the verbal distortions, the use of language as a tool of evasion, and the almost theatrical structure—along with the curious disappearance of the putative protagonists—render the question of social order the primary issue. To put it another way, the lack of novelistic conflict and the absence of dominant, well-developed characters prompt the reader to approach the text as both representation and metaphor. *Rinconete y Cortadillo* is both embodiment and critical vision of a festive, grotesque world. It is also a subtle code for speaking about social issues in the other, larger world.[6]

---

[5] Once again, see P. Dunn, "Cervantes De/Re-Constructs the Picaresque." See also A. Castro, *El pensamiento de Cervantes*, 228-44.

[6] Perhaps the most provocative and ingenious reading of this sort is that of C. B. Johnson, "The Old Order Passeth, or Does It? Some Thoughts on Community, Commerce, and Alienation in *Rinconete y Cortadillo*" (85-104).

In *Rinconete y Cortadillo* the problem of social orders, or sub-worlds, and of the borders between one social realm and another, is a question of languages as much as it is one of supposedly criminal actions and values. We enter the world of *Rinconete y Cortadillo* stage by stage, and at each point, language serves as a distinguishing marker, sometimes a barrier and often a device of initiation and identity. What Harry Sieber has said about the entry of the two boys into the sector dominated by Monipodio is applicable to the *novela* as a whole: "No es sólo que este mundo subterráneo tiene su conexión con el mundo comercial de Sevilla por el lenguaje aduanero, sino también su propio lenguaje interno, su propio código de ladrón. La entrada en el mundo de Monipodio es una entrada lingüística; . . ."[7] In *Rinconete y Cortadillo* language is a code in both senses of the word: a terminology that simultaneously communicates to the initiates and hides from the excluded outsider, and a system of laws or protocols that gives social order (hierarchy but also "law and order") and identity, collective as well as individual, to a specific stratum of society.

Concerning the structural features of this *novela*, we first note that, in what is becoming a familiar pattern, there is a doubling of the male protagonist: Rincón and Cortado are simultaneously similar yet deliberately non-identical. This doubling of the rogue reminds us slightly of Avendaño and Carriazo in their assumed disguises and roguish role-playing in *La ilustre fregona*. The obvious difference is that for the latter pair the roles of marginal low-life characters are a temporary detour from an aristocratic identity and place. For Rincón and Cortado, in contrast, their condition is not role playing, in the same sense. The text clearly indicates that there is no respectable or noble identity from which the boys have taken momentary leave. Rather, what little background is provided is at first kept ambiguous. In this initial inclination toward anonymity we are reminded of another evasive introduction in the *Novelas ejemplares*: that of Tomás at the beginning of *El licenciado Vidriera*. Tomás's reticence is moti-

---

[7] "Introducción" I, 27; throughout his introductory notes to the *Novelas*, Sieber has very incisively pointed out the relationship of the verbal to the sociocritical.

vated (or so he tells us) by a desire to attain honor and accomplishment before revealing his background, so that he might then bring credit to his family.[8] For the two young vagabonds of this third *novela*, however, their initial refusal to link themselves to place or family is part of a deliberate strategy of self-protection, a logical move, given the dangers and vicissitudes of criminal life.

As the *novela* opens, we are on the road, at what in terms of symbolic geography is an intermediate zone. Appropriately, we are at an inn.[9] Moreover, the boys are headed south, toward Sevilla. In the "moral geography" symbolized by place and direction, this means that we are headed toward a more lawless world, given the reputation of Sevilla as Spain's capital of picaresque criminality. The first words of the *novela* introduce this sense of place and suspension within a larger trajectory: "En la venta del Molinillo, que está puesta en los fines de los famosos campos de Alcudia, como vamos de Castilla a la Andalucía, un día de los calurosos del verano se hallaron en ella acaso dos muchachos de hasta edad de catorce a quince años; . . ." (I, 191). The narrator dwells upon the visual description of the boys, but not so much their physical features as their lack of cleanliness and the condition of their clothing. This description has both atmospheric and moral overtones. The two boys are young, tattered, and dirty. From this, we infer their moral marginality as well as the rootlessness of their identities. The first words between the two—the first of the many exchanges that structure the *novela*—are so conventional that one might miss the emphasis put on the problem of identity, here defined in terms of place of origin. The older boy speaks first:

> —¿De qué tierra es vuesa merced, señor gentilhombre, y para adónde bueno camina?

---

[8] See the *Novelas*, II, 43; see also Chapter Five, below.

[9] The importance of the inn as more than a mere arbitrary setting in the *Quijote*, Part I, hardly needs to argued. On the contrastive significance of the pauses implied by the roadside inn and the encompassing travel that defines this place of hiatus, see Hutchinson, *Cervantine Journeys*.

—Mi tierra, señor caballero —respondió el preguntado—, no la sé, ni para dónde camino, tampoco.

—Pues en verdad —dijo el mayor—que no parece vuesa merced del cielo, y que éste no es lugar para hacer su asiento en él: que por fuerza se ha de pasar adelante.

—Así es —respondió el mediano—; pero yo he dicho verdad en lo que he dicho; porque mi tierra no es mía, pues no tengo en ella más que un padre que no me tiene por hijo y una madrastra que me trata como alnado; el camino que llevo es a la ventura, y allí le daría fin donde hallase quien me diese lo necesario para pasar esta miserable vida. (I, 193)

In addition to the obvious desire to evade revelations, the most notable aspect of this first interchange is a certain verbal elegance and wit couched in colloquial simplicity. These two kids like to use words. A little further on (I, 194-98) Rincón and Cortado gain each other's confidence sufficiently to reveal their names and places of origin. Their backgrounds, while ambiguous, are not nearly as troubling as the sort found in the opening of the conventional picaresque narrative, in which the juxtaposition of blunt declarations and the impulse to distort the truth generally defines the genre. The contrast with the usual picaresque narrative—with its explicit, if deceptive, focus on lineage—is striking: where the opening of the *Lazarillo de Tormes* or the *Buscón* is relatively clear (if distorted or mendacious), the analogous section in *Rinconete y Cortadillo* is evasive.

This first dialogue—along with what follows (I, 194ff), in which the two boys gradually reveal their specific skills—sets the pattern for the entire *novela*. Recurrently throughout this text, two or more characters engage in dialogues that deploy and explore various verbal games, or in which the initial strangeness of a word, plus its subsequent explication, becomes a core part of the process of initiation, the act of crossing a boundary. Thus, while there are obvious instances of puns, malapropisms, and shared (i.e., mutually controlled and enjoyed) verbal play, a major role in *Rinconete y Cortadillo* is also played by the acquisition of the totally new jargon, the code of another "world."[10] The special, foreign language—the discourse as code—of the new social group is both a necessary tool and a verification of authentic belonging.

The idea of entering different worlds is a determining feature of this *novela*. As Harry Sieber has pointed out, the concept of the *aduana*, the customs house, and the notion of controlling the movement of goods and people through the gates of the city are key to both structure and theme in this *novela*.[11] From our anachronistic, late-twentieth-century perspective, the idea that the entrance to a city would need to be controlled or that a "duty" would need to be paid on transported goods seems odd. But aside from the historical authenticity of this detail, it is also crucial to the thematic dimension of the *novela*. Control, exchange, payment of duties, and the concept of borders and of entry into a "foreign" zone combine to reinforce the primary socio-critical point of the *novela*.

After the boys' first act of collaborative swindling (the episode of the card game at the inn; I, 198), they take up with a group of travelers who are going to Sevilla. As the group enters the city through the customs house gate, Cortado can no longer resist doing a little purse-cutting: "Con todo esto, a la entrada de la ciudad, que fue a la oración, y por la puerta de la Aduana, a causa del registro y almojarifazgo que se paga, no se pudo contener Cortado de no cortar la valija o maleta que a las ancas traía un francés . . ." (I, 199). Immediately thereafter, the two boys explore the city (during which, the narrator gives us a hint of the complex mercantile/criminal dynamic of this major port city[12]). They quickly decide to work as "muchachos de la esportilla"—in effect, delivery boys—since this

---

[10] On the question of languages in this *novela*, see A. W. Hayes, "Narrative 'Errors' in *Rinconete y Cortadillo*," *BHS* 58.1 (1981): 13-20.

[11] See H. Sieber's introductory comments, I, 26-27.

[12] Sevilla figures significantly in several of the *Novelas ejemplares*—*La española inglesa*, *El celoso extremeño*, *El coloquio de los perros*, etc.—and as I shall suggest in a later chapter, the moral implications of Cervantes's particularly rendered Spanish geography are quite important (see Chapter 8, "Identity and Social Order: *La ilustre fregona*").

profession will not only provide income directly, but will also allow them entry to houses so that they can, as we might say, "case the joint" for purposes of future theft.

As they quickly find out, however, Sevilla's criminal world is not the free-ranging, entrepreneurially fluid ambit of operations that they have known heretofore, on the road, and that they briefly enjoyed at the inn of el Molinillo. The boys barely have time to contract a catering job with a soldier (I, 202) and to perform a theft (Cortado's) upon the hapless student-sacristan (I, 203-205), when they are spotted and approached by one of Monipodio's *mozos* ("y más abajo estaba otro mozo de la esportilla, que vio todo lo que había pasado y cómo Cortado daba el pañuelo a Rincón, . . ." [I, 205]). The exchange between Monipodio's underling and the two new boys is emblematic of the intersection of language and subgroup social boundaries. The entry of this essentially minor character into the narrative and the mutual introductions of the three boys follow the pattern of the gradual presentation of a new discourse, of terms that are foreign to the two outsiders and that thus require explanation—in effect, translation—as we see in the following:

> —Díganme, señores galanes: ¿voacedes son de mala entrada, o no?
> —No entendemos esa razón, señor galán —respondió Rincón.
> —¿Que no entrevan, señores murcios? —respondió el otro.
> —No somos de Teba ni de Murcia —dijo Cortado—. Si otra cosa quiere, dígala; si no, váyase con Dios.
> —¿No lo entienden? —dijo el mozo—. Pues yo se lo daré a entender, y a beber, con una cuchara de plata: quiero decir, señores, si son vuesas mercedes ladrones. Mas no sé para qué les pregunto esto, pues sé ya que lo son. Mas díganme: ¿cómo no han ido a la aduana del señor Monipodio? (I, 206)

This dialogue of misunderstanding (and Rincón's first words protesting non-comprehension can be taken as a case of willful "playing dumb") begins with a question of semantics—"de mala entrada" and its *germanía* significance, which has to be explained—and ends with an allusion to the issue of social structure: "la aduana del señor Monipodio." The smallest detail of style and rhetorical form subtly embodies the underlying issue: the inextricable connection of language and social place or identity. What the text is telling us is that the proper admittance of the two neophytes into the *hampa* of Sevilla demands their acquisition of a new language. It also requires the proper paying of one's "duties," something that is both a ceremony and a material obligation.[13]

Between this first encounter with the *mozo* and the actual entry into the house of Monipodio, the process of linguistic initiation continues. In a directional sense, the *mozo* is a guide, as Cortado notes: "así puede vuesa merced guiarnos donde está ese caballero que dice, . . ." (I, 206). But the *mozo* also takes them into a new discursive or linguistic realm. The more experienced *mozo* in effect serves as an interpreter or educator for Rincón and Cortado. The initiations of language are a primary function of this transitional passage. Each new detail about this new world prompts curiosity and questions. To enter is to be forced to learn.

When the *mozo* speaks of Monipodio's virtues and talents as being such that "en cuatro años que ha que tiene el cargo de ser nuestro mayor y padre no han padecido sino cuatro en el *fini-busterrae*, y obra de treinta envesados y de sesenta y dos en gurapas" (I, 207), the bewildered Rincón replies, "En verdad, señor . . . que así entendemos esos nombres como volar" (I, 207). Rincón's response serves as a kind of cue, a signal to the *mozo* (but also to the reader) that a linguistic as well as a physical transition is to be made. Rincón's words invite the *mozo* to continue the process of leading and explicating. The boy thus responds: "Comencemos a andar, que yo los iré declarando por el camino . . . , con otros algunos que así les conviene saberlos como el pan de la boca" (I, 207). Walking and talking—learning new language, while strolling to the new realm—are subtly but tellingly connected. The narrator's brief transitional paragraph further ties the two concepts together: "Y así,

---

[13] This is clearly indicated in the next exchange: "¿Págase en esta tierra almojarifazgo de ladrones, señor galán? —dijo Rincón.

" Si no se paga —respondió el mozo—, a lo menos regístranse ante el señor Monipodio, que es su padre, su maestro y su amparo; . . ." (I, 206).

les fue diciendo y declarando otros nombres de los que ellos llaman *germanescos* o *de la germanía,* en el discurso de su plática, que no fue corta, porque el camino era largo" (I, 207).[14] The *mozo's* manner of talking to the two boys is self-consciously pedagogical. In explaining how the religious devotion of one member of Monipodio's band helped fortify him against torture by the authorities, for example, the youth narrates as follows:

> . . . porque los días pasados dieron tres ansias a un cuatrero que había murciado dos roznos, y con estar flaco y cuartanario, así las sufrió sin cantar como si fueran nada. Y esto atribuimos los del arte a su buena devoción, porque sus fuerzas no eran bastantes para sufrir el primer desconcierto del verdugo. Y porque sé que me han de preguntar algunos vocablos de los que he dicho, quiero curarme en salud y decírselo antes que me lo pregunten. Sepan voacedes que *cuatrero* es ladrón de bestias; *ansia* es el tormento; *roznos,* los asnos, hablando con perdón; *primer desconcierto* es las primeras vueltas de cordel que da el verdugo. (I, 208)

That Cervantes is both showing off his personal knowledge of *germanía* and also giving authentic color to the tale is obvious. At the same time, on a more subtle level, the attention given to this special verbal repertoire and, more importantly, the manner in which the language is presented reflect the themes of crossing borders, initiation, and entry that are central to the *novela.* But something else is happening during this verbal and spatial transition to Monipodio's den. Although the essential mode of the *dialogue* is maintained and although Rincón and Cortado continue very much a part of it, the process of the diminution, displacement, or what I would call disappearance of the two title characters has already begun. Through this literal "passage"—from their roles as the ostensibly central *pícaros,* first to that of newcomers, then to that of eager students, and finally to that of initiates—the two boys gradually become what they will most significantly be by the end of the story: spectators, listeners, and occasional commentators upon the actions

---

[14] On the highly pregnant implications of (verbal) discourse and the discourse or coursing of physical movement, see again Hutchinson, *Cervantine Journeys,* especially 3-17, "Motion in Language, Language in Motion."

that ensue. In Monipodio's world they are curious visitors, almost marginal onlookers.

The arrival at the house of Monipodio marks a significant change in the story. Monipodio's patio is the place in which the prior transitional action stops, the place toward which the introductory stages of incident and new language have been heading. The house itself functions as a defining social space. It is not merely a retreat or dwelling, but a place where business is transacted, disputes settled, and festivities celebrated. As much as Monipodio himself, the house represents not only the anti-social realm of the criminal, but also a place of an idealized yet grotesque, carnivalesque nature. The house, along with most of what goes on in it, is not in the literal sense a *carnival*; nor does every aspect of it and its inhabitants conform precisely to the Bakhtinian notion of the carnivalesque, with the extremes of license, exuberance, and controlled chaos of festival inversions that Bakhtin attributes to the carnival.[15] But with the prominence of food, the musical interlude, and the general atmosphere of celebration, the section that takes place in Monipodio's den suggests a subworld whose "order" is at once coarse and exuberant. The discursive space defined by Monipodio's house makes most sense seen from the perspective that P. Stallybrass and A. White have outlined in their treatment of the theatre and the fair in seventeenth-century England. As they put it,

> Patterns of discourse are regulated through the forms of corporate assembly in which they are produced. Alehouse, coffee-house, church, law court, library, drawing room of a country mansion: each place of assembly is a different site of intercourse requiring different manners and morals. Discursive space is never completely independent of social place and the formation of new kinds of speech can be traced through the emergence of new public sites of discourse and the transformation of old ones. Each 'site of assembly' constitutes a nucleus of material and cultural conditions which regulate what may and may not be said, who may

---

[15] See in particular Bakhtin, *Rabelais and His World*; see also Stallybrass and White, *The Politics and Poetics of Transgression*.

speak, how people may communicate and what importance must be given to what is said. (80)

Very clearly, Monipodio's lair is a defining social and cultural space, legitimizing the discourse and laws of the underworld. It also establishes a special space of social gathering and of somewhat formalized performance.

A sense of the grotesque pervades this *novela*. Yet it is not concretized in a single conventional figure, such as the carnivalesque clown, a "Lord of Misrule," or even a masking as in the "Rey de gallos" episode in Quevedo's *Buscón*. The most significant embodiment of the grotesque is Monipodio himself. The detailed physical description of Monipodio is not only one of Cervantes's most memorable passages of portraiture in the grotesque genre, but is also emblematic of the nature of his world. The wildness and earthy animality of this parallel criminal world is embodied in the leader of the *cofradía*.

At this point, it is worth noting certain tendencies of physical description in Cervantes's writing. With a few notable exceptions, descriptions of the beautiful characters, and in particular descriptions of body and face, are rarely detailed or concrete. The beautiful women and men in Cervantes, if they are described at all, are usually rendered in terms of conventions and clichés. Often, as we have seen and will see again, Cervantes lavishes more attention on the clothes and jewels of the women (e.g., Leonisa's arrival as a captive on Cyprus in *El amante liberal*, Isabel in *La española inglesa*, or for a male counterpart example, the first appearance of don Juan de Cárcamo in *La gitanilla*). By contrast, the physically unattractive, be it the grotesque, the merely old (e.g., don Quijote), or the rustically comic (e.g., Sancho Panza), elicits more detail. Cervantes's "beautiful people" do not need extensive describing, in part because they represent an ideal. The unbeautiful, meanwhile, may be merely amusingly "ill-favored"—as in the case of Maritornes—or fully hideous, usually for deliberately symbolic purposes, as with the witch Cañizares in the *Coloquio*.[16] With the ugly or grotesque, Cervantes is not plugging into a set of familiar conventions; thus each creation of the non-beautiful allows for the exercise of special descriptive creativity. By extension, the specific details and visual elements of the grotesque portrait take on greater symbolic meaning.

The presentation of Monipodio is Cervantes's most detailed portrait in *Rinconete y Cortadillo*. As the leader of this particular criminal band, Monipodio reflects the crudeness, criminality, and anti-social, anti-ideal essence of his subworld. But he also has certain curiously positive aspects. First and foremost, he is presented in a way that emphasizes his physically imposing, earthy, and yet paternal nature, while also underlining the carnivalesque aspect of this criminal world. Cervantes describes him as follows:

> Parecía de edad de cuarenta y cinco a cuarenta y seis años, alto de cuerpo, moreno de rostro, cejijunto, barbinegro y muy espeso; los ojos, hundidos. Venía en camisa, y por la abertura de delante descubría un bosque: tanto era el vello que tenía en el pecho. Traía cubierta una capa de bayeta casi hasta los pies, en los cuales traía unos zapatos enchancletados, cubríanle las piernas unos zaragüelles de lienzo, anchos y largos hasta los tobillos; el sombrero era de los de la hampa, campanudo de copa y tendido de falda; atravesábale un tahalí por espalda y pechos, a do colgaba una espada ancha y corta, a modo de las del perrillo; las manos eran cortas, pelosas, y los dedos, gordos, y las uñas, hembras y remachadas; las piernas no se le parecían; pero los pies eran descomunales, de anchos y juanetudos. En efeto, él representaba el más rústico y disforme bárbaro del mundo. (I, 211)

Monipodio's characterization, or what the text stresses, is well summed up in the phrase "el más rústico y disforme bárbaro del mundo." His physical features emphasize roughness and a hirsute masculinity that dramatically differs from, and in fact opposes, the handsome apearance of the smooth, usually fair-haired, and ephebic male protagonist found in other Cervantine fictions.[17] Monipodio is

---

[16] See Forcione, *Cervantes and the Mystery of Lawlessness*, especially 59-99. See also Chapter Ten below.

[17] Consider, for example, the portrayals of Ricaredo in *La española inglesa* or the ambiguously, androgynously beautiful Periandro /Persiles of the *Persiles*.

presented as possessing a masculinity of age and virility: he is tall ("alto de cuerpo") as well as dark and rough in this anti-idealized way: "moreno de rostro, cejijunto, barbinegro y muy espeso" (I, 211). The realistic detail of Monipodio's chest hair—"un bosque: tanto era el vello que tenía"—not only accords with the man's roughness, his older virility, but also underlines the wildness of this subworld: this demi-monde is a jungle, "un bosque." Monipodio's chest thus symbolizes the realm over which he presides. But Monipodio is also a rough-edged father figure. As such, the emphasis on his virility is as significant as the lack of any conventional male attractiveness.

Monipodio's coarse maturity contrasts with and overshadows the extreme youth of the two boys. This contrast reminds us that the symbolic implications of the different degrees of sexual development of the male characters, throughout the *novelas*, are of considerable importance. The youthful, ephebic, still putatively chaste male character is almost invariably associated with a high degree of virtue and sincerity. This is the case with don Juan de Cárcamo in *La gitanilla*, or Ricaredo in *La española inglesa*. Others—e.g., Ricardo in *El amante liberal*, Rodolfo in *La fuerza*, or Campuzano in the *Casamiento*—who are usually older or more experienced sexually, have less of an aura of untainted virtue, however manly and heroic they may seem. Finally, the oldest important male figure—Carrizales in *El celoso extremeño*—is, among other things, a figure of impotence and self-destructive folly. Within the possibilities of this spectrum, Rincón and Cortado occupy a place of ambiguous identity. Their presexual youth grants them a certain exemption, a kind of innocence. Yet they are emphatically not virtuous young male suitors or lovers. Thus, age and physicality, as well as the shift in the focus of the *novela*, subtly marginalize the boys, while Monipodio's maturity and presence establish the imaginative focus.

Monipodio's entry into the narrative shifts the center of gravity, the center of concern. With his entrance, the *novela* moves from a focus on the two young boys and their involvement in a string of minor incidents, and opens up into a space of suspended time. This space is both a theatre and a place of festivity. In the "court" of

Monipodio the members of this underworld congregate to settle disputes, report on their affairs, and regroup. But they also come to celebrate. It is both a refuge from and also a complex parody of the putatively law-abiding, orderly mainstream society. Monipodio's house recreates a critical anti-model of the respectable surfaces and rules of the society above and outside of this den of thieves.[18] The first order of business at the arrival of Rincón and Cortado is their presentation, by the *mozo*, to the bandit chief. This ceremony of introduction gives Rincón yet another opportunity to remind us that one's true identity is often best left ambiguous. The presentation of the two to Monipodio also allows the latter to rename the boys, revealing again the exigencies of his paternal role. With this rebaptism, however, Monipodio not only "adopts" but also subordinates the two youths—yet another step in their displacement from the *novela*'s central focus.[19] The renaming reminds us of the pervasive question of identity as potential liability and not just as source of stability. In the boys' evasion of giving information on their identities, moreover, we have a sly comment upon a rather serious socio-critical issue: the well-known and excessive importance of genealogy in the *honra*-driven regulations and protocols of the outer, respectable world. Rincón's remarks make this quite clear: "la patria no me parece de mucha importancia decilla, ni los padres tampoco, pues no se ha de hacer información para recebir algún hábito honroso" (I, 212). The play on words, in this case an irony of evaluative terms, is obvious: the "hábito honroso" to which Rincón refers is here the profession—and identity—of the thief, something that the two boys are seeking to obtain by presenting themselves to Monipodio. Indeed, this sort of "hábito" is hardly "honroso"; much less does it require an extensive family background check. Yet the

---

[18] For a most original reading, one that begins with this obvious connection and then goes significantly further, see again Johnson, "The Old Order Passeth," especially 90-91 and 102-04.

[19] As El Saffar puts it, the boys "become transformed, like so many of the early characters of Cevantes, from creators to observers of the reality in which they find themselves" (*Novel to Romance*, 31).

term "hábito honroso" immediately suggests the highest level of social valuation and respect, i.e., the possible acquisition of a title of nobility and specifically being named to one of the chivalric orders. The obtaining of such a distinction was much sought after in the Spain of Cervantes and it was rigidly guarded by much bureaucratic red tape and the requirement of a documented, unblemished lineage.[20] In this light, Rincón's witticism continues the verbal and evaluative games that make of this underworld a parodic counter-part to and comment on the higher strata of respectable society. It also subtly reminds the reader of the excesses and abuses of genealogy (real or fabricated) in a society obsessed with *honra* and social rank.

With the two youths duly installed into Monipodio's society of thieves, prostitutes, swindlers, and other low-lifes, the remaining action of the *novela* centers upon the affairs brought to Monipodio for his attention. In his role as bandit chief, Monipodio is obliged to intervene and settle disputes, and this becomes the main action in the central part of the *novela*. Monipodio's section of the *novela*, from the renaming of the two boys until the conclusion, subdivides as follows: the first part is characterized by festivity (beginning with food, and ending with music) and by the series of problems brought to Monipodio to be resolved. Then, there follows the passage devoted to a reviewing of accounts, or assignments, as listed in the "libro de memoria." The final paragraph serves as an epilogue. In it the narrator seems to filter his own comments through Rinconete's perspective in order to make a dismissing, distancing judgment on the world that has just been portrayed.

Immediately after the renaming and official induction of the two new boys into the *gremio*, the first problem to be resolved is brought into this court. In what will be the familiar pattern, there is a hasty interruption ("Estando en esto, entró un muchacho corriendo y

---

[20] On the rich—and troubling—implications of this issue of lineage and the acquisition of the *hábito* of a chivalric order, see in particular ter Horst, "Une Saison en enfer: *La gitanilla*," especially 96-100.

desalentado" [I, 216]) and the "alguacil de los vagabundos" comes in, demanding the return of a stolen purse. It turns out to be the one filched that morning by Cortadillo. The point of this first incident is to underscore the importance of obedience, order, and Monipodio's authority. The latter explains why the purse must be restored: "¡La bolsa ha de parecer, porque la pide el alguacil, que es amigo y nos hace mil placeres al año!" (I, 217). Not knowing that no regular member of his band had done the theft, and thus railing at them all, Monipodio is justified in his anger, as the text notes, "viendo que se rompían sus estatutos y buenas ordenanzas" (I, 217). Rinconete's prudent decision to tell Cortadillo to give up the stolen purse signals the boys' acceptance of the new authority, thus further defining their new limitations and obligations.

Monipodio's authority displays itself in various ways in the passages that follow. After the return of the stolen purse, the main focus of the episodic action shifts significantly from the fairly straightforward and impersonal business of theft, to the more complex and emphatically interpersonal concerns of whores and their pimps. After leaving to give the purse to the *alguacil*, Monipodio returns to the patio in the company of la Gananciosa and la Escalanta, "dos mozas, afeitados los rostros, llenos de color los labios y de albayalde los pechos, cubiertas con medios mantos de anascote, llenas de desenfado y desvergüenza: señales claras por donde, en viéndolas Rinconete y Cortadillo, conocieron que eran de la casa llana" (I, 218). Here again we find Cervantes's tendency, in describing people, to ignore the specificity of faces and bodies, and instead to fix on clothing and, as in this case, cosmetics. No clear sense of the women's possible physical beauty or ugliness is given, except in the most indirect ways. As opposed to the special case of the physique of Monipodio himself, the two prostitutes are, in effect, neither beautiful nor ugly because, for the purposes of this text, they don't need to be so identified. Their accessories and their comportment ("llenas de desenfado y desvergüenza") identify them as whores, and this is evidently sufficient. At the same time, the entire section dealing with the interactions between the *rameras* and their *rufianes* brings into the story whatever there is of a sexual dimension. It is the closest thing to romance or at least domestic comedy in this story: the lovers' quarrel of la Cariharta and el Repolido is—however farfetched it might seem—the grotesque echo and parallel to the trials and tribulations of such "romance-genre" lovers as Ricardo and Leonisa.

The entry of these two women, and the brief interchange with the *vieja*, la señora Pipota, serves as a lead-in to the spontaneous banquet (I, 222ff). We are, at this point, reminded of similar festive eating scenes in Cervantes's works, notably the meal shared by the *pastores* with don Quijote and Sancho (*DQ* I, 11). The menu is simple but, unlike the hard cheese and acorns of the *pastores* in *Don Quijote*, abundant, suggesting a certain sensual indulgence:

> y lo primero que sacó de la cesta fue un grande haz de rábanos y hasta dos docenas de naranjas y limones, y luego una cazuela grande llena de tajadas de bacallao frito. Manifestó luego medio queso de Flandes, y una olla de famosas aceitunas, y un plato de camarones, y gran cantidad de cangrejos, con su llamativo de alcaparrones ahogados en pimientos, y tres hogazas blanquísimas de Gandul. (I, 222-23)

The setting out of the food is a gesture that affirms the unity of the band and the inclusion of the two novices. The festivity underscores their inclusion. Likewise, the passages of the *novela* that run from the arrival at Monipodio's house to the end of the action, at the end of the penultimate paragraph, reflect this displacement into a festive, carnivalesque space. This central part, however, gives this dimension to a special level of intensity.

During this festive interlude, the sentimental affairs of men and women briefly take center stage. The main couple involved—Cariharta and her pimp, Repolido—are hardly the conventionally ideal, romantic archetypes. Yet the resolution of their conflicts and the expression of their fidelity and fondness toward each other are not undermined by satire. Except for the troubling (to our more enlightened sensibility) reference to "girl-friend beating," explained away as a sign of affection, the authenticity of the sentiments of Cariharta and Repolido seems credible. All that is "wrong with this picture" is the fact that positive, male-female love and devotion has been cast in terms of what the contemporaneous (and the modern) reader would have to consider low-life persons in a comically marginal realm.

It strikes me that there is no great intrinsic significance to the relationship between Cariharta and Repolido as far as the larger thematic structure of this *novela* is concerned. Yet, however comic and crude the sexual and domestic affairs of the two may be, this episode presents an important contrast between the world of human interactions partially represented by Monipodio and his house, on the one hand, and the viewpoint of the two young boys whose wanderings have led us there, on the other. Just as the entrance of Monipodio into the story—with his clearly delineated role as the paternal authority figure—has effectively upstaged the two youths, the emergence of a couple who are advanced in their sexual maturity further marginalizes the two sexually inexperienced boys. At the risk of belaboring the obvious, I would point out that *Rinconete y Cortadillo* is the only one of the *Novelas ejemplares* in which the putative main characters are uninvolved in any problem dealing with love or sex. By contrast, even the sexually aloof and uninterested Tomás in *El licenciado Vidriera* is at an age in which amorous interests and actions are possible.[21] Given this sexual and amorous noninvolvement, Rinconete and Cortadillo are most appropriate guides or vicarious viewers of Monipodio's world. But at the same time, their incompleteness of development means that they can't fully participate in this world. One might suggest that their status as mere boys is in part that which displaces them from the vitality of the comic episodes of the people who enter and leave Monipodio's patio. This pre-sexual innocence also undercuts the impact of the curiously disembodied and strangely moralistic commentary offered up in the concluding paragraph.

---

[21] See Chapter Five, on the strangely central yet disconnected role of the sexual conflict in *El licenciado Vidriera*.

The conclusion of the episode involving Repolido and Cariharta is marked not only by a reconciliation of the two lovers (I, 229), but also by Monipodio's successful prevention of a fight among his men (I, 230). The section thus reiterates Monipodio's role as the keeper of order and the protector of social harmony. The outcome of this incident likewise underscores the importance of group solidarity and fraternal friendship. As Maniferro puts it, "No hay aquí amigo . . . que quiera enojar ni hacer burla de otro amigo; y pues todos somos amigos, dense las manos los amigos" (I, 230). To which Monipodio adds, "Todos voacedes han hablado como buenos amigos, y como tales amigos se den las manos de amigos" (I, 230). This moment of comedic peacemaking and reconciliation is immediately punctuated by the impromptu musical interlude (I, 231-32). Monipodio and the three prostitutes each contribute a pair of lines to the *seguidilla*, first Escalanta, then Gananciosa, Monipodio, and finally Cariharta. The words of the last two in particular connect this celebratory musical moment with the prior subtheme of amorous conflict and the necessary resolution of same. Monipodio's contribution restates the paradoxical assertion made earlier by Gananciosa, who has said that "a lo que se quiere bien se castiga; y cuando estos bellacones nos dan, y azotan, y acocean, entonces nos adoran" (I, 225). Thus Monipodio sings: "Riñen dos amantes; hácese la paz: / si el enojo es grande, es el gusto más" and Cariharta adds, comically alluding to the flesh-of-my-flesh notion of the ideal married pair: "Detente, enojado, no me azotes más: / que si bien lo miras, a tus carnes das" (I, 232).

The festive conclusion to the section of the *novela* that centers on the sexual, amorous, and domestic relationships (however parodic or distorted) of grown-ups is then followed by the arrival of "un caballero mozo," what we might call a dissatisfied customer. With this, we come to the section dealing with Monipodio's "libro de memoria" and, thus, to a focus on business, accounts, and assignments.[22] What is most intriguing about this passage—and about the

---

[22] Concerning the role of this curious text, see K.-L. Selig, "Cervantes' *Rinconete y Cortadillo* and the Two 'Libros de memoria'," *Revista Hispánica Moderna* 40.3-4 (1978-

whole idea of there being a "libro de memoria"—is the reminder that Monipodio's band not only engages in prostitution and various kinds of theft and swindles, but also hires out its services for selected jobs of thrashing, slashing, and retaliatory vandalism.[23] Monipodio's memo book is ostensibly just the list, schedule, and accounting of completion of such hit jobs. But at the same time, the book (like any book) is a privileged symbol of order and authority, as well as a subtle reminder of the annals of history. That a book exists and is consulted, obeyed, and kept up to date lends yet another dimension of parodic similarity to this anti-social substratum. Specifically, since the retaliatory acts commissioned and listed in this comic catalogue have to do with the "settling of scores," or redressing of grievances, this book is yet another element of Monipodio's world—like the latter's functioning as a judge and settler of disputes among his underlings—that parallels and parodies the legal system of the respectable, law-abiding sectors of society from which Monipodio and his minions are supposedly separate and yet, as the text suggests, with which they are simultaneously very much in league.

The "libro de memoria" is an authority symbol in another more ironic way. It turns the tables on the preestablished notion of Monipodio's power and authority. As we will recall, after reaching a compromise with the young *caballero*, Monipodio calls his group together, and "poniéndose Monipodio en medio dellos, sacó un libro de memoria que traía en la capilla de la capa, y dióselo a Rinconete que leyese, porque él no sabía leer" (I, 235). The amusing but hardly unrealistic or surprising detail of Monipodio's illiteracy not only brings Rinconete (now needed as a reader—i.e., interpreter-translator of the necessary and thus privileged "code") back from his prior marginality to a position of importance. This slightly absurd state of

---

1979): 126-27.

[23] Concerning the possibility of a lack of connection between this text and the putative external reality of the story, see A. W. Hayes, "Narrative 'Errors' in *Rinconete y Cortadillo*," especially 17-18.

affairs also changes our sense of the legitimacy and extent of Monipodio's authority. While all the previous actions have validated the bases of his power and authority (in terms of his physical presence, good judgment, and ability to settle disputes among his subordinates), we now realize that, before this ultimate symbol of intellectual and "legal" authority, he is impotent—in effect, alienated from a foreign language, the written word.

The situation of power vs. impotence manifested in Monipodio's ambiguous relationship to his own book—possession and inaccessibility—on one level seems to de-authenticate or de-authorize his legitimacy. But at the same time the book itself and the care with which Monipodio and his band attend to its accounts rearticulates the question of social order, this time both within the roguish band and also beyond, out and into the surrounding, putatively respectible society. While the previous passages and episodes have dealt mainly with the issues of domestic friction and resolution, thus calling upon Monipodio for his skills as mediator, the brief section given over to the "libro de memoria" turns to questions of what one might call the dispensing of more elaborate justice. The tasks of mayhem and vandalism commissioned by various people to be carried out by Monipodio and his henchmen in effect represent the distribution of various kinds and degrees of justly deserved punishment.[24] In a way similar to the fact that Monipodio's group cultivates cordial and profitable relations with the *alguacil* (however conventionally disreputable such an officer of the law may have been in Golden Age literature and historical fact, he is nonetheless an official part of a legal system), the detail of the "libro de memoria" reminds us that at least one facet of underworld activity is directly tied to the respectable world's more serious needs, specifically the redress of grievances.

Yet Monipodio's incomplete understanding of this crucial text also hints at the lapses of justice and administration in the other

---

[24] Cf. the episode of Pablos's beating—actually a double beating—in the *Buscón*, Book III, Chapter 7.

social realm. Monipodio's illiteracy is not meant to suggest an identical illiteracy in the political and judicial hierarchy in the respectable social order. Nonetheless, the irony of power seen in the light of less than full competence resonates with the state of affairs in much of Spanish society of the time, a world in which, for example, Quevedo's satiric treatment of the judicial and political system was not without foundation.[25] The fact that Cervantes cleverly introduces a memo book into this unlikely scenario throws our expectations off balance: the putatively picaresque world of Rinconete and Cortadillo and of Monipodio and his gang is given another dimension of significance. They become, through the inclusion of the book, simultaneously part and parody of the society's legal systems and the laws that, however flawed, we are supposed to respect and obey.

The conclusion of the *novela* is, as I have suggested earlier, a peculiarly distanced leave-taking, very much an open ending. There are in effect two phases to the fade-out. First, the action comes to an end, with something like a formal ceremony of "clausura" (I, 239). Then, there is the curious epilogue of the final paragraph (I, 239-40).[26] In the penultimate paragraph, we are reminded again of the almost mock-pastoral harmony of this subworld, specifically as it touches on the domestic love relationships of members of the group. Monipodio once again brings people together and reestablishes harmony, and in appreciation, "Todos le volvieron [a Monipodio] las gracias. Tornáronse a abrazar Repolido y la Cariharta, la Escalanta con Maniferro y la Gananciosa con Chiquiznaque, . . ." He reiterates his gestures of inclusion and blessing with regard to Rinconete and Cortadillo: "Abrazó [Monipodio] a Rinconete y a Cortadillo, y echándolos su bendición, los despidió, encargándoles que no tuviesen jamás posada cierta ni de asiento, porque así convenía a la salud de todos" (I, 239). The final sentence of this paragraph brings us back to the narrative perspective of Rinconete and Cortadillo. We had not

---

[25] See, for example, the *Sueños*.
[26] See Casalduero, *Sentido y forma*, 99.

forgotten about the two youths, but their central involvement and
their critical perspective on the foregoing events had been more or
less pushed aside. With the termination of the action, the text
(perhaps a bit artificially) restores the boys to our attention. It also
puts them in a place of difference and separation from the world
they have supposedly joined and whose life and customs they have
just witnessed: "Con esto se fue [Monipodio], dejando a los dos
compañeros admirados de lo que habían visto" (I, 239).

The final paragraph elaborates on the suggestion of separation
and difference contained in the above sentence. But it goes further.
This peculiar epilogue does several things. Now that direct narration
of action and the attendant dialogues are concluded, the external
narrative voice reasserts itself, with the apparent aim of distinguishing the two title characters, on the basis of their moral and educational superiority, from Monipodio's world. Yet, at the same time,
the narrator—and the sensibility inherent in this particular
text—cannot quite pull itself away. Even though the condemnation
of the immorality of Monipodio's world would seem so easy to
make, the narrator's conclusion is ambiguous. The trouble seems to
be how to re-characterize our two young protagonists such that they
can be, if only for a while, plausibly a part of this world and yet can
also have imputed to them sufficient good judgment and culture to
be separate from it.

The narrator's dilemma is revealed in the structure and content
of the paragraph. It merits careful rereading. The first sentence,
somewhat long and rambling, attempts to recuperate for Rinconete
a degree of virtue and intellect. But it cannot escape reopening
problematic areas of doubt. As the narrator states, "Era Rinconete,
aunque muchacho, de muy buen entendimiento, y tenía un buen
natural" (I, 239). Yet if this were indeed so, one would have to
wonder at the boy's willingness to stay (given an evident lack of the
sort of material desperation found with, or claimed by, the more
familiar *pícaro*) with this disolute band. Likewise, to explain Rinconete's higher educational level, his cultural superiority, as it were,
the narrator notes that, "y como había andado con su padre en el

ejercicio de las bulas, sabía algo de buen lenguaje, y dábale gran risa pensar en los vocablos que había oído a Monipodio y a los demás de su compañía y bendita comunidad" (I, 239-40). The fact that Rinconete had tagged along with his father in the latter's "ejercicio de las bulas" obviously links our young friend with the archetypical episode of cynical and hypocritical swindling immortalized in *Lazarillo de Tormes* and perforce undermines our sense of the boy's real innocence. Rinconete's good education and culture were acquired on the streets and "in the trade," as we would say. In addition, there is something gratuitous (given that the discreet and witty reader no doubt "got" the jokes and malapropisms the first time around) and perhaps condescending about the narrator's recapitulation, ostensibly through Rinconete's mind, of the mistakes, garbled language, and "otras mil impertinencias" of Monipodio and his colleagues. The narrator's comment—the attitude imputed to Rinconete—that "sobre todo, le admiraba la seguridad que tenían y la confianza de irse al cielo con no faltar a sus devociones, estando tan llenos de hurtos, y de homicidios, y de ofensas de Dios" (I, 240), seems likewise gratuitous. For, while the coarseness of their world is made clear from the very start, and while we have no confusion about the *cofradía*'s involvement in prostitution, robbery, and acts of punitive and retaliatory violence, the *novela* really has not shown us a level of extreme violence (out and out murder). Neither has it given us the sense that their "ofensas de Dios" are different in anything but degree from the presumably excusable actions of the two young boys.

In one of the most curious sentences of the epilogue, we are told that, for Rinconete, "No menos le suspendía la obediencia y respecto que todos tenían a Monipodio, siendo un hombre bárbaro, rústico y desalmado" (I, 240). What is peculiar here is the strange logic implicit in the statement: if all the rest of the group is "bárbaro" and "rústico," to say the least, why *wouldn't* they obey a person like Monipodio? From the moment of his entrance, through his interventions to settle disputes and reestablish order and harmony among his followers, Monipodio has surely justified his claim to power and authority. What, then, is Rinconete's—or any possible reader's—surprise? The subworld that Cervantes has portrayed for us is, on one level, yet another ironic idealization (in the manner of the gypsies of *La gitanilla*) of a marginal and grotesque but not totally repellant world.[27] Monipodio's realm is a plausible social stratum that is the logical, contingent extension of the respectable levels of society, while it is also a parody of this same upper world. In this regard, the next sentence is highly revealing. Again the narrator "reads" Monipodio's world through Rinconete's mind:

> Consideraba [Rinconete] lo que había leído en su libro de memoria y los ejercicios en que todos se ocupaban. Finalmente, exageraba cuán descuidada justicia había en aquella tan famosa ciudad de Sevilla, pues casi al descubierto vivía en ella gente tan perniciosa y tan contraria a la misma naturaleza, y propuso en sí aconsejar a su compañero no durasen mucho en aquella vida tan perdida y tan mala, tan inquieta, y tan libre y disoluta. (I, 240)

But the two boys have hardly dropped into this world "del cielo," as Pedro del Rincón put it near the beginning of the tale. In effect, this dissolute world is the one to which the two have belonged from before the beginning, and if there be anything especially "pernicioso" about Sevilla and Monipodio's world, it is more a matter of degree than of kind.

What we might indeed find distinct about the subworld into which our two semi-innocents enter is the violence and sexuality of it. Yet there has been no real sense anywhere in the *novela* that Sevilla and the lives and actions of Monipodio and his *cofradía* are anything other than plausible, strangely familiar, and coherent with a society slightly beyond its borders and in which Cervantes's contemporaneous readers—and we ourselves—inevitably live.

The significant point about Cervantes's portrayal of this world and its moral implications is that there is in *Rinconete y Cortadillo* a peculiar ambivalence or softening of the full force of the critique.

---

[27] Once again, the contrast with a profoundly grotesque world such as the one created by Quevedo, for instance, in the *Buscón*, is highly revealing.

The complexity of attitude in this *novela* becomes evident when it is reread in light of the language and form of Cervantes's most harsh and penetrating (though hardly simplistic) socio-critical text, the *Coloquio de los perros*.[28] The vision of *Rinconete y Cortadillo* hovers between a certain half-innocent acceptance, or "decriminalizing," of Monipodio's and the boys' roguish world, and a conventional, perfectly respectable, morally offended rejection of the entire criminal enterprise—the tone and point of view tacked onto the *novela* at the very end. What both redeems *Rinconete y Cortadillo* and at the same time makes it a problem of interpretation is the fact that the text takes more interest in its play of language than in the real implications of the putative lives or problems of its characters. Because there are hints of such issues in the text, we search for a sense of more complex identity in the two boys, in the other characters, and certainly in the unforgettable Monipodio. But all of them are masquers, actors in an *entremés*. They live, as much as they do, only in their language and they evaporate as soon as the clatter of the stage and the banter of dialogue ceases—as the flatness of the final paragraph so tellingly reveals. But in this festive and sometimes grotesque play of words, Cervantes nonetheless slyly offers a view of a world that is part and parodic shadow of our own.

---

[28] See below, Chapter Ten, on the *Coloquio*; see also Forcione, *The Mystery of Lawlessness*.

Chapter Four
The Sins of the Father
La española inglesa

Within the *Novelas ejemplares*, *La española inglesa* represents the best example, in highly abbreviated form, of the romance or *novela bizantina*.[1] Along with *El amante liberal*, the other text of the collection that most closely approaches the familiar romance conventions, it contains idealized, beautiful protagonists, sea voyages, the clash of hostile cultures, and the rather improbable resolutions of thorny problems of personal and cultural conflict. If anything, *La española inglesa* ventures even further than *El amante* into the realm of the romance. Although it eschews the quasi-magical and unrealistic world of the *Persiles*, it is very much like a fragment of Cervantes's posthumous book.[2] Yet there is a most unromantic, or un-romance-like, counter-current in the text. In particular, in those aspects having to do with the question of identity defined in terms of social rank and forms of economic activity, this text raises the most troubling questions.[3] More than any of the others it works a series

---

[1] El Saffar places her commentary on this *novela* near the end of her study, reflecting her judgment that this is one of the last written. Numerous subsequent studies concur with the notion that *La española* fits more or less well into the romance, *novela bizantina* or *novela de peregrinaje* category. Concerning the romance structure in Cervantes, see also E. I. Deffis de Calvo, "El cronotopo de la novela española de peregrinación: Miguel de Cervantes," *Anales Cervantinos* 28 (1990): 99-108. Although I accept, for purposes of simplicity, the notion of novel and romance as different forms, I am more and more convinced that clear and absolute distinctions between the two so-called genres may be impossible to maintain; in this I find myself inclined to agree with M. A. Doody's position (*The True Story of the Novel*) that the distinction novel vs. romance has outlived its usefulness.

[2] On the nature of Cervantine romance and the *Persiles*, in particular, see Diana de Armas Wilson, *Allegories of Love*, especially 3-23; on the romance elements of *La española inglesa*, see S. Zimic, "El *Amadís* cervantino (apuntes sobre *La española inglesa*)," *Anales Cervantinos* 25-26 (1987): 467-83.

[3] H. Sieber's introductory note already points out the peculiarly extensive attention given to details of financial transactions (see the "Introducción," I, 28-30). These

of fascinating inversions. As I shall illustrate in what follows, the action of the *novela* begins with an inversion of the conventional expectations of virtue and social hierarchy: a nobleman behaves in a most ignoble manner, setting up a long process that begins in erotic tension, opens up to the possibility of sincere yet still erotically charged love, and achieves a subtly problematic resolution of the problems of both love and the initial crime of abduction. At the same time, the socio-cultural content of the *novela* and the socially defined identities of the principal characters propose a reversal of the assumptions about the ascending order of virtue and value usually expected as one moves from the rank of the commoner to that of the aristocrat. *La española inglesa* questions the nature of identity as it investigates the problematic of what legitimizes wealth and what determines social position. Specifically, it examines the concept of identity as based upon lineage and the traditional military duties of the nobility, as opposed to the social rank characterized and determined by a commercial mode of acquiring wealth. Combat versus commerce. But we shall begin with the erotic and end with the economic.

As is conventional to the romance genre, *La española inglesa* deals with the loss and restoration of a beautiful young woman and with the love story that involves her and a heroic young man. Fundamental to the plot, and once again resembling *El amante liberal*, are the historical specificities of time and place, along with the conflict of cultures and religions, here defined in terms of Spain and England.[4] But *La española inglesa* is distinct from the other Cervantine *novelas* for the moral transgression and repressed erotic motives that set the

---

issues have been even more extensively elaborated in two articles—to which this study is much indebted—by C. B. Johnson: "Catolicismo, familia y fecundidad: el caso de 'La española inglesa'," 519-24 in S. Neumeister, ed., *Actas del IX Congreso de la Asociación Internacional de Hispanistas*, vol. I; and "*La española inglesa* and the Practice of Literary Production," *Viator* 19 (1988): 377-416.

[4] On the question of England and Spain, particularly in terms of the problem of mutual perceptions and the condition of English Catholics, see Albert J. Loomie, *The Spanish Elizabethans: The English Exiles at the Court of Philip II*, especially 3-13.

story in motion. The initiating act of the plot is a troubling inversion of the norm: in a complete reversal of the analogous case in *La gitanilla*, the kidnapping of an innocent young girl is here the inexplicable deed of a supposedly virtuous English aristocrat. The motive (his admiration of the child's beauty) is never convincingly justified. In the text's insufficient concern for this element of the man's motivation, there is something crucial missing, a disquieting shadow projected through the entire story. What subsequently happens in the *novela* is a series of losses and recuperations, all of which center on the trials and triumph of the sincere, chaste love between Isabela and Ricaredo, a love that will redeem the initial crime of the latter's father, Clotaldo.[5] But Isabela's sufferings and Ricaredo's adventures are not only the conventional adversities of the romance genre. Rather they are part of a complex symbolic structure that encloses a displaced eroticism, one that is both masked and revealed by the father's initiatory crime. In *La española inglesa* the actions of the main characters, through the testing of love and the process of deferral—the erotic sufferings (*erotika pathemata*) of Ricaredo and Isabela—redeem, though perhaps not completely, Clotaldo's evil deed.

Alongside this purification of the father's repressed erotic desires and consequent crime, and through Ricaredo's and Isabela's love and suffering, there is yet another Cervantine exploration of the conservative, aristocratic rightness and the inevitable, material ironies of social class identity. The juxtaposition of aristocrats (Ricaredo and his family) alongside commoners—specifically from the mercantile class (Isabela and hers)—recalls the situation of don Fernando and Dorotea in Part I of *Don Quijote*, where the happy resolution of their conflict suggests Dorotea's upward social movement and her increased status. In *La española inglesa*, however, there is an ironic leveling effect: although he is a nobleman, Ricaredo is English, thus implicitly lacking a degree of status due to his alien identity. Isabela,

---

[5] On Ricaredo's redemption of his father's initial transgression, see especially El Saffar, 153-55.

although not an aristocrat, has the implicit superiority of being Spanish. Thus, while Isabela would seem to ascend, by marrying Ricaredo, into the aristocracy, in fact his non-Spanish status dilutes the putative value of his class identity. Likewise, his final arrival in Spain represents both a successful reunion with his beloved (as well as the freedom to be openly Catholic) and also a renunciation of his nationality, within which his aristocratic status would be both more powerful and unquestioned. This ironic reversal, meanwhile, is tellingly related to the question of material wealth and how it is acquired—by aristocrats (who are, after all, the latter-day version of the "warrior class") and by the socially inferior but possibly more "productive" merchant class with their more socially affirmative activities.[6] In no other of the *Novelas ejemplares* is the relationship between one's social class and the respective mode of acquiring wealth and one's economic and social activity so clearly and actively dramatized.

In *La española inglesa* there is a marked and at times seemingly digressive preoccupation with money, material goods in general, and even the details of international financial transactions (the *cédulas, cartas de crédito,* and so on).[7] Although the subtheme of money and material versus the ideal is in no way alien in the context of the other *Novelas ejemplares,* in *La española inglesa* this element acquires a particular intensity. In this *novela* the pervasive meaning of material wealth takes form on two levels. The first consists in the marked reification of the woman. The second level is reflected in the unconventional nature of the respective families' social class rank, that of Isabela being merchants, or non-aristocrats, and that of Ricaredo being of a noble house, but not Spanish, and thus alien.

From the beginning, with the first words of the *novela,* there is an obvious reification of the stolen child. The language leaves no room for ambiguity: "Entre los *despojos* que los ingleses llevaron de la

---

[6] Once again, this aspect of the text has been most interestingly pursued by Johnson; see especially "*La española inglesa* and the Practice of Literary Production."

[7] In addition to Johnson's two studies, see H. Sieber's introductory notes, I, 28-30.

ciudad de Cádiz, Clotaldo, un caballero inglés, capitán de una escuadra de navíos, llevó a Londres una niña de edad de siete años" (I, 243; emphasis added). A little further on, after noting that this act of kidnapping was done against the express orders of the commander of the English forces, the narrator repeats the image of woman as material object: "Finalmente, sus padres [de Isabel] se quedaron sin ella, tristes y desconsolados, y Clotaldo, alegre sobre modo, llegó a Londres y entregó *por riquísimo despojo* a su mujer a la hermosa niña" (I, 244; emphasis added). The *novela* thus begins with a clear connection between the main female character (Isabela) and material goods that are literally robbed and considered the spoils of war. But in addition, the *riqueza*, the *joya* referred to so repeatedly here, represents the metonymic sign of sexual purity, chastity, and desire. This emphasis on riches and spoils of war serves as both a sign and a deferral of the ultimate possession: the woman herself as sexual object. In the peculiar semiotic of this text (and in ways both similar to and distinct from *La gitanilla* and *El amante liberal*), the woman links the economic and the erotic, value and desire.

At certain points in the story, Isabela is presented in a less negatively materialized manner. When she appears for the first time at the Court of Queen Elizabeth I of England, for example, the girl's presentation follows the conventions of underlining the young woman's natural beauty with the symbolic material objects of wealth and art:

> . . . acordaron que Isabela no fuese vestida humildemente, como prisionera, sino como esposa, pues ya lo era de tan principal esposo como su hijo. Resueltos en esto, otro día vistieron a Isabela a la española, con una saya entera de raso verde acuchillada y forrada en rica tela de oro, tomadas las cuchilladas con unas eses de perlas, y toda ella bordada de riquísimas perlas; collar y cintura de diamantes, y con abanico a modo de las señoras damas españolas; sus mismos cabellos, que eran muchos, rubios y largos, entretejidos y sembrados de diamantes y perlas, le sirvían de tocado. Con este adorno riquísimo y con su gallarda disposición y milagrosa belleza se mostró aquel día a Londres sobre una hermosa carroza, llevando colgados de su vista las almas y los ojos de cuantos la miraban. (I, 248)

The family is in essence making a statement, underscoring and legitimizing the identity of the girl as fiancée to their noble son. But even here the materialization of the woman and the illegitimate implications of the material in question become once again evident. Specifically, the English queen is herself quite taken by Isabela's beauty and, in a highly revealing move, commands Ricaredo to prove his love for the girl and justify his own worth by participating in an expedition of *corsarios*, that is to say, in an action of state-sanctioned robbery. With this assignment, Ricaredo is not only engaging in an act meant to prove himself as a worthy warrior-aristocrat but is also repeating in a modified form his father's earlier expedition against Spain. Yet because Ricaredo both demonstrates his devotion and also purchases the woman he loves in a dramatic, if slighlty modified echo of his father's first action, the younger man's actions do not completely redeem the questionable motives and values of the father. The identification of Isabela with material wealth is pervasive and profound, conventional yet disturbing, and the son cannot fully separate himself from the world of his father.

We begin, then, with the patent fact that the father, the English nobleman Clotaldo, is a thief, an abductor. We necessarily return, then, to the most notable, irrational, and inexplicable element of this *novela*: the kidnapping and the troubling motives of this act. The explanation given by the narrator is unsatisfactory and evasive. Although the text, by way of justification, affirms that Clotaldo's motivation was that he found himself "aficionado, aunque cris-tianamente, a la incomparable hermosura de Isabel" (I, 243-44), at no time is it explained what, in this context, the mysterious ad-verb—*cristianamente*—might mean. What seems like a discreet way of excusing the older man of any lascivious motive in fact cannot close off these same troubling implications. For, without doubt, there can be no other motive for such an abduction—a kidnapping inspired by "la incomparable belleza"—than carnal desire, however thinly disguised or displaced as aesthetic appreciation. Ironically, then, by expressing the motive in this manner, the text's attempt at excusing becomes a subtle accusation.

When Clotaldo brings the girl to his home in London, the identity of Isabel becomes quite problematic and dangerously destabilizing.[8] The implicit intention of Clotaldo and Catalina is to incorporate the girl into the family, even though they make special efforts to keep her in contact with her language and her original culture. Yet Isabela continues to be a captive, and it is noted that she attends those in the family almost like a servant. Implicitly and ideally, however, she is incorporated into the family as sister and daughter. In this way, the initial repressed desires of Clotaldo have been displaced (for him) from a lust for the "other," available female, sublimated to the sentiments of paternal affection. The guilt of his first action, and thus his identity as impulsive abductor, is softened by the refuge behind the identity of substitute father. Yet, given the power of the father in the patriarchal societies of England and Spain, Clotaldo supresses one kind of possession while keeping or intensifying another.

This same ideal and figurative incorporation of Isabela into the family sets in motion the gradual development of Ricaredo's complex feelings of love. As I have suggested above, it is precisely the chaste love, sufferings, and trials experienced by the youth that redeem the original sin of the father. At the beginning, however, Ricaredo's growing love is, for him, the cause of considerable pain and uncertainty. It even produces in the youth a certain "illness."[9] The text describes the process of this evolution of sentiments quite realistically, noting that "como fue creciendo Isabel, que ya cuando Ricaredo ardía tenía doce años, aquella benevolencia primera y aquella complacencia y agrado de mirarla se volvió en ardentísimos

---

[8] Or Isabela; at this point in the *novela*, the girl is "renamed" and this other version is kept throughout the rest of the text. The subtle change, and vacillation, in the form of her name underlines the problematic nature of this part of the theme: the issue of identity, which for her will change and then be restored, but for Ricaredo will undergo a one-way transformation.

[9] As the text puts it, "Y así, perplejo y pensativo, sin saber qué camino tomar para venir al fin de su buen deseo, pasaba una vida tal, que le puso a punto de perderla. . . .

"Andaban todos los de casa tristes y alborotados por la enfermedad de Ricaredo, . . . " (I, 245).

deseos de gozarla y de poseerla" (I, 244). The narrator indicates that the principal reason for Ricaredo's anxiety in the face of his own love for Isabela is the fact that Clotaldo had already arranged for him a marriage with a Scottish noblewoman. However, the reader's attention is, by the curious tone of the narration, drawn to the fact that the closeness and Isabela's implicit identity as "sister" introduce a marked element of discomfort and confusion for Ricaredo. But also for the reader. Although Ricaredo's purer aspiration seems to redeem the initial crime of the father by offering the possibility of a carnal yet legitimatized love, this approach of the brother to the semi-adopted sister has certain echoes of the incestuous. The family's decision to permit this same union, however, serves paradoxically to clarify the lines of distinction between the English family and their Spanish guest-captive. Yet while this permission reiterates and partially restores the virtuous dimension of Ricaredo's love, the criminal circumstances of the girl's arrival in England and incorporation into the family continue to haunt the putatively virtuous character and motives of the son.

Within the general question of identity implicitly set forth in this *novela*, there are certain obvious elements that require attention. In the first place, it is notable that the main female character shares the name of the English queen. This effects a symbolic doubling or amplification of the girl, whose situation of relative weakness and captivity contrasts so markedly with the power of the "other" Isabela, Queen Elizabeth. In addition, it is the queen who at first prevents the scheduled marriage of the two young people by postponing it until after Ricaredo proves his worthiness by the *corsario* expedition. It is likewise important to note that at this moment of the story the young Isabela is, by order of the queen, taken out of the more secure, less visible ambit of Clotaldo's home and placed into the world of the court, a place in which the young woman comes to be the object of envy and where her true identity as Spanish and Catholic emerges once again as a basic problem of acceptance or rejection.

The entrance of the English queen into the narration and the complex symbolic suggestions that she occasions deserve an attention that they have rarely received. Elizabeth the First of England (1533-1603), who reigned for forty-five years, had died ten years before the publication of the *Novelas ejemplares*. For the Spanish reader of Cervantes's day, this historical figure would inevitably have inspired certain antagonistic sentiments, in view of recent history, including the defeat of the Armada in 1588 and the religious conflicts and dynastic complications within England that had drawn Spain into these same problems.[10] In this light, the rather positive portrait that Cervantes gives of the queen is curious, even though it is clear that the way in which Elizabeth I is characterized responds more to implicit artistic requirements than to the facts of history.

Yet, despite the needs of story over the requirements of historical fidelity, what does Cervantes's Queen Elizabeth represent? Both the truth and the legend in this case serve the needs of the *novela*. By this I mean that the complex system of relations and inversions of the erotic, identity, and the representation of gender find appropriate form in the particular characteristics of the English queen. Elizabeth embodies both the positive and also the disturbing implications of the famous "Virgin Queen." Cervantes's Queen Elizabeth, just as the historical personage, is the Matriarch who is both Virgin (positive) yet also Sterile (negative), that is to say, without descendants. She is also the valiant (female) warrior who rules a nation, through times of war and peace, with an iron hand. This fictionalized Elizabeth thus serves as a polar opposite to the weak yet desirable young Spanish woman. The queen is the virgin yet slightly monstrous mother, implicitly "adopting" the younger woman. In this regard, the queen's entrance into the story also represents a shift or displace-

---

[10] On the historical background of Spanish-English relations at this time, see J. Lynch, *Spain 1516-1598: From Nation State to Empire*, especially 418-28; also G. Mattingly, "International Diplomacy and International Laws," Chapter VI of *The New Cambridge Modern History*, vol. III, 158ff, and in the same volume H. G. Koenigsberger, "Western Europe and the Power of Spain," Chapter IX, especially 308-18.

ment of the center of power, control, and conflict from a purely male-dominated sphere and toward a context more influenced by the feminine principle. The queen literally takes possession of the Spanish girl, thus replacing the "second" mother, Catalina. At the same time, with her command to Ricaredo, the queen also appropriates the role and authority of the father. Clotaldo, too, has been diminished, surpassed.

The queen's world also contains, and opens the way to, other female forces. We now find ourselves in a world of mothers—or more precisely, of maternal forces—in a state of conflict. The young Isabela now sees herself captured for a second time; Queen Elizabeth has elevated her to a state of importance not completely exempt from danger. First, there is the threat of the revelation of the Clotaldo family's religious loyalty: as the illicit adoptive mother, Catalina, is displaced, she experiences the fear that, by this move, the Catholic identity of her family might be revealed. Then, ironically, as a consequence of Ricaredo's highly successful and materially profitable expedition, Isabela's real mother reappears, rescued or captured from the defeated Turkish forces along with the captive Portuguese treasure ship. At about this point, there enters yet another mother. Due to the threatening and unwanted love of Count Arnesto, the latter's mother provokes the major crisis of Isabela's near death by poisoning. In sum, the manner in which the women appropriate power and active roles within the story is startling and curiously destabilizing. The strength and the mechanisms of female power (something more possible in "art" than in the "real-world" society of Cervantes's day) bring us to the world of fairy tale and myth. It is also the nocturnal world of men's nightmares in the face of the magical and the irrational, the power of the imaginary female. Arnesto's mother, in her attempt to kill Isabela, gives her a poison that, in a way not unlike the ineffective drugged quince (*membrillo*) in *El licenciado Vidriera*, does not have the intended result but rather works a kind of transformation. Isabela's cure, the saving of her life, is the result of the queen's intervention and the skill of her medical team.[11] The nearly mortal illness and the transformation of the girl, from a state of beauty to a condition of supposedly ugly deformity, thus represents a struggle between two mothers—the figurative good mother, the queen, and the evil mother of Arnesto.

The most obvious consequence and function of Isabela's temporary transformation could be considered a test of her lover's devotion and idealism.[12] But from another perspective, Isabela's transformation—as in the change to madness experienced by Tomás in *El licenciado Vidriera*—represents not so much the imposition of an alien nature or condition, but rather the uncovering of a more profound essence, something inherent yet grotesquely disturbing, something revealing of an ulterior nature.[13] What we have is a vision of the fundamental female principle, the fertility of the earth goddess[14] that usually must hide itself behind the conventions and the cultural but also self-protecting idealizations of the male imagination of "the feminine," the idealized beautiful woman thus reified into the aesthetic and possessable object.

The conclusion of the *novela* brings the conventional happy ending, the restoration of that which was lost—both people and material—and the promise of a harmonious future based upon the fulfillment of the love now established and painfully tested by the adventures and adversities of Ricaredo and Isabela. As we will remember, after her recovery, Isabela returns with her parents to

---

[11] See I, 268-69; curiously, this is the one passage in the *novela* where complete and careful realism is breached, since Isabela's cure involves the Queen's doctors administering "cantidad de polvos de unicornio," among other drugs.

[12] On this thematic aspect, see El Saffar, *Novel to Romance*, especially 157-62; as El Saffar notes, "In *La española inglesa* the major characters do not invent the situation in which they find themselves. Their exemplarity derives from the constancy and devotion to eternal principles they display when assaulted by the challenges of a reality characterized by corruption, flux, and decay" (161).

[13] On the question of transformation as the actual revelation of essence, see my discussion of *El licenciado Vidriera*, Chapter Five below; see also J. R. Sampayo Rodríguez, *Rasgos erasmistas de la locura del licenciado Vidriera*, 120-26.

[14] In fact, Isabela's bloated condition is reminiscent of prototypical fleshiness of the Venus of Willendorf; on this question of the essential female versus the "refined" versions of the feminine, see C. Paglia, *Sexual Personae*, especially Chapter One.

Spain, while Ricaredo employs the pretext of a pilgrimage to Rome in order to get out of the arranged marriage with the Scottish gentlewoman. Having secretly promised Isabela that he will come to Spain and be reunited with her within the space of no more than two years, Ricaredo undergoes a series of adventures and episodes—among them a brief period of captivity in the hands of the Turks (clearly alluding to the plot of *El amante liberal*) and an unsuccessful assassination attempt by Arnesto and his henchmen. Ricaredo finally arrives in Sevilla, rather late, at the moment in which Isabel, believing him to be dead, is about to enter the convent.

With his words of interruption and *anagnorisis*—"Detente, Isabela; detente, que mientras yo fuere vivo no puedes tú ser religiosa" (I, 277)—Ricaredo closes the circle of love and commitment between the lovers. At the same time, we are presented with yet another articulation of Ricaredo's own differentness and beauty, one that partially reminds us of the intentionally ambiguous vision of his triumphant return to London after the privateering mission.[15] In contrast to the slightly androgenous tone of the earlier description, however, Ricaredo's beauty is here emphasized in terms of ethnic and national difference: "habiéndosele caído un bonete azul redondo que en la cabeza traía descubrió una confusa madeja de cabellos de oro ensortijados y un rostro como el carmín y como la nieve, colorado y blanco, señales que luego le hicieron conocer y juzgar por extranjero de todos" (I, 277). More striking than the reiteration of the physical aspect (which has already been established with the earlier

---

[15] As we will recall, this previous portrait—the most detailed visual description of the youth—is remarkable for its specificity and also for its explicitly ambiguous play with gender. It begins with a quite masculine, heroic vision: "Era Ricaredo alto de cuerpo, gentil hombre y bien proporcionado." But it concludes with a most curious composite image: "Con este adorno, y con el paso brioso que llevaba, algunos hubo que le compararon a Marte, dios de las batallas, y otros, llevados de la hermosura de su rostro, dicen que le compararon a Venus, que para hacer alguna burla a Marte de aquel modo se había disfrazado" (I, 259). For a reading that finds Ricaredo's visual portrayal more positively idealizing, rather than sexually ambiguous, see M. Alcázar Ortega, "Palabra, memoria y aspiración literaria en *La española inglesa*," *Cervantes* 15.1 (1995): 33-45.

description and which has put him in curiously ambiguous category, with regard to the conventions of sexual identity—very much in the manner of the presentation of Persiles/Periandro in the *Persiles*) is his identity as a foreigner. Ricaredo's loss—or, more properly, renunciation—of his original, authentic identity in order to incorporate himself into another culture is underscored here through the element of physical appearance. He arrives free but impoverished, figuratively stripped of his culture, nation, wealth, and also of the specific privileges of position within English nobility, aristocratic privileges that he now has only in theory. The ultimate purification or compensation for the "original sin"—the kidnapping of the young girl and her temporary captivity in England—is the renunciation of national identity and the willing subordination of the now mature and tested man, the son of the first transgressor. Moving, then, from the initial crime (Clotaldo's) of a suppressed eroticism, replaced in turn by an authentic, chaste love, which itself is forced to endure erotic sufferings (*erotika pathemata*)—conventional to the romance form, but in this case appropriate to this world of cultural and religious conflict and displacement—we arrive at the conclusion. The union and reunion of Isabela and Ricaredo thus represents something unique in the context of the Cervantine *novela*: a completed circle of loss and restoration for Isabela, but a dramatic, one-directional arc for Ricaredo. For the latter, the story enacts a transformation, renunciation, and reconstruction of identity. This transformation, justified by the power of love, appears to redeem the original sin, converting the incompleteness of the initial erotic urge and displacement by means of the realization of the chaste love and the dramatic sacrifice of one identity in favor of commitment to another.

But at this point we must step back once more from the superficial and comfortable reading of the resolution of the story and its conflicts in terms of love tested and triumphant, of initially impure erotic impulses transformed by chaste and deferred erotic sufferings. We must also step back from the easily readable, positive triumph of the rightness of the Spanish culture over the English. For, as indicated at the beginning, we not only have the English versus Spanish contexts of cultural identity, but we also have the obvious differences of social class and economic activity. As opposed to the don Fernando and Dorotea resolution in *Don Quijote*, where the woman (while arguing for an inherent *nobleza* of character rather than lineage) clearly ascends through marriage into an established aristocratic family, in *La española inglesa* we have something of the reverse. Ricaredo "ascends" only in the figurative sense of incorporation into the privileged culture. He ascends through a peculiar yet undeniable renunciation of status.

The concept that the English aristocrats, while endowed with the supposed virtue and moral superiority pertinent to higher social rank, essentially acquire and otherwise deal with material wealth through acts of plunder and violence is reiterated throughout the *novela*. As I noted at the beginning of this commentary, Clotaldo's initiatory act of theft-kidnapping, while clearly masking an erotic intention, is expressed in terms that tightly link the human prize with the concept of stolen riches. Ricaredo's purer motives, sufferings, and more chaste love seek to redeem the father's initial erotic impulses, but the mode by which the son proves himself is essentially the same. The ironies of this more deeply embedded structural connection become most apparent in the passages following Ricaredo's successful return from the privateering expedition. Once again, above and beyond the obvious symbolism of his return—not only laden with the twice-stolen material goods but also with the young girl's fortunately included parents—the language of Ricaredo's dealings with the Queen fascinatingly weaves together the material and the human elements:

> Aquella nave es de las que vienen de la India de Portugal, la cual por tormenta vino a dar en poder de los turcos, que con poco trabajo, por mejor decir sin ninguno, la rindieron, y según dijeron algunos portugueses de los que en ella venían, pasa de un millón de oro el valor de la especería y otras mercancías de perlas y diamantes que en ella vienen. A ninguna cosa se ha tocado, ni los turcos habían llegado a ella, porque todo lo dedicó el cielo, y yo lo mandé guardar, para Vuestra Majestad, que con una joya sola que se me dé quedaré en deuda de otras diez naves; la cual

joya ya Vuestra Majestad me la tiene prometida, que es a mi buena Isabela. Con ella quedaré rico y premiado, no sólo deste servicio, cual él se sea, que a Vuestra Majestad he hecho, sino de otros muchos que pienso hacer por pagar alguna parte del todo casi infinito que en esta joya Vuestra Majestad me ofrece. (I, 260)

The appropriately "romantic" reading of this passage, as in the case of the entire *novela*, would be that Ricaredo humbly declares that the object of his love, Isabela, is "worth" far more than the extravagant contents of the treasure ship. As in this sort of quest-motif story, the man goes forth to prove himself (meeting the Queen's challenge) and returns having done so. There is something slightly crass about considering this action as Ricaredo's purchase of his lover. But the metaphor—"la joya"—is insistently repeated. What Ricaredo has done is a logical extension of what, in Cervantes's day and even more pointedly in an archaic, more chivalric past, noblemen were expected to do: military action. The importance of the material connection—persons to things; persons as things—is made explicit in the text itself, as we see in the following passage, where Ricaredo's favored position before the Queen arouses a certain envious cynicism among other courtiers:

No consintió la reina que Ricaredo estuviese de rodillas ante ella; antes le hizo levantar y sentar en una silla rasa, que para sólo esto allí puesta tenían, inusitada merced para la altiva condición de la reina, y alguno dijo a otro:
—Ricaredo no se sienta hoy sobre la silla que le han dado, sino sobre la pimienta que él trujo.
Otro acudió y dijo:
—Ahora se verifica lo que comúnmente se dice, que dádivas quebrantan peñas, pues las que ha traído Ricaredo han ablandado el duro corazón de nuestra reina. (I, 262)

The obvious point throughout this section of the *novela* is the growing envy and hostility of the others in the Queen's court, those who will envy and resent Ricaredo for his success, along with those others who mistrust Isabela for her foreign identity, and the main antagonist, Arnesto, whose impulsive love for Isabela is in itself tinged with a sense of greed and competition.

The antagonistic emergence of Arnesto into the story continues and underscores the materialization of Isabela, on the one hand, and the larger dramatization of the action and identity of the English warrior class as centered upon wealth acquired through physical conflict, on the other. This part of the story also brings in the slightly archaic touch of disputed questions or the search for a "truth" being settled by dueling. Arnesto's formal challenge to Ricaredo returns us to this archaic, yet still fundamental aspect of the aristocrat. At the same time, his language once again underlines the concept of woman as object whose value transcends mere material only because the material in question can be brought in for purposes of contrast. As Arnesto states,

> Tú fuiste, y volviste cargadas las naves de oro, con el cual piensas haber comprado y merecido a Isabela. Y aunque la reina mi señora te la ha prometido, ha sido creyendo que no hay ninguno en su corte que mejor que tú la sirva ni quien con mejor título merezca a Isabela, y en esto bien podrá ser se haya engañado; y así, llegándome a esta opinión que yo tengo por verdad averiguada, digo que ni tú has hecho cosas tales que te hagan merecer a Isabela ni ninguna podrás hacer que a tanto bien te levante; y en razón de que no la mereces, si quieres contradecirme, te desafío a todo trance de muerte. (I, 266-67).

This revealingly worded challenge allows Ricaredo to relocate the emphasis of value, both abasing himself and affirming the supposedly unmaterialistic nature of his love: "En ninguna manera me toca salir a vuestro desafío, señor conde, porque yo confieso, no sólo que no merezco a Isabela, sino que no la merecen ninguno de los que hoy viven en el mundo" (I, 267). But the entire system, and in fact the curious dynamic of Arnesto's proclaimed love for Isabela, echoes the earlier problems of desire, greed, impulsive acts, and woman as object. In other words, Arnesto's ham-handed entry into the story reiterates, in another key, the problem of the "afición" that manifests itself in the literal taking and possession of the woman, the woman as possession. We are back once again with the crime of the father, Clotaldo, with which the story began.

Arnesto's intrusion leads to his mother's attempted murder of Isabela and the consequent physical transformation, as discussed previously. But on the level of underlying structures, something else happens here. Isabela's temporary transformation is, as noted above, yet another test of Ricaredo's love. It also prompts a falling off of interest on the part of the queen and, in effect, a return to a sense of reality for all of the persons involved. The queen and everyone else implicitly come to realize that, if the marriage between Ricaredo and Isabela has been cancelled (since the young man's parents reject the now ugly Isabela and bring the Scottish noblewoman back into the picture), it now only makes sense to restore the girl to her parents and to allow all of them to return to Spain. In the process of this shift, the texture of the story itself also changes. We are still in a material world, but the mode of interacting with wealth is subtly yet radically modified.

First and foremost, the queen's punishment of Arnesto's family includes a kind of financial sanction that aids Isabela and her parents. As the text explains, the punishment of Arnesto's mother is partly in the form of reparations or damages: "la condenó en que no sirviese más su oficio y en diez mil escudos de oro para Isabela" (I, 272). This reparation comes in addition to the money given to the girl and her family by Clotaldo, who gives them "tanto haber y riquezas que recompensasen sus pasadas pérdidas" (I, 270). In marked contrast to the previous actions of plunder and piracy carried out by members of the aristocracy, the transfer of wealth now becomes orderly, precise, commercial, and more than a little bureaucratic. Wealth is now figured in precise amounts of money, countable coinage, and documents of credit—thus, in objects that, in some cases, have intrinsic value and a regulated sign function and, in others, represent wealth through mechanisms of exchange. Thus, it is not only the orderliness of coinage that now takes precedence in the narrative. It is also another mode, another way of thinking and acting. We are now in a world of merchants and bankers, a world in which the concept of credit, the use of documents, and the basic necessity of mutual trust are fundamental. The queen sets this process in motion:

> La reina llamó a un mercader rico que habitaba en Londres, y era francés, el cual tenía correspondencia en Francia, Italia y España, al cual entregó los diez mil escudos y le pidió cédulas para que se los entregasen al padre de Isabela en Sevilla o en otra playa de España. El mercader, descontados sus intereses y ganancias, dijo a la reina que las daría ciertas y seguras para Sevilla sobre otro mercader francés, su correspondiente, en esta forma: que él escribiría a París para que allí se hiciesen las cédulas por otro correspondiente suyo, a causa que rezasen las fechas de Francia y no de Inglaterra, por el contrabando de la comunicación de los dos reinos, y que bastaba llevar una letra de aviso suya sin fecha, con sus contraseñas, para que luego diese el dinero el mercader de Sevilla, que ya estaría avisado del de París. En resolución, la reina tomó tales seguridades del mercader, que no dudó de ser cierta la partida; . . . (I, 272)

I quote this passage at length in part because it is worth noting the detail that Cervantes gives to specifying the process of the transfer of the money. In fact, from this point on in the story such orderly and essentially peaceful financial transactions will completely replace the violent and risky methods of Clotaldo's and Ricaredo's aristocratic world. Thus, not only are Isabela and her family restored to their native country, but also their mode of economic activity and their implicit social status (that of the merchant class) are validated, their values subtly approved.

The gradual but still quite miraculous restoration of Isabela's original physical beauty coincides with—and is underscored by—the return of the family to Spain and the recuperation of their former way of life and status, in large part due to the monies given to them by Clotaldo, by the damages exacted from Arnesto's mother, and by the English queen's own generosity. As the narrator tells us, "Ya Isabela en este tiempo comenzaba a dar grandes esperanzas de volver a cobrar su primera hermosura. Poco más de un mes estuvieron en Cádiz, restaurando los trabajos de la navegación, y luego se fueron a Sevilla por ver si salía cierta la paga de los diez mil escudos que librados sobre el mercader francés traían" (I, 273). There is, however, some delay in the functioning of the mechanisms of international finance. But the family waits patiently and with the trust that is an essential part of their financial-commercial world.

After a period of time, the transactions are completed, and the text makes it clear that this fulfillment coincides with Isabela's recuperation:

> Otros cuarenta días tardaron de venir los avisos de París; y a dos que llegaron el mercader francés entregó los diez mil ducados a Isabela, y ella a sus padres, y con ellos y con algunos más que hicieron vendiendo algunas de las muchas joyas de Isabela, volvió su padre a ejercitar su oficio de mercader, no sin admiración de los que sabían sus grandes pérdidas. En fin, en pocos meses fue restaurado su perdido crédito y la belleza de Isabela volvió a su ser primero, de tal manera que en hablando de hermosas todos daban el lauro a la española inglesa: que tanto por este nombre como por su hermosura era de toda la ciudad conocida. (I, 274)

The restorations take place all but simultaneously, coming together in a kind of celebration of both the virtue and rightness of Isabela and her long-suffering family and also of the dignity of their socially-defined identity within a larger structure of hierarchies. This restoration, meanwhile, causes "admiración" among the friends and acquaintances of Isabela's father, given their knowledge of the magnitude of the family's initial material losses. Their recovery of wealth and success is not due solely to their own efforts, but is also a result of the highly improbable and fortunate coincidences of fate. Mostly, however, it is due to the generosity and interventions of the people in England, the same people who, at an earlier time, victimized and kept captive their own daughter. Yet, although the plundered wealth of the warrior class here serves (through acts of justice and open generosity) to rebuild the lives of a merchant family, it is hard to avoid the implication that the *novela* is subtly arguing for the moral superiority of this putatively lower class, as one world and way of economic life is subtly replaced by another.

This distinctly unaristocratic mode of dealing with wealth, moreover, not only touches Isabela and her family—who have been, after all, merchants and commoners from the outset. It also becomes Ricaredo's own new method of dealing with what for him is a profoundly changed reality. As was mentioned earlier, Ricaredo's plan to avoid the wedding arranged for him by his family and to be reunited with Isabela requires him to leave England. His pretext for this journey is a pilgrimage to Rome. But other romance-type adventures take place during his two years on the road, including Arnesto's assassination attempt (which leaves him badly wounded), capture by Turkish pirates, and a period of captivity in Algiers (I, 281). During all this time, but especially after his departure from Rome and with his capture by the Turks and subsequent ransoming, Ricaredo is essentially in disguise. That is to say, he is a just another man, now without the power or prestige that he previously had enjoyed in England, either as a recognized nobleman or as the heavily armed commander of a naval expedition. Having voluntarily shed his former identity and its usual activities and inherent privileges, Ricaredo thus finds himself in a position where what remains of his wealth has necessarily had to be transformed—so that it may be transferred—into documents, into instruments of credit. Ricaredo too now finds himself enmeshed in, and in need of, the services of this other world, that of commerce, banking, documents, and trust.

In Ricaredo's narration of his adventures and adversities, he makes the significance of this new way of dealing with money very clear. He has become dependent upon the documents and protocols of the mercantile world. Speaking of his worries when captured by the Turks, he states that

> Bien se me podrá creer si digo que sentía en el alma mi cautiverio, y sobre todo la pérdida de los recaudos de Roma, donde en una caja de lata los traía, con la cédula de los mil seiscientos ducados; mas la buena suerte quiso que viniese a manos de un cristiano cautivo español, que los guardó: que si viniera a poder de los turcos, por la menos había de dar por mi rescate lo que rezaba la cédula, que ellos averiguarían cúya era. (I, 281)

The documents, in other words, represent the money that Ricaredo would later need, but they also necessarily *identify* him and, as he points out, thus indicate what would have been his ransom "value." As luck will have it, however, he is not only successfully ransomed by the Trinitarian Fathers, but also manages to recuperate his documents: "Por añadidura del bien de mi libertad hallé la caja perdida, con los recaudos y la cédula" (I, 281).[16] In short, Ricaredo's happy arrival in Sevilla and reunion with his beloved are accompanied by the safe transfer of at least a certain amount of the money with which he left England. But his reunion with Isabela is, as I stated previously, a renunciation of previous elements of his identity as an Englishman and as an aristocrat of some prominence. His integration into Isabela's Spanish world signals his acceptance of what she and her family represent socially. However noble Ricaredo may still be in theory, in fact he will implicitly live under the practical, material shelter of the prosperous merchant family of his in-laws.

The conclusion of *La española inglesa* contains the conventional happy ending. It is also one of the few conclusions that provides an explicit articulation of the "ejemplo." The short final paragraph is quite to the point; but it is also (yet again) unsatisfactory:

> Esta novela nos podría enseñar cuánto puede la virtud y cuánto la hermosura, pues son bastante juntas y cada una de por sí a enamorar aun hasta los mismos enemigos, y de cómo sabe el cielo sacar de las mayores adversidades nuestras, nuestros mayores provechos. (I, 283)[17]

The triumph of love and the fortunate restorations and reunions are the central stuff of the comedic and the romance pattern.[18] We expect this, and the level-headed reader might object that it goes quite

---

[16] It is worth noting Ricaredo's remark about the potential danger of his having been taken all the way back to Istanbul, a situation that, as I noted in the discussion of *El amante liberal*, would have been much more dire for him. As he states, "a conocerme los turcos por aquél que había echado a fondo sus dos bajeles y quitádoles de las manos la gran nave de la India, o me presentaran al Gran Turco o me quitaran la vida; y de presentarme al Gran Señor redundara no tener libertad en mi vida" (I, 282). Here we could well speculate on possible overtones of (homo)sexual "use value" or else simply Ricaredo's warrior potential in the context of the Ottoman practice of external recruitment, as outlined in Chapter Two above.

[17] On this issue, see especially A. Parodi, "*La española inglesa* de Miguel de Cervantes y la poética de las adversidades provechosas," *Filología* 22 (1987): 49-64.

[18] Again, see N. Frye, *Anatomy of Criticism*, especially "The Mythos of Summer: Romance" (186-206).

beyond the bounds of legitimate literary criticism to ask or speculate about a hypothetical "life" of the protagonists after the end of a given *novela*. This is to say, we don't and generally shouldn't ask: What did they *do* to earn money? How did they get on in life? But in the case of *La española inglesa* the text itself has brought this issue into question. The penultimate paragraph—a passage of notable simplicity and of a certain practical, domestic verisimilitude—puts this issue clearly into focus:

> Por estos rodeos y por estas circunstancias los padres de Isabela cobraron su hija y restauraron su hacienda, y ella, favorecida del cielo y ayudada de sus muchas virtudes, a despecho de tantos inconvenientes, halló marido tan principal como Ricaredo, en cuya compañía se piensa que aún hoy vive en las casas que alquilaron frontero de Santa Paula, que después las compraron de los herederos de un hidalgo burgalés que se llamaba Hernando de Cifuentes. (I, 282-83)

The specificity and detail of the above passage are so simple that their implications easily may be glossed over. Good fortune is rendered in terms of the family's recovery of their daughter, but also of their material wealth. Isabela's own good fortune is partly defined in terms of finding a husband of such fine aristocratic lineage ("marido tan principal"). She thus, in a sense, marries up. But the couple live, and must live, in a practical, material world. They are able to rent and then purchase a substantial home from the heirs of "un hidalgo burgalés." This is only possible as a result of the same material wealth with which the *novela* began and now ends: the wealth of this unaristocratic, modest but orderly merchant class.

What, then, does one make of *La española inglesa*? For Ruth El Saffar, this *novela* is one of the most fully realized examples of the romance, the most "idealized" of the whole collection.[19] In contrast, for Carroll B. Johnson, this text is, in terms of what it implies about class structure and the virtues of their respective economic activities, the most "revolutionary" of the *Novelas ejemplares*.[20] Clearly, the

---

[19] See once again *Novel to Romance*, especially 150-62.

[20] As Johnson puts it ("Catolicismo, familia y fecundidad: el caso de 'La española

novela can be read from a variety of critical perspectives and with quite distinct thematic interests. It is, simultaneously an all but fantastic romance of suffering and quest, on the one hand, and also an intriguing text that keeps offering up details—the simple but necessary stuff of life—that question or disrupt our normal novelistic expectations, on the other. The triumph of love and virtue is rendered by means of a story that also suggests a quite radical inversion of social hierarchical values, identities, and conventional beliefs. The triumph is thus not without its shadows, chief among which may be the question of whether Ricaredo's love fully redeems the initial "sin of the father" or whether the youth remains caught in that same mentality and merely repairs in part the first crime by his sacrifice of identity and his submerging into an alien culture and "inferior" social status.

---

inglesa'"), "El texto de Cervantes es, pues, un texto revolucionario. Invierte las normas genéricas de su época y anuncia una visión social subversiva—la plena integración de la clase burguesa mercantil cambista—precisamente por unas operaciones de cambio y sustitución. Tres conceptos estrechamente vinculados con la ideología oficial nacionalista y antimercantilista dejan su lugar acostumbrado y, al trasladarse, se revelan como soportes de una visión social y humana muy distinta" (524).

Chapter Five
Anonymity, Madness, and
the Decadence of Empire
El licenciado Vidriera

The fifth *novela* is one of the most memorable and studied of the collection.[1] The basic concept and central image of the story—a young man who goes mad and believes himself to be made of glass—is haunting. It both amuses and disturbs. During Tomás's period of madness and under his new identity as "el licenciado Vidriera," Cervantes offers a series of darkly satiric comments on the society of his time.[2] In Tomás Rodaja, when he is no longer Rodaja but the licenciado Vidriera, Cervantes creates his second most famous madman.[3] But unlike don Quijote, whose madness (the

---

[1] The following commentary is much indebted to Forcione's magisterial study, Chapter III of *Cervantes and the Humanist Vision*, "*El Licenciado Vidriera* as a Satirical Parable: The Mystery of Knowledge" (225-316). See also El Saffar, *Novel to Romance*, 50-61; and J. R. Sampayo Rodríguez, *Rasgos erasmistas de la locura del licenciado Vidriera de Miguel de Cervantes*.

[2] See Sampayo Rodríguez, especially 171-74; also M. A. Cruz Camara, "Cervantes como analista de la conducta humana: La inseguridad ontológica del protagonista de *El licenciado Vidriera*," *Explicación de Textos Literarios* 20.1 (1991-1992): 13-23. See also A. Redondo, "La folie du cervantin licencié de Verre (traditions, contexte historique et subversion)," 33-44 in *Visages de la folie (1500-1600)*. A highly inventive and incisive reading of this *novela* is provided by E. M. Gerli in "The Dialectics of Writing: *El licenciado Vidriera* and the Picaresque," *Refiguring Authority*, 10-23.

[3] Concerning this often made comparison, see especially V. E. Munguía García, "*El licenciado Vidriera* y don Quijote," *Anales Cervantinos* 30 (1992): 157-62; also L. Rosales, *Cervantes y la libertad*, vol. I, *La libertad soñada*, especially 183-213; and R. Ruiz, "La 'tres locuras' del licenciado Vidriera," *NRFH* 34.2 (1985-1986): 839-47. As Forcione has noted, concerning Cervantes's two creations, "If in the *Quixote* he is able, through the fantasies and frustrations of his mad protagonist, to enter the forbidden realm of the illegitimate marvelous of romance, where art molds experience in accordance with man's most extravagant desires for perfection, in *El Licenciado Vidriera* he can, through his mad scholar's vision of evil, explore the forbidden world portrayed by what Scipio designates 'satires of blood' as opposed to 'satires of light,' an imaginary world that is designed according to the logic of man's deepest fears concerning what he should not be" (290). On the *licenciado*'s

product of too much credulous reading) involves a complex and often inconsistent process of seeing the world as consonant with the fantastic conventions of the *libros de caballerías*, Vidriera's derangement (the result of a misfiring love potion)[4] manifests itself in hostile outbursts and bitterly alienated views of a real, existing society. If don Quijote's vision distorts what he sees into something more ideal, however detached it may be from worldly reality, Vidriera's vision purports to see critically that which is really there. But Vidriera's view of society takes in only its darkest aspects and possibilities, and this vision is, arguably, nearly as inadequate or incomplete as is that of the deranged *hidalgo*.[5]

For all of these reasons, *El licenciado Vidriera* has received a good deal of scholarly attention.[6] But whereas certain of the other *Novelas ejemplares* (e.g., *El amante liberal, La española inglesa, La ilustre fregona,*

---

madness in general, see D. L. Heiple, "Cervantes' Wise Fool: A Study of Wisdom and Fortune in *El licenciado Vidriera,* and "*El licenciado Vidriera* y el humor tradicional del loco," *Hispania* 66 (March 1983): 17-20.

[4] On the question of the pertinence, or thematic "impertinence" of the love potion, see W. Schleiner, "The Glass Graduate and the Aphrodisiac that Went Wrong: New Light from Old Texts," *Forum for Modern Language Studies* 24.4 (1991): 370-81.

[5] In this regard, see Rodríguez-Luis, *Novedad y ejemplo,* 204-05; concerning the ultimate inadequacy of Vidriera's/Tomás's madness for dealing with his own situation, Rodríguez-Luis quotes Avalle-Arce (*Three Exemplary Novels,* 20) to the effect that Vidriera's period of passive observation and critique "serves him well to unmask the circumstantial world from its appearance and to show it in all its sordid reality. But that kind of intellectual knowledge is totally ineffective when he tries to come to grips with his own suffering reality." See also Rodríguez-Luis, 208-09; and Forcione, 231-37. I would add that Vidriera's "vision" of reality is in itself less than efficaciously balanced, as I shall discuss later.

[6] In addition to the previously cited studies, see F. P. Casa, "The Structural Unity of *El licenciado Vidriera,*" *BHS* 41 (1964): 242-46; G. Edwards, "Cervantes's 'El licenciado Vidriera': Meaning and Structure," *MLR* 68.3 (1973): 559-68; A. K. Forcione, "El desposeimiento del ser en la literatura renacentista: Cervantes, Gracián y los desafíos de *Nemo,*" *NRFH* 34.2 (1985-1986): 654-90; J. Joset, "Bipolarizaciones textuales y estructura especular en *El licenciado Vidriera,*" *Cervantes: su obra y su mundo,* 357-63; E. C. Riley, "Cervantes and the Cynics (*El licenciado Vidriera* and *El coloquio de los perros*)," *BHS* 53 (1976): 189-99; and G. Speak, "*El licenciado Vidriera* and the Glass Men of Early Modern Europe," *MLR* 85.4 (1990): 850-65.

among others) resist and challenge commentary due to an excess of thematic subtlety or their seeming lack of a single, central image or concept, *El licenciado Vidriera* virtually demands and determines ingenious interpretation. The intriguingly fertile idea of the aloof student who coolly rejects a woman's amorous overtures, believes himself turned to glass, and then moves through sectors of Spanish society, reflecting and inspecting in a most negative and somber manner, invites our speculation.[7] The fascination that this text has long held for its readers, however, has been accompanied by a marked diversity of interpretations. As Forcione has noted, "The madness of the glass licentiate is fundamentally paradoxical, and Cervantes's balanced treatment of him as visionary and fool is attested by the widespread disagreement among Cervantists as to whether or not he is to be taken as a reliable spokesman for his author."[8]

The two central phenomena of the text—one individual's madness and the revelation of society's own ills—are impossible to overlook. These two dominant elements are consistent with the *novela*'s relative lack of action. Once again, as in *Rinconete y Cortadillo*, we have a *novela* without much of a conventional novelistic

---

[7] As Forcione (*Cervantes and the Humanist Vision*) reminds us, "As a critic the licenciate is obsessed with man's evil and hypocrisy, sees them in absolute clarity, and exposes them mercilessly. Clairvoyance in dealing with human evil, that whole realm that Cervantes probably had in mind when he wished that the *Celestina* had concealed *lo humano* a bit more than it did, is a traditional quality of the Cynic, but it can, even when it is operating most persuasively and disturbingly, present no more than a partial view of truth, and it can easily lead its possessor into the traditional intellectual and moral errors of the Cynic—undiscriminating generalization and hatred of man" (263).

[8] *Cervantes and the Humanist Vision*, 243; see also 262-63. In addition, see Sampayo Rodríguez, *Rasgos erasmistas*, especially 134-39; and El Saffar, *Novel to Romance*: "Tomás, through the image of glass, merges with the narrator to mediate between the reader and the environment. He protects Cervantes from censure, as the madness protects him, in his unmitigated attack on the variety of pretentions and misrepresentations that make life in the city and in the court impossible for the literate man" (55).

plot.[9] The complementary elements of madness and social critique make the need for the familiar story elements superfluous. Under the heading of madness, meanwhile, the problem of sex and sexuality figures significantly in the mechanisms and textures of this narrative. Tomás's sexual indifference and the equally improbable infatuation of the mysterious woman inevitably evoke speculations on such questions as Tomás's already neurotic tendency toward avoidance. The peculiar instigation of the madness—we recall that Tomás's rejection of the woman's advances is pointedly not based on his love for another woman, as is Andrés's rejection of Juana Carducha in *La gitanilla*, but rather stems from an unlikely yet all the more symbolically significant male frigidity—prompts a broader consideration of how his behavior is in many ways the logical extension of the mind-body dichotomy or the Apollonian versus the Dionysian, the primordial "male/intellectual" in tense and hostile relationship to and distinction from the "female/physical."[10] At the same time, this extreme of the male principle as pathology is, as

---

[9] On this structural tendency in the *Novelas*, see Rodríguez-Luis; as he suggests, "Cervantes demuestra aquí [*Rinconete y Cortadillo*], según ha visto Hainsworth, que es posible componer una narración basada en la reproducción de la realidad, o *sin argumento*; es decir, que salta por encima de la evolución normal del género que las demás Novelas tanto contribuyen a definir a través precisamente del ahondar en caracteres y situaciones dramáticas, para rechazar ambos procedimientos. Algo semejante sucede en *El licenciado Vidriera* y en el *Coloquio de los perros*, que por ello recuerdan también la técnica picaresca" (192).

[10] On the question in general, see C. Paglia, *Sexual Personae*, especially Chapter One (1-39). As El Saffar has stated, "The principal characteristic of the mad Licenciate and the young Tomás Rodaja is fear of the other. . . . The illness simply induced the crisis that all the other activities of Tomás's life had been designed to avoid, for the illness brought him forcibly, and for the first time, into confrontation with his contingency, his dependence on time and chance occurrences, his limited position in life, and his necessary recognition of death. In study Tomás had sought to escape not only his past and the obscurity to which it threatened to condemn him, but all of life's conflict and, implicitly, death itself" (*Novel to Romance*, 56-57). Forcione similarly notes that "The scholar's fanatical devotion to the mind and the spirit is grotesquely caricatured in his removal from his body and in the terribly high price which, in his state of constant anxiety, he must pay for his knowledge. In other words, the madness of the licentiate is, in one very important sense, a precise objectified image of his foolishness" (*Cervantes and the Humanist Vision*, 242).

many critics have suggested, already more than latent in Tomás and his personality, his style of involvement with others, and his all too narrowly focussed ambitions and goals.[11]

Above all, *El licenciado Vidriera* clearly invites a reading from the perspective of the questions of personal identity and social order. Taking the theme of identity first, it is obvious that Tomás's beginning and his end trace out a bitter parable. To focus on Tomás—with his mutations, madness, and ultimately frustrated yet ironically heroic end—is to realize that this is perhaps the most pathetic of the *novelas*.[12] From the perspective of the individual, the elements of Tomás's pathos outline a parable of identity, or identities: one never quite revealed (his mysterious origin) and another that is desired, yet never quite attained (the coveted fame as a scholar). We ask implicitly, but we never find out, who *is* Tomás Rodaja-Rueda? Is the second, final patronimic, *Rueda*, a return to, and hence a revelation of, the true family link evaded at the outset? Is it thus an open identification of self now possible with Tomás's achievement of both full maturity and a return to sanity? Or is it yet another invention, an attempt to begin anew, to separate himself from not one but two pasts: that of his humble and anonymous, if academically successful, boyhood and that of his more recent and now, seen in retrospect, quite embarrassing madness?

But if this particular mystery is never resolved to our satisfaction, there is much about the *novela*—and much in Tomás's life, madness, and death—that opens up a critical vision of the Spain of Cervantes's day. Much has been made of Vidriera's strange outbursts and their relevance to the socio-cultural aspect of Cervantes's Spain. But I would suggest that this *novela* inevitably goes beyond cultural commonplaces and reveals much about a larger political, historical situation. To begin with the obvious, Tomás is—before, during, and

---

[11] See Sampayo Rodríguez, especially 68-69; also Forcione, 273.

[12] A very suggestive reading from this perspective is given by J. V. Ricapito in "'El licenciado Vidriera' or 'La historia de un fracaso'," *Cervantes's* Novelas ejemplares: *Between History and Creativity*, 69-95.

after his vitrious phase—most significantly if problematically revealing of, although marginally involved in, the Spanish socio-political reality of Cervantes's day. Through Tomás's studies in Salamanca, his travels with the soldiers, and his period of madness in Salamanca and Valladolid, this *novela* touches on both the smaller social arena of the two Spanish cities (symbolic respectively of university and royal court) and on the larger issue of Spain's extended empire. The text as a whole thus has to be read both in terms of, but also beyond, Tomás's pathetic story. It is simulta-neously the tracing of one of the saddest personal life trajectories in the *Novelas ejemplares* and is also Cervantes's coldest, most Que-vedian, satiric projection of language against the many-levelled decadence of his society and the empire that it struggled to sustain.[13]

The *novela* begins in a deceptively simple yet curious way: the introduction of the title character is striking in the context of the collection for its radical ambiguity regarding Tomás's origin. The disturbing implications of the scene of Tomás's initial entrance, or discovery, and presentation have been variously remarked and explored, and a fair number of the most penetrating studies have drawn the obvious inference of a marked resonance with the picaresque.[14] Two young aristocratic students and their servant

---

[13] See Forcione, *Cervantes and the Humanist Vision*, 292-93, where he points out that Cervantes "could already see the spirit of the Licenciado Vidriera clearly emerging in the literary and cultural life of Spain—in the nightmarish fantasies of Quevedesque satire, as well as in the desolate vision of the popular picaresque narratives, with their panoramic surveys of human failings, their cultivation of railing abuse, and their antagonistic engagement with their readers."

[14] This element has been commonly noted; see Rodríguez-Luis, especially 193, where he notes the resonance of the location; also 201-202: "El objeto de su visión es, sin embargo, la maldad y la corrupción del hombre; el mismo, por lo tanto, de la picaresca. Porque en esta censura de la vida de la época, el autor está verdaderamente dibujando el contenido intelectual, el esqueleto, por decirlo así, de una novela picaresca despojada de la acción que podría poner en movimiento su característica visión del mundo. La descarnada crítica de Tomás, incluido el humor—ausente, en general, del *Guzmán*, pero desbordante en el *Buscón*—, es en esencia semejante a la del pícaro, aunque potenciada en su caso por la vocación intelectual del crítico y por la ausencia de contacto directo con la realidad, gracias

discover Tomás alone and asleep on the banks of the Río Tormes, dressed in the garb of a peasant (*labrador*). Tomás is, in effect, found in the middle of nowhere, precariously alone and defenselessly unconscious on a river bank. Likewise, as Tomás takes pains to assert, he is *from* nowhere—that is to say, from no place that he will ever name. His subsequent introduction of himself is both an evasion of the truth of his identity—an evasion far more radical and complete than the similar reluctance of Rincón and Cortado at the beginning of their story—and also a declaration of an ambition distinctly tinged with hubris and a certain intellectual vainglory.[15] The text presents this moment, in part, as follows:

> Mandaron a un criado que le despertase; despertó, y preguntáronle de adónde era y qué hacía durmiendo en aquella soledad. A lo cual el muchacho respondió que el nombre de su tierra se la había olvidado, y que iba a la ciudad de Salamanca a buscar un amo a quien servir, por sólo que le diese estudio. Preguntáronle si sabía leer; respondió que sí, y escribir también.
> —Desa manera —dijo uno de los caballeros—, no es por falta de memoria habérsete olvidado el nombre de tu patria.
> —Sea por lo que fuere —respondió el muchacho—: que ni el della ni el de mis padres sabrá ninguno hasta que yo pueda honrarlos a ellos y a ella.
> —Pues, ¿de qué suerte los piensas honrar? —preguntó el otro caballero.
> —Con mis estudios —respondió el muchacho—, siendo famoso por ellos; porque yo he oído decir que de los hombres se hacen los obispos. (II, 43)

As the conclusion of the *novela* emphasizes, Tomás will not achieve worldly success on the basis of any due recognition of his intellect and study. Rather, after he is cured of his mania and returns to the court as the renamed Tomás Rueda, his attempts to find employment

---

a ser de vidrio el licenciado y a tener, por lo tanto, que rehuir cualquier contacto con la gente que no sea oral." See also E. M. Gerli, "La picaresca y *El licenciado Vidriera*: Género y contragénero en Cervantes," 577-87 in M. Criado de Val, ed., *La picaresca: Orígenes, textos y estructuras. Actas del I Congreso Internacional sobre la Picaresca.* Gerli further refines his analysis in "The Dialectics of Writing: *El licenciado Vidriera* and the Picaresque," where he sees the *novela* as a profound subversion and reconfiguration of the picaresque.

[15] See, again, Rodríguez-Luis, 194; see also Sampayo Rodríguez, especially 68ff and 136ff; and Forcione, 307ff.

as a man of letters (in effect, as a lawyer or civil servant) are met with failure. In utter frustration and with some bitterness, he abandons the court, returns to the military sector, this time as a full participant and not just as a detached camp-follower, and dies in battle.

"The Death of Tomás Rueda"

At this point it is appropriate to skip ahead to the conclusion of the *novela*. In many ways, *El licenciado Vidriera* is a text that profits from a reading in reverse. This is especially so when one reconsiders the complex device of this curious, deeply frustrated, and anonymous identity as a pointed instrument of social examination. Tomás's much emphasized final rejection by and failure at the court is worth citing at length:

> Salió otro día, y fue lo mismo; hizo otro sermón, y no sirvió de nada. Perdía mucho y no ganaba cosa, y viéndose morir de hambre, determinó de dejar la Corte y volverse a Flandes, donde pensaba valerse de las fuerzas de su brazo, pues no se podía valer de las de su ingenio.
> Y poniéndolo en efeto, dijo al salir de la Corte:
> —¡Oh Corte, que alargas las esperanzas de los atrevidos pretendientes y acortas las de los virtuosos encogidos, sustentas abundantemente a los truhanes desvergonzados y matas de hambre a los discretos vergonzosos!
> Esto dijo y se fue a Flandes, donde la vida que había comenzado a eternizar por las letras la acabó de eternizar por las armas, en compañía de su buen amigo el capitán Valdivia, dejando fama en su muerte de prudente y valentísimo soldado. (II, 74)

This finale has inspired a peculiar and frankly contradictory variety of interpretations. As is well known, Cervantes himself—as one may infer from the autobiographical comments in his prologues and from relevant passages in his texts—considered the calling of the authentic soldier (as opposed to the vocation of his crazed knight errant) a most worthy and virtuous one. Thus, some have suggested that Tomás's death in battle provides a heroic and affirmative ending. Not only, then, is "la acabó de eternizar por las armas" meant without a hint of irony or bitterness, so it is argued, but his heroic death is a personal triumph, an authentic achievement that more than compensates for his ostensible failure at the corrupt, insensitive court.[16]   Others have suggested that his abandonment of the court—which is, in effect, his rejection by this world, his expulsion from a possible life, one that he truly wanted—is a defeat, a bitter failure.[17]

Tomás's denunciation—which is to say Cervantes's—of the hypocrisy and moral bankruptcy of the court is a kind of satiric commonplace.[18] But the court, however corrupt it may be, is—in fact and in symbol—the seat of national power, the place of political authority, and thus the key center from which the decisions of empire are projected out to the world. The simple fact is that Tomás not only dies in battle, in some generalized and universal act of military heroism; rather, he dies in Flanders. He dies in that particular "theatre of war" that was the curse and the hemorrhage of Spain's imperial policies under Felipe II and Felipe III, and that (despite the twelve-year truce with the Dutch in 1609) would continue to plague the Spanish Habsburgs through much of the

---

[16] Such a view seems implicit in Casalduero's final comments on the text; see *Sentido y forma*, 148-49.

[17] This seems to be the view of El Saffar throughout, although her interpretation leans toward a reading of Tomás as a projection or symptom of Cervantes's own struggle with the nature and limits of narrative.   Toward the end of her commentary, El Saffar states that "The Licenciate fails both in life and in letters. In life he cannot make meaningful contact with society. He has no friends outside of the intellectual community and finds only sickness and death in alternative roles" (60). Clearly, for El Saffar, Tomás's death in battle is yet another failure.

[18] One thinks immediately of Quevedo's satires, for example the passage on the pretensions and hypocrisy of ambitious noblemen in *El mundo por de dentro*: "Aquel caballero, por ser señoría, no hay diligencia que no haga y ha procurado hacerse Venecia por ser señoría, sino que, como se fundó en el viento, para serlo se había de fundar en el agua. Sustenta, por parecer señor, caza de halcones, que lo primero que matan es a su amo de hambre con la costa y luego el rocín en que los llevan, y después, cuando mucho, una graja o un milano" (*Sueños y discursos*, 280). See also Quevedo's letters, especially that passage from one of his many to Osuna (1615) in which he remarks that "Andase tras mí media corte y no hay hombre que no me haga mil ofrecimientos en el servicio de vuecelencia; que aquí los más hombres se han vuelto putas, que no las alcanza quien no da" (*Epistolario*, 142).

seventeenth century. In this manner, however much Cervantes's intention may have been to unironically "eternizar" his protagonist, the world that the text opens up to us reveals the inescapable irony of heroic blood spilt in a futile endeavor, one that was both symptom and cause of the imperial decadence that began with the régime of Felipe II and that would contribute to the crises of his two successors.[19]

In effect, then, Tomás's death—whatever specific personal meaning or value one might attach to or infer from it—subtly brings us out of the narrowness of the fiction and points to a much larger world, one whose texture is that of a palpable political anguish. It is not only Tomás's death that reminds us of imperial decline, however. It is also his life, its peculiar evasive nature, and the wanderings of his earlier years. Therefore, before returning to the implications of the *novela*'s conclusion, we should examine its beginning and what the well-known actions and statements reveal when read through the optic of the political, the politics of imperial decline.

The opening pages of *El licenciado Vidriera* frame the issues of identity and social order in a way that tellingly juxtaposes an individual alienation with the subtly glimpsed but much larger picture of a political world already revealing signs of fracture and decadence. Both identity and social order (in the sense of orderliness, as well as class strata) are introduced in the first paragraph: an anonymous, apparently vagrant boy is found by two young aristocratic students and their servant. The most sharply yet subtly drawn aspects of the identity question are here dramatized in the social rank distinctions and in the dialogue. In terms of both individual identity and socially stratified relationships, the first striking element is the fact of marginality. We are on the banks of the Tormes, a margin both geographic and thematic, with its rich picaresque allusions. The questions of marginality and social class

---

[19] Concerning Spain's situation in the late sixteenth century and the first half of the seventeenth, see H. Kamen, *Spain 1469-1714: A Society of Conflict*, especially 122-256; also J. H. Elliott, *Imperial Spain 1469-1716*, chapters eight and nine (285-360).

are also underlined by the distinction of the *caballeros* versus the *labrador*. The question of Tomás's marginality and social separation is stressed further by Tomás's refusal to identify himself in any way except in terms of his claimed talent and his future goals: an assertion of radical individuality in profound tension with the notion of group belonging. Social margins and the frustrated desires for, and *engaños* of, a radically self-made identity will continue implicitly to manifest themselves throughout the *novela*.

The opening section of *El licenciado Vidriera*, which for the purposes of this present commentary I will consider the passages up to and including Tomás's ingestion of the drugged *membrillo*, deals with the young man's formation and education. It also reveals his peculiar style of relationship and involvement. Tomás's manner is marked by paradox: he is charming yet distant; agreeable yet disinclined to make commitments. The ambiguity of commitment, relationships, and identity is carefully established from the outset of the *novela*, as Tomás is integrated into the intellectual and social context of his two new patrons and protectors. As the texts states,

> A pocos días le vistieron de negro, y a pocas semanas dio Tomás muestras de tener raro ingenio, sirviendo a sus amos con toda fidelidad, puntualidad y diligencia que, con no faltar un punto sus estudios, parecía que sólo se ocupaba en servirlos. Y como el buen servir del siervo mueve la voluntad del señor a tratarle bien, ya Tomás Rodaja no era criado de sus amos, sino su compañero. Finalmente, en ocho años que estuvo con ellos se hizo tan famoso en la universidad por su buen ingenio y notable habilidad, que de todo género de gentes era estimado y querido. (II, 43-44)

Although we are dealing with something of a commonplace—i.e., the notion that the boy's skill and good will as a servant win his masters' hearts to the extent that he is considered a companion, if not an equal—this passage also suggests the blurring of boundaries. In this case, distinctions of one's role (Tomás was able to be both an excellent student and a perfect servant) and also of class-based norms of interaction remain somewhat ambiguous.[20] Tomás has profited from his diligence and charm. But he has emphatically not been integrated into the family or social stratum of his protectors. He therefore has few qualms about leaving their service to return to Salamanca and his studies, and they have no hesitancy in endowing him financially so that he may finish his studies ("Ellos, corteses y liberales, se la dieron, acomodándole de suerte que con lo que le dieron se pudiera sustentar tres años" [II, 44]). Revealingly, Tomás will not return to these people, nor will they have any further role in the *novela*.

Something of this same ambiguity of identity and commitment is evident, though explored in a very different manner, in the next stage of Tomás's education, his initiatory travels with the soldiers. Relevant, but not often remarked, is the fact that, in this section of the *novela*, Tomás is on his way back to Salamanca, but that this time he fails to reach his destination. His chance encounter with another traveller, captain don Diego de Valdivia, changes his plans. Worth considering is the fact that Tomás's decision to postpone his return to his beloved studies is prompted by the captain's glowing description of the military life—a life whose true and profoundly unromantic nature the narrator is quick to underscore. The text quite effectively expresses this combination of ingenuousness and harsh reality: "En resolución, tantas cosas le dijo, y tan bien dichas, que la discreción de nuestro Tomás Rodaja comenzó a titubear y la voluntad a aficionarse a aquella vida, que tan cerca tiene la muerte" (II, 45). Tomás is, in effect, successfully seduced by his own curiosity and also by the captain's words.[21]

---

[20] Something of this ambiguous nature recalls the case of the mysterious *paje-poeta* Clemente in *La gitanilla*; in this latter case, however, Clemente's role and importance within the *novela* is radically different from the central position of Tomás in *El licenciado* (see Chapter One above).

[21] As the text presents it, the captain's invitation plays upon the intellectual curiosity that is part of Tomás essential nature: the captain "le rogó que se fuese con él a Italia, si quería, por curiosidad de verla; . . . " (II, 45).

In thinking about the captain's offer ("haciendo consigo en un instante un breve discurso . . ."), Tomás rationalizes his decision to accompany the soldiers by reminding himself that "las luengas peregrinaciones hacen a los hombres discretos . . . " (II, 46). This is to be yet another phase of his education. But this time there is a notable difference. For, while Tomás's university education was a direct and involved encounter with books and study, his learning experience with the soldiers is distanced and detached. The tour of parts of Italy and the journey (overland along the "Spanish Road") to Flanders are the experience of the tourist or the hanger-on. Tomás will learn of the soldiering life from the relatively safe distance of the camp follower. As the text puts it, from the very beginning of his travels with the soldiers and while still in Spain, at Antequera, Tomás is the calm observer:

> Allí notó Tomás la autoridad de los comisarios, la incomodidad de algunos capitanes, la solicitud de los aposentadores, la industria y cuenta de los pagadores, las quejas de los pueblos, el rescatar de las boletas, las insolencias de los bisoños, las pendencias de los huéspedes, el pedir bagajes más de los necesarios, y, finalmente, la necesidad casi precisa de hacer todo aquello que notaba y mal le parecía. (II, 46)

The young Rodaja defines himself as, and is able to remain, a detached observer, learning, or perhaps not really learning, about the profession in which he will ultimately earn his ironic fame. It is a subtly but significantly different sort of education.

For the purposes of this present commentary, however, the telling aspect of Tomás's sojourn with the soldiers, as well as his travels on his own in Italy, and finally his brief visit to Flanders, has less to do with the putative educational value of the tour, or with the extra-textual, biographical relevance of the Italian travels to Cervantes's own life.[22] Rather, this set of travels, the particular places visited, and certain allusions within the narration evoke the reality of a Spanish political empire of immense geographical extension and

---

[22] See Rodríguez-Luis, *Novedad y ejemplo*, I, 196-97, note 1.

hopelessly irresolvable conflicts.[23] Some critics have fixed on the evident superficiality of the narration at this point, and indeed, at times Tomás's travels in Italy seem more like an annotated wine list than either the recounting of significant action or the precise description of places. But the very fact that Spanish soldiers are coming and going to and from Italy reminds us of the specific political possessions of the Spanish Habsburg monarchy in Italian territory, not to mention Spain's interests and conflictive relations vis-à-vis the Papal states and other political entities in the northern half of the peninsula.[24] In effect, Tomás's brief and superficial tourist junket is only made possible by the simple, unstated but utterly crucial detail that the Spanish monarchy of Cervantes's day included a vast, geographically irregular, and profoundly troubled European empire.

The manner in which the text integrates and reveals the imperial theme and its paradoxes is deceptively light-handed and allusive. The seemingly most trivial rhetorical turn, or throw-away remark, opens up a glimpse of the imperial problematic. In speaking of Tomás's visit to and assessment of Venice, for example, the text states that Tomás

> fue a Venecia, ciudad que a no haber nacido Colón en el mundo no tuviera en él semejante: merced al cielo y al gran Hernando Cortés, que conquistó la gran Méjico para que la gran Venecia tuviese en alguna manera quien se le opusiese. Estas dos famosas ciudades se parecen en las calles, que son todas de agua: la de Europa, admiración del mundo antiguo; la de América, espanto del mundo nuevo. (II, 50-51)

Venice, a more or less independent political entity, is compared for aesthetic reasons to a most famous part of Spain's overseas empire. Cervantes's Mexico is known as both history and legend. It is also

---

[23] See in particular H. Kamen, *Spain 1469-1714: A Society of Conflict*, 205-10; also J. Lynch, *Spain 1516-1598*, 386-418.

[24] See H. Kamen, *Spain 1469-1714*, 83ff; also H. G. Koenigsberger, "Western Europe and the Power of Spain" (in *The New Cambridge Modern History*, vol. III, 234-318), in particular 254-63.

all but a metonymy for the New World wealth that helped finance the monarchy's political involvements and military actions in the Old World.[25]

Within just a few lines of the above allusion, Tomás's European journey continues as he rejoins the captain and goes to Flanders. The brief passage referring to this part of the travels reduces the reality of the endemic strife in the Low Countries region of the monarchy to the most unassuming aside; as the narrator puts it,

> Fue muy bien recibido de su amigo el capitán, y en su compañía y camarada pasó a Flandes, y llegó a Amberes, ciudad no menos para maravillar que las que había visto en Italia. Vio a Gante, y a Bruselas, y vio que todo el país se disponía a tomar las armas para salir en campaña el verano siguiente. (II, 51)

The offhand manner in which Cervantes alludes to the anticipated military conflict almost normalizes the chilling fact that, in the latter part of the sixteenth century and in the first years of the seventeenth, violence in these parts of Spain's European possessions was the norm.[26] Likewise, when Tomás returns to Spain (once again, a decision taken with his characteristic detachment: "Y habiendo cumplido con el deseo que le movió a ver lo que había visto, determinó volverse a España y a Salamanca a acabar sus estudios") and this journey takes him through France, we are again reminded of the grim side of European history: "y por Francia volvió a España, sin haber visto a París, por estar puesta en armas" (II, 51). What will, at the conclusion of the *novela* be the fitting and glorious theatre of Tomás's heroic end, the field of battle and the whole endeavor of war, is here the slight inconvenience of the uninvolved traveller. If we restrict our view to a narrow and exclusive focus on Tomás, then, the historical reality that surrounds him is interesting but incidental.

---

[25] This all but commonplace allusion has important resonance in other key moments of the *Novelas*. Cervantes's New World is not just a source of wonder but is also the combined refuge and source of questionable material "renewal" of Spain's lost souls, as we will see in *El celoso extremeño*; see Chapter Seven below.

[26] On this question, see H. G. Koenigsberger, "Western Europe and the Power of Spain," especially 264-318.

However, with a view of Tomás's whole career and especially of his two professions and his ambiguous passage through Spanish society, the details of this early travel phase become more significant. Once again, this broader and more inclusive meaning arises from contexts and curious juxtapositions. And for this we must continue to trace Tomás's pathetic trail—or trial—through sexuality, madness, and social vision.

Career of a Mad *Licenciado*

The infamous agent of Tomás's madness, and thus his Vidriera phase, is the mysterious woman, the "dama de todo rumbo y manejo," whose interaction with Tomás has been commented upon largely in terms of the implications of Tomás's rejection of the sexual and of the physical in general.[27] As I have suggested above, Tomás's rejection of the woman's advances—while hardly remarkable in and of itself[28]—cannot escape the reader's tendency to impute to this otherwise simple act, or non-act, more portentous symbolic content and purpose. Tomás is not merely uninterested in *this* woman; he shows and has shown a truly remarkable lack of interest in any woman. Whether one would then read this action as a troubling symptom of frigidity or irregular sexual orientation, on the one hand, or as a more symbolically-intended dramatization of the mind-body dichotomy, with Mother Nature punishing the vainglorious male/intellectual's failure to render due attention, on the other, one has to remark that Tomás's rejection of the woman is consistent with his entire being, insofar as we know it.[29]

---

[27] On this problem, see W. Schleiner, "The Glass Graduate and the Aphrodisiac That Went Wrong: New Light from Old Texts," *Forum for Modern Language Studies* 27.4 (1991): 370-81; see also El Saffar, *Novel to Romance*, 56-57.

[28] For example, consider the case of Marcela in *Don Quijote* I, or Andrés and Juana Carducha in *La gitanilla*.

[29] See, among others, Sampayo Rodríguez, especially 120-24.

But what about this shady lady herself? We know, of course, that she is a big hit with all the other students. Her role in the story, however, seems to be mainly functional: she enters in order to fall madly in love with Tomás, to be rebuffed, and hoping for a more favorable, aphrodisiac-inspired response, to give him the drug that will turn him into the man of glass. The narrator presents the woman and the subsequent problem with great economy, but the details merit attention: "Dijéronle a Tomás que aquella dama decía que había estado en Italia y en Flandes, y por ver si la conocía, fue a visitarla, de cuya visita y vista quedó ella enamorada de Tomás" (II, 52). Of course, no truly respectable woman, however attractive, would be unattached and spend her time "holding court" for all the local students. Much less would she have travelled idly through Italy and Flanders. She is obviously understood to be a prostitute. But the detail that she too had—though for other reasons—made the grand tour suggests that she was a camp follower of the female gender (one more revealing contrast with Tomás's own status and behavior as a more detached, uninvolved camp follower with the captain). The mysterious woman, then, is yet another symptom and revelation of Spain's European imperial problematic and of its wastes and futilities. Warring and whoring have always gone hand in hand, of course, but the reminder that the glorious, heroic, and noble calling of the soldier is not only heir to physical danger but also to moral corruption subtly undermines the possibility of taking the military finale of this *novela* as a pure and unambiguous ennoblement of Tomás's final endeavor, his heroic death. In short, the unnamed and seemingly insignificant woman points to an external context, a world of both familiar, universalized corruption and complexity, and also a specific historical moment, the reality of Spain in its history and in the individual human wanderings across a troubled European landscape of religious and political strife.

Tomás's career ("Dos años o poco más duró en esta enfermedad") as the crazed licenciado Vidriera dominates the central section of the *novela*. Appropriately, a fair amount of critical commentary has been devoted to this part of the text. The diversity or lack of tonal and ideological unity in the Vidriera phase, however, has prompted divergent judgments about whether Tomás as the licenciado is a projection of Cervantes's own views, a fair and consistent critic of social ills, or whether his own inconsistency and ill will, if not downright mean-spiritedness, place the pathetic madman himself rather beyond the pale, in an area of cynical marginality.[30] Much critical debate has also fixed on the structural implications of this central section. Does the passage dominated by Vidriera's peculiar critical pronouncements—some highly compact and aphoristic, others quite long and involved—contribute to a desired or expected novelistic unity, or does this section in effect blow the story apart?[31] Such considerations, of course, beg the question of how one might ever adequately define "unity" in the context of a Cervantine text. Nonetheless, I find myself largely in agreement with Rodríguez-Luis's sense that this part of the *novela* both destabilizes and distinguishes the text.[32]

Vidriera's part of the *novela* is clearly reminiscent of satiric works such as Quevedo's *Sueños*.[33] But as Cervantes has composed this section, the satiric career of the licenciado lacks the conciseness and

---

[30] With this phase, we are, as Forcione and Redondo, among others have noted, in the world of Quevedo's satires; see for example *El mundo por de dentro* and *La hora de todos*.

[31] On the thorny question of structural unity versus disintegration, see F. P. Casa, "The Structural Unity of *El licenciado Vidriera*," *BHS* 41 (1964): 242-46; G. Edwards, "Cervantes's 'El licenciado Vidriera': Meaning and Structure," *MLR* 68.3 (1973): 559-68; and Forcione, *Cervantes and the Humanist Vision*, 225ff.

[32] As Rodríguez-Luis has noted, "El peso del material aforístico, que no es a la postre tan original ni tan agudo como cabría esperar, desequilibra definitivamente la narración, paralizando el desarrollo de la novela propiamente dicha, hasta que una vez curado el loco-sabio se despacha el relato del fin de Tomás en un par de párrafos que definen primero que nada la lección negativa de la obra: fracaso del que confía demasiado en su voluntad sin cuidarse de las trampas del mundo; falta de caridad de los hombres; agudeza en la visión de la sociedad de quien vive fuera de ella; de qué poco, en fin, sirven la ambición, el saber y la madurez (en contraste con la anterior inocencia del protagonista)" (208).

[33] Again, compare especially the *Sueño del infierno* and *El mundo por de dentro* or the domestic-theme fragments of his *La hora de todos*, or similarly, Vélez de Guevara's *El diablo cojuelo*.

symmetry of Quevedo's satiric technique. Instead, more in the spirit of what we will find in *El coloquio de los perros*, Vidriera's remarks and judgments vary in length and character, from very short witty criticisms, or insults, to long, fairly complex investigations of a given subject. In part for this reason, the critical career of licenciado Vidriera is difficult to characterize. It is inconsistent and brings us into a logic or vision of fragmentation and perplexity.

Yet amid the satiric commonplaces—e.g., on poets, women, druggists, and physicians—Vidriera's bitter remarks include both indirect allusions and direct confrontations that reveal the causes and symptoms of the decadence that permeated the Spanish society on all levels, especially the political. How one gets from the relatively low socio-political level of Vidriera (or Tomás Rodaja-Rueda) as an individual to the level of the problematic of imperial decline involves a process of meta-thematic reading. We must, moreover, turn our attention to the intertextual connections in and across the rest of the *Novelas*. In Vidriera's invective we hear fragmentary echoes from other *novelas*, those brief moments in which hints of a jarring, troubling narrowness or chauvinism in the narrative voice are difficult to dismiss. For example, one of Vidriera's first wisecracks, his biblical-citation reply to the *ropera*, raises the issue not only of the questionable legitimacy of her children, but also the *limpieza de sangre* problem.[34] The otherwise quite innocent biblical quotation—"*Filiae Hierusalem, plorate super vos et super filios vestros*" (II, 55)—figuratively brings the woman, and the other women within earshot, into the questionable, ambiguous context of a possible Jewish community, but more disturbingly, of the Jewish traces within the real community.[35] The text's opening up of the *limpieza* question, however, is much more direct and obvious in a subsequent passage:

> Estando a la puerta de una iglesia, vio que entraba en ella un labrador de los que siempre blasonan de cristianos viejos, y detrás dél venía uno que

---

[34] See Sieber's note no. 43, 55, to the effect that the woman's children "no eran los hijos del marido."

[35] On this question, see Forcione, 277-78.

no estaba en tan buena opinión como el primero, y el Licenciado dio
grandes voces al labrador, diciendo:
—Esperad, Domingo, a que pase el Sábado. (II, 56)

The text gives us nothing more, i.e., nothing concerning the reactions
of anger or embarrassment of either or both men. But it is easy to
see, first, how the remark is a racist slur on the second man, and
second, how the *labrador* himself, as one of those who "siempre
blasonan de cristianos viejos," can be imagined to be both a bigot and
also possibly one who, as we might say, doth protest too much. The
larger political relevance of this teasing and sniping at the *converso*
question, meanwhile, is not hard to see. First, we will recall the
reflexive relevance of a hypersensitivity to *limpieza* that could easily
be imputed to Tomás himself, in his initial refusal to reveal his
background, coupled with his slightly suspect high level of education. The fear of association with the despised group, the people of
the Book, had led to an avoidance of cultivating those skills—in
letters and in administration and finance—traditionally linked to the
Jewish community and whose absence from the government of
sixteenth- and seventeenth-century Spain would prove detrimental
to the economic health and administrative efficacy of the monarchy.[36]

While it might appear that the lines of connection drawn above
are tenuous at best—and tendentiously speculative at the least—I
would nonetheless argue that the line of transmission and relevance
between ideological preoccupation, ambiguous individual aspiration,
governmental incompetence, and the ultimate follies and tragedies
of the empire all run directly through Cervantes's main character,
Tomás. Tomás embodies the paradoxes and absurdities of the needs
and fears of the imperial mechanism itself. Although there is, at the
beginning, Tomás's allusion to "obispos," it is soon clear that his own

---

[36] On this issue, see J. H. Elliott, *Imperial Spain*, especially 212-320; also H. Kamen,
Spain 1469-1714, 196-256. Concerning the economic consequences of the expulsion
of the Jews and the continuing persecution of the *conversos*, see A. Girard, "Les
étrangers dans la vie économique de l'Espagne aux XVIe et XVIIe siècles," *Annales
d'Histoire Économique et Sociale* 24 (1933): 567-78; and A. A. Sicroff, *Les Controverses
des Status de «Pureté de Sang» en Espagne de XVe au XVIIe Siècle*.

career path will not be religious but rather civil. This anonymous and mysterious but talented young man will either make his way, and his "name," through law, in or out of civil service, or he will not make his way at all. Thus, Vidriera's reluctance and satiric aversion when he is first invited to the Court (more as entertainment than as a serious intellectual resource) is a crucial part of a larger pattern:

> Las nuevas de su locura y de sus respuestas y dichos se extendió por toda Castilla, y llegando a noticia de un príncipe o señor que estaba en la Corte, quiso enviar por él, y encargóselo a un caballero amigo suyo que estaba en Salamanca que se lo enviase, y topándolo el caballero un día, le dijo:
> —Sepa el señor licenciado Vidriera que un gran personaje de la Corte le quiere ver y envía por él.
> A lo cual respondió:
> —Vuesa merced me excuse con ese señor, que yo no soy bueno para palacio, porque tengo vergüenza y no sé lisonjear. (II, 56)

This posture is, of course, a satiric commonplace: the Court seen as a place of flattery and hypocrisy (cf. Quevedo's letters to Osuna). But the only meaningfully successful destination for Tomás (as opposed to "Vidriera") is precisely this same Court, the government, in which—idealistically and supposedly beyond, or despite, corruptions and parasites—his ability would be recognized and rewarded, where he would, in effect, make a positive contribution to the good functioning of the monarchy.

The cured and restored Tomás, in other words, will have to return to this same despised place. And he will come back, though with quite unhappy results. But here, during his period of license as Vidriera the madman, Cervantes's creature can criticize the government as if it were nothing but abuse and corruption. One of his wisecracks will foreshadow Vidriera's own fate, although here, it would seem intended as comic word-play:

> Otro le preguntó qué remedio tendría para salir con una comisión que había dos años que la pretendía. Y díjole:
> —Parte a caballo y a la mira de quien la lleva, y acompáñale hasta salir de la ciudad, y así saldrás con ella. (II, 63)

The core of the joke is both trivial, on the one hand, and serious, though loaded with the time-worn critique of the frustrations of politics and the injustice of judgments of individual merit, on the other. This allusion to "una comisión que . . . pretendía" is, however, very much like the goal that implicitly lies at the heart of the young Rodaja's aspirations and that the mature, restored Rueda will fruitlessly seek. It is also, and quite pertinently, an echo of the situation of don Juan de Cárcamo's father at the Court, as alluded to in *La gitanilla* by the boy.[37] The issue of merited or parasitical entreaties to the court, meanwhile, also foreshadows intertextually a key satiric moment near the very end of the collection: the passage in the *Coloquio*, at the hospital of Mahudes in which the *arbitrista* appears and speaks of his *memoriales* and schemes.[38]

A couple of other passages from Vidriera's career of crazed, and thus indulged, critique merit brief mention for their subtle but pertinent connection to the political question. In these two places, however, the link to Tomás/Vidriera is less intimate. Instead, we are dealing with jokes that, however innocent or slight they may appear on their own, implicate the larger problems of the empire. Spain's economic condition—frankly quite dire during the closing years of the 1500s and the first years of the 1600s—is, as we have suggested, a result of fiscal and administrative incompetence but also a quite expectable consequence of the chronic need for military action in places like Flanders. The monarchy's acute need and excessive dependence upon foreign financiers and loans, was not only recognized by the serious writers of the age but was also a favorite

---

[37] As don Juan de Cárcamo expresses it, in his first presentation of himself—to "sell himself," as we might now say—to Preciosa, "Mi padre está aquí en la Corte pretendiendo un cargo, y ya está consultado, y tiene casi ciertas esperanzas de salir con él" (I, 84).

[38] See the *Coloquio*, especially II, 355-57; on the issue of *arbitristas* in general, see J. Vilar Berrogain, *Literatura y economía: La figura del arbitrista en el Siglo de Oro*.

topic of satire, especially for Quevedo.[39] We find Cervantes echoing some of that same concern in one of Vidriera's most concise jokes:

> En la acera de [San] Francisco estaba un corro de ginoveses, y pasando por allí, uno dellos le llamó, diciéndole:
> —Lléguese acá el señor Vidriera y cuéntenos un cuento.
> Él respondió:
> —No quiero, por que no me le paséis a Génova. (II, 65)

Once again, the connection is apparently slight, arbitrary, and seemingly trivial. The well-recognized problem of Genoese bankers, in effect a metonymy for Spain's national indebtedness, is easy material for satire and puns. But the core question of "cuentos" or "cuentas"—as repeatedly played upon by Quevedo—points to a deeper disease, less a problem of human nature than of the peculiar circumstances an empire's historical reality.

There are several longer and more complex disquisitions amid Vidriera's catalogue of critique. But perhaps the most interesting passage is the one having to do with *escribanos*. Vidriera begins by defending this frequently despised profession, in effect saying that *murmuradores* (backbiters) actually begin their training in the evil art of slander by reviling *escribanos*: "así los maldicientes, por donde comienzan a mostrar la malignidad de sus lenguas es por decir mal de los escribanos y alguaciles y de los otros ministros de la justicia . . ." (II, 69). This is curious. Once again, looking ahead, we will recall that the familiar entrapment scam recounted to us by Berganza in the *Coloquio* not only requires the complicity of an *escribano* with the corrupt *alguacil* and his prostitute accomplice, but that this sort of abuse strikes us as all too probable both in Cervantes's Spain and, occasionally, in our own society. Vidriera's defense of *escribanos*—not just in the general terms of the profession itself, but in the

---

[39] For example in *El alguacil endemoniado*, where the possessed *alguacil* states that "Y habéis de saber que en España los misterios de las cuentas de los genoveses son dolorosos para los millones que vienen de las Indias, y que los cañones de sus plumas son de batería contra las bolsas; y no hay renta que, si la cogen en medio el tajo de sus plumas y el jarama de su tinta, no la ahoguen" (*Sueños*, 175).

concrete terms of the men who are or who should be in such positions—recalls, moreover, the most peculiar passage of *Don Quijote* I, chapter 22, and the knight's strange praise and justification of *alcahuetes* (pimps).[40] As Vidriera puts it,

> Es el escribano persona pública, y el oficio del juez no se puede ejercitar cómodamente sin el suyo. Los escribanos han de ser libres, y no esclavos, ni hijos de esclavos; legítimos, no bastardos ni *de ninguna mala raza nacidos*. Juran de secreto fidelidad y que no harán escritura usuraria; que ni amistad ni enemistad, provecho o daño les moverá a no hacer su oficio con buena y cristiana conciencia. Pues si este oficio tantas buenas partes requiere, ¿por qué se ha de pensar que de más de veinte mil escribanos que hay en España se lleve el diablo la cosecha, como si fuesen cepas de su majuelo? No lo quiero creer, ni es bien que ninguno lo crea; porque, finalmente, digo que es la gente más necesaria que había en las repúblicas bien ordenadas, y que si llevaban demasiados derechos, también hacían demasiados tuertos, y que destos dos extremos podía resultar un medio que les hiciese mirar por el virote. (II, 69-70; emphasis added)

Although Vidriera's putatively sincere, even touching plea for the importance of virtue in the legal profession may strike us as appropriate to Spain's condition at the time, it has about it more the tone of the generous-spirited reformer than that of the mordant satirist. At the same time, we cannot overlook the curious fact that this same Vidriera—who has denounced whole professions without reservation—now defends en bloc the majority of men in a profession that, in practice, gave little reason for such defense. Amid all the "standard qualifications" for the job that Vidriera enumerates, moreover, we notice that he pointedly includes, along with legitimacy of birth, that other notorious marker of *honra/deshonra*, the question yet again of *limpieza*: "no bastardos ni de ninguna mala raza nacidos" (II, 70). Thus, while Vidriera seems to be allowed a moment of affirmation and a forbearance of the dark cynicism that marks most of his discursive existence, the text once again reveals

---

[40] As Cervantes's deranged *caballero* so eloquently states, the function of *alcahuete* "es oficio de discretos y necesarísimo en la república bien ordenada, y que no le debía ejercer sino gente muy bien nacida; . . . " (*Don Quijote*, I, 274).

more than standard critique or commonplace defense. Rather, it discloses the cracks and fissures in the broader society and culture. The desire for virtue and rectitude in the legal profession—and especially among the proverbially distrusted class of the *escribanos*—casually incorporates the same anti-*converso* prejudices and discrimination that had already undermined the quality and impartiality of this same profession.

Vidriera, in sum, presents us with a most curious program, a strange critical vision, if that is what it is, without coherence. But at the same time, amid its mean-spirited and diverse attacks the text itself—in its fragments, ambiguities, and strange, arbitrary inconsistencies—recurrently points to a reality beyond the clear and compact center, the case of the wretched and unfortunate Tomás. To the extent that Tomás and his individual human problem can become meaningful or interesting to us, *El licenciado Vidriera* is readable as a story of bizarre and ironic misfortune, of frustrated dreams or imprudent hubris (depending upon one's judgment of Tomás's ambitions), or perhaps of the almost mythic, deeper theme of the poignant rebellion of mind against body, intellect against nature. But Tomás lives and dies within a specific and complex historical situation and moment. He is the aspirant, perhaps the parasite, and surely the ultimate victim of the requirements, the policies, and the frustrations not just of his own individual self, but of the society and the empire of Spain itself.

With this we return to the end—or almost the end—of the *novela*. We return to the no longer quite so rhetorical question: Who is Tomás Rueda? Tomás is cured, as we are told, by "un religioso de la Orden de San Jerónimo, que tenía gracia y ciencia particular en hacer los mudos entendiesen y en cierta manera hablasen, y en curar locos . . . " (II, 73).[41] This same kindly cleric also sets Tomás back on his original path: "Y así como le vio sano, le vistió como letrado y le

---

[41] On Tomás's cure, see W. Schleiner, "Renaissance Exempla of Schizophrenia: The Cure by Charity in Luther and Cervantes," *Renaissance and Reformation* 9.3 (1985): 157-76.

hizo volver a la Corte, adonde, con dar tantas muestras de cuerdo como las había dado de loco, podía usar su oficio y hacerse famoso por él" (II, 73). Of course, Tomás, though cured and restored to his previous—and unremarkable, unentertaining—state, is still recognizable as the man who had made a name for himself as the indulged madman, the court fool or eccentric "seer" who claimed to be glass. Much has been made of the idea that the cold rejection of Tomás, his total inability to get a job, to regain any credibility, as we now might say, underlines both the irony of Tomás's whole career and original ambition, while also unmasking the cynicism of the Court itself. And so it does. But Tomás, both at the end and from the beginning, had essentially wished to be integrated into, and construct his name and his worth as an individual in, this same arena. Tomás's rejection by the Court can be seen as a statement of his superfluity: yet another *letrado* seeking entry into a vast and no doubt corrupt bureaucracy that already had more than enough *letrados*, not to mention various other competent and incompetent office-seekers. The empire was not just the court, the capital and the governmental headquarters, as the early section of the *novela* and Tomás's previous travels have reminded us. It was also its own geographical extension: the lands and political-military strife that would eventually bleed the empire to near ruin. Tomás dies in its service; as expressed in the concise and moving, aphoristic words of the last lines, he dies in Flanders "donde la vida que había comenzado a eternizar por las letras la acabó de eternizar por las armas" (II, 74). In this way, rhetoric allows Cervantes's ostensible redemption of Tomás's bitter disappointment to dramatize—in a subtle, slightly obscured circumstantial context and in the strange career of a solitary, alienated, and ultimately all but anonymous man—the many-faceted decadence of an empire.

Chapter Six
Redemption and Identity
La fuerza de la sangre

La fuerza de la sangre is the shortest of the collection, and in many ways it is the most unified and focussed of the *Novelas ejemplares*.[1] But despite its brevity and simplicity of plot, it presents daunting challenges to the reader, though more of an ethical than an intellectual sort.[2] *La fuerza de la sangre* is a kind of "Black Hole" of interpretation: it absorbs and obliterates any and all readings that seek to explain, justify, or find a rational, meaningful message in the events of the story. The main difficulty stems from the improbability of the motivations and psychological reactions, on the one hand, and the troubling moral implications of the resolution, on the other.[3] As we will recall, the insolent, violent, and sexually unbridled Rodolfo, inflamed at first sight by Leocadia's beauty, forcibly abducts her.

---

[1] Concerning the unity of structure, see R. P. Calcraft, "Structure, Symbol and Meaning in Cervantes's *La fuerza de la sangre*," *BHS* 58.3 (1981): 197-204. See also Casalduero, *Sentido y forma*, 150-51.

[2] The following reading is especially indebted to Forcione, *Cervantes and the Humanist Vision* (317-97), whose lengthy chapter on this *novela* gives the most detailed exposition of the cultural and religious context of late sixteenth-century Spain, but whose specific treatment of the text itself, disappointingly, gives us little more than the widely accepted—and convenient—notion that we are dealing with a "secularized miracle."

[3] See, for example, Calcraft, who notes that although most agree on the issue of structural symmetry, "the majority of critics see the consequent 'unreality' as a serious defect in the *novela*, and unwillingness to accept so balanced and contrived a story is increased by the equally criticized lack of effective explanation for such matters as Rodolfo's apparent change of character, Leocadia's warmth of response to her erstwhile seducer [sic; rapist would be more correct] and the sequence of coincidences that prepare for the happy outcome of the story" (197). For a refreshingly hard-nosed and perhaps cynical reading of this same text, see S. Zimic, "Demonios y mártires en *La fuerza de la sangre* de Cervantes," *Acta Neophilologica* 23 (1990): 7-26; Zimic sees Rodolfo as an unredeemed, unchanged brute and the resolution as a martyrdom-like capitulation of Leocadia and all concerned to the demands of social *honra*—in effect, as the perpetuation of the crime itself, or at least of the guilt.

With Leocadia having fainted into an improbably deep unconsciousness, Rodolfo rapes her and soon thereafter abandons her on the
street. Pregnant as a result of this violation, Leocadia gives birth to
a boy, whom her family, maintaining the fiction that he is a nephew,
raises for seven years. When the boy, Luis, is knocked down in the
street by a violently galloping horse, he is aided by Rodolfo's father,
who takes the boy back to the same house—and the same bedroom—in which Leocadia was raped. This brings Leocadia back to
the scene of her victimization and into contact with the rapist's
family. She reveals her own and her son's identity to Rodolfo's
mother, who then orchestrates a harmonious resolution by ordering
her son back from Italy, on the pretext of having arranged a marriage
for him. At the climactic dinner scene, Leocadia makes a grand,
ceremonial entrance and Rodolfo sees Leocadia again; yet it is as if
he had never seen her before. He falls immediately in love with her,
this time in love in the best sense of the word. The two are then
married, and as the narration puts it, live happily ever after.[4]

The concluding, putatively happy marriage of Leocadia and
Rodolfo—and thus the restoration of the woman's lost honor and the
possible redemption (in the reader's eyes) of some shred of virtue for
the man in question—gives the story an affirmative, harmonious
ending.[5] But the almost complete lack of conscience or moral
responsibility on Rodolfo's part produces a feeling of incompleteness
and undermines our sense of true or complete justice in this same

---

[4] As the narrator states, connecting the simple, mundane act of the characters going
to bed after the ceremonies with an encompassing moral and predictive historical
conclusion, "Fuéronse a acostar todos, quedó toda la casa sepultada en silencio, en
el cual no quedará la verdad deste cuento, pues no lo consentirán los muchos hijos
y la ilustre descendencia que en Toledo dejaron, y agora viven, estos dos venturosos
desposados, que muchos y felices años gozaron de sí mismos, de sus hijos y de sus
nietos, permitido todo por el cielo y por *la fuerza de la sangre*, que vio derramada en
el suelo el valeroso, ilustre y cristiano abuelo de Luisico" (II, 95; italics as in the
original).

[5] See Sears, *A Marriage of Convenience*, especially Chapter 5, "The Marriage Plot:
Structures of Social and Narrative Order" (149-65).

happy conclusion.[6] To deal with this, the reader is tempted to abandon the assumption of realism for a more symbolically inclined approach or for a recourse to the notion of divine intervention and purpose. The commentaries of Forcione, El Saffar, and Casalduero share a certain agreement with regard to the idea that the logic of the *novela* corresponds to the miraculous, be it religious in the strict sense, or a more secularized miracle.[7] This miracle embraces as much the narrative coincidences of the action as it does the unrealistic fact that the ill-intentioned young man of the beginning is, to all appearances, transformed and redeemed at the end.

But the moral and practical problems of Rodolfo's crime and the fortunate, if improbable happy ending are not the only concern of this *novela*. The question of identity is also very much at issue in this text. *La fuerza de la sangre* represents not only a tale or exemplum of miraculous redemption, but also presents the story of identities caught up in a complex process of loss, recovery, transformation, and affirmation. The identities and relationships of social rank established at the outset, as well as the process by which Leocadia's honor is restored, have to do with the ways in which a sense of self is constructed. Partly drawn from an individual's often private struggle with virtue, identity is also the result of the opinion or repute conferred by one's community and the social structures within which one must live. Seen from this perspective, the text sets forth the problem of the basic constitution of any identity and the importance of internalized virtue, as opposed to and yet in dynamic, complex interaction with the external pressures and "opinión" of the community. The resolution of the problem and crime that begin the tale include the ability for a tarnished and suppressed identity to emerge into the public sphere with honor restored. Leocadia's

---

[6] With regard to the structure and the problem of Rodolfo and his apparent lack of change, from the beginning of the story to the conclusion, see David M. Gitlitz, "Symmetry and Lust in Cervantes' *La fuerza de la sangre*," in *Studies in Honor of Everett W, Hesse*, 113-22.

[7] See Forcione, *Cervantes and the Humanist Vision*, 317-97; El Saffar, *Novel to Romance*, 128-38; and Casalduero, *Sentido y forma de las* Novelas ejemplares, 150-60.

recovery of her honor and the restoration of her identity—which in turn effects, or coincides with, the redemption of Rodolfo—comes, however, at a steep price. Along with the crime visited upon the woman at the beginning, the ostensibly happy ending restores a microcosmic social order by affirming the rule of male authority and the necessity of female silence and submission.

The drama of Leocadia's rape and the miraculous redemption at the end of the story can be read not only as an example of an act of merciful rather than retributive justice, but also as the idealization of the possible relations between persons as members of their respective social classes. The resolution of Leocadia's problem and the restoration of her (and her family's) lost honor is integral to the establishment of a bridge between two families of markedly different social rank.[8] However, the text also opens up the question of identity in the uniquely individual sense. The latter is presented as a complex issue from the beginning of the *novela*. The problem of individual identity is underscored by the darkness and ambiguity that predominate from the very first scene. The simple, mundane action of one person knowing and recognizing another is made highly problematic. As Forcione has noted, there is a complex structure of "light" and "darkness," "vision" and "blindness," especially in the opening scenes.[9] From the outset, the text establishes a deliberate vagueness of definition and recognition of one person by another, a confusion that parallels the moral chaos of Rodolfo and the dark suppression of the truth that, for Leocadia's family, dominates the central part of the story.

---

[8] As S. Zimic has pointed out, we could consider not just Leocadia, but her entire family as a kind of collective protagonist, and this being the case, the same could be said of Rodolfo's family. Zimic states that "La familia entera de Leocadia es, en realidad, la protagonista de esta novela; familia buena, honrada-virtuosa, cristiana, pero de humildes recursos económicos, víctima inerme de una poderosa y desmandada clase alta, a cuya riqueza se plegan hasta las autoridades civiles . . ." (10).

[9] See *Cervantes and the Humanist Vision*, 356-57.

The second important entry into the question of individual identity is prompted by the act and consequences of the rape itself. The rape both symbolizes and causes Leocadia's pathetic loss of identity, the recuperation of which is central to the story. The final resolutions engineered by doña Estefanía bring about a simultaneous restoration of both honor and identity, on Leocadia's part, and the full emergence of Rodolfo's own defined, individual identity. It is only at the end that he appears as a person and not just a representation of an evil force (as he is at the beginning) or a narrative device needed to produce the initial violent acts.[10] *La fuerza de la sangre* thus presents the problem of identity dramatized in terms of social harmony established between and within groups (persons as representatives of their respective social ranks), on the one hand, and also the conflict and discord between individuals, on the other.

The plot itself underlines the problems contingent upon the obvious social inequality of the two families. This differential of power and thus of the ability to defend or justify oneself is made clear in the aftermath of Leocadia's rape and her own and her family's response to the crime. From the beginning, and in several key passages, the narration reiterates the fact that Leocadia's family occupies a position socially inferior to Rodolfo's. The quality of *lo honrado* of Leocadia's family is based, in principle, on their sense of moral worth and noble heritage rather than on great material wealth or a high position within the aristocracy. The inferior social situation of Leocadia's family thus puts them in a position of relative weakness from the outset. This is further compounded by the complex human and moral dilemmas created by the nature of Rodolfo's crime, the rape. Then as now, the aftermath of rape would involve public shame, as well as the difficulty of trying to find and identify

---

[10] As has been pointed out, it is only after his return from Italy, and specifically in his conversation with his mother, that Rodolfo finally speaks; in effect, we have a final, and long overdue, emergence of his personality, his individuality, if one can use such terms; see Rodríguez-Luis: "El verdadero Rodolfo empieza a revelarse en el discurso que dirige a su madre a propósito de la mujer que querría para esposa, ocasión además en que lo escuchamos hablar por primera vez" (63).

the guilty man, all of which further tend to silence the victim. The power conferred by superior social rank, along with the license evidently granted to the men of the aristocracy, underscores the relative "silencing" that is already the conventional situation of the woman in this society. But in addition to Cervantes's evident belief that these distinctions of social rank can be partly equalized by the force of inner virtue (as in the case of Dorotea and don Fernando in *Don Quijote*, Part I), in *La fuerza de la sangre* Cervantes also explores the theme of a social harmony that is broken as the result of the initial crime and that is then restored at the end, or more precisely, that achieves a putatively more ideal state. This more ideal state, however, is not without a bitter and ironic aftertaste, given that not only is Rodolfo redeemed without a full realization on his part, but also that the admirable virtue and fortitude of the women affirm and restore a patriarchal structure that continues to excuse and redeem men even in such circumstances of egregious abuse.

The obscuring of individual identities, juxtaposed to the question of identity as determined by the community's perception of one's honor constitutes the dilemma of Leocadia and her family after the rape. The conclusion of the *novela* would appear to permit the affirmation of the validity of virtue as the source of honor, instead of honor as merely the product of the "opinión" of the community. But it is highly questionable, and much debated, whether the happy conclusion and the triumph of Leocadia—and of doña Estefanía, of course—is really such a bold affirmation of the power of inner virtue over the norms and assumptions of the community and the importance of hierarchy.[11]

In its manner of narrating the events and describing what is seen and what isn't, the *novela* begins by accentuating ambiguity and anonymity. At the outset, for example, the narrator describes Leocadia's family without specific visual details but with precision

---

[11] See Sears, *A Marriage of Convenience*, especially 156-58, and S. Zimic, "Demonios y mártires en *La fuerza de la sangre*."

concerning their social position: "un anciano hidalgo con su mujer, un niño pequeño, una hija de edad de diez y seis años y una criada" (II, 77). As we know, this unfortunate group ("el buen hidalgo con su honrada familia") is laboriously climbing uphill on foot, from the Río Tajo to Toledo, when Rodolfo and his companions, descending this same hill on horseback, encounter them. The first description of Rodolfo likewise omits concrete details of his physical appearance. Instead it underscores his social status and moral character:

> Hasta veinte y dos tendría un caballero de aquella ciudad a quien la riqueza, la sangre ilustre, la inclinación torcida, la libertad demasiada y las compañías libres, le hacían hacer cosas y tener atrevimientos que desdecían de su calidad y le daban renombre de atrevido. (II, 77).

Another detail of considerable importance, as much symbolic as functional to the exigencies of the plot, is the fact that Rodolfo and his friends are wearing masks: "Rodolfo y sus camaradas, cubiertos los rostros, miraron los de la madre, y de la hija, y de la criada" (II, 77). The inequality of social status, much like the opposition of movement (the family laboriously climbing up to the city; the young men, on horseback, descending), is thus repeated in the inequality of the ability to see and recognize. Those of the innocent group, with their faces uncovered and quite visible, find themselves even more weak and victimized in their state of visibility before the more powerful and anonymous, faceless aggressors.

From the beginning, then, Rodolfo is radically anonymous. Even with regard to proper names, the text imposes a deliberate ambiguity.[12] The names of the two main characters are presented by the narrator as pseudonyms. Speaking of the man, he states that: "Este caballero, pues—que por ahora, por buenos respectos, encubriendo su nombre, le llamaremos con el de Rodolfo" (II, 77); similarly, in the case of the young woman, the narrator proceeds even more laconi-

---

[12] This device of pseudonyms has led some to speculate on the possibility that Cervantes is here giving a rather faithful, if fictionalized, version of events that actually happened in sixteenth-century Toledo; on this issue, see Amezúa y Mayo, *Cervantes, creador de la novela corta española*, vol. 2, 203ff.

cally: "Leocadia, que así quieren que se llamase la hija del hidalgo" (II, 77). But the complex interplay of identity and anonymity that dominates the first half of the *novela* goes beyond the question of names. The text also puts into darkness many important visual elements. For example, if the initial portrayal of Leocadia is a little generalized (the only reference to her physical appearance is quite conventional: "la mucha hermosura del rostro que había visto Rodolfo"), the visual description of Rodolfo is even more ambiguous. Rodolfo is here and throughout the *novela*, or at least until the last scene, a man without a face, without distinction of physical appearance or personality. Ironically, in the crucial scene of the sexual violation and what follows in Rodolfo's bedroom, emphasis is put on the visual, but only to stress the obscurity of the scene, the difficulty of seeing. In the first moments after Leocadia regains consciousness, she is unable to see anything clearly and cannot even distinguish the face of her rapist. Only when the man leaves the room and Leocadia opens a window to the moonlight, is she able to make out certain elements of the room, most significantly the crucifix.

In this same scene—so central and so disconcerting—the narration emphasizes the juxtaposition of Rodolfo's total silence and Leocadia's long, complex speech. In a peculiar reversal of expectations, the text gives us the victim's discourse in the face of the malefactor's silence, thus establishing an inverse relationship to the powers of vision and possession that Rodolfo has—or more precisely, had at first—over the visually and physically vulnerable Leocadia. The passage that includes her long speech is important for two reasons: first, what Leocadia says continues the development of the theme of the nature of honor. Very much reflecting the prevalent beliefs of her culture, for Leocadia honor exists in either a positive or negative condition not only as a consequence of what one does, but as a product of public awareness of what has happened. As Leocadia says, "venturosa sería yo si esta escuridad durase para siempre, sin que mis ojos volviesen a ver la luz del mundo, y que este lugar donde ahora estoy, cualquiera que él se fuese, sirviese de sepultura a mi honra, pues es mejor la deshonra que se ignora que la honra que está puesta en opinión de las gentes" (II, 79). The central problem of the loss of Leocadia's "honor" is here (as throughout the text) defined largely in terms of perception. Fortunately, then, Leocadia and her family have the choice of hiding the act from the community, instead of responding to the crime as a challenge that demands vengeance or other acts of retribution, thus making public the question of honor. They take the first option: silence.

Leocadia's words to Rodolfo and this curious moment in the story also represent the beginning of a process of covering over not only the shameful fact of Leocadia's dishonor, but also the truth of her identity. The crime perpetrated against Leocadia would render questionable the community's view of her, were the act to become public, despite her innocence and integrity in the context of Rodolfo's exploitation of her unconsciousness. After returning home and speaking to her family, and later with her pregnancy and the birth of her son, Leocadia descends step by step to a level of social withdrawal and anonymity. The term "encubrir" and the concept of covering over arise with frequency in the text. The rape of Leocadia thus initiates the process of a (temporary) loss of authenticity as much as the (permanent) loss of her virginity.[13] The entire family draws inward to protect and conceal the wronged woman and also to construct, for a time, the façade of a false but ostensibly honorable identity and set of relationships for both Leocadia and Luis, her illegitimate son, as aunt and nephew. This fiction, however, distorts the reality of self for all the members of the family.

The pregnancy and subsequent birth of Luis also initiate an inverse process, the recuperation of authenticity. The child's injury and the impulsive, spontaneous reaction of Rodolfo's father to aid the boy allow the truths of origin to come forth. Before Luis's unfortunate accident, he exists unwittingly in a problematic state of identity. In order to maintain the fiction of Leocadia's virginity, Luis

---

[13] See for example II, 84: Leocadia "gimió y lloró de nuevo, y se redujo a cubrir la cabeza, como dicen, y a vivir recogidamente debajo del amparo de sus padres, con vestido tan honesto como pobre."

has been living with his own mother believing her to be his aunt. Luis, too, is someone necessarily marginalized and consigned to a false identity from the family's fear of revealing the original crime and dishonor. He thus represents the more fundamental problem: the authenticity of one's being versus the fiction of anonymity and feigned relationships. The child's true identity, just like that of his mother, is only fully restored with the resolution of the honor problem and the reunion of his two parents.

Despite his putative individuality, Luis is also a reflection and a reproduction, as much of the individual (i.e., his father Rodolfo) as of the "noble" qualities that, according to the ideology implicit in the epoch and explicit in Cervantes's writings, are presumed to be inherent in persons of noble blood. For this reason, in the description of the boy—after speaking in very conventional terms of the physical ("de rostro hermoso")—the text states that "en todas las acciones que en aquella edad tierna podía hacer, daba señales de ser *de algún noble padre engendrado*" (II, 85; emphasis added). In this way, Luis represents yet another subtle statement of the Cervantine ideology concerning social position and inherent, stratified virtue. He also functions as a bridge between the two families and their distinct social ranks, as well as between the two main characters, Leocadia and Rodolfo. At a moral and symbolic level, meanwhile, the child connects the two states of Leocadia's identity: an initial state of shame, occlusion, and marginality; at the end, a state of restored honor, full recognition, and authenticity.

This denouement only succeeds in occurring as a consequence of the accident and the subsequent partial yet providential recognition of the boy by Rodolfo's father. After the accident, when Leocadia's father thanks the gentleman for his efforts to aid the child, the text presents the nobleman's reactions as follows: "que no tenía que agradecelle, porque le hacía saber que cuando vio al niño caído y atropellado, le pareció que había visto el rostro de un hijo suyo, a quien él quería tiernamente, y que esto le movió a tomarle en sus brazos y a traerle a su casa" (II, 86). A bit later, doña Estefanía expresses a similar sentiment, in effect telling Leocadia that "aquel niño se parecía tanto a un hijo suyo que estaba en Italia, que ninguna vez le miraba que no le pareciese a su hijo delante" (II, 87). This last declaration gives Leocadia both the occasion and the courage to reveal to doña Estefanía the heretofore suppressed story. What Leocadia tells the woman is the first revelation, to anyone outside of her immediate family, of what happened and the truth about both Luis's and her own identity. In this way, Luis is the key, connecting piece of the mystery of sin and of the temporary suppression of his mother's identity.

But if the miracle or coincidence of Luis's accident occurs through the grandfather's partial and intuitive *anagnorisis*, the larger resolution of the *novela*'s conflict happens on the basis of yet another *anagnorisis*—one that is more complex and gradual and that begins with an improbable but total lack of recognition, on Rodolfo's part. The *novela*'s conclusion contains the final connection and reunion necessary for the redemption of Leocadia's honor and identity. These final scenes effect another redemption, that of Rodolfo. When the rapist returns home after more than seven years in Italy, he seems to be a very different person in comparison with the violent, unbridled, and immoral youth of the beginning of the story. For the first time we hear him speak. In fact, Rodolfo's reaction to the portrait of the woman supposedly chosen as his wife is his first discourse of any importance.

When Rodolfo sees Leocadia, in the markedly ceremonial and theatrical moment of her entrance at the dinner party, the most jarring, improbable detail is the fact that he does not recognize the very same woman whose beauty, some seven or eight years ago, had incited in him lascivious desires. Instead, this same beauty, this same woman, now awakens in him a supposedly profound, sincere, and honorable love. How is this possible? From one perspective, accepting the predominant role of the miraculous, the simple explanation is that the evil man of the beginning has been transformed into a virtuous person. But from another perspective, one could argue that for the first time the real person emerges. Rodolfo is only now the man who finally has, and can thus reveal, a full and authentic self. The fact that Rodolfo has changed so radically can indeed be seen as a miracle, of course. At the same time, another way to read the conclusion of the *novela* (following the approach suggested by M. Welles[14]) would be to recognize the role of the female characters, Leocadia and in particular doña Estefanía, in the working of an almost miraculous integration of Rodolfo into a more perfect social and familial circle.

In the final scene, orchestrated by doña Estefanía, one finds something of the device and the magic of restoration of the seemingly lost person that takes place toward the conclusion of Shakespeare's *The Winter's Tale*. In this play, the lady Paulina unveils to King Leontes what appears to be a painted statue of his own wife Hermoine, supposedly dead for sixteen years.[15] In the face of this vision, Leontes once again expresses his sense of guilt, sadness, and remorse for his jealous rage that, so he has thought, caused Hermoine's death, and in this moment, the statue comes to life. It is, of course, Hermoine herself, seemingly lost for so many years, but in fact long hidden under the protection of Paulina. This restoration completes the scene that began with the return of Hermoine's and Leontes's banished daughter, significantly named Perdita. The play concludes with an act symbolic of forgiveness and renovation: a reintegration of the family, including Perdita's princely young suitor.

Despite the obvious differences of detail, the ending of *La fuerza de la sangre* presents a reunion and a reconciliation similar to what we find in *The Winter's Tale*. As Welles has argued, the resolution of

---

[14] See Marcia L. Welles, "Violence Disguised: Representation of Rape in Cervantes' 'La fuerza de la sangre'," *Journal of Hispanic Philology* 13.3 (1989): 240-52. See also Adriana Slaniceanu, "The Calculating Woman in Cervantes' *La fuerza de la sangre*," *BHS*, 64.2 (1987): 101-10.

[15] The length of time is all but absurdly long, given the expectations of realism. But it is necessary for the development, the transformation of the baby girl into the marriageable-aged teenager. See *The Winter's Tale*, IV, 1, where Time enters as "Chorus" and states in part "Impute it not a crime / To me or my swift passage that I slide / O'er sixteen years, and leave the growth untried / of that wide gap, since it is in my power / To o'erthrow law, and in one self-born hour / To plant and o'erwhelm custom."

Cervantes's *novela* reveals the redeeming and transforming power of the female. By her virtue, patience, and suffering, Leocadia has in effect redeemed the act of violence and violation. That which was, from one point of view, a sinful act acquires, in this redemptive present, a positive character. The rape itself comes to be that which leads to the solid social link of marriage between the two persons. The magic of patience and of female fortitude makes this highly unrealistic miracle possible. The ending of *La fuerza de la sangre* thus closes the circle of incomplete events. The texture and logic of magic and miracle help explain certain unrealistic elements of the action, especially toward the conclusion of the tale. For instance, the rather curious moment of the double fainting (II, 93) can, in this light, be seen as a symbolic revelation of Leocadia's emotional state and Rodolfo's own anxiety in the presence of this "new" love. The double loss of consciousness is a symbolic threshold between a shameful past, a redeemed present, and a virtuous future. As the creator of this brief moment of theatre, doña Estefanía, tells her son, "esta desmayada que en los brazos tengo es tu verdadera esposa; llamo verdadera porque yo y tu padre te la teníamos escogida, que la del retrato es falsa" (II, 93-94). The clarification of the term "verdadera" has the obvious function, on the literal level, of explaining the artifice of the false portrait. But the declaration by Rodolfo's mother that Leocadia is the "verdadera esposa" has a more important symbolic and ceremonial value as well. It illuminates and redefines a deed from the past in the light of the present, revealing another level of family identity.

Rodolfo's crime was a violation on many levels. But with the redemption effected by time, by the virtue of the victims (Leocadia and Luis), by the miracle of transformation, recognition, and the revelation of true identity, and by the unifying power of the female element (as much that of doña Estefanía as that of Leocadia herself), the initial act is redefined. It becomes the beginning and the basis of a union now consecrated by love and by the idealized and social structure of a new family.[16] Yet the creation of this new family—through Leocadia's marriage to Rodolfo, which (with or without love on the part of the woman) restores her honor—with which the *novela* ends, is marked by a retreat into a kind of magical silence: "Fuéronse a acostar todos, quedó toda la casa sepultada en silencio, en el cual no quedará la verdad deste cuento, pues no lo consentirán los muchos hijos . . . " (II, 95). The discreet silence fades into the formulaic note of the many noble offspring, the future family. But this silence reminds us of the larger meaning of the women's ironic triumph: if order and honor have been restored, if identities have reemerged, however much due to the women's strength and patience, it all takes place within and under the prerogatives of the fathers, including the man who sinned and was given forgiveness without having asked. Once again, the men of the story will represent authority and, through the institution of family, the core of identity. In *La fuerza de la sangre*, it is this final return to silence and conventional submission that, despite the dramatic restorative powers of female will and endurance, leaves us so peculiarly disturbed.

---

[16] On the centrality of marriage, as both a goal of the comedic plot structure and a symbol of the socially conservative value system of the Cervantine *novela*, and especially of this most problematic one, see Sears, *A Marriage of Convenience*, in particular 80-81.

Chapter Seven
Eros, Material, and the Architecture of Desire
El celoso extremeño

The seventh *novela* begins—and could be seen at its core—as one of the most conventional of the whole collection.[1] A very old, suspicious, wealthy yet impotent man marries an extremely young woman. This May-December marriage contains within itself the seeds of its own destruction, and the inherent contradictions of the situation promise to play themselves out in the form of either farce or tragedy.[2] In contrast to Cervantes's own farcical treatment of this plot concept in his *entremés*, "El viejo celoso," the exploration of the mismatch device in *El celoso extremeño* leads to a conclusion both pathetic and ambiguous.[3] Once again, however, a possibly simple story reveals—in both the larger trajectory of its action and the seemingly less significant details of setting and characterization—a rich and troubling parable of social structures and individual conceptions of self. Although the story indeed encompasses the necessary central triangle of husband, wife, and intrusive seducer, along with the supporting cast of servants and slaves, the *novela* offers itself to us as the fevered projection of one person, Carrizales.

[1] See, for example, Forcione: "Of all the tales in the collection none is more directly indebted in form and content to the central tradition of the European short story, which found its classical expression in the *Decameron*, and none reveals more clearly Cervantes's mastery of the narrative techniques which Boccaccio perfected and left as the classical standard for future short story writers" (*Cervantes and the Humanist Vision*, 31). The present commentary is much indebted to Forcione's chapter on *El celoso* (31-92); see also J. B. Avalle-Arce, "*El celoso extremeño* de Cervantes," 199-205 in *Homenaje a Ana María Barrenechea*; J. Casalduero, *Sentido y forma*, 167-89; El Saffar, *Novel to Romance*, 40-50; P. Dunn, "Las «Novelas ejemplares»," *Suma Cervantina*, especially 98-106; T. R. Hart, *Cervantes' Exemplary Fictions*, 75-96; J. Rodríguez-Luis, *Novedad y ejemplo*, vol. II, 1-39; and Leo Spitzer, "Das Gefüge einer cervantinischen Novelle: *El celoso extremeño*," in *Die Romanische Novelle*, 175-213.
[2] See C. Stern, "*El celoso extremeño*: Entre farsa y tragedia," 333-42 in *Estudios sobre el Siglo de Oro en homenaje a Raymond R. MacCurdy*; and A. Weber, "Tragic Reparation in Cervantes' *El celoso extremeño*," *Cervantes* 4.1 (1984): 35-51.
[3] On the ambiguity of the *novela*'s ending, see especially Hart, 89-96.

El celoso extremeño is essentially a paranoid and hallucinatory nightmare.[4] It enacts the ironies, impossibilities, and fears of eros and material, the things that we believe we need and try to possess and yet that we can never contain or shape to our own wills. Cervantes's text reminds us how our lust for possession and control ultimately destroys us.

When the *novela* settles into its principal action of enclosure, fear, and penetration from the imagined outside, it becomes the most static and claustrophobic of the collection. Carrizales's house is not just the fortress and prison that he designed it to be. Rather, it all but takes on the role of a character, a presence that is both an integral part and a neurotic projection of Carrizales's own imagination. The house is also the deceptive device whose promised protection is, at bottom, the inevitability of betrayal.[5] But in this most static of narratives there is, at the very beginning, a highly significant—if also highly compressed—stretch of time and set of travels involving the protagonist. With striking economy and precision, the first four paragraphs set forth the basic problems of Carrizales's nature: the juxtaposition and paradox of a man's fearful old age and his profligate youth, one that will not be corrected but rather will be punished by the foolish endeavors and reactions of old age. The early stages of the man's life, so succinctly recounted in these first pages, stress his wastefulness. At the same time, this swiftly outlined "Cervantine journey," in a slight echo of the young Tomás Rodaja's European travels, alludes to the deceptive illusion of power

---

[4] As El Saffar puts it, "Like Don Quixote, Carrizales created the protagonists of his imagined world. The characters who emerge out of the monomania of his jealousy are embodiments of Carrizales himself. . . . When Carrizales considers marriage, the vision of the handsome seducer presents itself before him simultaneously with the vision of the wife. Leonora and Loaysa were born simultaneously in Carrizales's imagination" (42).

[5] For a most exhaustive and penetrating study of the role of Carrizales's house and its spatial, visual, and erotic implications, see M. Molho, "Aproximación al *Celoso extremeño*," *NRFH* 38.2 (1990): 743-92. See also Casalduero, 175-79; and Forcione, 35-36.

seen against the background reality of the decadence of Spain's empire:

No ha muchos años que de un lugar de Extremadura salió un hidalgo, nacido de padres nobles, el cual, como un otro Pródigo, por diversas partes de España, Italia y Flandes anduvo gastando así los años como la hacienda; y al fin de muchas peregrinaciones, muertos ya sus padres y gastado su patrimonio, vino a parar a la gran ciudad de Sevilla, donde halló ocasión muy bastante para acabar de consumir lo poco que le quedaba. (II, 99)

What Carrizales does in his own small, personal way could be read as a figure for the ultimately profligate, if putatively "prudent" and serious endeavors of a monarchy trying to hold on to the rebellious fragments of an impossible empire.[6] But more to the point, what will finally be the entrapment and confinement of the main story and of Carrizales himself is first defined and thrown into implicit contrast by the man's passage through a vast geography, one that here as elsewhere is subtly presented in moral terms.

As the text clearly suggests, Sevilla once again plays its complex role as Spain's capital of criminality and commerce.[7] Here Sevilla's conventional character as a world of morally ambiguous social activities and class boundaries is further underscored by the crucial geographical and moral connection between this main Spanish port of embarcation and the New World. As the narrator puts it, inserting the protagonist emphatically into this larger fabric of immorality, loss, scheming, and illusions, Carrizales

---

[6] In a sense, this possible symbolic aspect of the story recalls that analogous subtheme of El licenciado Vidriera; see Chapter Five above. On the relevance and resonance of Carrizales's time in the New World, see James D. Fernández, "The Bonds of Patrimony: Cervantes and the New World," PMLA 109.5 (1994): 969-81.
[7] The implications of Sevilla and its multiple appearances in the Novelas ejemplares would merit a separate study. One recalls that Sevilla figures prominently in Rinconete y Cortadillo and will provide the starting point for Berganza's autobiography in the Coloquio de los perros (see Chapter Ten, below). In most cases, this important city carries implications of instability and questionable morality. Only as the final, happy destination of Isabela and Ricaredo, in La española inglesa, is Sevilla relatively innocent of ethically complex or negative overtones.

se acogió al remedio a que otros muchos perdidos en aquella ciudad se acogen, que es el pasarse a las Indias, refugio y amparo de los desesperados de España, iglesia de los alzados, salvoconducto de los homicidas, pala y cubierta de los jugadores a quien llaman *ciertos* los peritos en el arte, añagaza general de mujeres libres, engaño común de muchos y remedio particular de pocos. (II, 99)[8]

For Carrizales the Indias, and specifically Peru, will prove to be the source of material renewal. But it is a renewal that is ironically destructive to the individual hoping also for a true regeneration of his behavior and spirit. Equally crucial is the not trivial fact that, after his success in America, Carrizales will return to settle in this same city. Thus the "New World" fails to renew, and the city in which the forty-eight year old Carrizales found himself materially bankrupt will be the same one in which he will die from his illusions and the insidious sterility of his old-age riches.[9]

The journey, Carrizales's transatlantic passage, is initially presented as a kind of figurative death ("su matalotaje y su mortaja de esparto") from which he will be reborn. But the suggestion of a "sea change" is illusory, as we shall see. Meanwhile, the moment of his journey from Spain to the New World gives occasion for the narrator to hint at Carrizales's possibly, but questionably, redemptive critical view of himself. The paragraph merits quotation in full:

---

[8] Cf. the ending of Quevedo's *Buscón*, where the frankly irredeemable protagonist makes a similar decision: "no de escarmentado . . . sino de cansado, como obstinado pecador, determiné, consultándolo primero con la Grajal, de pasarme a Indias con ella, a ver si, mudando mundo y tierra, mejoraría mi suerte. Y fueme peor, como v. m. verá en la segunda parte, pues nunca mejora su estado quien muda solamente de lugar, y no de vida y costumbres" (*La vida del Buscón*, edición crítica de F. Lázaro Carreter, 280).

[9] Sterility of material and of persons lies at the heart of this *novela*'s mystery; as Forcione notes, "Carrizales confines his wife in the gloomy house with the same confidence with which he hoards his countless bars of gold in a bank, and his absurd belief in the effectiveness of locks and keys as a guarantee of predictability in human behavior is symptomatic not only of his tyrannical nature but also of the failure to discriminate between things and people in his life, a failure that is one of the most frightening forms of egotism" (63).

Iba nuestro pasajero pensativo, revolviendo en su memoria los muchos
y diversos peligros que en los años de su peregrinación había pasado, y el
mal gobierno que en todo el discurso de su vida había tenido; y sacaba de
la cuenta que a sí mismo se iba tomando una firme resolución de mudar
manera de vida, y de tener otro estilo en guardar la hacienda que Dios
fuese servido de darle, y de proceder con más recato que hasta allí con las
mujeres. (II, 100)

The two crucial terms, *hacienda* and *mujeres*, wealth and women, are
connected here in ways already suggesting that Carrizales has
tended, and will continue, to fuse and confuse both. Not only will he
treat women as property, but he will treat his property as something
charged with its own erotic, and hence (for Carrizales) threatening,
dimension. As the text's development of Carrizales's house and
domestic world reveals, this sexualizing of space is less far-fetched
than it might at first sound.[10]

But to return to the preliminary paragraphs, in which the core
story of the pathetic and monstrous marriage is set up, we note
something peculiar about Carrizales's remarkable material success
after his twenty years in Peru. Although it is simple arithmetic that
leaving Spain at age forty-eight, the man would be sixty-eight upon
his return after twenty years, the narration goes further. It stresses
that this return, however renewed Carrizales seems to be materially,
is a return to a world no longer his. Too much time has passed.
Despite the deceptive promise of renewal gained through material
success, the text makes it clear that Felipo is returning to a world
transformed by death: "llegó a Sevilla, tan lleno de años como de
riquezas; sacó sus partidas sin zozobras; buscó sus amigos: hallólos
todos muertos; quiso partirse a su tierra, aunque ya había tenido
nuevas que ningún pariente le había dejado la muerte" (II, 101).
With all friends and family dead, Carrizales is radically—and
somewhat improbably—alone. The extreme of his wealth only

---

[10] On this question, see Beatriz Colomina, "The Split Wall: Domestic Voyeurism,"
in *Sexuality and Space*, 73-128; and in the same collection, Mark Wigley, "Untitled:
The Housing of Gender" (327-89).

underscores more painfully the irony of his situation: wealthy and potentially comfortable, yet profoundly isolated, bereft.

The wealth itself likewise brings with it a further kind of alienation, a troubling of the spirit.[11] Carrizales now has something that is his but is not himself, not part of him. His money can be, in a sense, possessed. But as in all such cases, it can only be had up to a point. The more one attempts to have it, the more it takes on a life of its own. Thus, in another sense and as if in revenge or belated punishment, Carrizales's money possesses him. It demands to be used, transformed in some way:

> Contemplaba Carrizales en sus barras, no por miserable, porque en algunos años que fue soldado aprendió a ser liberal, sino en lo que había de hacer dellas, a causa que tenerlas en ser era cosa infrutuosa, y tenerlas en casa, cebo para los codiciosos y despertador para los ladrones. (II, 101)

But beyond his understandable fears, there is the anxious desire for that spurious hint of immortality—which itself is yet another variety of the desire to possess—the immortality that takes form in the wish to create and bequeath one's wealth to a following generation. Thus, having largely made up his mind to withdraw from the active business world (II, 101-02), Carrizales entertains the idea of creating a family: "Quisiera tener a quien dejar sus bienes después de sus días, y con este deseo tomaba el pulso a su fortaleza, y parecíale que aún podía llevar la carga del matrimonio; . . . " (II, 102). But this thought is immediately followed by an ironic twist, or twisted afterthought. The mere idea of marriage arouses his jealous fears: "y en viniéndole este pensamiento, le sobresaltaba un tan gran miedo, que así se le desbarataba y deshacía como hace a la niebla el viento;

---

[11] As the narrator puts it, "Y si cuando iba a Indias, pobre y menesteroso, le iban combatiendo muchos pensamientos, sin dejarle sosegar un punto en mitad de las ondas del mar, no menos ahora en el sosiego de la tierra le combatían, aunque por diferente causa: que si entonces no dormía por pobre, ahora no podía sosegar de rico; que tan pesada carga es la riqueza *al que no está usado a tenerla ni sabe usar della*, como lo es la pobreza al que continuo la tiene" (II, 101; emphasis added). Thus does the text subtly introduce the suspicion that Carrizales will inevitably "invest poorly" in affairs both material and human.

porque de su natural condición era el más celoso hombre del mundo" (II, 102). Of course, this dilemma of wanting marriage and, in the moment of thinking such thoughts, of being overcome by irrational fears, is a kind of elaborate joke. From one perspective, it renders the protagonist, potentially, an object of ridicule. But in the specific portrayal of his character and the manipulation of the ostensible actions of the *novela*, the narrator presents a man whose seemingly ridiculous dilemmas and paradoxes of personality are more profoundly expressive of an imagination consistently centered upon its own materialized eros and its eroticized material world.[12]

Carrizales is not simply a jealous, fearful old man. Given the errors and profligacy of his earlier years and the ironic untimeliness of his old-age material success along with his belated hope to procreate, he is a creature of inversions and perversions in the natural order of things. At the point where he marries Leonora and creates his monstrous household, he represents the man as sterile woman. As Paglia (citing K. Stern) observes, "Karl Stern diagnoses as 'a caricature of femininity' the self-thwarting of neurotic men 'whose attitude toward life was one of hoarding and retentiveness, with a tendency to unproductive accumulation, a kind of unending pregnancy of material inflation, which never came to creativeness or 'birth'.' He calls this syndrome 'accumulation without issue'."[13] The combination of Carrizales's motive for marrying (to produce an heir) and his actual impotence (after a year, there is still no sign of issue and reason to suspect that Leonora is still a virgin) make Felipo a

---

[12] On this particular aspect, see A. Weber, "Tragic Reparation in Cervantes' *El celoso extremeño.*" My own reading of the *novela* is greatly indebted to this most provocative and convincing study.

[13] *Sexual Personae*, 92. Paglia refers to Stern's book *The Flight from Woman*, in which he deals with the tendency, mostly of men, to deny feelings, to fear being loved, and to be "driven" by or into some endeavor to achieve such avoidance. This sort of pathology is not irrelevant to the condition of Carrizales. See also Weber, "Tragic Reparation," and in particular her assertion that "In his relationship with his wife, Carrizales develops a different but equally manic reparative strategy—he re-creates in himself an omnipotent all-nurturing parent. His house, a stomach-womb populated with the offspring of his self-impregnation, is an oral paradise" (43).

prime candidate for placement in this category the self-thwarting, material-obsessed yet sterile male.

Carrizales's madness and the complex symbolic language of this entire *novela*, its language of materiality and eros, center around two conceptions, each being both figurative and concrete: the human body and architecture.[14] The ulterior relationship between both elements involves the question of sight. As the narrator tells us, "la primera muestra que dio de su condición celosa" is the not totally absurd refusal to let his wife—more specifically his wife's body—be measured by a tailor (II, 103). With Leonora's body in effect "off limits," Carrizales sends in a substitute, as we might now say. On the level of verisimilitude, this expedient is both logical and ludicrous. But from a more suggestive point of view, the implications of this act are troubling: bodies are simultaneously sacred, or we might say privileged, as personal possessions, and yet here they are rendered as also interchangeable. For Carrizales they are objects of exchange and substitution, whose only importance is endowed from without, given to them by virtue of whether or not they are "owned" by a certain man. Bodies—touched and not touched, seen and not (quite) seen—become later on in the *novela* both a central image of hallucination and an ironic device for the undoing and punishment of Carrizales's unnatural obsessions and hopes.[15]

But to get to the body, we need also the interplay and the structures of seeing and concealment. Structure and sight bring us to the most important and memorable non-human element of this *novela*: architecture.[16] Given that Carrizales is a paranoid, fearful

---

[14] This aspect of the *novela* has been widely recognized by critics and general readers, as Casalduero has remarked (see *Sentido y forma*, 176); a most incisive analysis of this aspect is given by Molho, "Aproximación al *Celoso extremeño*," especially 753-56.

[15] Concerning one important aspect of the unnatural, see E. Urbina, "Incesto en *El celoso extremeño* de Cervantes y en *L'école de femmes* de Molière," 709-21 in *Homenaje al Profesor Antonio Vilanova*; see also Casalduero, who puts it in moral rather than "natural" terms: "Carrizales no está desobedeciendo los dictados de la naturaleza que la razón descubre, sino la ley de Dios" (179).

[16] As Colomina (while speaking about the twentieth-century architect, Adolf Loos)

man where his wife is (now) concerned, he connects, confuses, and interfuses her with his wealth. This is actually not so much a mistake or a confusion, given the customs and ideology of the time, as it is an extreme but logical extension of the normal. Because of—and within—this sexual, material, and cultural web, Carrizales becomes Cervantes's most fascinating architect. Cervantes's narrator makes the significance of the architectural especially clear: "La segunda señal que dio Felipo fue no querer juntarse con su esposa hasta tenerle puesta casa aparte, la cual aderezó en esta forma . . . " (II, 103). The protagonist will literally postpone consummation of the marriage until after the conclusion of his architectural precautions. The basic design and set up of the house—its enclosure and guarded entrance, its self-sufficiency, etc.—are little more than a slight inten-sification of the typical design of a Spanish house. What calls itself to our attention as perhaps extreme is the question of the visual: Carrizales "cerró todas las ventanas que miraban a la calle, y dióles vista al cielo, y lo mismo hizo de todas las otras de casa" (II, 103). The concern with the windows facing the street, of course, pointedly echoes and reminds us of the beginning of Carrizles's involvement with Leonora. He is seduced—or, as the terminology more precisely puts it, overcome, defeated—by sight, by a vision:

> quiso su suerte que pasando un día por una calle, alzase los ojos y viese a una ventana puesta una doncella, al parecer de edad de trece o catorce años, de tan agradable rostro y tan hermosa que, sin ser poderoso para defenderse, el buen viejo Carrizales rindió la flaqueza de sus muchos años a los pocos de Leonora, que así era el nombre de la hermosa doncella. (II, 102)

The fact that Leonora is at the window, and thus available to be seen, is (as M. Molho has pointed out) already a subtle undermining of the

---

states, "Architecture is not simply a platform that accommodates the viewing subject. It is a viewing mechanism that produces the subject. It precedes and frames its occupant" ("The Split Wall: Domestic Voyeurism," 83). And in a phrase even more insightful and pertinent to the systems and structures of El celoso, "At the intersection of the visible and the invisible, women are placed as the guardians of the unspeakable" (82).

possibility of the uncomplicated simplicity, the woman's virgin sensibility, desired by Carrizales.[17] Thus, the juxtaposition—within the space of only two pages—of the man's seeing the woman at a window followed by his desire for possession and his attempt to complete this possession by blinding his own windows is powerful in its irony. This juxtaposition already suggests, as well, the core futility. Both moments (the first sight and the subsequent attempt to ban sight) remind us that, along with protection from the elements and from human intrusions, houses are architectural systems that guide, frame, allow, or prevent sight.[18] The interplay of framing and blocking, moreover, immediately evokes the concept of voyeurism, the corrupting or energizing of the visual by the power of eros. And this, of course, will be the central, motivating dynamic of *El celoso extremeño*, once the novelistic problem of the story (the interest and efforts of the intruder) come to the fore.

The house, then, as M. Molho has most convincingly argued, is a world and a system of confusions and erotic enticements that will destroy the unnatural tranquility that Carrizales foolishly attempts to establish.[19] But in addition to the paradoxical effect of the material

[17] See Molho, "Aproximaciones," 751-52. On the issues of the nature of Leonora's putative innocence, see also Casalduero, who notes that "En Leonora, [Carrizales] no buscaba un ser virtuosamente inocente, sino inocentemente ignorante que no echara de menos la libertad" (179).

[18] Once again, see B. Colomina's study "The Split Wall"; see also M. Wigley's "Untitled: The Housing of Gender," which is especially pertinent to the Cervantine context given that Wigley comments on the concepts of Leon Battista Alberti, who has much to say on the male vs. female, exterior vs. interior proprieties of life and architecture. Alluding to Xenophon, whose ideas would be seconded by Alberti, Wigley notes that "The spaces literally produce the effect of gender, transforming the mental and physical character of those who occupy the wrong place: compelled to sin indoors, the body becomes effeminate and mind loses its strength" (334). Wigley further states, in a passage most suggestive for *El celoso* and for Cervantes's *novelas* in general, that "The threat of being in the wrong place is not just the feminization of the man, but the feminine per se. If the woman goes outside the house she becomes more dangerously feminine rather than more masculine.... The woman on the outside is implicitly sexually mobile. Her sexuality is no longer controlled by the house" (335).

[19] See "Aproximaciones," especially 758-72.

and visual preventions embodied in the house, the human element of Carrizales's world also reflects a perverse reaction to the biological, and mainly the sexual, reality of human nature and the old man's chronic tendency to treat the autonomously human as the containably material. Carrizales's slaves and servants are prisoners, like his wife. They are also—in the case of Luis and the slaves, both black and white—mutilated in one way or another (II, 104). On the most literal, common-sense level, the idea of having a eunuch as a kind of a gate-keeper is unremarkable, although Luis's position and function is considerably more ambiguous: he is emphatically not trusted as a gate-keeper; he has no access to keys, is not allowed into the interior, female center of the house, and cannot go out of the house. Luis's situation conjures up images of the fabulous tale set in a Middle-Eastern, Islamic locale; it suggests the world of the fairy tale. In his simple-minded behavior, Luis lends some comic relief to the otherwise mostly gloomy ambiance of the story. But Luis's castration is also appropriate thematically. Luis—Carrizales's mutilated servant-prisoner and the "intermediate object" of Loaysa's musical seductions—is, however minor his role may seem, one of three impotent men, each one impotent in a different but meaningful way. We should not ignore completely the obvious but attenuated homosexual implications of Loaysa's seduction and manipulation of Luis. This element is not without some pertinence, however: Luis is a eunuch; Loaysa will prove to be less than adequately powerful, and the emphasis upon his slightly effete physical beauty is a bit disturbing. Fittingly, Carrizales's own impotence-driven sexual fears will be embodied and "realized" in and by another sexually ambiguous figure, with the help of yet a third.

If Luis's sterility is the consequence of an act of mutilation visited upon him (we assume) against his will, Carrizales's sterility is the effect of both advanced age and a perverse displacement of values. Although his initial motive, as the text presents it, was emphatically that of engendering an heir, as soon as he is married and his self-contained, autarchical household is in operation, Carrizales's satisfaction seems to shift and come to rest on a kind of static enjoyment of things as they are. What physical pleasures he allows himself and Leonora fall far short of those sexually vigorous enough to bring about what was, supposedly, his primary goal. This peculiar short-circuiting of his initial goal and the re-centering and limiting of Carrizales's desires is well captured in the following passage:

> Hecha esta prevención y recogido el buen extremeño en su casa, comenzó a gozar como pudo los frutos del matrimonio, los cuales a Leonora, como no tenía experiencia de otros, ni eran gustosos ni desabridos; y así, pasaba el tiempo con su dueña, doncellas y esclavas, y ellas, por pasarle mejor, dieron en ser golosas, y pocos días se pasaban sin hacer mil cosas a quien la miel y el azúcar hacen sabrosas. Sobrábales para esto en grande abundancia lo que había menester, y no menos sobraba en su amo la voluntad de dárselo, pareciéndole que con ello las tenía entretenidas y ocupadas, sin tener lugar donde ponerse a pensar en su encerramiento. (II, 105)

As A. Weber has noted in her very incisive commentary on this *novela*, the perverse, enclosed world created and evidently desired by Carrizales is a kind of paradise of oral pleasure.[20] The seemingly "innocent" pleasures of eating are allowed to displace—and in Carrizales's ill-advised opinion, to fully compensate for—both freedom and the actualization of other, equally or more important physical pleasures. What is thematically significant about this replacement of sexual fulfillment by an endless supply of candy is the implication that whatever can be controlled or satisfied by material in generous supply ("Sobrábales para esto en grande abundancia lo que había menester") can indeed insure the tranquility

---

[20] Again, as Weber has stated, Carrizales's house "is an oral paradise" ("Tragic Reparation," 43). Weber goes on to point out the implications and consequences of this: "By encouraging the infantile, oral behavior of his wife and her numerous servants, Carrizales treats them as the good possessions he needs in order to feel safe and full. His specially adapted house, with its boarded up windows, its enclosed stable, and its self-sufficient supplies of water and food becomes an undifferentiated body cavity which denies the need for elimination. In short, this aspect of Carrizales' manic reparative strategy consists of *becoming* the depleted parent, then replenishing himself" (44).

of one's world and can win the loyalty of those who are, already, under one's ostensible control.

The narrator makes it clear that Carrizales's generosity, however pleasant his disposition, has a certain smothering, tyrannical quality (see II, 105-06). This is especially the case in the peculiar relations between Carrizales and Leonora's parents. The following passage aptly sums up the chilling combination of generosity and iron-bound control: "Los días que iba a misa, que, como está dicho, era entre dos luces, venían sus padres, y en la iglesia hablaban a su hija, delante de su marido, el cual les daba tantas dádivas que, aunque tenían lástima a su hija por la estrecheza en que vivía, la templaban con las muchas dádivas que Carrizales, su liberal yerno, les daba" (II, 105). The term "liberal" (in its sense of "generous") is repeated obsessively in relation to Carrizales (e.g., "por ser de condición llana y agradable, y, sobre todo, por mostrarse tan liberal con todas" [II, 106]). But in the total context of the story and, above all, in light of the man's character and compulsive behavior, it is clear that this "liberalidad" is completely and sinisterly limited to things material, things that he can give, hold on to, and above all, control. "Liberal" will, for Carrizales, have nothing to do with the realm of the spirit or with human freedom of will or movement. And, of course, Carrizales's paranoia, possessiveness, and inordinate desire for protection and control all combine and conspire to construct that object of material and erotic desire—the house—that will attract and in fact "create" its own destruction, its own penetrating force and figure. But, as we shall see, this figure is also a creature of perversions, and not the liberating, healthy force of nature and love.

At this point in the *novela* ("Desta manera pasaron un año de noviciado, . . . ; y así fuera si el sagaz perturbador del género humano no lo estorbara, como ahora oiréis" [II, 106]), and as the tale is about to take its turn into the action and complications of Loaysa's penetration quest, there appears one of the narrator's several fascinating and disturbing intrusions. Cervantes's narrator interrupts, becoming a slightly intrusive "first person," as he turns to address and implicate the reader. In a summation or reiteration of the perverse architecture and motivation of Carrizales's world, the narrator begins with the rhetorical question: "Dígame ahora el que se tuviere por más discreto y recatado qué más prevenciones para su seguridad podía haber hecho el anciano Felipo, . . . " (II, 106). There is something more than unnecessary about this peculiar apostrophe. The reader is slightly put on the spot. We are nearly as trapped within the narrator's perverse control of story and sightlines as are the hapless creatures of the text. The narrator's own control and knowledge, as critics have noted, is mysteriously incomplete.[21] But at this crucial transitional moment, the voice operates with surgical precision. The turning of Carrizales's world from a device of largely material protection into an object of definitively eroticized mystery is pointedly enacted in one pivotal paragraph: "No se vio monasterio tan cerrado, ni monjas más recogidas, ni *manzanas de oro* tan guardadas; y con todo esto, no pudo en ninguna manera prevenir ni excusar de caer en lo que recelaba; a lo menos, en pensar que había caído" (II, 106; emphasis added).[22] It is at this point that the intruder Loaysa enters, or is created in the fevered paranoid imagination of the story.

The figure of Loaysa is, in its ostensible narrative function, quite conventional.[23] Were this *novela* to have a comedic structure and tone

---

[21] On the question of the baffled narrator, see especially Forcione, *Cervantes and the Humanist Vision*, 85-87; see also El Saffar, *Novel to Romance*, 48-49, who considers this phenomenon "characteristic of the early works." She suggests that "When the narrator becomes interpreter, his fallibility becomes apparent. Just as Loaysa's words and Leonora's deeds are unimportant as isolated facts, the changed ending allows us to see that the very words which make up the story do not entirely contain its meaning. No facts are possible isolated from a perceiver and interpreter of them" (48).

[22] The image of the golden apples is hard to overlook; and at this point, the connection of architecture and the erotic is clear. As C. Paglia has noted, "Mystery shrouds woman's sexuality. This mystery is the main reason for the imprisonment man has imposed on woman. Only by confining his wife in a locked harem guarded by eunuchs could he be certain that her son was also his" (*Sexual Personae*, 22).

[23] Much has been written on the nature and implications of Loaysa; is he a pale, or twisted, repetition of Carrizales? Or is he something quite distinct? A most

(in the Fryean sense), Loaysa would be the liberating sexual and love interest. Were the text more farcical, as in Cervantes's own *entremés*, Loaysa might play a very minor, perhaps all but mute, functional role.[24] But *El celoso extremeño* is neither romantic comedy nor quasi-obscene farce. The Loaysa of this text is a major, but highly ambiguous figure given what he does—and fails to do—and how he does it, what he suggests and how he is described. In light of the recurrent themes of the present study, identity and social order, Loaysa simultaneously points outward (as the text clearly notes: "Hay en Sevilla un género de gente ociosa y holgazana, a quien comúnmente suelen llamar gente de barrio" [II, 106]) to the complex, fluid, expectedly immoral world of Sevilla, and also inward, back toward Carrizales himself.

The long, many-staged process of Loaysa's successful penetration into Carrizales's world dominates the center and main portion of the text. Loaysa is obviously more a trickster figure than a love interest or *galán* in the conventional mode.[25] Between him and Leonora there is very little sentiment—other than a mutual curiosity—and certainly no love. In the power and charm of his musical abilites (which in themselves are of questionable quality), the text refers to him as an

---

provocative interpretation of Loaysa is offered by Molho, "Aproximaciones" (see especially 763-72). See also Forcione, *Cervantes and the Humanist Vision*, 47-55; and Weber, "Tragic Reparation," who suggests that "Loaysa incarnates Carrizales' past as seducer and will repeat his exile in the New World" (45). Weber, however, also notes the troubling inversion to which Loaysa lends himself, the question of a gender ambiguity to which Carrizales would in no way be appropriate: "Loaysa, though aggressive in his initial assault on the house, is no longer the seducer but the object of seduction once he gains admittance. The dueña, Marialonso, and the servant girls admire him, not as a phallus, but as a dismembered assortment of feminized body parts" (45).

[24] On the difference of the young seducer figure in the *entremés* and the *novela*, see Casalduero, 169-71.

[25] As Forcione—in what one might consider an understatement—puts it, "Loaysa's interest in sexual pleasure is seldom mentioned, and he appears to be motivated primarily by curiosity and a perversely misdirected will to power, which finds satisfaction in the *'proezas'* of coldly manipulating reactions in other people" (55).

"Orfeo."[26] But this is surely ironic and intentionally misleading on Cervantes's part. Loaysa has no "Eurydice" whom he rescues by charming the powers of Hades; nor does he meet anything like the tragic, emblematic fate of the original mythological figure, torn to pieces by the Bacchantes. Rather, Loaysa is more a perversion of Hermes than a version of Orpheus. He is also, in yet another of Cervantes's few but significant cases of same, a markedly androgynous figure, someone of questionable masculinity. More than a little reminiscent of Cornelio in *El amante liberal*, Loaysa is presented in such a way that, whenever the visual focus comes to rest upon him, his attractiveness is described in ways that have more than a little of the epicoene. From the beginning of Loaysa's disguising-seduction quest, the manner in which the text deals with him, his appearance, and his tactics, creates a subtle and disquieting displacement of emphasis. The reader is led away from the first-level reality of sex and sexuality as action, force, and fertility, and instead becomes aware of the attenuated, second-level suggestiveness of the erotic as it takes form in appearances, games, deferrals, and hallucinations.

Once Loaysa is completely within the house and able to be made the object of display—in two key scenes, first glimpsed through the door, with Luis passing the candle along his body, and then once he is inside, in immediate contact with the women—the text plays with the conventions of beauty in a way that transgresses and blurs the line between male and female norms. The first visual presentation is less detailed. Instead, it emphasizes the reversal of the usual voyeuristic relationship. Loaysa is the visually devoured object, and the act of illumination underscores the eroticism of the moment:

> Era mozo y de gentil disposición y buen parecer; y como había tanto tiempo que todas tenían hecha la vista a mirar al viejo de su amo, parecióles que miraban a un ángel. Poníase una al agujero para verle, y

---

[26] On this aspect, see M. Gómez-Reinoso, "El mito recurrente en *El celoso extremeño*," 281-87 in *Festschrift José Cid Pérez*.

luego otra; y por que le pudiesen ver mejor, andaba el negro paseándole el cuerpo de arriba abajo con el torzal de cera encendido. (II, 117)

The second instance of Loaysa's erotically charged physical presentation, a moment in which the reversal of the usual voyeuristic gaze (i.e., male upon female) is as emphatic as is the troubling and slightly perverse undertone of eating, implicit in the term *pepitoria*, begins again with the part-by-part illumination of the body, this time with the *dueña* doing the candle job:

Y tomando la buena Marialonso una vela, comenzó a mirar de arriba abajo al bueno del músico, y una decía: «¡Ay, qué copete que tiene tan lindo y tan rizado!» Otra: «¡Ay, qué blancura de dientes! ¡Mal año para piñones mondados que más blancos ni más lindos sean!» Otra: «¡Ay, qué ojos tan grandes y tan rasgados! Y por el siglo de mi madre que son verdes, que no parecen sino que son de esmeraldas!» Ésta alababa la boca, aquélla los pies, y todas juntas hicieron dél una menuda pepitoria. (II, 125)

The enthusiastic visual dismemberment of the youth is simultaneously plausible and yet troublingly inverted. The prolonged enclosure and isolation of the women of the household partly justify such transports of pleasure at the sight of this novelty. But the text leaves no doubt that, either in fact or in the women's feverish vision, Loaysa's physical beauty is more "pretty" than maturely "handsome." Only Leonora, at this point, resists joining in with quite the same degree of exuberance as her colleagues, though her interest is obvious: "Sola Leonora callaba, y le miraba, y le iba pareciendo de mejor talle que su velado" (II, 125). Once again, her reaction is more one of curiosity than unbridled desire. But even before this moment, Leonora has emerged as a disturbingly autonomous person and has taken actions more bold and "masculine" than her innocent years might have suggested. She has already drugged her husband, which, as Weber has pointed out, is the only real physical violation in the entire *novela*.[27]

[27] As Weber notes, "Carrizales will be rendered impotent in a total physical and psychological sense by an aggressive, invasive female—his own Leonora. For it is Leonora who makes the final assault on the inner sanctum of Carrizales' bedroom.

The character of Leonora herself presents a particular problem—or set of problems—for the critical interpretation of this *novela*.[28] In some ways, she is the most perplexing of the three main characters, and the changes that Cervantes evidently made from the earlier Porras manuscript version to that of the 1613 published text only serve to complicate the question further. As most readers have agreed, the most important change from the previous version of the story is the fact that Leonora, in sharp contrast to the Isabel of the previous version, changes her mind and, once in bed with Loaysa, successfully fights off his attempts to consummate the seduction sexually. But what else about this strangely simple—or surprisingly complicated—heroine? She was chosen by Carrizales on the basis of her extreme youth and putative innocence; she is thus the symbol of Carrizales's profound folly in thinking that one can "educate" another individual into radical innocence. At the same time, as Molho has pointed out, in the circumstances of her very first appearance in the *novela*, there is subtle evidence of her complexity, her curiosity. Leonora has a far stronger claim to the role of Pandora than Loaysa has to that of Orpheus. In general, she emerges as a far more interesting and complex figure than that which would be required for the simple irony of the fitting and deserved defeat of Carrizales and his bizarre, fearful attempts at control and possession.

The most significant and controversial interpretative question involving Leonora—one which also involves Carrizales—concerns

---

... This narcoleptic embalming, this mucuous intimacy, is the real violation of the story; it is the inversion of and retaliation for what Carrizales has done to Leonora" (46-47).

[28] El Saffar, for example, finds an emergence of character and selfhood in Leonora: "Leonora and Carrizales remained locked up within themselves during most of the story because their lack of true self-awareness gave them no perspective from which to view anyone else. Leonora, captured for the first time in the story in outgoing gestures of concern for her husband [i.e., at the conclusion], has emerged from her experience with Loaysa more clearly self-defined" (46-47). Forcione, by contrast, finds less character definition: "Leonora's presence remains elusive and mysterious to the end, when she slips out of her narrator's control and disappears behind the confining walls of a nunnery" (58). See also 62ff.

the ending of the story. The main question has to do with what, if anything, has been learned by the two. It also touches on the question of human freedom and the possibility of transcendence. Coming at the issue from markedly different perspectives, both El Saffar and Forcione seem to agree that, in the 1613 version, the ending brings a level of knowledge and change for both Carrizales and Leonora. In Forcione's view, there is at once the attainment of a self-transcendence for the two, as well as a full realization, on Carrizales's part, of the true nature of his folly and misguided desires.[29] For El Saffar, there is a degree of sincerity and autonomy achieved by both and especially by Leonora.[30] But I would argue that the text is far too ambiguous in its final pages to allow an indisputable assertion of such conclusions. Rather, in ways not unlike what we find in the situation of Anselmo and the end of the chapters containing the "Curioso impertinente" in *Don Quijote*, Part I, we have, with Carrizales, someone who gains at best a limited knowledge, a realization of his failure and defeat, without a *full*, adequate understanding of the flaw within his original desire. To put this question back into perspective, we must return to the last stages of the story.

The troubling moment is, it would seem, a vision—in effect a posture. We come upon this vision in two stages. First, as the text so improbably presents it, Leonora and her curiosity, aided by the corrupting arguments of the *dueña*, entice her into going to bed with Loaysa. But she then resists his supposed main intention of sexual intercourse: "Pero, con todo esto, el valor de Leonora fue tal, que en el tiempo que más le convenía, le mostró contra las fuerzas villanas de su astuto engañador, pues no fueron bastantes a vencerla, y él se

---

[29] See *Cervantes and the Humanist Vision*, especially 72-84.

[30] As El Saffar puts it, "Carrizales, equally selfish and possessive, suggests Loaysa's destiny, just as Loaysa reveals Carrizales's past. And Carrizales's self-transcendence offers hope for Loaysa's ultimate salvation." And a little further on: "Carrizales and Leonora, in the published version of the story, both confront and transcend the limitations they have imposed on themselves and have had imposed on them" (50).

cansó en balde, y ella quedó vencedora, y entrambos dormidos" (II, 130). As mentioned earlier, the fact that the bold and resourceful Loaysa proves too weak or resolute to finish the job of his sexual conquest raises a variety of questions touching on his real strength and on his essential interests (is he more in love with the game of trickery itself than he is interested in sexual gratification?). It also raises a question or two about Leonora's sense of integrity. She "triumphs" in fighting off her seducer, but she is not sufficiently offended to then decamp the field of battle. Falling asleep in the same bed with her defeated aggressor suggests a troubling casualness about the whole question of fidelity and virtue. This posture, in any case, is the one in which the two ambiguous adulterers are found by Carrizales. As the text describes it, Carrizales, "abriendo la puerta muy quedo vio lo que nunca quisiera haber visto, vio lo que diera por bien empleado no tener ojos para verlo. Vio a Leonora en brazos de Loaysa, durmiendo tan a sueño suelto como si en ellos obrara la virtud del ungüento y no en el celoso anciano" (II, 130).[31] Much is usually made of the fact that, in this second version, Leonora has preserved her *honra*.[32] The text thus underlines the peculiar irony of Carrizales drawing the "wrong" inference from this scandalous sight. Carrizales does indeed draw certain wrong conclusions, and Leonora's unfortunate faintings and her inability to tell what did and did not happen compound the irony of the situation. But the real violations and the most meaningful betrayals have in fact happened.[33] Given Carrizales's wish for a peaceful, protected world, and given Leonora's sufficiently Pandora-like curiosity (which has already resulted in her own "violation" of her husband's body when she administers the drug), the destruction of his world is more than complete.

---

[31] As the text goes on to reiterate, this idea of "los nuevos adúlteros enlazados en la red de sus brazos" (II, 130) is given special emphasis. Regardless of the (also ambiguous) facts of the case, the eroticism of the image is hard to deny.

[32] Again, see El Saffar, 47-50.

[33] See Weber, "Tragic Reparation," especially 46-51.

Carrizales does not, however, do the conventional thing. He does not kill wife and seducer. Rather, due partly to a convenient fainting fit of his own and partly to a strange sense of magnanimity, he decides to pardon them both, and knowing that he will soon die of a broken heart and thus free his wife, he gives Leonora even more money. Given this state of affairs, Carrizales's long discourse to Leonora and her parents is of particular importance. It is simultaneously an index of his mercy in not killing his betrayers (yet another expression, or so he thinks, of his generosity) and also a clear indication of what he has *not* learned, how he has in fact not changed. Carrizales has learned the futility of trying to "protect" that which he thinks is his, but he is still firmly ensconced in his self-involved material world. His language is saturated with the troubling combination of sentiment and materiality:

> Bien se os debe acordar, que no es posible se os haya caído de la memoria, con cuánto amor, con cuán buenas entrañas, hace hoy un año, un mes, cinco días y nueve horas que me entregastes a vuestra querida hija por legítima mujer mía. También sabéis con cuánta liberalidad la doté, pues fue tal la dote que más de tres de su misma calidad se pudieran casar con opinión de ricas. (II, 132)

The quantitative precision of Carrizales's reference to the length of time of the marriage is either a ludicrous excess of sentimentality or yet another sign of his obsession with that which is countable. Or both. But the main disturbing undertone of his whole speech is the continual return to himself, to *his* generosity, to *his* concerns. Carrizales's arguments are a strange mixture of simple fact and alarming obtuseness, as we see in the following: "Dile criadas y esclavas que la sirviesen; ni les negué a ellas ni a ella cuanto quisieron pedirme; *hícela mi igual*; comuniquéle mis más secretos pensamientos; *entreguéle toda mi hacienda*" (II, 133; emphasis added). For Carrizales to say that he made Leonora his "equal" or that he handed over to her his entire wealth is a stunning but totally characteristic revelation of his continuing inability either to see what he has really done to another person, or to separate persons from material, to de-materialize the human.

Carrizales's revenge ("la venganza que pienso tomar desta afrenta no es ni ha de ser de las que ordinariamente suelen tomarse, pues quiero que, así como yo fui estremado en lo que hice, así sea la venganza que tomaré, tomándola de mí mismo como del más culpado en este delito; . . ." [II, 133]) is yet another act of compulsive, smothering generosity. In a gesture that could well be read less as forgiveness than as intensifying his wife's shame and pain, he increases her inheritance and magnanimously urges her to marry her presumed young lover.[34]   And here, the irony of ignorance is especially telling. It is of importance that Carrizales knows nothing of the facts of the case—specifically, that there is no rival lover. Carrizales neither foresaw nor understood the inevitable consequences of what he had tried to do: to mold a supposedly empty, virgin soul to his own desires.   Now, seeing the failure of his preventions, he still can only talk in terms of money and material. He feels sorry for himself and accepts the guilt, but he still places himself in the middle of his shattered world: "Mas como no se puede prevenir con diligencia humana el castigo que la voluntad divina quiere dar a los que en ella no ponen del todo en todo sus deseos y esperanzas, no es mucho que yo quede defraudado en las mías y que yo mismo haya sido el fabricador del veneno que me va quitando la vida" (II, 133). His concept of himself as fabricator, as maker of his own disaster is, of course, both fitting and more than a little conventional.[35] This architectural concept of fabricator is repeated again, soon after the above passage, but in an image that is even more resonant to the case of materialism and blind self-involvement: "Yo fui el que, como el gusano de seda, me fabriqué la casa donde muriese, . . . " (II, 133). The man was the creator of his "house"—a house that would be not the refuge from which the reborn and

---

[34] As the text puts it, Carrizales says that he will rewrite his will, "en el cual mandaré doblar la dote a Leonora y le rogaré que después de mis días, que serán bien breves, disponga su voluntad, pues lo podrá hacer sin fuerza, a casarse con aquel mozo, . . . " (II, 134).

[35] Cf., for example, the situation and state of awareness of Anselmo at the end of the episode, or *novela*, of "el curioso impertinente" in *Don Quijote*, Part I.

transformed insect would emerge, but rather the winding sheet that others would turn into an object of value. Carrizales, in any case, is still the center of things, as far as he is concerned. Even more to the point, the above passage does not end with that peculiar image and formula of maker, house, and death. Rather, the phrase continues with Carrizales's magnanimous but still unenlightened "forgiveness" of his wife: "y a ti no te culpo ¡oh niña mal aconsejada! . . . no te culpo, digo, porque persuasiones de viejas taimadas y requiebros de mozos enamorados fácilmente vencen y triunfan del poco ingenio que los pocos años encierran" (II, 133). True, the efforts and corruptions of the *dueña* and Loaysa played a role. But what happened really came about as much because an autonomous, curious, and active individual—Leonora—also emerged.

The final lines of the *novela* underscore the pathos and irony of the outcome of this grim story. Despite the assertions of El Saffar, Forcione, and others, I find precious little enlightenment or attainment of freedom, as the text represents it, in the final situations of any of the three main characters.[36] The penultimate paragraph is as definitive and precise as the final paragraph is bizarrely ambiguous and confused. The narrator's clear report of what happens to the principals is as follows: "Quedó Leonora viuda, llorosa y rica; y cuando Loaysa esperaba que cumpliese lo que ya él sabía que su marido en su testamento dejaba mandado, vio que dentro de una semana se entró monja en uno de los más recogidos monasterios de la ciudad. Él, despechado y casi corrido, se pasó a las Indias" (II, 135).[37] Leonora's decision to enter the convent is hard to read as the

---

[36] In this regard, and given the openness of the text, I find myself more in agreement with Hart's position. As he has stated, "*El celoso extremeño* has sometimes been seen as an example of Baroque *desengaño*, a term often translated as 'disillusion.' Desengaño, however, does not suggest disappointment but rather something positive, a stripping away of illusion, an awakening to reality. Whether Carrizales experiences anything of this kind is questionable" (*Cervantes' Exemplary Fictions*, 89). As with this lack or incompleteness of such an awakening, so too (in my opinion) is there a lack of transcendence or freedom for Carrizales and Leonora.

[37] The rest of the paragraph paints a picture of last-minute generosity that nonetheless has about it a resigned and melancholy air: "Quedaron los padres de

assertion of bold, new-found awareness or autonomy. Given her total lack of love for Loaysa and her profound shame at what has happened, this move strikes me as the least dishonorable way out. Loaysa's fate is rather more teasingly suggestive of a reflection of, or upon, Carrizales. The fact that Loaysa runs off to las Indias (also, let it be noted, somewhat shamed at the outcome of the affair) suggests that he will, or might, repeat Carrizales's life pattern. But it is clear that Loaysa, the immoral trickster from Sevilla, is from the outset very different from the young Felipo Carrizales, the noble but wasteful aristocrat from Extremadura.[38] In other words, as pathetic as the total life trajectory of Carrizles has been, it is hard not to suspect that Loaysa is less pathetic than, morally, despicable. His departure for the New World has more an element of punishment than promise in it.

The final paragraph is one of the most curious endings of any of the *Novelas ejemplares*. On its surface, it is a strange combination of a flat-footed and slightly unsatisfying "ejemplo" (one of the few explicit examples or moral lessons to be found in the collection), on the one hand, and an absurd and frankly unnecessary expression of narratorial bafflement, on the other. While the narrator does acknowledge—as Carrizales does not—"lo poco que hay que fiar de llaves, tornos y paredes *cuando queda la voluntad libre*" (II, 135; emphasis added), he again blunts the point by taking another parting shot at that conventional target of satire and criticism, the "dueñas de monjil negro." The core of the lesson has to lie somewhere between Carrizales's perverse delusions and the inevitable but unexpected complexity of Leonora's will and imagination. Thus, in

Leonora tristísimos, aunque se consolaron con lo que su yerno les había dejado y mandado por su testamento. Las criadas se consolaron con lo mismo, y las esclavas y esclavo, con la libertad; y la malvada de la dueña, pobre y defraudada de todos sus malos pensamientos" (II, 135).

[38] We will recall the narrator's subtle, ambiguously incriminating remark when, after finally getting into Luis's hayloft, the latter gives Loaysa some food: "dio de comer a Loaysa tan bien como si comiera en su casa, y aun quizá mejor, pues pudiera ser que en su casa le faltara" (II, 115). Clearly Loaysa is of a social group and level that, in things material, is anything but noble or materially comfortable.

light of the deeper significance and pathos of the *novela*, the circumstances of the story's ending—that which "baffles" the narrator—are
in fact artistically effective. The *novela* ends with the narrator saying
that "Sólo no sé qué fue la causa que Leonora no puso más ahínco en
disculparse y dar a entender a su celoso marido cuán limpia y sin
ofensa había quedado en aquel suceso; pero la turbación le ató la
lengua, y la priesa que se dio a morir su marido no dio lugar a su
disculpa" (II, 135). Given the real violation of trust that Leonora's
curiosity and actions have already amply proved, and given Carrizales's incurable solipsism, it is unlikely that the woman's explanation would either have been believed by her husband, or if it had
been, that it would have made any difference. Was it fully consummated sexual adultery, or presumed adultery, that brought on
Carrizales's death? Or was it the more unequivocal and fully evident
fact that his world of control, material safety, and strangely displaced
desire had been proven to be an architecture of impossible delusions? There is no mystery to Leonora's ironic, and convenient,
silence. Rather, in what is a brilliant addition by Cervantes, it makes
even more powerful the representation of Carrizales's obsessed and
pathetically frightened nature.

In terms of identity and social order, who or what, then, is Felipo
Carrizales? Given what we know about the tendencies of Spanish
culture in Cervantes's time, and certainly in light of what Spanish
Golden Age literature would present to us, Carrizales's jealousy can
be seen, simultaneously, as a monstrous and pathetic perversion and
also as an only slight exaggeration of the preoccupation with the
sexual purity dimension of the familiar *honra* theme. But, at this
point, it is worthwhile to return to an issue raised at the beginning of
this commentary, i.e., to the sharp contrast of Carrizales's two (or
three) worlds: the travels of his profligate youth, the recuperative
journey to the New World of his mature years, and his attempt to
create an enclosed, perfectly controllable miniature world in his old
age. In terms of the possibilities of cultural norm and social order,
Carrizales is an example of a series of ultimately failed and foolish
economic structures and modes. His youth is wastefulness; subse-

quently, and in a kind of betrayal of the norms of his aristocratic class, his financial and mercantile success in Peru is both concrete and delusive; his old age is sterile misuse of wealth and human potential. The geographical pivot-point, Sevilla, is symbolically crucial on this level of the theme. As the port, the city of thieves, and the link between the exploitable, fantastic possibilities of the New World and the rigidities, limits, and decadence of the Old, Sevilla is the appropriate setting and symbol for Carrizales's initial exhaustion of his wealth, his illusion of return and success, and his final destruction. Carrizales's perversions and self-deceptions are unique, extreme. But they are also resonantly telling within the fabric of a culture that Cervantes knew well. In this world, the difficulty of striking a balance between generosity and oppression, between a high-minded transcendence of material greed and the prudent investment of material and human effort, between possessive erotic desire and the purification of the sexual by the trials and sacrifices of love, was not unknown. Carrizales's nature and fate ends up by being a sad eccentricity that nonetheless holds up an incisive if artfully distorting mirror to a society quite prone to the contradictions of material and sexuality, of possession and free will.[39]

---

[39] On the question of freedom, both artistic and moral, see H. Percas de Ponseti, "El 'Misterio escondido' en *El celoso extremeño*," *Cervantes* 14.2 (1994): 137-53. As she concludes, "La psicología tanto de Leonora como de Carrizales, tan verídicamente reflejadas en la invención novelística, precisamente por dársenos desprovistas de explicaciones puntualizadoras y por mantener en pie el misterioso mecanismo de la interioridad humana, constituyen la base de la proyección moral de la novela. ... El 'misterio escondido' que encierra y 'levanta' la novela, como nos advierte Cervantes en el prólogo a sus *Novelas ejemplares*, nos lleva a meditar sobre la impredecible naturaleza humana: cada ser humano tiene la capacidad de escoger entre los dilemas que le presenta la vida y de redefinirse a cada paso mediante la acción redentora o condenatoria así como la de reconocer el error moral" (152-53). See also E. Williamson, "El 'misterio escondido' en *El celoso extremeño*: Una aproximación al arte de Cervantes," *NRFH* 38.2 (1990): 793-815: "En esta acepción un misterio es como una vía de comunicación trascendental, un hacer presente ciertas verdades no asequibles a la razón humana. Si transferimos esta idea al fenómeno literario, el 'misterio' al que alude Cervantes al final del Prólogo significaría los ritos mismos de la creación literaria, la actividad creadora en sí" (813).

In the focussed simplicity of its plot, juxtaposed to the troubling ambiguity of its implications, *El celoso extremeño* is similar to *La fuerza de la sangre*. We know precisely what happens, but we are unsure about what we should make of the ending, about its lessons or implications for personal identity, moral values, or social order. If *La fuerza* disturbs us because the putatively happy ending fails to conceal the fact that appearances and social conformity must prevail, *El celoso extremeño* likewise leaves unresolved the question of the boundaries between love and delusive self-love, between open generosity and blind possessiveness. Carrizales is the architect and victim of his own fearful material world, and at the end his enlightenment is pathetically incomplete. Perhaps this *novela* especially disturbs its reader because we simultaneously feel superior to and separate from the follies of its protagonist and yet recognize a part of ourselves in his all too plausible desire for certainty, contentment, and peace.

Chapter Eight
Identity and Social Order
La ilustre fregona

La ilustre fregona is one of the least studied of the *Novelas ejemplares.* Yet despite its apparent simplicity of action and its lack of an overridingly memorable image, it brings clearly into focus the issues of identity and social order that underlie all of the *Novelas.*[1] As in the case of the *novelas* discussed previously, a disturbance in society's rules and structures, along with a case of mistaken or displaced identity, provides Cervantes with his point of departure. This eighth text combines two of the principal plot devices common to the *Novelas ejemplares*: a woman who is kidnapped as a child, and thus temporarily robbed of her social and personal integrity, must regain or discover her true identity; two men in disguise, meanwhile, encounter adventures, detouring from their appropriate moral rectitude or social place. But they too will conform to the same requirement: that questions of social and personal identity be resolved as the *novela* concludes.[2] In *La ilustre fregona*, as in so many of the other *novelas*, resolution means the restoration of the main

---

[1] The following interpretation is much indebted to A. M. Barrenechea, *"La ilustre fregona* como ejemplo de estructura novelesca cervantina," *Actas del Primer Congreso Internacional de Hispanistas*, 199-206; J. M. Diez Taboada, "La estructura de las *Novelas ejemplares, Anales Cervantinos"* 17 (1979-80): 87-106; J. Lowe, *Cervantes: Two "Novelas Ejemplares:" La gitanilla* and *La ilustre fregona*, especially 56-74; and F. Pierce, "Reality and Realism in the *Exemplary Novels,"* BHS 30 (1953): 134-42. See also *Lenguaje, ideología y organización textual en las "Novelas Ejemplares." Actas del Coloquio celebrado en la Facultad de Filología de la Universidad Complutense en mayo de 1982*, which contains eight provocative commentaries on this work: A. M. Maestro, "Conjunciones y disyunciones en *La ilustre fregona*," 69-79; J. Paulino, "El espacio narrativo en *La ilustre fregona*," 93-108; A. Redondo & C. Sainz de la Maza, "*La ilustre fregona*: cuatro cuartos y una cola," 109-18; M. Débax, "Ser y parecer," 163-70; M. Ezquerro, "Tres por dos son seis," 171-78; M. Ramond, "'Yo soy la ilustre fregona' o la simbolización de un delirio," 179-90; C. Chauchadis, "Los caballeros pícaros: contexto e intertexto en *La ilustre fregona*," 191-97; and J. Alsina, "Algunos esquemas narrativos y semánticos en *La ilustre fregona*," 199-206.

[2] See El Saffar, *Novel to Romance*, 25-26.

characters to their proper places and thus conclusion brings affirmation of the rightness of the established social order.[3] Or so it would
seem.

La ilustre fregona is, on its surface, a conservative and socially
legitimizing *novela*, since it culminates in the restoration of social
harmony symbolized by the new microcosmic, harmonious society
of the marriages of Costanza and Tomás and the two other young
couples. The *novela* also embodies the structural and typological
distinctions of social levels that Cervantes incorporates throughout
the *Novelas*. While one could characterize the social in *La ilustre
fregona* as a total, complex society composed of numerous levels and
sectors among which the main characters wander, one could also
argue that, against the permanent and real society of their past and
future lives in Burgos, Cervantes sets the temporary and complex
"fictional" society of Toledo and the inn. Such juxtapositions
underscore a particular vision of the right ordering of relationships
not only between two or more individuals (love), but between an
individual and the larger defining group (one's social role).

On an initial reading, *La ilustre fregona* seems somewhat disorga-
nized and random. In particular, the two young men whose
adventures and desires dominate the narrative bring with them two
very different kinds of action and hence two distinct, generically
determined tendencies of discourse. As Harry Sieber has stated, "*La
ilustre fregona* es una de las novelas ejemplares más curiosas. Hay en
realidad dos novelas de dos amigos: las aventuras picarescas de
Diego de Carriazo y la historia de amor de Tomás de Avendaño."[4]
Sieber's mention of the picaresque element of the text reminds us of

---

[3] El Saffar, 14-17; given the basic theoretical framework of her book and the reliance
on a plausible chronology of the composition of the *novelas*, El Saffar speaks of
"earlier" vs. "later" texts, but many of her observations fit with my slightly looser
categories based on a more or less Fryean scale of comedic/positive vs.
ironic/negative; see N. Frye, *Anatomy of Criticism*, especially 43-49. On the question
of rigid social classes and privileged justice, see also A. Castro, "La ejemplaridad
de las novelas cervantinas," in *Hacia Cervantes*, 451-74; see also F. Pierce, "Reality
and Realism in the *Exemplary Novels*."
[4] See H. Sieber's introductory note, the *Novelas ejemplares*, II, 21.

the peculiar ways in which the essentially negative and narrowing aspects of the picaresque perspective and its usual modes of discourse are modified as they are incorporated into a Cervantine text.[5] In *La ilustre fregona*, the composite of its picaresque and comedic-amorous actions serves less to establish the limited perspective of the *pícaro* than to allow a certain juxtaposition of individuals and social ranks. This juxtaposition, in turn, suggests a world in which the presumption of aristocratic virtue and order both allows and requires happy endings; this story and its discourses are not an optic that magnifies only society's hypocrisies and the problems of its marginalized persons and groups.[6]

Perhaps the most important point raised by Sieber's observation is the problem of the text's heterogeneity, the markedly free manner in which Cervantes incorporates into this *novela* certain elements of the picaresque, on the one hand, and, on the other, the central action of a tale of love interwoven with a larger comedy of loss and restoration.[7] Some critics, however, have seen the picaresque elements as a crafty distraction, masking the text's quite different generic nature. As Robert M. Johnston has suggested, the principal

---

[5] In this regard, I find myself largely in agreement with A. Castro's position as outlined in his section on "Lo picaresco" in *El pensamiento de Cervantes*, 228-235. The picaresque, when it can be said to be present at all in a Cervantine text—e.g., here or in *Rinconete y Cortadillo*—represents the inclusion into a larger context of episodes or characters that evoke the lower reaches of society, rather than the elaboration of a total and exclusive picaresque vision, the basically alienated and critical view of society. For more specific considerations of the integration of picaresque elements into *La ilustre fregona*, see M. Joly, "Para una reinterpretación de *La ilustre fregona*: Ensayo de tipología cervantina," in *Aurem Saeculum Hispanum: Beiträge zu Texten des Siglo de Oro*, 103-16, and R. M. Johnston, "Picaresque and Pastoral in *La ilustre fregona*," in *Cervantes and the Renaissance*, 167-77.

[6] In this light, Carriazo's picaresque sub-plot functions as a temporary excursion from his authentic identity and social rank, curiously reaffirming his inherent nobility, rather than as the meaningful immersion of the youth into the picaresque world or, even less, his transformation into a *pícaro*.

[7] This latter structure largely conforms to the notion of the "romance" genre, as El Saffar has argued (*Novel to Romance*), though *La ilustre fregona* would still be, in El Saffar's scheme, a problematic, transitional text, still very much tied to novelistic realism.

setting of the *novela* (the inn), along with a good deal of the ways in which the characters interact and talk to each other, allows us to see this text as a kind of pastoral, understood in a loosely Empsonian sense.[8] *La ilustre fregona* is not the full-blown, conventional Renaissance pastoral of Cervantes's own *Galatea*. Rather it belongs to that group of more open-ended and ambiguous forms in which the pastoral space exists within the text in a way that reveals its edges, both its separateness from and its points of contact with contingent and surrounding societies.[9] There are, however, some fundamental, if intriguing, difficulties in an approach that sees *La ilustre fregona* as mainly pastoral. In particular, the quintessential thematic focus of conventional Renaissance pastoral—the discussion of the nature of love—is largely absent. Romantic love plays a part in this text and is given some notable passages, but it exists as a necessary *given* of the story, not as a problem or as the central, dominant theme.[10]

By raising this point, I do not mean to deny the pastoral elements of the text, but rather to suggest that the pastoral has been incorporated in a partial manner. We grant the presence of the pastoral (e.g.,

---

[8] See Johnston, "Picaresque and Pastoral in *La ilustre fregona*." William Empson's classic study—*Some Versions of Pastoral*—is very much a product of its epoch and reflects a refreshingly inventive response to what he saw as the stultifying excesses of the "socialist realist" vein of some Marxist literary criticism; nonetheless, Empson's highly original redefining of the pastoral genre renders the term susceptible to being applied to a vast range of works of fiction. In my opinion, Johnston's use of the concept brushes, though perhaps does not overstep, the boundaries of the justifiable use of the term.

[9] Consider the subtle and specifically modified pastoral of the Grisóstomo and Marcela episode in *Don Quijote*, Part I. As Johnston has so carefully put it, "the true pastoral of *La ilustre fregona* is an internal sort of pastoral. Instead of happening in a place resembling the earthly paradise or the Golden Age, it exists within the characters as a state of mind" ("Picaresque and Pastoral," 174). On the pastoral in Cervantes, and especially in the *Galatea*, see D. Finello, *Pastoral Themes and Forms in Cervantes's Fiction*, in particular 41-57.

[10] If, however, one steps back from the more restricted conventions of Renaissance pastoral and considers the more inclusive Empsonian notion of "the pastoral process of putting the complex into the simple" (see Empson, 3-23), one is still left with the question of what *is* the concentrated and "simple" discourse of *La ilustre fregona* into which a complexity has been placed? And what is the complexity?

in the intercalated poetry and in the conventional motif of courtship) in *La ilustre fregona*. But it is clear that a version of pastoral discourse has been intertwined with elements of the picaresque and the familiar comedic discourse of loss and recovery, sin and restitution. *La ilustre fregona* embodies the plurality and coexistence of discourses that, under the concept of *heteroglossia*, Bakhtin has proposed as a fundamental defining feature of the modern novel.[11] In dealing with the generic diversity of the text, we must understand how the comedic-amorous component serves as the essential organizing principle of the *novela*, while the low-comic and picaresque episodes, however much they may seem assignable to the status of sub-plot, retain an importance that resists their subordination to mere supporting or digressionary roles. This heterogeneity of actions is reflected in the linguistic diversity seen in the juxtapositions of verse fragments and courtly formulas alongside the slang of muledrivers and less-than-chaste serving-girls.

This combination of distinct types of discourse representing different social strata harmonizes with the other main structural and thematic devices of the text. First, there is the concept of *excursions*, understood literally as travels and figuratively as disguisings. Second, there is Cervantes's richly suggestive and familiar device of the *inn*, a place that both allows the ambiguities of disguise and also promotes the reunions and revelations that, in turn, resolve old

---

[11] See M. M. Bakhtin, *The Dialogic Imagination: Four Essays*, especially the essays "From the Prehistory of Novelistic Discourse" (41-83) and "Discourse in the Novel" (259-422). What Bakhtin states as a general case seems especially appropriate to the situation of language and genre in *La ilustre fregona*: "The prose writer as a novelist does not strip away the intentions of others from the heteroglot language of his works, he does not violate those socio-ideological cultural horizons (big and little worlds) that open up behind heteroglot languages—rather, he welcomes them into his work. The prose writer makes use of words that are already populated with the social intentions of others and compels them to serve his own new intentions, to serve a second master. . . . Diversity of voices and heteroglossia enter the novel and organize themselves within it into a structured artistic system. This constitutes the distinguishing feature of the novel as a genre" (299-300). See also 320-21, on "incorporated genres."

problems and establish the new, "fortunate" society.[12] As in *Don Quijote*, Part I, the *posada del sevillano* in Toledo not only provides the plausible place for actions ranging from the farcical to the sentimental, but also establishes what Sieber (speaking of an element fundamental to all the *Novelas ejemplares*) has called the "parenthetical space" into which people may enter freely and in which the novelistic action can unfold.[13] These parenthetical actions, within the parenthetical space of the inn, create an interlocking series of wanderings and displacements. In the same way, there is also established a linguistic, discursive matrix for the juxtapositions of persons and their respective voices. Within the world created by this subtle textual heterogeneity, the problems of identity and of immoral actions (on the part of the elder Carriazo) will be resolved. The interaction of these disparate genres and voices (picaresque, pastoral, comedic), moreover, leaves, as a residue, a sense of a larger society, one that is more realistic and convincing than the fortunate but improbable coincidences and adventures of the principal characters of the *novela*.

The *novela* begins with the narrator identifying the main characters, first the two fathers and then their sons, with special attention given to social rank: "En Burgos, ciudad ilustre y famosa, no ha muchos años que en ella vivían dos caballeros principales y ricos: el uno se llamaba don Diego de Carriazo, y el otro, don Juan de

---

[12] The centrality of the inn as a setting for disguise, mistakes, and final *anagnorisis*—as well as its more subtle function as a device for the temporary bringing together of diverse social sectors and their discourses—is not only fitting in light of the narrative exigencies of this *novela*, but it also suggests a significant allusive connection between this shorter work and *Don Quijote*, Part I, where the inn setting frequently discharges similarly complex and crucial functions. For a highly insightful analysis of this aspect, see J. Paulino, "El espacio narrativo en *La ilustre fregona*." Concerning the importance of journeys and the relationship of language to movement across space, see S. Hutchinson, *Cervantine Journeys*, especially 3-37.
[13] In this regard, the *posada* is emphatically that which Sieber has characterized as the typical space and moment of the Cervantine *novela*'s action: "Casi todas las *Novelas ejemplares* presentan personajes en una situación, digamos, entre paréntesis," and thus the Cervantine *novela* "tiene lugar para los personajes y para los lectores en este espacio parentético" (*Novelas ejemplares*, I, 15).

Avendaño. El don Diego tuvo un hijo, a quien llamó de su mismo nombre, y el don Juan otro, a quien puso don Tomás de Avendaño" (II, 139). Although such an opening passage is quite conventional, in this case the emphatic linking of fathers and sons—particularly of the two Carriazos, who are given the same first name—and the emphasis on social position are crucial to the structural and thematic exigencies of the *novela*. The two youths' relatively innocent excursions and disguisings will correspond to and help redeem the previous and more grave moral detour of Carriazo senior. The evocation of an "ilustre y famosa," aristocratic Burgos is particularly significant since the city does not figure directly in the *novela*. Rather, it is presented at both beginning and end invested with a special emblematic weight, as the locus of the main characters' real lives as well as a metonymy for the values of sobriety and decorum, orderliness and wealth.[14]

The interactions and implicit contrasts of personality of the two young men, Diego and Tomás, are also important to the allusive evocation of a textually absent, external world. The presence of the two youths—a doubling of the young male lover role[15]—also allows greater complexity of comedic plot. This doubling makes the final recognitions and restorations more inclusive and social. But given the fact that the young Carriazo will not play the part of Costanza's suitor (he is, as we will learn, her half-brother), his importance in the *novela* might at first seem secondary. In light of the basic thematic questions of identity and social order, however, he in fact has a central role. Carriazo's complex personality and his semi-picaresque adventures serve to demonstrate that the meaning of what one does

---

[14] As J. Paulino ("El espacio narrativo") states, "El narrador, al seleccionar y combinar sus menciones y comentarios, está oponiendo Burgos, Valladolid y Salamanca (lugares de vida noble, honrada, recta y de estudio) a Madrid, Toledo y Sevilla, centros de la picaresca y el engaño. Con esto se configuran dos espacios globales en el relato y una incursión a un espacio límite al que no se llega otra vez" (99).

[15] See Casalduero, *Sentido y forma*, 191; see also Barrenechea, "*La ilustre fregona* como ejemplo de estructura novelesca cervantina," 202.

in this particular world is not simply determined on its own merits as an action, but rather is judged in the context of the social identity of the person who does the action.[16] The summary of Carriazo's first period of wanderings, which begins with the second paragraph and occupies the first several pages, establishes this context of valuation. In this section, the narrator emphasizes the willful deliberateness, along with the curiously distanced innocence of Carriazo's decision to leave home and of his subsequent adventures: "Trece años, o poco más, tendría Carriazo cuando, llevado de una inclinación picaresca, sin forzarle a ello algún mal tratamiento que sus padres le hiciesen, sólo por su gusto y antojo, se desgarró, como dicen los muchachos, de casa de sus padres, y se fue por ese mundo adelante" (II, 139). His voluntary excursion through a picaresque world is not, however, his transformation into the conventional *pícaro* since the essence of his more noble identity continues to manifest itself. As the narrator puts it: "a tiro de escopeta, en mil señales, descubría ser bien nacido" and "En fin, en Carriazo vio el mundo un pícaro virtuoso, limpio, bien criado y más que medianamente discreto" (II, 140)—clearly something of a pointed oxymoron. Carriazo's dominance of the introductory section thus sets the stage, opening up the possibilities of place and language, for the larger question of the relationships between one's origin in the social hierarchy and one's individual, autonomous—or perhaps not fully autonomous—virtue and moral character.

---

[16] The character of young Carriazo / "Lope Asturiano" is in itself worth extensive commentary. He is, obviously, a kind of complementary expansion or unfolding of the all-too-patient, well-behaved Avendaño; at the same time, while the narrator is at pains (near the opening of the *novela*) to insist on Carriazo's noble character, good nature, and good judgment (*discreción*), in his encounters with fellow *aguadores* and others of the town, the youth shows himself to be rather hot-tempered and violent. And after the second encounter, the reader is apt to wonder how the boy might have fared at the hands of "la justicia" if his aristocratic identity had not, providentially, come to light. For some highly original, and somewhat negative, readings of his character and its implications, see J. Alsina, "Algunos esquemas narrativos y semánticos en *La ilustre fregona*" and C. Chauchadis, "Los caballeros pícaros: contexto e intertexto en *La ilustre fregona*."

Carriazo's seemingly arbitrary picaresque inclination also serves to connect the temporarily severed threads of a larger story. The young man not only convinces Avendaño to leave home and join him in his second excursion, thereby setting up the encounter of Tomás and Costanza. Carriazo's willful wanderings from his home, his social rank, and his true identity also echo, in a significantly modified way, the moral wanderings of his father. Once again, as in *La española inglesa*, we have a case of "the sins of the father," though here with significantly different details. The older Carriazo's rape and abandonment of the unidentified aristocratic woman (who from this dishonorable act becomes pregnant and subsequently bears a daughter) engenders the central character, the *fregona*; the crime also prompts the guilt-driven conclusion. In the symbolic moral implications of this relationship of father to son, the marked differences in the spirit of their respective actions are difficult to overlook. In essence, the wandering of the father's lust demonstrates the man's weaker, baser side, while the exuberant wanderlust of the son serves to underscore his virtue, as his noble character shows forth—or so the narrator suggests—even more against the backdrop of the plebeian, picaresque settings. Once again, however, the moral differences may be less extreme than one would think.

The young Carriazo's significance to the structure of the *novela* goes beyond his role as the initiator of actions necessary to the comedic-amorous development of the plot. He also leads his friend Avendaño—and along with Avendaño, the reader—through different worlds of language.[17] Carriazo himself is presented as a master of more than one particular social discourse. Such mastery is crucial to his successful disguising and his skillful navigation through the lower reaches of society. The presence of the socially differentiating discourses through which Carriazo leads us is, moreover, subtly dialogic in nature.[18] The heterogeneity of language

---

[17] In this, we are reminded of the picaresque and linguistic diversity of *Rinconete y Cortadillo*; see Chapter Three above.

[18] See Bakhtin, *The Dialogic Imagination*, 331 ff ("The Speaking Person in the Novel")

is not only manifested, as one would expect, in the separate discourses of persons from distinct social sectors; rather, even within a given character's speech we find the interpenetration of different discourses.

A revealing instance of such discursive interplay occurs early in the *novela* when Carriazo and Avendaño meet the two Andalusian *mozos de mulas*, one of whom describes the beautiful *fregona* of Toledo. The muledriver, who has seen Costanza and whose gross advances have been fittingly rebuffed, describes the girl, in part, as follows:

> Es dura como un mármol, y zahareña como villana de Sayago, y áspera como una ortiga; pero tiene una cara de pascua y un rostro de buen año: en una mejilla tiene el sol, y en la otra, la luna; la una es hecha de rosas y la otra de claveles, y en entrambas hay también azucenas y jazmines. No te digo más sino que la veas, y verás que no te he dicho nada, según lo que te pudiera decir, acerca de su hermosura. (II, 148)

The language of this supposedly crude *mozo* combines an expectedly low-level, colloquial register with a brief and sudden shift into a more poetic, if rather clichéd and shop-worn, metaphoric style. Such shifts contribute to the satiric, undercutting effect of the *mozo*'s comments, as is evident when the youth, acknowledging Costanza's unattainability, pays her his highest compliment: "En las dos mulas rucias que sabes que tengo mías la dotara de buena gana si me la quisieran dar por mujer; pero yo sé que no me la darán: que es joya para un arcipreste o para un conde" (II, 148). The allusion to the illicit amorous activities of an *arcipreste* strikes the chord of a familiar picaresque *topos* and thus clearly falls into a certain satirical convention, however "unironically" it may have been intended by the *mozo*. Through this peculiarly hetergeneous discourse, the girl is both

---

and in particular his statement that "The speaking person in the novel is always, to one degree or another, an *ideologue*, and his words are always *ideologemes*. A particular language in a novel is always a particular way of viewing the world, one that strives for a social significance. It is precisely as ideologemes that discourse becomes the object of representation in the novel, and it is for the same reason novels are never in danger of becoming a mere aimless verbal play" (333).

valued and devalued by the ambiguous resonances of a seemingly maladroit and rufianesque, but deceptively complex, language.

Costanza herself presents a problem of recognition and valuation for others and not only for the rustically comic muledriver. For nearly everyone in the *novela*, the evident disharmony of her beauty, grace, and discretion, on the one hand, and her emphatically plebeian duties and environment, on the other, is more than a little disconcerting. Even for young Avendaño, whose love-at-first-sight response to his first encounter with the *fregona* is a necessary, unambiguous given, the incongruity of such a beautiful woman in such a mundane setting is a problem. Avendaño cannot overlook, or fail to mention, the issue of the difficulties implicit in the difference of their social positions; as he says to Carriazo: "Mira, amigo: no sé cómo te diga . . . de la manera con que amor *el bajo sujeto desta fregona*, que tú llamas, me le encumbra y levanta tan alto, que viéndole no le vea y conociéndole le desconozca" (II, 164; emphasis added). For Avendaño, although love conquers all—or so it would seem—the caste distinction hardly goes unnoticed. As in the case of don Juan de Cárcamo in *La gitanilla*, by acknowledging its existence, Avendaño partly emphasizes and validates the force and sincerity of his love, while subtly reiterating the significance of his presumed social superiority.[19]

Carriazo's reaction to his friend's declaration of love for Costanza, in turn, is marked by a tone of good-natured mockery. As Carriazo states: "¡Oh amor platónico! ¡Oh fregona ilustre! ¡Oh felicísimos tiempos los nuestros, donde vemos que la belleza enamora sin malicia, la honestidad enciende sin que abrase, el donaire da gusto sin que incite, y la bajeza del estado humilde obliga y fuerza a que le suban la rueda de la que llaman Fortuna!" (II, 165). His apparently joking allusions to "Platonic love" and to the convention of Neo-Platonic pastoral, moreover, resonate with even deeper irony, given the comedic-amorous core of the *novela*, since a

---

[19] On this issue, see A. Weber, "*La ilustre fregona* and the Barriers of Caste," *Papers on Language and Literature* 15 (1979): 73-81.

good deal of such neo-Platonic values and of the novelesque machinery of Fortune will indeed prove to be operative. What is most significant about this passage and about the relationship of speaker to discourse, however, is the way in which Carriazo ironically gives this mock-pastoral apostrophe, clearly marking it off as artificial discourse. The reader, with a more inclusive comprehension of the text, has already grasped the unintended if partial validity of this statement. This passage and its larger context demonstrate the by-now familiar Cervantine tendency to juxtapose strikingly distinct discourses. The final effect, in this case, is less a sense of romantic artificiality than an intimation of the plausibility of a world in which such languages—as devices of disguise, desire, persuasion, or wit—are so variously deployed.

The central section of the *novela* is both peculiarly static and frenetically busy. After the two boys decide to stop off at Toledo in order to see the beautiful young *fregona*, not much of great significance to the main comedic-amorous plot appears to happen. Once the two youths arrive at the inn and Avendaño is smitten by Costanza's beauty, the narrative becomes dominated by this apparently random, episodic world. Things do happen, of course, because this inn, like any other, is a quintessentially "parenthetical" space where people stop off for indeterminate periods of time, meeting by chance or on purpose, and where disguises and deliberate or accidental confusions of identity are likely to occur. The *posada del Sevillano*, moreover, is a kind of theatrical space in the sense that, as much as non-verbal actions and gestures, the games of language and the interplay of contrasting discourses become of prime importance.[20] Kinds of discourse will be the vehicles by which people play roles,

---

[20] Again, one of Bakhtin's fairly general ideas seems especially relevant to *La ilustre fregona*, as he notes, speaking of highly dialogic texts: "The plot itself is subordinated to the task of coordinating and exposing languages to each other. The novelistic plot must organize the exposure of social languages and ideologies, the exhibiting and experiencing of such languages . . . In a word, the novelistic plot serves to represent speaking persons and their ideological worlds" (*The Dialogic Imagination*, 365).

try to introduce themselves or verify their true identities, and, finally, seek to uncover the central, mysterious identity: that of Costanza.

Given these characteristics of the inn (a place of random encounter, ambiguous identity, and complex verbal games), it is fitting that this is the temporary world of Costanza, the still unidentified, or misidentified, child of the likewise unidentified *señora peregrina*. Although remarkably passive and uninvolved in the action of the story, Costanza emerges as the unifying thread, linking the past (the lust-inspired, illicit acts of the elder Carriazo) with the future (the virtuous love interest of young Avendaño). But while the development of the love interest between Costanza and Tomás—a sentiment that appears far more lively on his side than on hers—dominates much of the center of the *novela*, the courtship that takes place is a peculiar one. For one thing, it involves very little direct interaction and no special tasks or challenges for the young man. Rather than the series of tests and tribulations found in *La gitanilla, La española inglesa,* or *El amante liberal,* courtship is here rendered as the process of a gradual revelation of identity (Avendaño's) and as the working out of a larger structure of dialogic interplay. Significantly, textual discourse comes to play a role alongside mere orality. For example, it seems that Avendaño's greatest success in gaining Costanza's genuine interest comes when he reveals, in *writing,* his true aristocratic rank. Likewise, the aristocratic lineage of the girl is revealed not ony through the oral discourses of the inn-keeper and of Carriazo senior, but also textually, in the reuniting of the divided parchment. Only at this point, with a text undergirding the spoken word, is the heretofore relatively silent and non-involved Costanza finally free to exercise an automomous will, paradoxically affirming her own identity by accepting and thus subordinating herself to Tomás's marriage proposal.[21]

---

[21] On the curious nature of Costanza's character, Barrenechea states that "para Costanza, que vive en una posada de Toledo, no rigen las convenciones estéticas de lo pastoril, ni la libertad real y literaria de lo gitano; está dentro de las reglas sociales y aún conviene que se extreme su recato como contraste con el tráfago que la rodea. Cervantes ha construido con ella un personaje en hueco, que el lector sólo

The first meeting of Avendaño (or "Tomás Pedro," as he has renamed himself) and Costanza is marked by both deliberate and unintended confusions of identity. To the girl's innocent question about who the young man is—"¿Es por ventura criado de alguno de los huéspedes de casa?"—Avendaño wittily replies that "No soy criado de ninguno, sino vuestro" (II, 150). This declaration of interest is met with apparent indifference by the girl. As the comic episodes multiply and he realizes that he has a serious rival in the person of the local Corregidor's son, Avendaño, in an attempt to emphasize and authenticate the sincerity of his sentiments, expresses his intentions in a letter that begins by clearly stating his true rank. He thus moves from the ephemeral spoken word to the peculiarly authoritative realm of the written text. The first half of this letter reads as follows:

> Señora de mi alma: Yo soy un caballero natural de Burgos; si alcanzo de días a mi padre, heredo un mayorazgo de seis mil ducados de renta. A la fama de vuestra hermosura, que por muchas leguas se extiende, dejé mi patria, mudé vestido, y en el traje que me veis vine a servir a vuestro dueño; si vos lo quisiéredes ser mío, por los medios que más a vuestra honestidad convengan, mirad qué pruebas queréis que haga para enteraros desta verdad; y enterada en ella, siendo gusto vuestro, seré vuestro esposo y me tendré por el más bien afortunado del mundo" (II, 178)[22]

Costanza, who has been told by Tomás that the note was a prayer efficacious for curing toothache, reacts in a discreet but ambiguous way by tearing up the letter and telling the youth, evasively, that "tu oración más parece hechicería y embuste que oración santa . . ." (II, 178-79). But Tomás is slightly encouraged since she neither rejects him outright nor does she denounce him to the "authorities" (i.e., the innkeeper). The implication of this crucial but curious moment in the

---

conoce a través de los otros personajes por el influjo que ejerce en ellos, como un astro que arrastra hacia su órbita a los que se cruzan en su camino" (199-200).

[22] It should be pointed out that Tomás is significantly twisting the truth, with regard to his motives for leaving home in the first place: the one notable—and interesting—lie in an otherwise quite frank presentation of himself and his background.

narrative is that this partial revelation of identity cannot yet fully resolve the question of love and union. Not only has Avendaño, or Tomás Pedro, not yet returned to his true personal and social place. More importantly, Costanza has not been restored to her proper place either. Equally significant are the candor and specificity of the letter's content, in which Avendaño bluntly states his wealth as well as his social rank. While this information can be seen as simply another way to gain the woman's interest, one cannot overlook the sense in which it also represents a natural part of Avendaño's definition of his identity. It is yet another necessary aspect of his most fundamental concept of self.[23]

The full and final revelations and restorations of identities, in true comedic fashion, await the coming together of all the principal characters. The climactic moment comes soon after the arrival of the two fathers, Carriazo and Avendaño. An important step in the process of revelation occurs when the local Corregidor comes to the inn, also in search of the *fregona*. The Corregidor's motive is to meet and see for himself the young woman who has rendered his son so totally lovestruck. After he meets her, he questions the innkeeper about her origin, and the man fills in a substantial part of the history (II, 186ff). Following this narration, the innkeeper produces the incomplete gold chain and the jaggedly cut parchment with its cryptic string of letters (II, 190). The combining of this fragmentary document with its missing half, soon to be supplied by the elder Carriazo, will reunite the father with his long-abandoned daughter. Once again, it is appropriate that a text, a document of identity—one simultaneously more ambiguous and yet more authoritative than Avendaño's letter—plays such an indispensable role. While the establishment of Costanza's true identity might have been possible through a simple deductive review of the circumstances, in the dynamics of this *novela* the revelation must proceed through a

---

[23] We are again reminded of the analogous passage in *La gitanilla*, when, in his first appearance in the story, don Juan de Cárcamo makes a point of stating this element of his identity as well; see Chapter One above.

sequential process of two complementary, intercalated *historias* followed by a final, culminating textual seal of authenticity. The uncovering of the truth demands the subtle and various interventions of discourse.

Soon after the appearance of the Corregidor, the two fathers, Carriazo and Avendaño, arrive on the scene (II, 191). It turns out that they have come, at Carriazo's insistence, not in search of their missing sons, but rather—moved by a long-overdue twinge of conscience—in search of Carriazo's illegitimate child. The elder Carriazo brings the crucial items that will "prove" the relationship: the missing links of the gold chain and the corresponding half of the parchment, whose fit with the other half validates the blood relationship by reuniting and literally restoring sense to a long divided sentence: "ESTA ES LA SEÑAL VERDADERA" (II, 193). What follows is the predictable comedic scene of *anagnorisis* and reunion: the elder Carriazo recognizes (in the sense of openly acknowledging) his daughter, the two fathers recognize their errant sons, and as a result, both the younger men and the long-lost young woman recognize (realize) their appropriate and foreordained roles in society. The familial, institutional resolution of the story is embodied in a somewhat complex mass marriage: Tomás Avendaño marries Costanza; young Carriazo marries the Corregidor's daughter (who seems to have magically appeared for just this purpose); and the disappointed son of the Corregidor is conveniently paired off with a daughter of the Avendaño family.[24] Needless to say, everyone lives happily ever after.

Near the very end, the narrator sums up the fortunate finale in the following way:

---

[24] A relationship perhaps all too close to the incestuous, since the senior Avendaño and the Corregidor are said to be *primos*. It might also be noted that, with these weddings, the three families are now all interlinked by marriage, dramatizing yet again the creation of the new and more tightly united "society." Once again, on the importance of the marriage theme, see Sears, *A Marriage of Convenience*.

Desta manera quedaron todos contentos, alegres y satisfechos, y la nueva de los casamientos y de la ventura de la fregona ilustre se extendió por la ciudad, y acudía infinita gente a ver a Costanza en el nuevo hábito, en el cual tan señora se mostraba como se ha dicho. Vieron al mozo de la cebada Tomás Pedro vuelto en don Tomás de Avendaño y vestido como señor; notaron que Lope Asturiano era muy gentilhombre después que había mudado vestido y dejado el asno y las aguaderas; . . . (II, 198)

The resolution of the fundamental problems of identity and social displacement is thus presented in a way that highlights appearance and the signifying function of costume, as we see especially in the emphasis on Costanza's "nuevo hábito." The vestments do not, as it were, simply transform their wearers, but the clothes do symbolize and reinforce the rightness of the given person's return to a preordained social place. In a similar way, the resolution of the ostensible main problem—the return of Costanza to her rightful place and the appropriate uniting of her and Tomás as husband and wife—is further "dressed" by the simultaneous weddings of the two other couples. Through this markedly festive conclusion, Cervantes deliberately enlarges the focus of the restoration theme, beyond the limited and individual, and outward toward the social.

In *La ilustre fregona* Cervantes has created one of the most deceptively subtle yet most broadly representative texts of the *Novelas ejemplares*. In this *novela*, the themes of individual identity and social order, along with the structural elements of generic and discursive heterogeneity, emerge as the prime defining features. In so doing they effectively present a conservative, if benevolent and forgiving, ideological perspective.[25] Yet the sense of magnanimous

---

[25] One should add that the apparent respect for the established hierarchies and norms of society manifested in the *Novelas ejemplares* is not the whole Cervantine picture; Parts I and II of *Don Quijote* would certainly have to be seen as complicating any notion of a simplistic acceptance, in Cervantes's social vision, of the unquestionable rightness of each and every element of the social structures of his time. Likewise, an ideological perspective that largely accepts aristocratic values and the social status quo is not inconsistent with the idea that the Cervantine vision is essentially "humanist," in the sense of the term employed by Forcione in *Cervantes and the Humanist Vision*.

forgiveness in the conservative Cervantine vision of social order is both affirmed and ironically destabilized in the various kinds and levels of freedom implicit in *La ilustre fregona*: the freedom of the two young men to change identities and play roles, the relative moral freedom of the elder Carriazo to sin and then, quite late, to make seemingly adequate restitution, and the freedom with which aristocratic families can make amends and reconstitute social harmony through their wealth and power and through fortunate, if hastily arranged, multiple marriages. The basic ideological need for such an affirmative resolution, or so one might suspect, requires these authorial manipulations, with all their happy improbabilities: a denouement whose willful artifice is impossible to overlook. The broader implications, meanwhile, are not without disturbing ironies. From one perspective, this tale affirms once again that love triumphs, and in so doing, restores a harmonious order. But the same result along with what leads up to it, seen from another angle, is really the affirmation once again that the aristocrat is not so much the pos-sessor of unquestioned moral superiority as he is the one who can make a mess, deviate from properly moral behavior, and finally (with society's patient indulgence) clean it up.

The temporary center of *La ilustre fregona* (the *posada* in To-ledo)—with its comic contrivances, transparent fictions, and highly improbable coincidences—validates by contrast the plausibility and reality of a world partially glimpsed in the text but largely distant from the immediate center: the "real" world of Burgos. In *La ilustre fregona*, the *posada*—as a stop-over on the excursions of life and identity—takes on its sociocritical significance, ironically, because it is *not* all of society and definitely not one's own authentic social place, because one returns *from* it to the familial home. Thus, when all the excursions have ended, when the golden chain has completed its circle of authenticity, and when the text has been reunited into sense, then the *historia* can disappear—or rather, the persons of the *novela* can in a way disappear from the *historia*, to return (in the reader's complicit imagination) to the real and external society of Burgos.

The *novela* ends with the very much distanced narrator giving a summation of the main characters' happy future lives, while also presenting deliberate echoes of the past events and of the abandoned, marginal worlds that these same characters temporarily inhabited. Yet, while the allusions to the characters are quite clear, the persons themselves seem, at this point, curiously absent, as if already replaced into their proper world. The final sentence of the text, a peculiar and deliberate mixing of discourses and worlds, suggests this removal:

> Dio ocasión la historia de *La fregona ilustre* a que los poetas del dorado Tajo ejercitasen sus plumas en solenizar y en alabar la sin par hermosura de Costanza, la cual aun vive en compañía de su buen mozo de mesón, y Carriazo ni más ni menos, con tres hijos, que sin tomar el estilo del padre ni acordarse si hay almadrabas en el mundo, hoy están estudiando en Salamanca; y su padre, apenas ve algún asno de aguador, cuando se le representa y viene a la memoria el que tuvo en Toledo, y teme que cuando menos se cate ha de remanecer en alguna sátira el «¡Daca la cola, Asturiano! ¡Asturiano, daca la cola!» (II, 198)

These concluding words of the *novela* reiterate the attenuated but still present picaresque element in their allusion to the roguish trick of Carriazo/"Lope Asturiano," the non-rogue. But since young Carriazo has been forgiven and reintegrated into his proper world, the subtle effect of this final colloquial fragment is the indirect validation of Carriazo's authentic belonging to the aristocratic world of Burgos to which he and the others have already returned.

Chapter Nine
Pathos and Melodrama
Las dos doncellas and *La señora Cornelia*

The ninth and tenth *novelas* lend themselves to a contrastive study of the marriage theme. Here, before we arrive at the memorable "deceitful marriage" of the eleventh story, we encounter two explorations of love entanglements that resolve into, and are resolved by, marriage. Once again Cervantes explores the problems of love and abandonment, of injustice followed by redress and harmonious reunion. In both stories, the establishing of justice in questions sexual and ethical is seen as requisite for social order. But these *novelas* also confront the issues of identity and social relationships, as manifested in sexual transgressions, broken promises, and the gender-crossing implications of disguise. If, as Sears has so persuasively argued, the marriage plot and its implicit conservative ideology represent a crucial theme and structuring device of the *Novelas ejemplares*, then the juxtaposition of these two texts provides a penetrating and unexpectedly disturbing return to the question.[1] Within (or despite) the seemingly happy endings of both stories, Cervantes's texts uncover two ironic and critical versions of the marriage resolution, the first story cast in a sentimentalized, slightly archaic, and unrealistic tone, and the second story suggesting an almost subversively farcical confusion of identities and socially stratified values.[2] Most significantly, however, *Las dos doncellas* and

---

[1] See Sears, *A Marriage of Convenience*, especially chapter six (175-95).

[2] As Sears has argued, "The marriage plot (and its two dominant constituents, the courtship and the seduction plot) creates a structure whose purpose is to replicate the paternal authority by casting it as a positive, benign order in whose favor a woman would freely decide . . . " (180); and also "Cervantes' repetition of the courtship pattern of marriage plots declares the greater comfort that exists in utilizing a genre that provides for a limited amount of narrative and atmospheric variety within a strong frame that advances narrative order and a recognizable albeit idealized social hierarchy" (188). Concerning the subtle ironies of language and situation in *Las dos doncellas*, ironies that render this text arguably a "romantic

La señora Cornelia employ and explore, each in its own distinct
manner, the theme of love and marriage in ways that not only affirm
the dominant social conventions and institutions as symbolized by
marriage, but that also simultaneously reveal the inconsistencies and
injustices of the aristocratic social order celebrated by and renewed
in these harmonious marriages.[3]

In the sequential context of the entire collection, these two *novelas*
propose a significant set of contrasts with regard to the institution,
implications, and ideology of marriage. If an ill-advised marriage is
the pathological beginning and self-destructive organizing principle
of *El celoso extremeño*, while a set of affirmative, putatively happy
marriages serves as the concluding thematic punctuation of the
patient, long-suffering love quest and the contingent restoration and
anagnorisis of *La ilustre fregona*, then the problem of marriage itself
stands at both the beginning and the end of *Las dos doncellas* and *La
señora Cornelia*. In each case—and each one echoing in distinct ways
the Cardenio-Luscinda, Dorotea-don Fernando entanglement in *Don
Quijote*, Part I—a promise of marriage (or a conflicting set of
incompatible promises) stands as the love pledge at the beginning of
the story while it also provides the temporary obstacle or ambiguity
that sets the action in motion. The stories begin with two women (or
one woman, in the case of *La señora Cornelia*) left in a state of
confusion and apparent abandonment by the man whose amorous
intentions have been supposedly sealed by a promise of marriage.
The particular tone and texture of each *novela*, however, are markedly different.

I begin with the first of the two, *Las dos doncellas*. This is yet
another text that benefits from a retrospective reading. Starting at
the conclusion, specifically with the strange scene and commentary

satire," see A. M. Beaupied, "Ironía y los actos de comunicación en *Las dos
doncellas*," *Anales Cervantinos* 21 (1983): 165-76.
[3] To an extent seconding the basic thesis of Sears's book, this has been one of the
main arguments of my own explications for certain key *novelas*, especially *La
gitanilla*, *La fuerza de la sangre*, and *La ilustre fregona*, as indicated in the previous
chapters.

found in the last pages, helps orient one's reading of the beginning of the narration. Near the end of the *novela*—with the conflict and confusion of the love triangle created by the vacillating, opportunistic Marco Antonio's promises to both Leocadia and Teodosia having been resolved into the marriages of the two pairs (Marco Antonio and Teodosia; don Rafael and Leocadia)—the happy group, after their pilgrimage to Santiago, nears their respective neighboring villages. From a hill overlooking the valley that separates the two towns they come upon a strangely archaic scene:

> Descubríase desde la parte donde estaban un ancho valle que los dos pueblos dividía, en el cual vieron, a la sombra de un olivo, un dispuesto caballero sobre un poderoso caballo, con una blanquísima adarga en el brazo izquierdo, y una gruesa y larga lanza terciada en el derecho; y mirándole con atención, vieron que asimismo por entre unos olivares venían otros dos caballeros con las mismas armas y con el mismo donaire y apostura, y de allí, a poco vieron que se juntaron todos tres y habiendo estado un pequeño espacio venido se apartó con el que estaba primero debajo del olivo; los cuales, poniendo las espuelas a los caballos, arremetieron el uno al otro, con muestras de ser mortales enemigos comenzando a tirarse bravos y diestros botes de lanza, ya hurtando los golpes, ya recogiéndolos con tanta destreza que daban bien a entender ser maestros en aquel ejercicio. (II, 234-35)

This peculiarly chivalric and theatrical episode is, in effect, the working out (on the level of the respective fathers) of the *honra* question initially provoked by Marco Antonio's unscrupulous actions. The fathers of Teodosia and Leocadia have each challenged and will fight, one at a time, Marco Antonio's father.[4] Before too much damage is done, however, don Rafael and the others come running down into the valley and stop the hostilities, telling the three

---

[4] As the narrator explains, "En el camino supieron don Rafael y Marco Antonio la causa de aquella pendencia, que fue que el padre de Teodosia y el de Leocadia habían desafiado al padre de Marco Antonio en razón de que él había sido sabidor de los engaños de su hijo, y habiendo venido los dos, y hallándose solo, no quisieron combatirse con alguna ventaja, sino uno a uno, *como caballeros*, cuya pendencia parara en la muerte de uno o en la de entrambos si ellos no hubieran llegado" (II, 236; emphasis added).

men that the apparent problem has been happily and honorably resolved. The rest of the *novela* recounts the conventionally happy resolution and future lives of all the characters, with the narrator's curiously apologetic note that Rafael and Marco Antonio

> luengos y felices años vivieron en compañía de sus esposas, dejando de sí ilustre generación y de[s]cendencia, que hasta hoy dura en estos dos lugares, que son de los mejores de la Andalucía; y si no se nombran es por guardar el decoro a las dos doncellas, a quien quizá las lenguas mal-dicientes o neciamente escrupulosas les [harán] cargo de la ligereza de sus deseos y el súbito mudar de trajes; a los cuales ruego que no arrojen a vituperar semejantes libertades hasta que miren en sí si alguna vez han sido tocados destas que llaman flechas de Cupido, que en efe[c]to es una fuerza, si así se puede llamar incontrastable, que hace el apetito a la razón. (II, 236-37)

The complete comedic resolution of the conflicts and the uniting of the pairs in marriage, then, is tempered by the narrator's sense (or slight anxiety) that the daring and possibly scandalous cross dressing of the two maidens ("el súbito mudar de trajes") reflects badly upon the women's character. As I shall suggest below, this question of disguise and the evident confusion of gender has deeper and more interesting implications, especially with regard to the theme of identity.

But the most peculiar elements about the scene of the combat between the three fathers, it seems to me, are the strikingly ana-chronistic tenor of the scene and the uncritical, unironic way in which the action is presented. Although no concrete historical time references are given in this *novela*, the description of the arrival of the galleys in Barcelona and the overall atmosphere of the actions and settings lead one to suppose that the tale is set in a time relatively contemporaneous to Cervantes's epoch. Yet the battle on horseback with lance and shield, over an affair of honor, is something out of the books of chivalry—or out of the crazed imagination of Cervantes's most famous *caballero*. The reader is thus subtly thrown off balance, presented with a vision of a relatively more legendary, slightly unrealistic world and time, a place of improbable behaviors and modes of resolving problems of honor. The deeper point of all this is that this particular *novela* is—among all those of the collection—the most stylized and unrealistic in its subtle but crucially important shift of tone, to a world of the legendary, the unrealistic, and the archaic. Of all the *Novelas ejemplares*, this ninth text explores the questions of identity and the obligations of love proved and resolved within the social institutions of marriage and *honra* in ways that restate once again the temporary nature of individual and specifically female autonomy, as opposed to the necessity of return and submission to the order of the patriarchal institutions—and collective will—of a society structured by aristocratic values and privilege.[5]

The opening of the *novela* is yet another instance of the combination of *in medias res* narrative structure and deliberate confusion of identities, in which regard we are reminded of the opening of *El amante liberal*. The device—quite conventional in Spanish Golden Age *comedia* and in Cervantes's own texts—of the woman-on-the-road disguised as a man is once again a starting point, and once again it signals a prior disturbance in both personal and more broadly community affairs.[6] Teodosia is on the road, in search of the man who has not only promised marriage, but has seduced and abandoned her, enjoying a bit too soon the prerogatives of legitimate matrimony.[7] Once again, we have the device of the initial stunning

---

[5] In this regard, *Las dos doncellas* reiterates the values of *La gitanilla* and *La ilustre fregona* (see Chapters One and Eight, above), among others, but in an even more unified, emphatic manner.

[6] On this particular question, not a great deal has been written; but the position stated by Casalduero is representative: "En *Las dos doncellas* el problema es distinto, no tanto porque se trata de mujeres solteras en lugar de casadas—lo que indudablemente hace más fácil el problema—, sino porque con esta novela vemos a Cervantes en un terreno completamente social" (*Sentido y forma*, 215). A most incisive study of this *novela*, especially in terms of the problem of the disturbance in social order is C. Schmauser's "Dynamism and Spatial Structure in *Las dos doncellas*," 175-203 in *Cervantes's 'Exemplary Novels' and the Adventure of Writing*.

[7] In the midst of Teodosia's long narration of the case, she states that "Llegóse a todo esto las promesas, los juramentos, las lágrimas, los suspiros y todo aquello que a mi parecer puede hacer un firme amador para dar a entender la entereza de su voluntad y la firmeza de su pecho, y en mí, desdichada (que jamás en semejantes ocasiones y trances me había visto), cada palabra era un tiro de artillería que

presentation—the suspiciously beautiful young man—followed by the gradual revelation of true gender identity, a process of disguise and partial revelation that suggests both a dangerous liberty and certain erotic boundary confusions.[8]   But in this particular text Cervantes has chosen to extend and complicate the device of mistaken identity, or misrecognition, to a point quite unprecedented in the *Novelas ejemplares*. Although inevitably the device of cross dressing, and especially the emphasis on the extreme beauty of the young man (who will sooner or later be revealed to be a woman), prompts questions of both gender boundaries and the nature of beauty as such, the usage of male disguise in *Las dos doncellas* has more to do with the question of confusion in the areas of true identity and of moral choice and responsibility, especially as defined in terms of the marriage commitment.

The *novela* begins with the breathless entrance of the first of the two disguised, cross-dressed women. The texture of this opening scene and of the improbable persuasiveness of Teodosia's disguise (as the young "Teodoro") suggests a prior state of chaos in the social order.[9] When a woman is found in flight and in male disguise, this usually means that there has been a problem of love and, usually

---

derribaba parte de la fortaleza de mi honra; . . . de tal suerte que acabó de consumir la virtud que hasta entonces aún no había sido tocada y, finalmente, con la promesa de ser mi esposo, a pesar de sus padres, que para otra le guardaban, di con todo mi recogimiento en tierra, . . . " (II, 207).

[8] See M. Garber, *Vested Interests*, especially 1-17. When Garber speaks of the idea that "one of the most consistent and effective functions of the transvestite in culture is to indicate the place of what I call 'category crisis,' disrupting and calling attention to cultural, social, or aesthetic dissonances" or when she speaks of "the extraordinary power of transvestism to disrupt, expose, and challenge, putting into question the very notion of the 'original' identity," she is, of course, speaking of a phenomenon distinct from the temporary "disguising" of Cervantes's two women. But the implicit overtones and suggestions set off by the extent to which Cervantes carries the illusion in this *novela* gives Garber's arguments a certain utility in the present discussion. On the history and implications of this device in Spanish literature, and specifically the theater, see C. Bravo Villasante, *La mujer vestida de hombre en el teatro español*.

[9] Compare, for example, not only the entry of Dorotea in the *Quijote*, but also the opening of *La vida es sueño*.

male, betrayal. Through a man's lies or vacillations, the ideal order of society—as symbolized and contained in love properly sanctified by marriage—has been broken. The woman, having through disguise seized the freedom and autonomy usually allowable only to men, appears in the story as both the heroically questing agent and the vulnerable victim of the initiating male transgression. In her arrival at the inn, Teodosia fully fits and satisfies this well-worn literary convention.

Not content with the obvious, first-level implications of this familiar identity shift, however, Cervantes extends the confusion beyond the limits of the probable. Despite Teodosia's payment for both beds and her insistence that she (still misrecognized as a "he") not be disturbed, the innkeeper is forced to lodge in the same room another man, who will prove to be Teodosia's brother, don Rafael. Yet, despite overhearing a long, revealing speech made by Teodosia (believing her fellow lodger to be asleep), don Rafael recognizes from the voice nothing more than the fact that this supposed man is a woman: "coligiendo por las razones que había oído que sin duda alguna era mujer la que se quejaba, cosa que le avivó más el deseo de conocella" (II, 205). Teodosia's soliloquy of complaint— "¡Ay sin ventura! ¿Adónde me lleva la fuerza incontrastable de mis hados? ¿Qué camino es el mío o qué salida espero tener del intrincado laberinto donde me hallo?" (II, 204)—provides quite enough information from which a semi-informed brother would have been able to discover his relationship to the person and his familial concern for her troubled affair. In particular, her mention of the name of the man at the heart of the problem should have registered with don Rafael: "¡Oh fementido Marco Antonio! ¿Cómo es posible que en las dulces palabras que me decías viniese mezclada la hiel de tus descortesías y desdenes? ¿Adónde estás, ingrato; adónde te fuiste, desconocido? Respóndeme, que te hablo; espérame, que te sigo; susténtame, que descaezco; págame lo que me debes; socórreme, pues por tantas vías te tengo obligado" (II, 205). But the revelation is only partial at this moment, at least for don Rafael. Cervantes, meanwhile, extends further the play of misrecognitions by having don Rafael speak to his roommate in a manner that disingenuously disguises his own realization of the other person's gender. His words to Teodosia merit quoting in full, as much for style as for content:

> —Por cierto, señor gentilhombre, que si los suspiros que habéis dado y las palabras que habéis dicho no me hubieran movido a condolerme del mal de que os quejáis, entendiera que carecía de natural sentimiento o que mi alma era de piedra y mi pecho de bronce duro; y si esta compasión que os tengo y el presupuesto que en mí ha nacido de poner mi vida por vuestro remedio, si es que vuestro mal le tiene, merece alguna cortesía, en recompensa ruégoos que la uséis conmigo declarándome, sin encubrirme cosa, la causa de vuestro dolor. (II, 205)

Leaving aside the improbable complication implicit in don Rafael's feigning the belief that his companion is male—after all, the voice has just been heard to lament the absent or lost affections of another man, which would suggest a disturbingly strange inclination, were this voice really that of a man—don Rafael's language displays a courtly and slightly archaic elegance. This tendency of language is characteristic and appropriate to this *novela*. From the very beginning and in more than just the unrealistic and slightly medieval, knightly gestures and combat, we are in a textual world of the chivalric.

We are also in a world marked by the distortions of dream and passionate instability. From one obvious perspective, the strange deferrals of accurate recognition and the improbable, overheard soliloquies, like the disguisings themselves, conform to the conventions of the theatrical: the soliloquy functions as "asides"; the improbably convincing disguise serves as costume. At the same time, these curious elements underscore the central thematic issue of disturbance in the spheres of social and individual relationships. Two people—ostensible strangers, one of them being at first taken for a man, but in fact brother and sister—lie half awake, in an anxiety-filled state, waiting for dawn. In the case of Teodosia, the emotions are not without fear concerning the intentions of the other lodger. Although with the coming of dawn and in the privacy of the inn room, don Rafael and Teodosia confront each other in their true identities, when they go back out into the world the woman resumes her male disguise and a very active, aggressive masculine comportment. From the very beginning, then, the curious fictional presuppositions of Las dos doncellas ask us to accept an intricate structure of improbabilities and archaisms.

If the situation of ironic non-recognition between Teodosia and her brother don Rafael in the darkened room at the inn is more than a little unrealistic, then the effective disguising and the subsequent, markedly "masculine" actions of the two maidens are even more so. Much has been made of the question of this evident doubling of the principal female character; critics have discussed the similarities and subtle distinctions between the two women, and so on.[10] The general inclination of critical commentary, in distinguishing between the two women, not only tends to contrast differences in character, but also confronts the question of which woman has the more legitimate prior claim upon Marco Antonio. Relatedly, critics have touched on the sincerity of the latter's love and the validity of the marriage proposal.[11] Somewhat lost in these critical discussions are the implications of the simple fact that Marco Antonio (1) has promised marriage to two women, (2) has seduced and slept with the first (subsequently promising but bowing out on a similar illicit tryst with the other woman), and (3) has abandoned both women, with the intention of going to Italy for a few years, both to enjoy himself and to let things cool down. In the sick-bed scene, where the gravely wounded Marco Antonio declares his true love and marriage intentions toward Teodosia and where he explains his prior behav-

---

[10] On these issues, see L. Britt, "Teodosia's Dark Shadow? A Study of Women's Roles in Cervantes' Las dos doncellas," Cervantes 8.1 (1988): 39-46; El Saffar, Novel to Romance, especially 111-14; and J. Thompson, "The Structure of Cervantes' Las dos doncellas," BHS 40 (1963): 144-50.

[11] See in particular J. Thompson, "The Structure of Cervantes' Las dos doncellas"; Thompson notes that "The cuestión which is now presented is: Who has the greater claim, legally and emotionally, on Marco Antonio—Teodosia, whose love was consummated, or Leocadia who was loved more recently than Teodosia? . . . This apparently insoluble cuestión is the centre of the whole work" (146).

ior, his words—however sincere they may be at this point—do nothing to justify his previous actions in terms of morality or simple good judgment. In fact, what is most striking in this particular *novela* is the eerie lack of anxiety or moral pain expressed or experienced by this young aristocrat.

We do not encounter Marco Antonio until about two thirds of the way through the text. But from the respective narrations of Teodosia and Leocadia, the reader is inclined to infer that this young man is sufficiently mature, desirable, and convincing to have won the love of Teodosia, with enough sincere commitment on her part for the woman to have yielded sexually. Likewise, Marco Antonio is supposedly attractive and sincere enough to Leocadia for her to have cultivated his interest and then believed in the validity of his proposal and thus of her subsequent claim. The written form of Marco Antonio's proposal—the *cédula*—is a curious and slightly ironic touch. It simultaneously casts Leocadia as a bit coldly legalistic, while making Marco Antonio's rejection of his signed and sealed word reflect back even less favorably upon his ethical character. That the man's pledge of marriage to Teodosia is the giving of an inscribed ring and the taking of her virginity sets up an unavoidable contrast of symbols and values. The priority of Teodosia's "claim"—given the price paid—is not in question. But the irresponsibility of the man's actions is not convincingly ameliorated by this priority. The fact that Marco Antonio will return to his first fiancée, Teodosia, and not to Leocadia, meanwhile, is more fundamentally necessary for the exigencies of symmetry and the larger resolution: Teodosia is, after all, don Rafael's sister, and were Marco Antonio to marry Leocadia, the latter would not be available to don Rafael. Since don Rafael obviously could not be paired in marriage with his own sister, the *novela* would have been left with these two abandoned and unsatisfied persons, thus symbolizing isolation and a lack of social reunion and harmony. And, as we have seen, the Cervantine concept of affirmative, comedic closure demands symmetry. But I shall return to don Rafael and Leocadia later.

What *Las dos doncellas* in effect presents in the figure of Marco Antonio is yet another case of a supposedly worthy and attractive aristocrat who can dally, deceive, and dishonor; then at the end he can make, or be moved to make, everything right. This pattern is familiar from the episode of Dorotea and don Fernando in Part I of the *Quijote*. We are also reminded (a bit chillingly) of such errant men as Rodolfo in *La fuerza de la sangre*, the elder Carriazo in *La ilustre fregona*, and as we shall see, the *duque* in *La señora Cornelia*. Each of these cases, of course, has its own distinctive features. Nonetheless, within this spectrum of Cervantine possibilities of male aristocratic errancy and final redemption, the case of Marco Antonio is unusual and a bit difficult to characterize.

Clearly not in the category of the initially monstrous and later miraculously transformed Rodolfo of *La fuerza de la sangre*, Marco Antonio is nonetheless in his own way troubling. Despite—or perhaps because of—the fact that Marco Antonio does not undergo the radical transformation of Rodolfo, and given that he has a less direct role than do either don Fernando in the *Quijote* or the duque de Ferrara in *La señora Cornelia*, the slippery ambiguity of his character is all the more notable and disturbing. Marco Antonio, as he is presented in the text, is a person of inversions of, and detours from, the conventional expectations attached to the principal male character. In his first direct entrance into the story, he is found in the midst of a battle in the port of Barcelona, a clash between rebellious galley slaves and townspeople. Although at first Marco Antonio is portrayed as valiantly holding his own, what is most striking is the bold intervention of the two cross-dressed women who race forward to join the battle. The presentation of the latter is clearly cast, once again, in quasi-epic and literary terms: "con gran ligereza saltaron de las mulas, y poniendo mano a sus dagas y espadas, sin temor alguno se entraron por mitad de la turba y se pusieron la una a un lado y la otra al otro de Marco Antonio, que él era el mancebo de lo verde que se ha dicho" (II, 224). A bit further on, as the group is being forced to retreat, the two women are referred to as "las dos valientes y nuevas Bradamante y Marfisa o Hipólita y Pantasilea" (II, 224). The remarkable masculine aggressiveness of the women not only puts them on a par with the men in general and Marco Antonio in particular, but their stature is further enhanced when their feckless lover is wounded by a thrown rock and rendered unconscious and the two women support his inert body in their arms. Leocadia in particular takes a physically vigorous part, as she continues to carry him to safety (II, 225). Through these actions, a reversal of the conventional gender roles and expectations is emphatically drama-tized and underlined.

Marco Antonio, from this point in the *novela* up to the resolution of the question of the conflicting marriage proposals and claims, is most tellingly placed into a debilitated and passive state.[12] Even though the authentic gender of Teodosia and Leocadia will eventu-ally be revealed, up to this point in the story they maintain their gender-crossed disguises. Partly as a result, Marco Antonio's character and vulnerability, as well as his nature as the object of the desires of others, are the prime focus; in light of the passivity of the man, the force and complexity of these other desires (the women's) largely determine our sense of him. The story thus decenters him from the norms of the powerful (if destructive) male and shifts him to the position of the (usually victimized) female. Marco Antonio's wounded condition, moreover, serves to bring the latent questions of love and compromise to a resolution, as if this subtle reversal or inversion of power made further lies, vacillations, or transgressions on his part impossible. In this condition, he is first confronted by Leocadia (II, 227-28), who reiterates her claims upon his promise and his honor. As she concludes, "Y así, os ruego primeramente por Dios, a quien mis deseos y intentos van encaminados, luego por vos, que debéis mucho a ser quien sois, últimamente por mí, a quien debéis más que a otra persona del mundo, que aquí luego me recibáis por vuestra legítima esposa, no permitiendo haga la justicia

---

[12] As Thompson states, "For the main part of the narrative Marco Antonio has been only the passive object on which the hopes and fears of all three characters have been centred" (149).

lo que con tantas veras y obligaciones la razón os persuade" (II, 228). Leocadia's claim on Marco Antonio's promise and, given the implications of union through marriage, on his aristocratic identity are certainly valid. But in his state of debilitation—in effect, Marco Antonio believes that he is near death—and with the temporary reversal of power differentials, the previously impulsive and unethical man has little choice but to confront the reality of his own sincere sentiments—or, more appropriately, he must find, if he can, the sincerity of his sentiments.

Marco Antonio's effort to extricate himself, which demands that he be honest and bring his own sentiments into focus, is a curious combination of admirable assertion and assumption of personal responsibility, on the one hand, and of troublingly cavalier indifference, on the other. When he finally gets to the heart of his speech, he is fairly blunt and definitive about his choice:

> Confieso, hermosa Leocadia, que os quise bien y que me quisistes, y juntamente con esto confieso que la cédula que os hice fue más por cumplir con vuestro deseo que con el mío; porque antes que la firmase, con muchos días, tenía entregada mi voluntad y mi alma a otra doncella de mi mismo lugar, que vos bien conocéis, llamada Teodosia, hija de tan nobles padres como los vuestros; y si a vos os di cédula firmada de mi mano, a ella le di la mano firmada y acreditada con tales obras y testigos, que quedé imposibilitado de dar mi libertad a otra persona en el mundo. Los amores que con vos tuve fueron de pasatiempo, sin que dellos alcanzase otra cosa sino las flores que vos sabéis, las cuales no os ofendieron ni pueden ofender en cosa alguna; lo que con Teodosia me pasó fue alcanzar el fruto que ella pudo darme y yo quise que me diese, con fe y seguro de ser su esposo, como lo soy. (II, 228-29)

The candor of this explanation is slightly tarnished by the man's open admission that he did in fact sign an agreement. As if it were a valid, mitigating element, he states that his amorous behavior and gestures "fueron de pasatiempo" and went less far than the stage that he reached with Teodosia, which is here acknowledged with surprising openness. But what Marco Antonio then says, his explanation for the decision to leave both women and go to Italy, is an admission nearly as troubling in its implications as is the similar action of Rodolfo in *La fuerza de la sangre*. As Marco Antonio so clearly states:

> Y si a ella y a vos os dejé en un mismo tiempo, a vos suspensa y engañada y a ella temerosa y, a su parecer, sin honra, hícelo con poco discurso y con juicio de mozo, como lo soy, creyendo que todas aquellas cosas eran de poca importancia, y que las podía hacer sin escrúpulo alguno, con otros pensamientos que entonces me vinieron y solicitaron lo que quería hacer, que fue venirme a Italia y emplear en ella algunos de los años de mi juventud, y después volver a ver lo que Dios había hecho de vos y de mi verdadera esposa. (II, 229)

Whether or not this strikes the reader as psychologically plausible, given the tendencies of either the time or of the Cervantine *novela*, there is more than a trace of cold egotism and a dishonorable lack of concern ("que todas aquellas cosas eran de poca importancia") in Marco Antonio's reasoning. In this light, one could even speculate upon the ultimate triumph of Teodosia, in winning back this man, a man who, other than his title and the relatively higher aristocratic status, could be seen objectively as being something of a cad and considerably less worthy in terms of honor and character than Teodosia's brother, don Rafael.

But with this moment of candid confession, the conflictive cases of the two marriage promises and of an all too familiar male perfidy are superficially resolved. But only in part: for, while Teodosia is restored to her proper and desired place as Marco Antonio's lawful and (one assumed) sincerely loved wife, Leocadia is left disappointed and disillusioned. It is worth noting, at this point, that Leocadia's deluded state, vis-à-vis Marco Antonio's real intentions, is echoed in her likewise less perspicacious recognition of the true identities of those around her. When Teodosia, previously lurking back in the shadows among the others, is brought by Don Rafael to Marco Antonio's bedside, it is clear that Leocadia has believed, up to this moment, that this person is a man.[13] Leocadia's incompletely

---

[13] As the narrator puts it, "Mas la desengañada y sin ventura Leocadia, que vio por sus ojos lo que Marco Antonio hacía y vio al que pensaba ser hermano de don

satisfied state of emotions and harmony corresponds to her incomplete and erroneous sense of her immediate world. Thus, although the harmony of the resolution to Teodosia's problem is obvious—even as her true identity, both personal and gender, is now clear to all, including Leocadia—the larger, more inclusive harmony has yet to be achieved.

This brings us back to Leocadia and to the highly ambiguous resolution of the love interest on her part: don Rafael's declaration of his love and his marriage proposal. While the sincerity of don Rafael's love interest has been clear to all (including Leocadia herself; see II, 230), it is here, in this moment of Leocadia's greatest disappointment, humiliation, and abandonment that don Rafael becomes most articulate. What we have here is, from one perspective, a highly compressed, foreshortened courtship. From another vantage point, this passage represents the remarkably clear, even blunt, articulation of the familiar Cervantine ideological triad of love, marriage as goal and institutional validation, and social position as embodiment of worth and identity. Don Rafael emerges more fully, and with this emergence and revelation of his love, there also arise various questions about the value and nature of the conflicting loves and commitments of all four main characters.

Don Rafael begins by emphatically declaring his love. He then becomes distinctly practical, pointing out to Leocadia the obvious: "Ya veis que Marco Antonio no puede ser vuestro porque el cielo le hizo de mi hermana, y el mismo cielo, que hoy os ha quitado a Marco Antonio, os quiere hacer recompensa conmigo, que no deseo otro bien en esta vida que entregarme por esposo vuestro" (II, 231). Don Rafael's invocation of divine providence is picked up by Leocadia a bit later. For don Rafael, God's will explains the rightness of what has happened, while for Leocadia it ameliorates her disillusionment and helps facilitate her resigned acceptance of the new reality.[14] But

---

Rafael en brazos del que tenía por su esposo, viendo junto con esto burlados sus deseos y perdidas sus esperanzas, se hurtó de los ojos de todos . . . " (II, 230).

[14] As she later says, "pues así lo ha ordenado el cielo, y no es en mi mano ni en la

just prior to Leocadia's acceptance of don Rafael's proposal (and, thus, of the reality of the case), don Rafael frames his offer in a manner that combines a romanticized sense of the moment and a clear reiteration of values defined in terms of aristocratic identity. He begins by asking for her acceptance: "—Acabad, señora de mi alma, de serlo del todo a vista destos estrellados cielos que nos cubren, y deste sosegado mar que nos escucha, y destas bañadas arenas que nos sustentan. Dadme ya el sí, que sin duda conviene tanto a vuestra honra como a mi contento" (II, 232). By bringing together her honor and his own happiness, don Rafael reminds us of the ambiguity of Leocadia's position. Can the woman's concern for her own *honra* be a meaningful element of this or any courtship? The evidence of this particular *novela* would suggest that the answer is yes. Meanwhile, don Rafael's verbal courtship continues by returning to the notion that identity and personal value are rooted in social position:

> Vuélvoos a decir que soy caballero, como vos sabéis, y rico, y que os quiero bien, que es lo que más habéis de estimar, y que en cambio de hallaros sola y en traje que desdice mucho del de vuestra honra, lejos de la casa de vuestros padres y parientes, sin persona que os acuda a lo que menester hubiéredes, y sin esperanza de alcanzar lo que buscábades, podéis volver a vuestra patria en vuestro propio, honrado y verdadero traje, acompañada de tan buen esposo como el que vos supisteis escogeros; rica, contenta, estimada y servida, y aun loada de todos aquellos a cuya noticia llegaren los sucesos de vuestra historia. (II, 232)

The clarity with which don Rafael pairs and all but equalizes his rank and wealth with his love (though giving some priority of importance to the latter) is no more remarkable than is his emphasis on identity and return to place. Don Rafael underscores the problematic aspect of the heretofore fundamental and necessary device of disguise, the "other" side of the cross dressing issue, the "hallaros sola y en traje que desdice mucho del de vuestra honra"; likewise he notes that the

---

de viviente alguno oponerse a lo que Él determinado tiene, hágase lo que Él quiere y vos queréis, señor mío; . . ." (II, 232).

solution to her problems would include "volver a vuestra patria en vuestro *propio, honrado y verdadero traje*" (emphasis added). The acceptance of the man's offer of love is thus complexly fused with the return to and restoration of one's place and identity. Of particular significance as well is the emphasis placed on the notion that, through the device of cross dressing, the identity detour has introduced a particularly serious problem of decorum and the integrity of one's honor.

To return to Leocadia and her acceptance of don Rafael's marriage proposal and declaration of love, we are reminded of the complexity of her character and motivations. In Leocadia we confront the one person in the *novela* who has tended to receive the most negative judgments.[15] Under the circumstances of Marco Antonio's confused, confusing, and definitely less than admirable behavior, it is arguable that Leocadia (ironically) has been spared marriage to a man of notably less stature and worth than don Rafael. But this irony does not help to account for the problem of the relationship between her true sentiments and the concrete resolution of the case—her marriage to don Rafael. As I mentioned above, Leocadia, in her reply to don Rafael, picks up the thread of the divine providence theme. She then—with remarkable candor—couches her acceptance of his marriage proposal in terms that, once again, build upon the notion of identity as largely defined by social position:

> mas sea como fuere, que en fin el nombre de ser mujer legítima de don Rafael de Villavicencio no se podía perder, y con este título solo viviré contenta; y si las costumbres que en mí viéredes después de ser vuestra [esposa] fueren parte para que me estiméis en algo, daré al cielo las gracias de haberme traído por tan extraños rodeos y por tantos males a los bienes

---

[15] On Leocadia, see El Saffar, whose interpretation places Leocadia in a slightly negative and surely secondary position, especially 111-15. As El Saffar states, "Like the other Cornelia in *La señora Cornelia*, or Carriazo in *La ilustre fregona*, Leocadia is Teodosia's dark shadow, exaggerating the dangers of her situation, the baseness of her motives, and the extent of her complicity in the destruction of her honor. . . . Leocadia is the image of Teodosia's self-doubts, having no real claim to a separate identity" (114). For a different view of the implications of the character of the two women, see L. Britt, "Teodosia's Dark Shadow?"

de ser vuestra. Dadme, señor don Rafael, la mano de ser mío, y veis aquí
os la doy de ser vuestra, y sirvan de testigos los que vos decís: el cielo, la
mar, las arenas y este silencio, sólo interrumpido de mis suspiros y de
vuestros ruegos. (II, 232)

Leocadia's expression of modesty and self-abasement ("si las
costumbres que en mí viéredes . . . fueren parte para que me
estiméis") is both conventional and in this case quite affecting. But
what is also crucial here is the sense of a possible happiness justified
and defined on the basis of an identity that will be in part a new
identity: "el nombre de ser mujer legítima de don Rafael de Villa-
vicencio" and "con este título solo viviré contenta." Leocadia's own
feelings, or let us say, the depth and sincerity of her love, is left more
than a little ambiguous. The final physical gesture of this scene is
telling: "Diciendo esto, se dejó abrazar, y le dio la mano, . . . " (II,
232). The woman passively lets herself be embraced by the man into
whose nobility and higher social status she will be, by this marriage,
incorporated.

As the *novela* ends, there is a coming together of levels and
values, a uniting of the individual happiness and future good fortune
and honor that both pairs will enjoy (see II, 236-37). As the narrator
expresses this happy conclusion and the "future" beyond the textual
ending, the two women are brought together in an equality of
beauty, character, and ethical value. The concluding phrase—that
"los poetas de aquel tiempo tuvieron ocasión donde emplear sus
plumas exagerando la hermosura y los sucesos de las dos tan
atrevidas cuanto honestas doncellas, sujeto principal deste extraño
suceso" (II, 237)—unites the two, equalizing their beauty as well as
justifying the daring and boldness of their actions. But as the
narration itself has dramatized and as various critics have pointed
out, there are considerable differences between the two women, as
well as between the two men.[16] The narrator, however, does not take
this moment to draw any distinctions. Nor does he worry over the
question of the various confusions and moral detours—the one that

---

[16] Again, see especially El Saffar; Britt; and Thompson.

set the novelistic actions in motion (Marco Antonio's duplicity), or the boldly unfeminine actions of the two women. Rather, the language and tone of the conclusion of this *novela* seek to relax any residual tensions, to retreat from any troubling dissonances or vexing questions of ethical superiority (or inferiority) between the four main characters. It papers over the frankly disturbing behavior and character of Marco Antonio. In her reading of the story, El Saffar finds a kind of achievement and progress in the character or spiritual development of Marco Antonio and Teodosia.[17] This is plausible, arguable. But at the same time it is equally clear, and even more striking, that the story ends with a return and restoration very much like what we have seen in some of the previous *novelas*, a restoration that entails submission and conformity to aristocratic and conventional values. The morally errant male and the abandoned, if not betrayed, female work out—through the events and processes of plot, language, and deeper narrative structure—the initial problem of disturbance. The conclusion of the story becomes the restoration of identities and, equally significant, the restoration of persons to their rightful social places within a structure that will continue to be harmonious and idealized, but only in a way consonant with an acceptable patriarchal culture and aristocratic privilege.

What happens in *La señora Cornelia* is profoundly different in its tone and the nature of its story. Yet the similarities of its ideology and basic assumptions are strikingly consistent with the world view of *Las dos doncellas*. Once again, the question of marriage lies at the beginning and the end of a story that, while it has some elements of

---

[17] See *Novel to Romance*; as El Saffar argues, "For his part, Marco Antonio must become passive, having conceived himself only in the active role. He must be saved in order to save. The two characters must, in other words, merge by discovering each other within themselves, thus seeing that their originally conceived selves are actually a composite of forces, some of which are suppressed in conformity with socially imposed roles, but all of which must be understood before the other can be accepted as equal. The equalization of author and character and of husband and wife results in the recognition of a higher controlling order and the rejection of license on the part of the apparently controlling half of the dialectic" (116-17).

intrigue, is basically uncomplicated. A problematic and less than proper marriage proposal again initiates a chain of events and problems touching on the twin themes of identity and honor.[18] But while the tone of the previous *novela* is one of archaic and perhaps somber, elevated seriousness, the atmosphere of *La señora Cornelia* combines a more realistic pathos with a markedly melodramatic sentimentality and a few swervings into, or dangerously close to, the realm of farce and questionable taste. The ostensible main characters—Cornelia herself and her fiancé, the duque de Ferrara—are simultaneously central and yet curiously secondary in this *novela*, one in which two unattached and seemingly uncompromised young Spanish students become the necessary agents of the plot's resolution. The references to these two men as angels are slightly eerie and totally fitting.[19]

The *novela* begins with a brief explanation and lead-in, describing the wanderings of the two young Spanish gentlemen, don Antonio and don Juan. In what is by now a familiar pattern, the two men are presented as student-soldiers, young aristocrats touring the Spanish-dominated parts of Europe, seeking to further their education and to find interesting military action. The first paragraph underlines the significance of the relationship between the exercise of arms and the essence of noble character:

---

[18] On this *novela*, see especially G. Bradbury, "Lope, Cervantes, A Marriage Trick and a Baby," *Hispanófila* 82 (1982): 11-19; E. Lacadena y Calero, "*La señora Cornelia* y su técnica narrativa," *Anales Cervantinos* 15 (1976): 199-210; F. Luttikhuizen, "Verdad histórica y verdad poética en *La señora Cornelia*," 265-69 in *Actas del Primer Coloquio Internacional de la Asociación de Cervantistas*; and S. Zimic, "*La señora Cornelia*: una excursión a la *novela* italiana," *Boletín de la Real Academia Española* 71.252 (1991): 101-20.

[19] After being taken in and helped by the two Spanish students, Cornelia refers to them as angels: "Allí fueron infinitas las lágrimas de alegría de Cornelia, infinitos los besos que dio a su hijo, infinitas las gracias que rindió a sus favorecedores, llamándolos ángeles humanos de su guarda y otros títulos que de su agradecimiento daban notoria muestra" (II, 255). Later, Lorenzo, speaking of the anonymous person who interceded to help the duque, uses similar terms: "pero fue socorrido de algún ángel, que no consintió que con su sangre sacase la mancha de mi agravio" (II, 257).

Don Antonio de Isunza y don Juan de Gamboa, caballeros principales, de una edad, muy discretos y grandes amigos, siendo estudiantes en Salamanca determinaron de dejar sus estudios por irse a Flandes, llevados del hervor de la sangre moza y del deseo, como decirse suele, de ver mundo, y por parecerles que el ejercicio de las armas, aunque arma y dice bien a todos, principalmente asienta y dice mejor en *los bien nacidos y de ilustre sangre*. (II, 241; emphasis added)

Unfortunately for the men, they find that peace has broken out in Flanders, and so they decide to return to Spain. But first, they make a detour through Italy. Impressed by the Colegio Español in Bolonia, they decide to stay and pursue their studies. Bolonia becomes the setting for most of the story. In this place and given their "foreign" identity, the two Spaniards can be detached outsiders and also agents of resolution, privileged with a marked degree of mobility and improbable trust.

La señora Cornelia is, in terms of its central conflict, a tale of a love confronted with a curious obstacle. Cornelia and the duque de Ferrara are in love and the duque has secretly proposed marriage to Cornelia. But he cannot go through with the marriage in the proper public way, given his own mother's opposition to such a match. Once again, we have the familiar device of the private, guarded marriage promise, leading up to the premature sexual consummation. However, unlike the cases of Dorotea in *Don Quijote* or Teodosia in *Las dos doncellas*, whose loss of virginity to their respective fiancés does not result in pregnancy, Cornelia is impregnated and soon after the *novela* begins, she gives birth. The new-born baby is not only the concrete and symbolic link and affirmation of the love between Cornelia and the duque; the child is also a crucial device of the plot intrigue. It should be noted as well that this detail also emphatically signals a substantial gap of time, at least nine months, during which the ostensible male hero of the tale has failed—or neglected—to work out the basic problems of his intended betrothal and marriage. The duque has in effect done nothing other than wait for his obstructive mother to die.

When we first encounter the duque in the text, it is at night, in the midst of a street fight marked by darkness and flashing swords. In this episode the duque is beset by Cornelia's brother and his henchmen. Outnumbered, the duque is on the verge of being overwhelmed and is only saved by the providential arrival and aid of don Juan. As both the fight scene and the duque's inability to make his case effectively to his mother indicate, despite his evident physical courage, he clearly lacks the moral courage to confront the challenge of making right his promises of love in the context of the entanglements of family influences. The problem of his mother's disapproval, moreover, is not just a convenient device of plot complication. Rather, it also returns us to the issue of social order and identity, given that the mother's objection is partly driven by considerations of social class. To a certain extent, then, the duque fits into the familiar Cervantine category of the slightly indecisive yet opportunistic aristocrat as lover. But the specific comedic obstacle that sets the intrigues of the plot in motion goes beyond the familiar problem of the perfidy or indecisiveness of the errant male. In effect, by involving the mother (who, not insignificantly, never appears on the scene), the details of this *novela* dramatize even more forcefully the issue of how individual desire is complicated by one's obligations to family and the expectations of one's social status.

This *novela*, then, is not just a love comedy; it is also about individual and class identity. The story uses the convenient device of mistaken and slightly marginalized identities (e.g., the two foreign students) to pursue the larger question of identity in terms of the individual, on the one hand, and the relationship of the individual to the hierarchies of society, on the other. Masking, obscurity, and confusion pervade the entire *novela*. The conflicts and complications of the tale involving the duque and Cornelia begin with the entry of one of the young Spaniards into the melodramatic entanglement. This chance intrusion is occasioned by a slightly bizarre and improbable identity error. As the text presents it, don Juan is walking one night down a dark street, when he hears someone calling softly to him:

al pasar por una calle que tenía portales sustentados en mármoles oyó que
de una puerta le ceceaban. La escuridad de la noche y la que causaban los
portales no le dejaban atinar al ceceo. Detúvose un poco, estuvo atento,
y vio entreabrir una puerta; llegóse a ella, y oyó una voz baja que dijo:
—¿Sois por ventura Fabio?
Don Juan, por sí o por no, respondió sí. (II, 243)

By impulsively and inexplicably claiming to be this "Fabio," don
Juan becomes the recipient of a mysterious little bundle, which he
soon discovers to be a baby and which he brings back to his residence. A misrepresentation of identity thus opens up another
confused story. It brings don Juan and his companion don Antonio
into someone else's "story" and connects the two Spaniards with the
identity mystery embodied and symbolized by this baby.

Another key episode of identity confusion occurs soon after don
Juan has left the baby in the care of his housekeeper. Returning to
the place where he was given the child, don Juan comes upon a
sword fight in progress. This of course is Cornelia's brother Lorenzo
and his men setting upon the duque de Ferrara, as noted above. Don
Juan knows nothing of the people involved or the cause of this
unequal battle. But moved by a chivalric notion of aiding the under-
dog, he comes to the duque's defense. After the attackers are driven
off, and still cloaked in darkness and confusion, don Juan and the
unrecognized duque pick up their hats, which had fallen off during
the fight. As we might anticipate, each man mistakenly takes ("mistakes") the other's hat. The duque's hat then becomes yet another
device of recognition and misrecognition. First, soon after the hat-
switch, don Juan meets up with his friend don Antonio. Still in the
darkness of the street, the latter narrates his own story to don Juan,
in this case, his finding of a beautiful woman, also in a situation of
need. Then, when they return to their residence and come into the
light, don Antonio notices the hat: "Llegaron en esto, y a la luz que
sacó uno de [los] tres pajes que tenían, alzó los ojos don Antonio al
sombrero que don Juan traía, y viole resplandeciente de diamantes;
quitósele, y vio que las luces salían de muchos que en un cintillo
riquísimo traía" (II, 248). To the two Spanish students, this richly

adorned hat tells them something fairly significant: "Aquí acabaron de conocer ser gente principal la de la pendencia . . ." (II, 248). But the obvious question of who its owner might be remains a mystery.

Within a very few lines, however, when don Juan looks into the room where the beautiful woman found and aided by don Antonio is resting, the woman, fixing more on the hat than on the face of its wearer, says "Entrad, señor duque, entrad, ¿para qué me queréis dar con tanta escaseza el bien de vuestra vista?" (II, 248). To which don Antonio replies that "Aquí, señora, no hay ningún duque que excuse de veros" (II, 248). This peculiar mistake forces the question and leads to the revelation that the hat's real owner is "Alfonso de Este, duque de Ferrara" (II, 249). From this, the woman herself is forced to uncover her own story and she confirms that she is "Cornelia Bentibolli, hermana de Lorenzo Bentibolli" (II, 252). In the midst of her narration, Cornelia alludes quite clearly to the question of the inequality of social rank that, so we come to suspect, is at the heart of the opposition of the duque's mother to the possible match. It may also be a concern for the duque as well. As Cornelia puts it, "Mil veces le dije que públicamente me pidiese a mi hermano, pues no era posible que me negase, y que no había que dar disculpas al vulgo de la culpa que le pondrían de *la desigualdad de nuestro casamiento*, pues no desmentía en nada la nobleza del linaje Bentibolli a la suya Estense" (II, 252; emphasis added).[20] The explicit confrontation of the question of social rank is carried to a length in this *novela* that is remarkable even in the context of such a conservative and class-conscious fictional world as the one we have seen portrayed in so many of the other *Novelas ejemplares*.[21]

---

[20] What immediately follows the above passage is more than a little telling, troubling; for Cornelia then states that the duque's response to her urgings was, both, evasive and opportunistic: "A esto me respondió con excusas, que yo las tuve por bastantes y necesarias, y confiada como rendida, creí como enamorada, y entreguéme de toda mi voluntad a la suya por intercesión de una criada mía, más blanda a las dádivas y promesas del duque que lo que debía a la confinaza que de su fidelidad mi hermano hacía" (252-53). It is difficult not to suspect that he too is troubled by the distinction of social rank.

[21] Consider, for example, the ways and extent to which the issue of identity

The problem of identity and recognition is not only treated through the device of the duque's hat. It is also represented in the case of the newborn child and the "ricos paños" in which he was first wrapped. When the baby, swaddled in other, poorer clothes, is first brought out to Cornelia (II, 250-51), she does not recognize the child as hers. Then, after Cornelia has told her story, don Juan instructs the housekeeper to bring the baby out again, this time dressed in his original clothes: "don Juan dijo al ama que entrase dentro y llevase la criatura con los ricos paños, si se los había puesto. El ama dijo que sí, y que ya estaba de la misma manera que él la había traído" (II, 254). When Cornelia sees the child for the second time, now dressed as he had first been found, she is astonished and questions the housekeeper as follows:

> —Decidme, señora, ¿este niño y el que me trajistes o me trujeron poco ha es todo uno?
> —Sí, señora —respondió el ama.
> —Pues, ¿cómo trae tan trocadas las mantillas? —replicó Cornelia—. En verdad, amiga, que me parece o que éstas son otras mantillas o que ésta no es la misma criatura. (II, 254)

The sense of confusion is deliberately prolonged and is in its own way acutely disorienting. Cornelia is confused about the child but definite about the identity of the clothes. As she states, "Digo que me digáis de dónde habéis habido estas tan ricas mantillas, porque os hago saber que son mías, si la vista no me miente o la memoria no se acuerda" (II, 255). Finally, to allay any further distress, don Juan confesses that "Esas mantillas y ese niño son cosa vuestra, señora Cornelia" (II, 255). In effect we have a situation not unlike the long concealed items of identification that, after many years, clarify and prove the identities of the two Costanzas, Preciosa in *La gitanilla* and the title character of *La ilustre fregona*. What is striking is the issue of the detail—the rich clothing—and the fact of belonging: who is this child and to what social world does he belong? The device or trick

---

understood in terms of social class background predominates in *La gitanilla*, *La ilustre fregona*, *La española inglesa*, and *La fuerza de la sangre*.

of the "changed clothes" is thus not only an enhancement of plot
development, as is the duque's hat. It also points up the importance
of social, as well as individual, identification. That the child's own
mother only recognizes the clothes and not the baby is, on the one
hand, somewhat realistic (given the relative indistinctness of any
baby's features), but it is also very penetrating and apt as a thematic
echo of the issue that lies at the heart of the *novela*. When the entire
story reaches its necessary resolution, all details—clothes, persons,
promises—will be returned to their proper places or fittingly
clarified. In the meantime, we are still in a world of haste, impulsive
action, nocturnal darkness, and ambiguity.

The sudden appearance, at this point, of Cornelia's brother
Lorenzo (II, 256) complicates the plot, of course. But it also thrusts
the two Spaniards further into the position of intermediaries. In
terms of what Lorenzo represents structurally and thematically, the
brother—although active and very much present in the story
itself—serves as the counterpart to the duque's mother. He represents, in more than one sense, the interests and identity of the
Bentibolli family. Lorenzo's arrival at the residence of the two
Spanish students causes acute fear and anxiety for Cornelia; as she
exclaims, "Sin duda debe de haber sabido que estoy aquí, y viene a
quitarme la vida; ¡socorro, señores, y amparo!" (II, 256). Lorenzo, as
we already suspect on the basis of the violent street encounter with
the duque, is taken by Cornelia to be the agent of a punishment to be
visited upon her for the *deshonra* of the woman's liaison with the
duque. Lorenzo is the sole representative and embodiment of the
family ("Quedé huérfano algunos años ha, y quedó en mi poder una
mi hermana"), and he does indeed come with the mission of
avenging a perceived dishonor. As Lorenzo understands the matter,
the duque cynically deceived his sister: "Finalmente, por acortar, por
no cansaros este que pudiera ser cuento largo, digo que el duque de
Ferrara, Alfonso de Este, con ojos de lince venció a los de Argos,
derribó y triunfó de mi industria venciendo a mi hermana, y anoche
me la llevó y sacó de casa de una parienta nuestra, y aun dicen que

recién parida" (II, 257).[22] Lorenzo continues his narration, and it is interesting that not only is he concerned about his sister's dishonor; he is also sensitive to the issue of differences in wealth and social standing:

> Hame dicho mi parienta, que es la que todo esto me ha dicho, que el duque engañó a mi hermana debajo de palabra de recebirla por mujer. Esto yo no lo creo, por ser *desigual el matrimonio en cuanto a los bienes de fortuna*, que en los de naturaleza el mundo sabe la calidad de los Bentibollis de Bolonia. Lo que creo es que él se atuvo a lo que se atienen los poderosos que quieren atropellar [a] una doncella temerosa y recatada, poniéndole a la vista el dulce nombre de esposo, haciéndola creer que por ciertos respectos no se desposa luego; mentiras aparentes de verdades, pero falsas y malintencionadas. (II, 257; emphasis added)

Ironically, Lorenzo has it only half right: there are "ciertos respectos" that intervene and that prevent the immediate and open betrothal. As will be pointed out by the duque later (II, 265), the impediment is linked to the "desigualdad" of the match itself. But at this point, Lorenzo's main focus is the element of insincerity, the "engaño" of the whole business, from which the taking of the woman's honor was made possible. Such behavior on the part of the duque—or anyone—demands retribution, as far as Lorenzo (which is to say, the Bentibolli family) is concerned.

We then learn that Lorenzo's arrival at the residence of don Juan and don Antonio is not occasioned by a search for Cornelia. Rather, he has come to ask don Juan to be his second in his planned challenge and duel with the duque. As Lorenzo expresses it, the mere fact that this stranger is Spanish is sufficient assurance that don Juan will be an effective and trustworthy second: "confiado en que lo haréis por ser español y caballero, como ya estoy informado" (II,

---

[22] Following immediately upon the above passage, Lorenzo makes the second of the references to the two Spaniards as "angels": "Anoche lo supe, y anoche le salí a buscar, y creo que le hallé y acuchillé; pero fue socorrido de *algún ángel*, que no consintió que con su sangre sacase la mancha de mi agravio" (II, 257; emphasis added). Of course, Lorenzo is speaking to this same "ángel" in the person of don Juan.

258). With this connection established between Lorenzo and don Juan, the latter is now able to be the advocate for both parties, Lorenzo and Ferrara. Thus when the two go off to find the duque, don Juan will be able to serve not as the duelist's second but as the fortunate mediator. The actual scene of the encounter on the road between Lorenzo and the duque is somewhat strange; first, the duque recognizes don Juan from a distance because of the diamond-studded hat. Then, don Juan is able to keep the two men apart, so that he can speak to each one separately (II, 264-66), in effect connecting and negotiating. When he explains to the duque the substance of Lorenzo's complaint, this gives Ferrara the chance to reaffirm his honorable commitment to Cornelia and also to indicate what the core problem has been. The duque states in part that

> yo no he engañado ni sacado a Cornelia, aunque sé que falta de la casa que dice; . . . si públicamente no celebré mis desposorios fue porque aguardaba que mi madre (que está ya en lo último) pasase désta a mejor vida, que tiene deseo que sea mi esposa la señora Livia, hija del duque de Mantua, y por otros inconvenientes quizá más eficaces que los dichos, y no conviene que ahora se digan. Lo que pasa es que la noche que me socorristes la había de traer a Ferrara, porque estaba ya en el mes de dar a luz la prenda que ordenó el cielo que en ella depositase; . . . (II, 265)

Somehow all of this, the duque's explanations and his sincerely expressed sentiments, is found to be acceptable. Thanks to the intervention of don Juan and thanks to the sense of trust and honor that he instills in both men, the case of Cornelia and the duque now comes into focus. It almost seems as if, without the agency of don Juan, this outcome would not have been possible. Most of all, the duque is able to make the sincerity of his and Cornelia's love and commitment convincing and acceptable to the woman's brother.

The emotional, tearful encounter of Lorenzo and the duque (II, 266-27) brings this antagonistic element of the story to a harmonious resolution. But the full resolution, the restoration of social order and the creation of the symbolic new family, has yet to be accomplished. Cornelia, still fearing that all is not well between her brother and the duque, and quite upset by the alarming and misleading imaginings of the housekeeper, has left the Spaniards' residence and fled to the home of a priest, known and trusted by the housekeeper; the priest will turn out to be a friend of the duque. But the significant aspect of this slight postponement of final and total resolution is the occasion that it gives for the insertion of a counter-current of unromantic and slightly roguish elements. The *novela* has heretofore portrayed a world of aristocratic persons, slightly melodramatic and improbable complications, supposedly sincere and intense love, problems of honor, and so on. Yet, alongside and within this serious, idealized world of the aristocratic and the semi-chivalric, there is the world of servants and rogues. The more complete insinuation of this world and its language into the story comes first by way of the *ama* (II, 261-62). After don Juan, Lorenzo, and don Antonio have all left the house, Cornelia confides in the housekeeper, telling her the whole story. In response, the *ama* becomes alarmist and rather disloyal to her two masters ("Oyendo lo cual el ama—como si el demonio se lo mandara, para intrincar, estorbar o dilatar el remedio de Cornelia— . . . " [II, 261]). After telling Cornelia that the whole business of Lorenzo and don Juan going to Ferrara is a ruse and that Lorenzo will return and kill his sister, the housekeeper goes on to undermine all confidence in the two Spaniards. Significantly, she first shifts attention to the reality of the level of the servants:

> Mirá debajo de qué guarda y amparo quedamos sino en la de tres pajes, que harto tienen ellos que hacer en rascarse la sarna de que están llenos que en meterse en dibujos; a los menos, de mí sé decir que no tendré ánimo para esperar el suceso y ruina que a esta casa amenaza. ¡El señor Lorenzo, italiano, y que se fíe de españoles, y les pida favor y ayuda! Para mi ojo si tal crea —y diose ella misma una higa —; si vos, hija mía, quisiéredes tomar mi consejo, yo os le daría tal que os luciese. (II, 262)

The housekeeper's bizarre suspicions not only frighten Cornelia into deciding to flee to the priest's house; they also serve to cast a different and much more negative light on the two foreign students. In effect, the putative honorableness of *los españoles* is turned on its head, and the element of sexual integrity and trust is comically but disturbingly underlined. As the *ama* puts it,

Y ya, señora, que presupongamos que has de ser hallada, mejor será que te hallen en casa de un sacerdote de misa, viejo y honrado, que en poder de dos estudiantes, mozos y españoles, que los tales, como soy buen testigo, no desechan ripio. Y agora, señora, como estás mala, te han guardado respecto; pero si sanas y convaleces en su poder, Dios lo podrá remediar, porque en verdad que si a mí no me hubieran guardado mis repulsas, desdenes y enterezas, ya hubieran dado conmigo y con mi honra al traste; porque no es todo oro lo que en ellos reluce; . . . (II, 262-63)

Whether or not the housekeeper's fears are well founded, we are inescapably reminded of the human—sexual—possibilities that shadow, test, or contradict the comforting assumptions of the virtue and restraint supposedly inherent to the sphere of idealized aristocracy and chaste love.

The suspicion cast upon the two Spaniards, however, is not as important as the fact that the housekeeper's alarming tirade opens up a window on the low-life, roguish aspects of a larger world, a world that contains aristocrats, but of which Cornelia, the duque, don Juan and don Antonio, and their respective affairs are only one part. This sector—with the allusion to mangy pages and opportunistic sexual aggressions—is radically different from the imaginable and perhaps imaginary sphere of beautiful, high-born ladies and gallant, noble gentlemen motivated only by the best values of love and honor. The texture of the ama's language itself clashes colorfully and effectively with the tone heretofore established by the narrator and in the speeches of the principal characters. We are reminded of similar interweavings of discourse and the complex relationships of language to social subworlds, as noted in such novelas as Rinconete y Cortadillo or La ilustre fregona.[23]

The more complex, morally questionable, and possibly scandalous social dimensions introduced here return toward the end of the novela in the form of two supposedly comic but frankly disturb-

---

[23] See Chapters Three and Eight above; the question of languages and society, considered from a quite different angle, and the issue of the picaresque or roguish dimension of the Cervantine vision will be dealt with in Chapter Ten.

ing *burlas* or cases of mistaken identity. The first case of confusion is based on the coincidence of the name (Cornelia) shared by both the heroine and another woman, one of a very different sort. When don Antonio arrives back at his residence, hoping to prepare Cornelia for the happy news of the resolution of the discord between her brother and her fiancé, he finds that Cornelia is gone. Don Juan and Lorenzo then arrive, and perplexed over the absence of Cornelia, the three men are told by one of the pages that "Santisteban, el paje del señor don Juan, desde el día que vuesas mercedes se fueron tiene una mujer muy bonita encerrada en su aposento, y yo creo que se llama Cornelia, que así la he oído llamar" (II, 269). This news causes the men great consternation. In effect, they fear that the mentioned woman may in fact be the *señora* Cornelia ("Alborotóse de nuevo don Antonio, y más quisiera que no hubiera parecido Cornelia, que sin duda pensó que era la que el paje tenía escondida, que no que la hallaran en tal lugar" [II, 269]). However, the woman surreptitiously ensconced with Santisteban is not the noblewoman, but rather a most ignoble woman. First, don Antonio calls through the door, thinking that it is the lady Bentibolli: "Abrid, señora Cornelia, y salid a recebir a vuestro hermano y al duque vuestro esposo, que vienen a buscaros." To which the woman on the other side of the door replies "¿Hacen burla de mí? Pues en verdad que no soy tan fea ni desechada que no podían buscarme duques y condes, y eso se merece la presona que trata con pajes" (II, 269). Don Antonio thus realizes that this is not Cornelia Bentibolli. But before he can bring this fact to the attention of his companions, the first page, evidently with a certain malicious intent, runs downstairs and perpetrates the same deception on the duque. The duque eagerly ascends the stairs, expecting to find his beloved; entering the room, he calls out

> —¿Dónde está Cornelia, dónde está la vida de la vida mía?
> —Aquí está Cornelia —respondió una mujer que estaba envuelta en una sábana de la cama y cubierto el rostro, y prosiguió diciendo—: ¡Válamos Dios! ¿Es éste algún buey de hurto? ¿Es cosa nueva dormir una mujer con un paje, para hacer tantos milagrones?
> Lorenzo, que estaba presente, con despecho y cólera tiró de un cabo de la sábana y descubrió una mujer moza y no de mal parecer, la cual, de

vergüenza, se puso las manos delante del rostro y acudió a tomar sus vestidos, que le servían de almohada, porque la cama no la tenía, y en ellos vieron que debía de ser alguna pícara de las perdidas del mundo. (II, 270)

The mistake of identity and the fact that the other Cornelia is a prostitute might be seen as little more than comic relief. It does serve as an amusing dilatory device, a postponement of the final reunion of the two lovers and the resolution of the conflicts and misunderstandings with which the story began. But this mistake of identity also prompts the question of what a name really means, how—or if—a name distinguishes persons. And if not by a name, how then is one person granted a certain distinction? The woman in Santisteban's room is, after all, nothing more nor less than a woman. As such, her essential human worth is surely as valid as that of any other woman. However, in the eyes of those sensitive to social hierarchy, the obvious difference in roles and social rank between the two Cornelias "reassures" the reader that this other woman has no relationship whatsoever to the aristocratic lady and her world. It is totally conventional, in Cervantes's writings and in the literature of his epoch, to relegate the lower classes, without irony or question, to a realm of human interactions untouched by the finer sentiments. But the sexuality of the common, putatively coarse man and woman, page and prostitute, reminds us that the love affair of the duque and the noble lady also has its physical dimension. And while one woman is nominally from a higher social rank, does not the mere coincidence of the name remind us that both are, finally, only women and that little more than an accident of birth has conferred virtue on one and denied it to the other?

The second incident of mistaken identity is basically a joke perpetrated by the duque, a strange and perhaps gratuitous provocation that, as in the case of the prostitute Cornelia, brushes the borders of a breach of decorum. After the final emotional encounter of Ferrara and Cornelia at the priest's house (marked by the duque's inexplicable, sudden, and wordless exit from the room, after first seeing Cornelia and the baby, and then his equally abrupt return), the duque sends for Lorenzo, don Juan, and don Antonio. The three men, who have been in Bolonia and still do not know Cornelia's whereabouts or the happy reunion, arrive at the duque's residence in Ferrara, and at this point the duque engages in a curious deception. In a move that very slightly recalls the "graciosa burla" of dangerously Turkish disguising near the end of *El amante liberal*, the duque announces to the three men that Cornelia has not appeared and that he therefore has decided to marry another woman. As the duque states,

> [Cornelia] no parece y mi palabra no ha de ser eterna. Yo soy mozo, y no tan experto en las cosas del mundo que no me deje llevar de las que me ofrece el deleite a cada paso. La misma afición que me hizo prometer ser esposo de Cornelia me llevó también a dar antes que a ella palabra de matrimonio a una labradora desta aldea, a quien pensaba dejar burlada por acudir al valor de Cornelia, aunque no acudiera a lo que la conciencia me pedía, que no fuera pequeña muestra de amor. Pero pues nadie se casa con mujer que no parece, ni es cosa puesta en razón que nadie busque la mujer que le deja por no hallar la prenda que le aborrece, digo que veáis, señor Lorenzo, qué satisfac[c]ión puedo daros del agravio que no os hice, pues jamás tuve intención de hacérosle, y luego quiero que me deis licencia para cumplir mi primera palabra y desposarme con la labradora, que ya está dentro desta casa. (II, 275)

This section of the duque's slightly cruel little deception is interesting for several reasons. For one thing, the duque feigns a kind of unworldly inexperience ("soy mozo, y no tan experto en las cosas del mundo") as a way of justifying what he claims is his impulsive inconstancy. In effect, he implicitly justifies amorous and sexual impulsiveness: this is what young and inexperienced men do. Secondly, the duque's fiction of a prior dalliance (the promise of marriage to "una labradora desta aldea") is both an eerie echo of don Fernando's behavior toward Dorotea in *Don Quijote*, Part I, and also reminds us of the hurtful duplicity of Marco Antonio in *Las dos doncellas*. The duque de Ferrara's provocative and cruel fiction, thus, plays with the more serious and damaging versions of the two-timing and mendacious male aristocrat whom we have met, under various names and in several contexts.

The duque's strange and offensive *burla* has the anticipated effect, angering Lorenzo, don Juan, and don Antonio. But before real trouble can happen, Ferrara goes into the next room and brings Cornelia out to meet her brother and the two Spaniards. Once again, happiness is shared all around, and the duque's joke is approved. As the narrator puts it, "Don Juan y don Antonio dijeron al duque que había sido la más discreta y más sabrosa burla del mundo" (II, 276). But the reader is prompted to wonder wherein lie the witty and delicious elements of this strange prank. The duque reiterates the concept of "labradora" when, as he presents Cornelia and his son to the three men, he says "Recebid, señor hermano, a vuestro sobrino y mi hijo, y ved si queréis darme licencia que me case con esta labradora, que es la primera a quien he dado palabra de casamiento" (II, 276). The concept of the country girl ("labradora"), now relieved of its function as provocation and deception, here takes on a metaphoric quality, almost as if it were an allusion to the pastoral ideal. Ostensibly ironic, it is, however, a term that does not quite accord with the true social position or character of the duque's beloved. Directly, it signals a very different world; implicitly and indirectly, however, it reminds us of the essentially unequal nature of the match between the house of Ferrara and the lower-ranked family of the Bentibolli's.

The *novela* ends happily for all, of course, but not without yet another curious touch, reminding us of the power and dissonances of the social order and implicit values that the story celebrates. As the text puts it, "la duquesa [Ferrara's mother] murió, Cornelia entró en Ferrara, alegrando al mundo con su vista, los lutos se volvieron en galas, las amas quedaron ricas, Sulpicia por mujer de Fabio, don Antonio y don Juan contentísimos de haber servido en algo al duque, el cual les ofreció dos primas suyas por mujeres con riquísima dote" (II, 276). The conventional and necessary comedic ending requires marriage, or marriages, as we have seen many times before. Here, however, the *novela* adds the intriguing detail that the duque, in a gesture of supposed generosity, offers the two helpful Spaniards a couple of his own cousins for wives. As if the women were available, disposable goods—like the "riquísima dote" of *La española inglesa*—which, we now are jolted into remembering, women in fact so often were in the culture and society of Cervantes's time.

Don Juan and don Antonio politely decline the duque's offer ("Ellos dijeron que los caballeros de la nación vizcaína por la mayor parte se casaban en su patria; . . . " [II, 276-77]), but the story ends on a note of general harmony distinguished by numerous marriages. What the resolution of this particular *novela*, the details of its action, and the agencies of reestablished harmony all suggest, however, is that the world of the privileged has certain capabilities, a peculiar license to err and manipulate. The melodramatic love entanglement of the duque and Cornelia are simultaneously affecting and more than a little banal. An aristocratic matriarch, having another match in mind, implicitly prevents her son's marriage to a woman of lesser rank. The son vacillates, falls in love with and seduces this disapproved woman. Pregnancy and the ire of the woman's brother ensue. The mother conveniently dies and the young aristocrat finds his voice, as it were, articulating his true sentiments, and all problems and acrimonies are overcome. What in *Las dos doncellas* leads to a situation of crisis and tension, to a dangerous transgressing of boundaries and decorum, the near-death condition of Marco Antonio, and the devastating rejection of Leocadia (only to a certain extent redeemed by don Rafael's profession of love), is in *La señora Cornelia* reduced to the smaller orbit of domestic intrigue, curiously extenuated pathos, and almost farcical, low-comic intrusions that both contrast with and slyly satirize the principal concerns of two noble but perhaps maladroit lovers. These intrusions and the peculiarly central yet uncommitted role and agency of don Juan and don Antonio make of this *novela* a text that is more plausible and yet less idealizing than *Las dos doncellas*. Both *novelas*, however, are in implicit accord when it comes to the issue of the necessity of the marriage resolution and also in terms of their values. In each text, the device of the resolving marriages (the signal of future concord and of social renewal) and the clear implication of the two stories—i.e., that nobility of rank ultimately allows one to redeem one's errors and indiscretions—fall comfortably within the conventions and tendencies of those Cervantine *novelas* in which the questions of love, identity, and social harmony can be answered in an affirmative way. Does love always triumph? Can any and all (male) transgression be absolved? Where aristocratic values are at issue, the answer is all but invariably yes. But love is not always the issue, and identity and social order have taken and will take other forms. This will be the challenge and the map of our reading in the concluding *novelas*: *El casamiento engañoso* and *El coloquio de los perros*.

Chapter Ten
Confession, Commentary, and the End of Fiction
El casamiento engañoso and *El coloquio de los perros*

Cervantes concludes his excursion through worlds of reality and imagination with a pair of *novelas* that constitute in fact a single double-tiered work. With the *Casamiento* and the *Coloquio*, the question of unity versus separability, the relationship of the frame tale to the included dialogue, is not just a curiosity of literary-critical debate. Rather, with these two texts, the ambiguity of textual connection versus independence lies at the heart of the work's theme: the nature of fiction, reading, and narrative form. The text has, however, been dealt with as two separate units. Especially with the *Coloquio*, one might limit an analysis to just one part of the whole.[1] Either section can be read, superficially, as coherent and sufficiently independent. The *Casamiento* at first appears to be a subtle but conventional tale of mutual swindling, while the *Coloquio* begins as the recounting of a quasi-picaresque life by means of the self-conscious, critically filtering medium of dialogue.

But the *Casamiento* and the *Coloquio* must be read as a unit, not only for the obvious reason that Cervantes implicitly leads us in that direction—having inserted one within the other, with the first serving as the frame tale of the second—but also for larger thematic and conceptual reasons. As El Saffar has argued, neither *novela* quite

---

[1] See for example J. Rodríguez-Luis, *Novedad y ejemplo*, in which he treats the two parts separately, the *Coloquio* in his vol. I, 211-50, and the *Casamiento* in vol. II, 39-53. As this critic notes, "A mi ver, sin embargo, la necesidad de explicar tan sutilmente la relación entre ambas novelas subraya su independencia mutua, o cómo, de no existir el epílogo de la historia de su matrimonio en que cuenta Campuzano a Peralta que escuchó y puso por escrito el curioso coloquio, la existencia de una novela no implica en modo alguno la de la anterior o la de la siguiente" (vol. I, 212).

makes sense without the other.[2] The movement through the *Casamiento*, then into the aptly titled *Novela y coloquio*, and finally back to the level of Campuzano and Peralta demonstrates how and to what extent the full text demands and justifies its claim to unity as a complex narrative essentially about reading.[3] Given this aspect of thematic focus and the nature of the text's structure, the *Casamiento/Coloquio* not only stands above the foregoing ten *novelas* by virtue of its density, but also returns us as more informed and critical readers of these same prior texts. It teaches us how to reread. Finally, the play of ambiguities in this closing text brings us back to the beginning, to the "Prólogo" itself and the purposes of the activity of *novelar*. Between the prologue and the last *novela*, then, we begin to perceive the outlines of the missing master frame tale of the whole collection.

The complexity of this double *novela* has provoked, as might be expected, an immense amount of scholarly study.[4] Among the scholars and critics who have dealt with this text, this double *novela* has prompted critical essays of remarkable penetration and quality.[5]

---

[2] See *Novel to Romance*, especially 68-72. As El Saffar notes, "The *Casamiento engañoso* is so clearly oriented toward the *Coloquio de los perros* that it is difficult to say much more about it in isolation from the story it appears designed to frame. For surrounding the *Coloquio* and the *Casamiento* is another story narrated in the third person. An unnamed narrator introduces the weak-legged and yellowed Ensign at the beginning of the *Casamiento*, and seals the *Coloquio* by telling of the Licenciate's approval of the story's artifice and invention. This unnamed narrator's presence adds yet another narrational layer to the double novela and makes a unity out of their separateness" (72).

[3] Various critics have dealt with this element of the *novela*, but perhaps the most ambitious approach of this sort is offered by M. Nerlich, "On the Philosophical Dimension of *El casamiento engañoso* and *El coloquio de los perros*," *Cervantes's 'Exemplary Novels' and the Adventure of Writing*, 247-329.

[4] The present reading is much indebted to the following studies: Casalduero, *Sentido y forma*, 237-63; El Saffar, *Novel to Romance*, 62-82, and also her monographic study, *Cervantes: El casamiento engañoso and El coloquio de los perros*; Forcione, *Cervantes and the Mystery of Lawlessness*; M. Molho's Introduction ("Remarques") to his edition and translation of the text, 11-88; and T. R. Hart, "Renaissance Dialogue into Novella: *El coloquio de los perros*," *Cervantes' Exemplary Fictions*, 97-109.

[5] Forcione's study (*Cervantes and the Mystery of Lawlessness*) must rank as the

In its philosophical and metafictional implications, the *Casamiento/Coloquio* is second only to the *Quijote* in terms of the significant and probing critical questions that it has inspired. While the *Casamiento/Coloquio* echoes and at times alludes to the problems and themes of the other *novelas* of the collection, it is not really like any of the others. In the context of the central issues that have motivated and shaped my own approach to the *Novelas* in the previous chapters—the themes of identity, language, and social order—the *Casamiento/Coloquio* offers a complex meditation on the limits and ethical responsibility of language and a penetrating exploration of identity as both deceptive device and symbolic mystery, while revealing Cervantes's most troubling vision of society and human interaction. A complex play of mis-read identities underlies the action and the ulterior themes of the *Casamiento*, as does the question of the dogs' possibly human or magical identity in the *Coloquio*. Likewise, both texts are deeply imbued with a sense of social order and the disorder that threatens it. In particular Berganza's autobiographical stories and the two dogs' dissection of their own discourse are emphatically concerned with social issues. But, as is the case with other critical approaches to this text, something seems to elude the ability of the critical discussion to explain and contain this work. The *Casamiento/Coloquio* absorbs and then transcends our attempts to read and explicate. While it shares with its predecessors the essential though superficial character of the text that merely tells a story (or set of stories, in the case of the *Coloquio*), this concluding text raises to the highest level, and explores as none of the others does, the nature of telling itself. The *Casamiento/Coloquio* is a text for which "stories" are a pretext. It is about narrative and imaginative authority, about the art of reading, the problem of writing, and (as I have explored in another but related context) the diseases of telling.[6]

---

touchstone for all subsequent treatments of this text; at the same time, I find El Saffar's monographic study and Molho's introduction quite unsurpassed for incisive clarity and inventiveness of reading.

[6] See my study "The *Quijote*, the 'Curioso,' and the Diseases of Telling," *Revista de Estudios Hispánicos* 28 (1994): 378-93.

The *Casamiento/Coloquio* is the most portentous and compelling *novela* of the collection. While not necessarily the most difficult, it is surely most significant in its implications. One reads the *Casamiento/Coloquio* with a sense of confusion and awe similar to that with which one reads the more perplexing of the foregoing *novelas*, but in this case, the sense of mystery is raised to a greater intensity. Our readings and interpretations of this double *novela* are saturated and haunted by the magisterial readings already established in those signal texts of the critical tradition. But even without a knowledge of such prior critical explorations, and as the very first readers of the *Novelas ejemplares* would have experienced, it is impossible to read the *Casamiento* and the *Coloquio* without a sense of the larger problem of prior readings and of critique and judgment. The text itself problematizes the issue of writing and reading, of telling and listening, the ethics of narrative, and the moral burden of assimilating and judging what one hears and reads. In the face of this ultimate master text, one is denied the possibility of an innocent reading and perhaps of innocence itself.[7]

It is not obvious at the opening of the *Casamiento engañoso* that this ostensibly conventional, uncomplicated *novela* of swindling, self-deluding vanities, and different types of imposture is really about something quite distinct. We only begin to realize, in the final passages of the *Casamiento* section (before the segue to the *Coloquio*), and then more fully appreciate at the end of the whole unit, that while the total text may contain "stories," it is really *about* the question of language and knowledge, fiction and authority. Likewise, although marriage is in the title and a marriage provokes Campuzano's medical and economic problems, the *Casamiento* is not really about marriage, or the marriage plot.[8] Rather, as in certain

---

[7] See M. Molho, "Remarques," especially 69-88; also C. Mazzucco, "The Doorways to the Maelstrom of Discourse in Cervantes's *El casamiento engañoso* and *El coloquio de los perros*," *Romance Languages Annual* 4 (1992): 516-20.

[8] See Sears, *A Marriage of Convenience*. Sears touches on the *Casamiento* and *Coloquio* in various passages of her study, but it is clear that the deeper ideological questions embodied in the institution of marriage that form the focus of her study are not

extended episodes of the picaresque classics, Campuzano's brief marriage to doña Estefanía serves to expose the deep corruptions (be they comic or pathetic) to which social institutions and the human trust upon which they must be based are prone. Campuzano's marriage is a swift and exemplary unmasking of greed and the extent to which greed and self-delusion tend to create their own placement and punishment.

The *Casamiento* section of this double *novela* is thoroughly saturated with a sense of irony and self-conscious discrimination. In a word, it deals with retrospective critique and judgment. The narrative moment of the *Casamiento*—and by extension, of the entire text—is a hypothetical present-future time, from the perspective of which both Campuzano's disastrous marriage and the canine colloquy (and thus the "life" recounted within the latter) are a fictional, or historical, past. This in itself is not unusual: the moment of narration is always already retrospective. Rather, what is significant are the details and circumstances deployed around the central presentation of first one story and then another. The ensign Campuzano emerges from a hospital, having suffered through the mind-altering experiences of disease and cure. Although Campuzano's case of syphilis might seem worthy only of relegation to the level of yet another comic-grotesque detail (a poetically just intensification of his punishment for greed and folly), his venereal disease is especially appropriate to the question of the telling of tales. The ignominy of his victimization in and through the marriage would, in itself, have justified the compulsion to tell a story. But the addition of this medical aftermath, the diseased souvenir of greed and sexual, sensual indulgence, makes the need to explain his case, to contextualize the shameful history, even more urgent. Campuzano's disease, moreover, is not only his punishment. It is also his reason for being in the hospital. Thus it represents his bridge to the

---

dealt with by Cervantes in these final texts. Sears points out quite succinctly the more self-consciously literary and critical focus of this text in her sixth chapter; see especially 183ff.

revelation—or fantasy—of the dogs' dialogue. Venereal disease, grotesquely but fittingly, becomes the metaphor for the problem and challenge of the art of fiction.

Campuzano's emergence from the aptly named Hospital de la Resurrección is both a restoration and a presentation of the transformed and chastened man. The first sentence is memorable in its bluntness and bitter humor: "Salía del Hospital de la Resurrección, que está en Valladolid, fuera de la Puerta del Campo, un soldado que, por servirle su espada de báculo y por la flaqueza de sus piernas y amarillez de su rostro, mostraba bien claro que, aunque no era el tiempo muy caluroso, debía de haber sudado en veinte días todo el humor que quizá granjeó en una hora" (II, 281). His changed and ruined appearance startles his friend Peralta ("el cual, santigüándose, como si viera alguna mala visión"), and this—the ravages of disease—more than anything else prompts the *licenciado*'s curiosity and the ensign's desire to tell. The dialogue of the two men then ensues. Peralta's question "¿Qué color, qué flaqueza es ésa?" elicits Campuzano's explanation that, in part, "salgo de aquel hospital, de sudar catorce cargas de bubas que me echó a cuestas una mujer que escogí por mía, que non debiera" (II, 282). The witty exchange between the two men immediately fixes upon the questions of marriage, love, and disease in a manner that reverses and thwarts the expectations and conventions of those previous *novelas* in which idealized love leads to happy, affirmative, and often restorative marriage. As Peralta comments, in reply to Campuzano's admission that he did indeed marry, "Sería por amores . . . y tales casamientos traen consigo aparejada la ejecución del arrepentimiento" (II, 282). But if love itself is wittily, perhaps bitterly, banished from the subworld of the ensign and the licenciate, the compulsion to tell and hear stories, to write and read, is not. Campuzano's reply to Peralta's foregoing remark starts with a view of his "caso," but it quickly evolves into a suspenseful, seductive invitation:

> —No sabré decir si fue por amores —respondió el Alférez—, aunque sabré afirmar que fue por dolores, pues de mi casamiento, o cansamiento, saqué tantos en el cuerpo y en el alma, que los del cuerpo, para entre-

tenerlos, me cuestan cuarenta sudores, y los del alma no hallo remedio
para aliviarlos siquiera. Pero porque no estoy para tener largas pláticas
en la calle, vuesa merced me perdone; que otro día con más comodidad le
daré cuenta de mis sucesos, que son los más nuevos y peregrinos que
vuesa merced habrá oído en todos los días de su vida. (II, 282)

Campuzano begins with verbal games ("amores" vs. "dolores";
"casamiento" playing against "cansamiento") that hardly enhance or
elicit the pathos or sympathy usually sought after in such cases. He
then slyly moves to the tease, the promise of future telling, of
"sucesos . . . más nuevos y peregrinos." Thus we are from the first
aware that this putative victim is also an artificer, a player and
manipulator of wit and *récit*.

Campuzano's account (II, 283ff) of his misbegotten adventure
with doña Estefanía works a subtle but telling variation on the
conventional device of love (or, as in the case of the first encounter
in *La fuerza de la sangre*, lust) at first sight. Sight is involved, but it is
a distorted, literally veiled perception, a first encounter in which
curiosity plays a greater role than the romantic and "romanticized"
display of female beauty that is usually presented in the form of the
face. As Campuzano presents the episode, the question of this
particular woman's identity—and the very concept of identity as
such—is underscored as being fundamentally ambiguous: "la otra se
sentó en una silla junto a mí, derribado el manto hasta la barba, sin
dejar ver el rostro más de aquello que concedía la raridad del manto;
y aunque le supliqué que por cortesía me hiciese merced de des-
cubrirse, no fue posible acabarlo con ella, cosa que me encendió más
el deseo de verla" (II, 283). That the face—the usual overture to a
sentimental interest, as well as the conventional symbol of both
beauty and communication (visual, vocal, auditory)—is so deliberately obscured already suggests that both identity and conversation
will be simultaneously central and problematic. Above all, we
suspect that they will be the products of artifice.

The *Casamiento* section of the *novela* places special emphasis on
language and the image of hands, which in turn reminds us of the
interlinked concepts of gesture and manipulation, of theft and the

"underhanded."   For the unfortunate, though hardly innocent, Campuzano, doña Estefanía's hands are a prime device of her deceitful stratagem.   As we are reminded, speaking of his curiosity and desire to see the woman's face, Campuzano states that "para acrecentarle más, o ya fuese de industria [o] acaso, sacó la señora una muy blanca mano, con muy buenas sortijas" (II, 283).   The woman thus reveals only a small, if symbolic and "promising," part of the whole.   The prominence of the hand intensifies, by contrast with the concealed face, the man's desire.   The exposed, ring-adorned hand beckons.   Campuzano quickly emphasizes his own folly and vanity, particularly the self-serving and self-regarding narcissism of his comportment.[9] But it is clear from the beginning—and in all fairness, retrospectively quite plausible—that the man's interest is largely spurred by curiosity.

Doña Estefanía, of course, manages to get Campuzano "hooked" into her strategy of deception and desire.   In the figure of doña Estefanía Cervantes has dramatized in a most telling way the problem of a fluctuating, enigmatic, and yet thematically revealing identity.   Estefanía might at first almost remind us of the nameless "dama de todo rumbo y manejo" whose sincere though irrational and unrequited love for the hapless Tomás Rodaja drives her to the destructive expedient of a love potion that misfires and renders the youth temporarily insane (see Chapter Five, above).   But doña Estefanía is neither irrational nor in love.   While she may seem to share with the shady lady of *El licenciado Vidriera* a certain mysterious past and a mobility, social and geographic, well lubricated by a casual sense of virtue, Campuzano's wife-to-be is not a victim of her own, or anyone else's, passions.   She is, rather, an artist, a certain kind of swindler for whom the techniques of *engaño* have been refined to the level of art.[10]

---

[9] As Campuzano himself puts it, "Estaba yo entonces bizarrísimo, con aquella gran cadena que vuesa merced debió de conocerme, el sombrero con plumas y cintillo, el vestido de colores, a fuer de soldado, y *tan gallardo a los ojos de mi locura*, que me daba a entender que las podía matar en el aire" (II, 283-84; emphasis added).

[10] The suggestion of a connection between the profession, or arts, of the prostitute

Like her gulled husband Campuzano, Estefanía also knows how to use and manipulate people by means of language. The extent of her artistry in this area is made plain in Campuzano's recounting of his first "unveiled," face to face meeting with the woman. When—after the woman sets up the ground rules and arranges the time and place for the meeting at what we suppose is her house—Campuzano finally sees Estefanía, he presents the scene as follows:

> Hallé una casa muy bien aderezada y una mujer de hasta treinta años, a quien conocí por las manos. No era hermosa en extremo; pero éralo de suerte que podía enamorar comunicada, porque tenía un tono de habla tan suave que se entraba por los oídos en el alma. Pasé con ella luengos y amorosos coloquios. (II, 284)

This passage is in many ways the most loaded and significant section of the entire *Casamiento* frame tale. We will later realize—but we already have reason to suspect—that Campuzano's own skills, and no doubt his own major attractions, are largely centered in the area of language. Of doing things with words, as it were. But in doña Estefanía he has not only found a match; he has clearly met his match. Her evident lack of the usual and (for a romantic story) requisite physical beauty is, so Campuzano asserts, more than compensated for by her mastery of the arts of language. The phrase "que podía enamorar comunicada" not only compliments her art and ability, but in fact characterizes precisely how the "love," or the sufficiently powerful attraction, between these two people develops. Or, we should say, how it is managed by Estefanía. The "luengos y amorosos coloquios" that ensue are, then, a combination (or so Campuzano suggests) of his own foolish detours and indulgences of vanity and of doña Estefanía's crafty, carefully restrained, and masterful ensnaring of her prey.

---

and the creator of illusory identity is not irrelevant here. The woman, or man, who serves another for what most of us would assume are merely purposes of immediate sexual gratification is also a kind of impostor and fulfiller of illusory desires and identity.

The gradual courtship or entry into this marriage of most inconvenient convenience begins, as Campuzano would have us believe, with the complex mixture of a man's short-sighted, egocentric vanity and greed and a woman's highly refined skills in the arts of language and the sensual aspects of housewifery. Their most explicit and detailed discussion of the question of marriage is curiously unsentimental. Doña Estefanía, taking more the stance of a marriage broker, presents the situation in bluntly practical terms. Her proposition is posed as essentially the pooling of material goods. Likewise, she "sells" her own housekeeping skills and seems to be frank about her checkered past. The passage merits quoting at length:

> Señor Alférez Campuzano, simplicidad sería si yo quisiera venderme a vuesa merced por santa. Pecadora he sido, y aún ahora lo soy; pero no de manera que los vecinos me murmuren ni los apartados me noten; ni de mis padres ni de otro pariente heredé hacienda alguna, y con todo esto vale el menaje de mi casa, bien validos, dos mil y quinientos escudos; y éstos, en cosas que, puestas en almoneda, lo que se tardare en ponellas se tardará en convertirse en dineros. Con esta hacienda busco marido a quien entregarme y a quien tener obediencia; a quien, juntamente con la enmienda de mi vida, le entregaré una increíble solicitud de regalarle y servirle; porque no tiene príncipe cocinero más goloso ni que mejor sepa dar el punto a los guisados que le sé dar yo, cuando, mostrando ser casera, me quiero poner a ello. Sé ser mayordomo en casa, moza en la cocina y señora en la sala; en efeto, sé mandar y sé hacer que me obedezcan. No desperdicio nada, y allego mucho; mi real no vale menos, sino mucho más cuando se gasta por mi orden. (II, 285)

The practical, materialistic focus of doña Estefanía's discourse of self-presentation is its most obvious aspect. The notion that marriage in general, and this marriage in particular, is a kind of investment opportunity is hard to overlook. This material dimension is unromantic and, in reality, such concerns have always been an important element of this social institution and its rules. What is most curious here, however, is the way in which Estefanía manipulates her victim and, in particular, her use of a fragment of truth to advance and strengthen her basic structure of deceit.[11] Her seeming frankness, along with the simple fact that she serves as her own marriage broker, preempts the possible suspicions about her past and her real motives. The fact that she admits to a sinful past serves, ironically and intentionally (on her part), to diminish the importance and the untidy implications of this obvious history of sexual indiscretion. As we might now say, doña Estefanía is very "up front" about her past, and in so doing, she is all the better able to obscure her present.

The woman's sales pitch, meanwhile, is completely successful. Through this, we are reminded that doña Estefanía is not just a sweet talker. She is a master—or mistress—of language, a corrupt but effective rhetorician. The verbal is, however, not her only "language." As various readers and critics have noticed, despite Campuzano's explicit desire and plan to sell off his new wife's ostensible *hacienda* and then move to comfortable retirement in the country, after the marriage he sinks into a kind of protracted honeymoon of indolence and sensual (especially gustatory) indulgence: "almorzaba en la cama, levantábame a las once, comía a las doce, y a las dos sesteaba en el estrado; . . . El rato que doña Estefanía faltaba de mi lado, la habían de hallar en la cocina, toda solícita en ordenar guisados que me despertasen el gusto y me avivasen el apetito" (II, 286-87). In Campuzano's case, the way to a man's heart is definitely through his stomach. What the narrative subtly achieves, meanwhile, is the further underscoring of a corruption and displacement of the faculties of sense and judgment. This emphasis echoes the confusion already stated bluntly by Campuzano himself: "Estaba yo entonces bizarrísimo, . . . y tan gallardo a los ojos de mi locura, . . . " (II, 283-84); and a bit later: "Yo, que tenía entonces el juicio, no en la cabeza, sino en los carcañares, . . . " (II, 285). The ensign begins by letting his eyes deceive him (first, the veiled face and bejewelled white hand; later, the less than prime woman herself) and by letting his narcissism contribute to his bad judgment. He

---

[11] See M. Molho, "Remarques," especially 72-75.

ends by handing over command and judgment to the realm of his body's nether regions. The prolonged dalliance in the bed at what he takes to be doña Estefanía's house is a fitting image of his "arrest" or entrapment in an intermediate space, a place of pleasure that will prove to be the site both of illusions and of a retributive sin whose consequences will only materialize later.

The core—both of its comedy and its deeper thematic exploration—of Campuzano's tale is once again the question of identity. A set of swindles is under way, of course, and the problems of judgment, corruption of the senses, sexual indulgence, and lies dominate the text. But the key question of the *Casamiento*, or at least that part devoted to Campuzano's narrative of the episode with doña Estefanía, is the question of imposture, of who one really is. Estefanía is a skilled artist of language and gestures; she plays with partial truths and, as we saw in a preceding passage, lets Campuzano know "who she is" but only to a certain extent. This is, once again, lying with the truth. Her identity as mistress of this house, as possessor of this particular estate or body of wealth, is what truly matters to Campuzano. Thus the untimely return of doña Clementa Bueso, with her fiancé don Lope and the housekeeper Hortigosa in tow, aptly brings the game of identity—specifically the question of who *is* the mistress of this particular house—back into central prominence. Despite the fact that Campuzano sees and hears with his own eyes and ears the "reality" of this deception, he continues to allow himself to be gulled by, but really incorporated into, the "story" that his wife continues to elaborate around the all-too-evident and plausible facts. Thus, Hortigosa's exclamation—"¿Qué es esto? ¿Ocupado el lecho de mi señora doña Clementa, y más con ocupación de hombre? ¡Milagros veo hoy en esta casa! ¡A fe que se ha ido bien del pie a la mano la señora Estefanía, fiada en la amistad de mi señora!" (II, 288)—fails to shake sufficiently Campuzano's credulity. As he explains to Peralta, his wife "me dijo que aquella su amiga quería hacer una burla a aquel don Lope que venía con ella, con quien pretendía casarse" (II, 288). Estefanía once again employs a partial truth to further obscure an immediate reality: there is indeed a game or *burla* of identity and rightful ownership being perpetrated for the purpose of securing a marriage. The reversability of identities, owner of the house versus the friend and house sitter, is not only an effective ploy to keep Campuzano gulled. It is also an apt figure for the larger question. Who is doña Estefanía? begs the question of Who really is Campuzano?

At this point in Campuzano's story, events—or more precisely, the revelation of truths—accelerate. Having had to decamp to a cramped garret, Campuzano and Estefanía find themselves embroiled in constant argument and conflict. Within a short time, Campuzano learns from Estefanía's putative friend that, indeed, doña Clementa is the owner of the house and that Estefanía is the fraud.[12] This sudden collapse of illusion, which does not quite register with the deluded and self-deluding man, reiterates the crucial question of identity in general and those aspects of identity most pertinent to social structure, in particular. We, of course, know that doña Estefanía is a fraud, an impostor, and that the other woman, doña Clementa Bueso is the true mistress of the house, the "authentic" lady. But the reader has to wonder about the too easy shifting and appropriation of identities in this small world of swindle, and perhaps in worlds more familiar to us.

Campuzano's tale ends (II, 292) with the wife having fled and robbed him, but having left him with her disease. Even here, however, Campuzano tempers misery with wit: "Halléme verdaderamente hecho pelón, porque ni tenía barbas que peinar ni dineros que gastar" (II, 292). Fleeced in every sense of the word, the ensign (whose own lack of innocence in this episode of mutual deceit is freely admitted) seems less bent on winning his friend's sympathy than on catching the latter's curiosity through the promise of further

---

[12] At this point, the imagery of the empty trunk (II, 290) is most telling, and it points inevitably to the corresponding irony of Campuzano's own fraudulent wealth (II, 291). The trunk, naturally, suggests a coffin—the death of the man's narcissistic illusions—but it also reminds us of the emptiness of stories and appearances promoted by disguise, clothing, gestures, and smooth talk.

stories.   To Peralta's expression of wonder and amazement at Campuzano's tale of personal misfortune, the latter replies that:

> —Pues de poco se maravilla vuesa merced, señor Peralta —dijo el Alférez—; que otros sucesos me quedan por decir que exceden a toda imaginación, pues van fuera de todos los términos de naturaleza: no quiera vuesa merced saber más sino que son de suerte que doy por bien empleadas todas mis desgracias, por haber sido parte de haberme puesto en el hospital donde vi lo que ahora diré, que es lo que ahora ni nunca vuesa merced podrá creer, ni habrá persona en el mundo que lo crea. (II, 292)

The fact that Campuzano could, even in jest, state that "doy por bien empleadas todas mis desgracias" simultaneously stretches credulity and sparks in Peralta an acute desire to know what he saw ("vi lo que ahora diré"). That a hospital would be a place of encounter for marvels of a positive sort, for wonders worth recounting to someone else, already challenges the usual assumptions.   Yet it ironically serves to ensure that Peralta will follow the lead and fall into the game or the rhetorical trap. Campuzano's story of his seduction by the deceitful and mysterious woman (as well as by his own greed) itself turns out to be a larger seduction, that of his friend Peralta, or more properly, of Peralta's curiosity and natural desire for the further pleasures of hearing or reading new narratives. Needless to say, Peralta's curiosity and seduction parallel our own.

Campuzano's orally narrated story (which is, for us, already a text) stresses its real-world plausibility. The wonder or amazement that the story supposedly causes Peralta stems in part from the improbable folly and credulousness of the man telling it. By contrast, what Campuzano, within the first or frame fiction, will now teasingly hook Peralta into is a text, which for Peralta and for us determines an act of reading. The source of this text, moreover, is, from the outset, a structure of paradoxical and endlessly elusive relationships of origin, of fictional versus "historical" authority. The manuscript that Campuzano gives Peralta to read is, so the ensign at first insists, the verbatim transcription of a conversation between two dogs that a possibly delirious and surely insomniac Campuzano overheard.[13] Slightly scandalized by the patent absurdity of Campuzano's claim, Peralta retorts "que hasta aquí estaba en duda si creería o no lo que de su casamiento me había contado, y esto que ahora me cuenta de que oyó hablar los perros me ha hecho declarar por la parte de no creelle ninguna cosa. Por amor de Dios, señor Alférez, que no cuente estos disparates a persona alguna, si ya no fuere a quien sea tan su amigo como yo" (II, 293). But the unquestioned belief of the reader or listener is not required for the story to be accepted or have its desired effect (II, 294). All that Campuzano—or any text, for that matter—demands or implicitly offers is a certain curiosity, or the satisfaction of curiosity.

What distinguishes this most subtle and memorable transition—this shift from the level and moment of the *Casamiento* to the at first textual, then immediately "present," dialogic level of the *Novela y coloquio que pasó entre Cipión y Berganza, perros del Hospital de la Resurrección*[14]—is the manner in which Campuzano both insists on the veracity of his report and yet slyly dismisses the importance of this same veracity. Campuzano neither has to win an argument (prove his outlandish assertion) nor capitulate to Peralta's flat rejection, thereby admitting his own role as creator. Rather, all he has to do is let the text be, let it speak, or be read, for itself. Campuzano's final overture to Peralta plays between these two extremes without having to settle down upon any one point. As Campuzano concludes, "Pero puesto caso que me haya engañado, y *que mi verdad sea sueño*, y el porfiarla disparate, ¿no se holgará vuesa merced, señor

---

[13] Cervantes has his character, or spokesman, introduce the moment as follows: "y es que yo oí y casi vi con mis ojos a estos dos perros, que el uno se llama Cipión y el otro Berganza, . . . estando a escuras y desvelado, pensando en mis pasados sucesos y presentes desgracias, oí hablar allí junto, y estuve con atento oído escuchando, por ver si podía venir en conocimiento de los que hablaban y de lo que hablaban, y a poco rato vine a conocer, por lo que hablaban, los que hablaban, y eran los dos perros Cipión y Berganza" (II, 293).

[14] On the implications and importance of both the title and the nature of the text itself, see L. A. Murillo, "Cervantes' *Coloquio de los perros*, A Novel-Dialogue," *Modern Philology* 58 (1961): 174-85.

Peralta, de ver escritas en un coloquio las cosas que *estos perros, o sean quien fueren*, hablaron?" (II, 294; emphasis added). Campuzano reiterates the play of ambiguities of origin, of narrative form, and of epistemological authority in his last words to Peralta as the former prepares to drift off (tellingly) into another sleep, while the licenciate reads:

> — Yo me recuesto —dijo el Alférez— en esta silla en tanto que vuesa merced lee, si quiere, esos sueños o disparates, que no tienen otra cosa de bueno si no es el poderlos dejar cuando enfaden. (II, 295)

Peralta reads, Campuzano returns to sleep, and (in effect) the reader falls into a double suspension—reading with Peralta and hallucinating retrospectively with Campuzano, listening to a pair of lucid, ludic dogs. Beginning with the obvious issue of reading, listening, and judgment, the ulterior mission of both the orally delivered story and the textually represented dialogue is Campuzano's sly and subversive lesson in how to read a strange text, both his "dream" and his artifice.

The transition from the moment of Peralta and Campuzano at the former's lodging, to the *Novela y coloquio que pasó entre Cipión y Berganza*, is unique in the context of the larger collection. It does, however, recall the transition in *Don Quijote*, Part I, from chapter 32 to chapter 33, in which the priest begins to read the *Novela del curioso impertinente*.[15] As in the case of the priest's comments at the end of his reading of the *Curioso impertinente*, the dogs' *coloquio* will raise

---

[15] As Cervantes sets up the situation in *Don Quijote*, at the end of chapter 32, the priest is persuaded by the others at the inn to read:

> —Pues desa manera —dijo el cura—, quiero leerla, por curiosidad siquiera; quizá tendrá alguna de gusto.
>
> Acudió maese Nicolás a rogarle lo mesmo, y Sancho también; lo cual visto del cura, y entendiendo que a todos daría gusto y él le recibiría, dijo:
>
> —Pues así es, esténme todos atentos; que la novela comienza desta manera:

From which the text opens immediately onto chapter 33 ("Donde se cuenta la novela del curioso impertinente"); *Don Quijote*, I, 394. Revealingly, this act of reading in *Don Quijote* is communal, out loud, while that of the *Casamiento/Coloquio* is silent and solitary.

questions about plausibility and the ethics of narrating. But in the latter case, the core concept—that dogs can and did speak—elicits especially perverse and insolubly self-referential questions about the nature of fiction and the locus of imaginative and epistemological authority. In a move that (again most teasingly) strikes us as an artificer's ploy rather than an element necessary to the construction of the story's plausible-impossible world, and in what we might call a "preemptive strike" of Campuzano's own sly devising, the colloquy begins with the dogs themselves taking up the issue of their sudden, miraculous ability to speak. Berganza answers Cipión's first wonder-struck words by noting that "óyote hablar y sé que te hablo, y no puedo creerlo, por parecerme que el hablar nosotros pasa de los términos de naturaleza" (II, 299). The dogs go on to discuss, in ways that play between ingenuousness and a bizarrely improbable and at times superfluous erudition, the basic question of speech in animals, the difference between merely mimicking human sounds and actually conversing (speaking in the concerted structures of discourse), the elusive yet wondrous gift of "reason," of human intelligence, something supposedly denied to even the most advanced members of the animal kingdom.

It might seem that, aside from a crafty and intentionally ironic look backward to the brief dispute between Campuzano and Peralta on the authenticity of the reported event, this detour on animal speech is more than a little gratuitous. The actual question about the miracle and impossibility of animal speech is partially a diversion. Yet it also touches upon the true thematic core and structural principle of this powerful and lucid, yet for many readers troubling, perplexing text. The *Casamiento* phase of this double text seems to enfold a fantasy within the "realist" recounting of a grotesque if mundane story. Yet the frame tale is really about the problem of telling and the relation of language to truth, of interpretation to meaning. Similarly, the embedded canine *Coloquio* at first appears to be a vision of, or excursion through, a world of nearly unrelieved human evil, culminating in the scene with the witch Cañizares, her grotesque body and putatively meaningful trance. But it is also—or perhaps more essentially—about the limits of language, the nature of knowledge in a work of verbal art, and the locus of imaginative authority.

Much has been made not only about the narrative content and thematic implications of the *Coloquio* (for example, the notorious critical question of whether the *Coloquio* is authentically picaresque or not), but also about the narrative structure and sequential logic of the colloquy as a whole.[16] The *Coloquio* seems to overwhelm its readers in a variety of ways. The sense of fragmentation and digression, the mixture of a linear narrative (Berganza's auto-biography) with the seemingly asymmetrical interruptions by Cipión and sometimes by Berganza himself, the interplay of an implicitly critical vision of human society and an explicitly autocritical dissection by the two dogs of their own process of telling and judging—all such elements have prompted some readers to see in this text an extreme of complexity. The embedded *Coloquio* is indeed subtle, digressive, and highly complex. But it is hardly baffling or ill organized.[17] Forcione—who, in addition, finds an extreme of the demonic in what I would class as a fairly plausible balance of familiar human treachery and vice and the occasional act of decency—states that "If we inspect the anatomy of Cervantes' literary monstrosity [the *Coloquio*] closely, we observe that it is swollen and bursting with objects, that there is tremendous variety

---

[16] In addition to the studies mentioned above by El Saffar (*Cervantes:* El casamiento engañoso *and* El coloquio de los perros) and Molho ("Remarques"), see O. Bellic, "La estructura de 'El coloquio de los perros,'" *Análisis estructural de textos hispanos,* 61-90; J. M. Pozuelo Yvancos, "Enunciación y recepción en el *Casamiento-Coloquio,*" in *Cervantes: su obra y su mundo,* 423-35; P. Waley, "The Unity of the *Casamiento engañoso* and the *Coloquio de los perros,*" BHS 34 (1957): 201-12; and L. J. Woodward, "*El casamiento engañoso y el coloquio de los perros,*" BHS 36 (1959): 80-87.
[17] On the rigor and precision of structure, see especially Molho, "Remarques." As Molho asserts, "On remarque, cependant, que toutes précautions semblent avoir été prises (et avec succès, si l'on en juge par le désarroi des exégètes) pour que la rigoureuse géométrie de l'édifice se dissimule au regard sous le tissu des propos qui paraissent s'échanger à bâtons rompus. Tout se passe, en effet, comme si la morphologie profonde de *Colloque* se voilait sous l'apparence d'une liberté, qui n'est, à vrai dire, qu'un habile trompe-l'oeil" (44).

in its substance, narrative shapes, subject matter, character types, ideas, styles, tones, and voices. Saturation and narrative chaos would appear to be its dominant general features."[18] This judgment is, to my mind, itself a bit baffling. The *Coloquio* is surely complex and varied, but it is anything but saturated and chaotic. Rather, once one recalls that Cervantes has proposed to us the simulacrum of a conversation within which one speaker, in a most realistic, plausible manner, recounts his life (with aleatory but quite convincing digressions and the occasional comment or interruption by his listener), the *Coloquio* is hard to see as anything other than an astonishingly well-organized, highly economical, and precise textual representation of its ostensible dialogic and narrative event. Frankly, I see neither chaos, confusion, nor excess in this text. Rather I find a peculiar, prismatic complexity contained in a discourse of great surface clarity. What Cervantes has created is a complex game of mirrors, illusions, and philosophical as well as narrative refractions.

What a given reader sees in or "gets out of" the text, depends to a great extent upon what philosophical baggage, generic assumptions, or thematic priorities he or she brings into the act of reading. The dogs themselves put this question into perspective, as Cipión decides that perhaps wondering about the phenomenon is less fruitful than simply accepting and taking advantage of it:

> Pero sea lo que fuere, nosotros hablamos, sea portento o no; que lo que el cielo tiene ordenado que suceda, no hay diligencia ni sabiduría humana que lo pueda prevenir; y así, no hay para qué ponernos a disputar nosotros cómo o por qué hablamos; . . . sepamos aprovecharnos della y hablemos toda esta noche, sin dar lugar al sueño que nos impida este gusto, de mí por largos tiempos deseado. (II, 301)

The curious, witty, and slightly absurd notion that the dogs had long desired to have the ability to talk is taken up immediately by

---

[18] *Cervantes and the Mystery of Lawlessness*, 22; see also Forcione's commentary, 26-35: "The Patterns of Narrative Disorder: Saturation, Variegation, Fragmentation: Dialogue as a Mode of Disarticulation" and 36-48: "The Patterns of Narrative Disorder: Dismemberment of Coherent Form Through Anticlimax and Parody: The Main Plot of the Colloquy."

Berganza: "Y aun de mí, que desde que tuve fuerzas para roer un hueso tuve deseo de hablar, para decir cosas que depositaba en la memoria, y allí, de antiguas y muchas, o se enmohecían o se me olvidaban" (II, 301). The idea that this particular dog (or any dog) has been itching to reveal and comment upon what he has seen is patently funny and absurd. It begs the question "Why?" and the related question "To whom?" These questions will be touched upon periodically in the course of Berganza's narration and Cipión's occasional interventions. But the emphasis placed upon the desire and the self-consciousness of speech simultaneously lifts this narrative far above the level of the traditional fable (in which animals may speak but usually don't wonder about it), thus rendering it more realistic yet also underlining its ambiguous self-referentiality.

In this early stage of the dialogue Cervantes's two speakers make clear their keen intention to employ the gift. But almost immediately they come up against two crucial, related issues concerning language itself: aesthetics and ethics. The first has to do with form, the consciousness of the use of language and the problems of shape and organization in the task of narration. Berganza (finishing the passage quoted above) first alludes to the problem: "pienso gozarle y aprovecharme dél lo más que pudiere, dándome priesa a decir todo aquello que se me acordare, *aunque sea atropellada y confusamente*, porque no sé cuándo me volverán a pedir este bien, que por prestado tengo" (II, 301; emphasis added). The business of well-planned, coherent order and structure is, needless to say, a problem, and many readers have fallen (as I would put it) into the craftily laid trap of seeing the structure and sequence of this section of the text as resembling the "pulpo" (be it in terms of Berganza's multiform, octopus-like additions and digressions, or in the imagery of the grotesque suggested by this animal) mentioned pejoratively by Cipión.[19] But Berganza's urgent desire to speak and his worry about

---

[19] To Cipión's insistence that Berganza cease digressing and *murmurando* ("que calles ya y sigas tu historia."), Berganza replies "¿Cómo la tengo de seguir si callo?" Prompting Cipión's much studied octopus allusion: "Quiero decir que la sigas de

jumble and confusion are not in fact the danger that he will encounter most often. If the dogs' two major concerns, as they embark on this adventure of speaking, are the aesthetic and the ethical, then it is clearly the latter issue that will most trouble and challenge them.

Cipión helps focus the ethical question, linking it to the problem of the structural and stylistic preoccupations of the speaker—or writer. After criticizing Berganza for one of his seemingly gratuitous descriptions and commentaries (in this case, on the butchers in the Matadero), Cipión says the following:

> Y quiérote advertir de una cosa, de la cual verás la experiencia cuando te cuente los sucesos de mi vida; y es que los cuentos unos encierran y tienen la gracia en ellos mismos; otros, en el modo de contarlos; quiero decir que algunos hay que aunque se cuenten sin preámbulos y ornamentos de palabras, dan contento; otros hay que es menester vestirlos de palabras, y con demostraciones del rostro y de las manos y con mudar la voz se hacen algo de nonada, y de flojos y desmayados se vuelven agudos y gustosos; y no se te olvide este advertimiento, para aprovecharte dél en lo que te queda por decir. (II, 304)

Cipión thus lays out the form vs. content problem, albeit in an oversimplified manner. In any case, we clearly sense that his comment on those stories where "es menester vestirlos" is meant as a negative criticism, a distinction of quality. The seemingly innocent remark about those stories "que aunque se cuenten sin preámbulos y ornamentos de palabras, dan contento" subtly but effectively echoes Campuzano's comment about his own stylistic decisions in the *writing* down of the dialogue (see II, 294: "lo escribí otro día, sin buscar colores retóricas para adornarlo"). Rhetoric and the ornaments and pleasures of language itself are called into question—even while, ironically, the reader and listener knows that this *novela* is deeply penetrated by a conscious sense of verbal aesthetics, the beauty of a rhetoric that eschews the conventional and superficial ornaments of language.

---

golpe, sin que la hagas que parezca pulpo, según la vas añadiendo colas" (II, 319).

But after Berganza's reply that he will try to keep to the point, Cipión continues, and with a seemingly low-key, general comment, he opens what will be the greater concern: the ethical. As Cipión advises, "Vete a la lengua, que en ella consisten los mayores daños de la humana vida" (II, 304). Quite aside from the obvious irony that "la humana vida" can (or should) only have for the dogs a distant, vicarious, and detached relevance, this comment brings up an even deeper set of ironies: language, the tongue, is a potentially dangerous faculty. To speak is thus always to run the risk of causing harm. To tell of one's life—or to report any story or history—is to enter a territory in which critical observation, and hence comment, is impossible to avoid. Is it not, after all, demanded by a loyalty to verisimilitude and the truth of events? Finally, how does one define and draw the line between acceptable critique, or the valid and useful correction of vice, and the unacceptable, abusive act of gossip and injurious back-biting?[20]

The term and preoccupation that runs through the dogs' colloquy is *murmuración*.[21] The usage of the specific terms—"murmuración," "murmurar," and "murmurador"—begins a little further into the dialogue. Berganza, after meeting up with the shepherds, thinks back one more time on his life in the Matadero and the evil doings of his former master; but he stops himself, saying "¡Oh, qué de cosas te pudiera decir ahora de las que aprendí en la escuela de aquella jifera dama de mi amo! Pero habrélas de callar, por que no me tengas por largo y por murmurador" (II, 306). This prompts Cipión's remark, linking the current problem (Berganza's impulse to digress and to

---

[20] On the dangerous and elusive line between the acceptable and the injurious, see C. Mazzucco's incisive study ("The Doorways to the Maelstrom of Discourse"); as she notes, "If prostitutes like Colindres or Estefanía suggest a venereal disease that literally and metaphorically weakens the power group through temptation to transgress the boundaries that separate the two groups, then gossip can be called the venereal disease of discourse" (518).

[21] On the concept and problem of language and satire, *murmuración*, see Forcione (*Cervantes and the Mystery of Lawlessness*), especially 170-86.

criticize) to a classical allusion and to the deeper issue of the
borderline between the proper and the hurtful:

> Por haber oído decir que un gran poeta de los antiguos que era difícil cosa
> el no escribir sátiras, consentiré que murmures un poco de luz y no de
> sangre; quiero decir que señales y no hieras ni des mate a ninguno en cosa
> señalada; que no es buena la murmuración, aunque haga reír a muchos,
> si mata a uno; y si puedes agradar sin ella, te tendré por muy discreto. (II,
> 306-07)[22]

If true wit and judgment ("discreción") lie in knowing and always
observing this limit between *señalar* and *herir*, then this will be a
boundary line of language, judgment, and tone that neither the dogs
nor their readers will ever be able to recognize with total certainty.
Like satire itself, the limits of the permissible in language and the
mere task of telling without hurting prove difficult first to determine
and then to negotiate.

The ostensible core of the *Coloquio* is Berganza's narration of his
life, from his earliest recollections up to the present moment and his
current, evidently happy situation of employment with Mahudes at
the hospital. Given the largely chronological form, the seemingly
arbitrary and disconnected character of the episodes, and the
preponderance of time spent with members of the poorer, criminal,
or otherwise marginalized classes, it is easy to see in Berganza's story
elements of the picaresque, whether or not one decides that the text
as a whole, or Berganza's role within it, accords with the main
tendencies of the rogue's tale genre.[23] In general, for Cervantes the

---

[22] This comment prompts Berganza's sly Horatian compliment to Cipión that "bien
se puede esperar que contará los suyos de manera que enseñen y deleiten a un
mismo punto" (II, 307).

[23] Considerable scholarly attention has been given to the question of the picaresque
in the *Coloquio*, or (perhaps more properly) the placement of the *Coloquio* into the
picaresque. I find myself most in agreement with the view reflected in El Saffar's
notion of how the dialogic structure divides this text from the picaresque genre:
"Although criticism of society is also a factor in the *novela*, Cipión's constant
intervention and the presence of certain mysterious elements make it impossible to
conclude that the *Coloquio de los perros* is a picaresque work" (*Cervantes:* El
casamiento engañoso *and* El coloquio de los perros, 15).

picaresque is less a genre that he chooses to explore than it is a source of motifs, character types, and self-conscious, literary allusions that he can cannibalize for fragments to be incorporated into his fictions. In the *Coloquio*, however, he not only takes this obvious and familiar course. He also steps back from the essential picaresque endeavor of the confession and the single-voiced address to a hypothetical judgmental reader, the "Vuestra Merced" or supposed, implied external reader. The device of the dialogue both breaks down the univocal, uncritical voice and also shifts the center of focus from the solitary and confessional discourse, to the skeptical and constantly critical dialogic mode.[24]

Berganza's life story—as well as Cipión's and Berganza's own commentaries upon it—and the dogs' ongoing, parallel discussion about the formal, aesthetic, and ethical challenges of narration are a lesson in reading. They are also a return to the beginning of the *Novelas ejemplares*. Berganza—or Campuzano, or perhaps Cervantes through Campuzano and Berganza—once again teaches us how to read by disturbing our act of reading. During his pre-articulate life, Berganza's mute interactions with and observations of the worlds of Sevilla's Matadero, of the nearby shepherds, of merchant families, corrupt cops and whores, and so on, combine to both influence and mirror the reader's view of and encounter with a society previously present (and presented) in the foregoing *novelas* but never seen from

---

[24] But although we can separate this text from full and authentic membership in the picaresque genre, it is nonetheless a story of a life experienced as a progression through time, an education, and a passage through the nether reaches of society. The ways in which Cervantes has distinguished the presentation of Berganza's life from that of, for example, Lazarillo or Pablos de Segovia are at times ambiguous. The obvious differences—such as the device of the dialogue and how the interruptions and commentaries distance the putative protagonist(s) and render their judgments fundamentally different from the socio-critical remarks of a Lazarillo or a Pablos—are balanced by those aspects that seem to fit all too well into the expansive genre of the picaresque narration. But most clearly, what Berganza's story embodies is a critical trajectory of observation and ambiguous encounters, rather than a confessional (explicatory) autobiography. Berganza, in effect, has nothing to confess, explain, or hide. On the implications of the dialogue form, see especially T. Hart, *Cervantes' Exemplary Fictions*, 106-07.

quite this perspective or with this peculiar luxury of time, intimacy, and detachment. The family of the *mercader sevillano*, for instance, is not the same as that of Isabel in *La española inglesa*, but it is in reality not very different. The distinction is that in the previous story, Sevilla and Isabel's family were the beginning and end points, the happy goal of Ricaredo, the terminus of a long-suffering love quest. Berganza experiences the more virtuous side of the merchant family's life, but he also sees what goes on in the darkness in the slave and servant quarters, after hours and on a very different social and sentimental level. Likewise, the *gitanos* whom Berganza encounters toward the end of his tale are perhaps a different group from those who made up the temporary world of the lost and found Preciosa in *La gitanilla*. But the harsh judgment rendered by Berganza would not be incomprehensible as a comment upon Preciosa's gypsy teachers and companions. Again, the difference is one of perspective and emphasis.[25]

The shape, sequence, and balance of Berganza's chain of encounters has about it a chilling precision and intensity. Despite the superficial digressions and the ostensibly disruptive but crafty and disingenuous asides and interruptions, the trajectory of Berganza's narrated life traces with penetrating economy a passage through a familiar society, a journey now retold with ineluctable commentaries. These commentaries seem to worry the question of aesthetic and ethical propriety in the act of telling a story, but they really concern the nature of literature more broadly, slowly and carefully peeling back the layers of narrative illusion and implicitly asking us what it is we do when we read. Contrary to what Forcione argues in his superb and exhaustive reading of the text, the overall effect of our adventure of reading this double *novela* is not the vision and revelation of a profoundly demonic evil (the episode with the witch) and the move through a demonic world, although we do indeed

---

[25] On the points of coherence and contrast between the gypsy world more fully represented in *La gitanilla* and the brief characterization of it in Berganza's story, see Forcione (*Mystery*), especially 131-33.

confront this crucial image and its implications. Rather, our experience can be characterized as a witty education, the sly manipulation of reader by text, through which we come both to question what and how we know anything and to see ourselves as reading participants in a world whose surfaces allow self-delusion but whose lessons also permit a healthy skepticism, one that might provisionally help and defend us. To arrive at this intimation, we must, however, consider the shape and content of Berganza's narrative.

The structure of Berganza's story has been much studied.[26] In essence it is composed of five main episodes prior to the central encounter with the witch Cañizares, followed by another five episodes that have more the character of tableaux or brief encounters. All of these episodes have been exhaustively analyzed, and it would be idle to paraphrase and add commentary to them. Suffice it to say that at every stage the persons and milieux encountered by Berganza either reveal different aspects of society or else raise pertinent ideological or philosophical questions. As El Saffar and Molho have pointed out, the first four episodes involve Berganza with professions and persons who, however base and violent they may (by nature) be, are integral to the functioning of society, while the episodes that follow the central encounter with Cañizares tend to focus on marginal, or marginalized, persons and races. The apparent progression in the first episodes, then, begins in a world of brutal but unremarkable violence and corruption (the slaughterhouse) and then moves, in the succession of Berganza's masters and jobs, to the revelation of evil and violence beneath the surfaces of more "respectable" vocations and social milieux. There is a curious yet effective lack of schematic uniformity to the first four (or five) episodes—and, in fact, to all the parts of Berganza's narrative. The grim realism of life at the Matadero, for example, contrasts subtly but

---

[26] Once again, I refer the reader to the studies mentioned in the previous notes; amid all the many examinations of the structure of Berganza's story, I find those by El Saffar and Molho to be the most useful and incisive.

undeniably with the ineluctably allegorical overtones, in form and language, of the episode with the shepherds. Likewise, the duality and strange (perhaps thickly veiled) ironies of Berganza's incidents and observations while he is with the *mercader de Sevilla* are not quite like any other section of the story.[27] Nonetheless, the entirety of the text serves to open up to scrutiny the persons, classes, professions, and putatively necessary structures and institutions of a society not unlike our own.

Despite the clear emphasis upon violence and various forms of human evil—all of which underscores the picaresque resonances exploited by Cervantes in this text—the world of this *novela*, which begins as Campuzano emerges from the Hospital de la Resurrección and which ends, within Berganza's level of the narrative, with both dogs working happily in this same hospital, is one in which humankind's better potential is also evident and even attainable. It would be something of a stretch to argue that love and virtue are shown to prevail at some end point in the lives and experiences of either the men or the dogs. But Campuzano's story does seem to move toward, and perhaps beyond, the possibility of physical recuperation and the attainment of a degree of chastened knowledge or human perspective, while Berganza and Cipión find themselves working happily, or so it would seem, with Mahudes in the laudable vocation of aiding the charitable and restorative mission of a hospital.

The central section of Berganza's narrative involves the meeting with the witch.[28] Cervantes's portrayal of Cañizares is one of the most memorable and astonishing moments in the *Novelas ejemplares*. Both for the level of grotesqueness in the physical depiction of the unconscious witch and for the implications of what she says and supposedly engages in, the episode of Cañizares has a hypnotic, disturbing impact on the reader. Understandably, this pivotal and

---

[27] On this episode, and with particular emphasis on the admixture of cleverly veiled negative comment on the seemingly idyllic nature and laudatory view of the Jesuit school, see M. Molho, "Remarques," especially 27-39.

[28] In terms of the narrative structure, both Molho and El Saffar combine the fifth and sixth episodes, the brief time with soldier-drummer and the scene with Cañizares.

artistically powerful moment has received considerable critical attention.[29] The fact that, alone among all the other human beings whom Berganza meets before or after, the old woman (believing him to be human) speaks to the dog, opens up several interlinked questions. Specifically, this episode helps focus the nature of human evil, as well as the issue of authentic identity, and what is for me the real ulterior question: the nature of fiction and the origins and bases of imaginative, fictional authority. The episode with Cañizares and the "story" that she gives Berganza—concerning the latter's supposedly true origin and identity—is without doubt a crucial yet deeply ambiguous section of the text. The elegance of Cervantes's fictional tactic here should be reiterated. The episode of Cañizares and everything that she reportedly says is narrated by a temporarily speech-endowed dog. Similarly, Berganza's words, and in fact the entire dialogue of the two dogs, have been transcribed, or so it is claimed, by a delirious syphilis victim, a soldier whose own credibility is more than a little questionable. Meanwhile, what the presumed witch in the center of this dizzying discursive labyrinth is saying is that the dog who listens to her story is not, in fact, a dog.[30] Every level, each internal reference serves to remind us of the provisionality of any fiction and prompts us to question the relationship between the "relation" (*el relato*), listened to or read, and the reality or possibility of the content of this "relation" as an event out in a world. In this specific case, the patent absurdity of talking dogs

[29] The thematic importance of Cañizares and her identity as witch occupies a major portion of Forcione's study (see *Cervantes and the Mystery of Lawlessness*, especially 59-99). See also P. Finch, "Rojas' Celestina and Cervantes' Cañizares," *Cervantes* 9.1 (1989): 55-62; A. Huerga, "El proceso inquisitorial contra *La Camacha*," in *Cervantes: su obra y su mundo*, 453-62; S. Hutchinson, "Las brujas de Cervantes y la noción de la comunidad femenina," *Cervantes* 12.2 (1992): 127-36; C. B. Johnson, "Of Witches and Bitches: Gender, Marginality and Discourse in *El casamiento engañoso y Coloquio de los perros*," *Cervantes* 11.2 (1991): 7-25; and Molho, "Remarques," 59-62.
[30] On the ironies and implications of the dogs' identity—are they "dogs"? are they men changed into dogs? are they dogs who, through the subtle power of a hallucinatory fiction that we almost do not register, have become more human than the human beings of their world?—see Molho, "Remarques," 63-65.

evidently affects some readers by lowering their skeptical defenses in the face of the possibility of witches and the latters' most outlandlishly claimed powers and adventures.

The transition from the level of the dogs' dialogue and from Berganza's heretofore first-level narration involves a masterful and subtle insertion of voices. Cañizares's story occupies a sizable portion of the text. Furthermore it represents the longest uninterrupted passage of Berganza's narration.[31] The descent from the level of Berganza's own narration to that of the witch is effected by the simple device of embedded citation. After describing the first moments of their time alone in the woman's room, and noting his own revulsion at the woman's aspect, Berganza (or rather Cervantes's text) moves as follows:

> Llegóse, en fin, el punto de verme con ella en su aposento, que era escuro, estrecho y bajo, . . . ; atizóle la vieja, y sentóse sobre una arquilla, y llegóme junto a mí, y, sin hablar palabra, me volvió a abrazar, y yo volví a tener cuenta con que no me besase. Lo primero que me dijo fue:
> «Bien esperaba yo en el cielo que antes que estos mis ojos se cerrasen con el último sueño te había de ver, hijo mío, y ya que te he visto, venga la muerte y lléveme desta cansada vida.» (II, 336)

Once again, with this crafty shift we have a voice within a voice, or what is actually a text within a text, which (in turn), since it is the text that Campuzano claims to have written and which Peralta is now reading, is enclosed within yet another (questionable) text. Each level of remove ought to alert us to a greater degree of unreliability, of authoritative ambiguity. Yet the multiplication of levels and putative sources somehow serves to lend an air of improbable credibility to each enclosing or enclosed narrative and textual level.

Despite the persuasiveness of the voice and the supposed importance of what is being told here by the witch, Cervantes systematically de-stabilizes the possibility of certainty. Cañizares

---

[31] Cañizares makes her appearance within Berganza's narration on page 335, and after one brief interruption by Cipión, Berganza speaks continuously about the witch, from page 336 to page 346, within which Cañizares's own "narration" runs from page 336 to the moment when she goes into her trance on page 343.

herself repeatedly casts doubt upon her own assertions, claims, and knowledge. In her first words to Berganza—her supposed recognition of the dog as one of the two human sons of the witch la Montiela who were converted at birth into dogs by a spell cast by the other infamous witch, la Camacha—Cañizares brings up the possibility that what she herself sees and believes may not be so. Speaking of la Camacha—"Tuvo fama que convertía los hombres en animales, . . . " (II, 337)—Cañizares combines the notion of witchcraft with the possibility of the more mundane enchantments of female sexual power:

> lo que se dice de aquellas antiguas magas, que convertían los hombres en bestias, dicen los que más saben que no era otra cosa sino que ellas, con su mucha hermosura y con sus halagos, atraían los hombres de manera a que las quisiesen bien, y los sujetaban de suerte, sirviéndose dellos en todo cuanto querían, que parecían bestias. (II, 337)[32]

But she then undermines the certainty of her own assertions by saying "Pero en ti, hijo mío, la experiencia me muestra lo contrario: que sé que eres persona racional y te veo en semejanza de perro, si ya no es que esto se hace con aquella ciencia que llaman *tropelía*, que hace parecer una cosa por otra" (II, 337; italics in the original). The witch claims to know and believe certain things. But, as she admits, she does not know for sure or believe without certain reservations. For what she sees (either) confirms her belief in the reality and power of magic and evil spells, or it is the product of *tropelía*, of the arts of deception, or self-deception. Cañizares repeats this essential and troubling admission of ambiguity later, when she speaks of what should be the climactic point of her episode: her participation in, and

---

[32] As El Saffar has noted, "The witch's narration touches on the central mystery of the double *novela*, the conversion of man into beast through the wiles of evil women" (*El casamiento engañoso* and *El coloquio de los perros*, 64). The subtle but haunting parallel, of course, is that what is grotesquely and self-evidently presented as a witch's questionable explanation (the dogs as originally men) is more true, though figuratively so, in the animalizing of Campuzano (his descent into folly and sensuality) by the far more bewitching but quite un-magical doña Estefanía.

the reality of, the grotesque rites of the satanic sabbath.[33] But the significant issue here for Berganza and for us as readers is that what Cañizares's voice, within Berganza's voice, within Campuzano's text, achieves is both the forward motion of the tale and also the further underscoring of an acutely metafictional self-consciousness. Cañizares and her statement participate, on the deepest level, in the deliberate questioning of the problematic elusiveness of fiction that lies at the heart of the larger, encompassing text.

Who or what is Cañizares? For many readers, she is essentially what she says she is: a hypocritical old woman publicly feigning virtue and proper Christian belief, yet secretly an unrepentant witch.[34] But she is also, simply, an old woman. As such, she presents the image of the female, past the stage of fertility but nonetheless (or all the more so) the symbol of earth, generation, and regeneration. The old woman, here as elsewhere in Cervantes, is the keeper of domestic and irrational connections, the teller of tales, and the repository of a kind of magic more mundane yet far more potent than the *tropelías* or old wives's tales of witchcraft.[35] As we gaze

---

[33] Speaking about her participation in these satanic gatherings ("Vamos a verle muy lejos de aquí, a un gran campo, donde nos juntamos infinidad de gente, brujos y brujas, . . . " [II, 339]), Cañizares immediately places the reality of such events and the certainty of her knowledge into a most ambiguous position: "Hay opinión que no vamos a estos convites sino con la fantasía en la cual nos representa el demonio las imágenes de todas aquellas cosas que después contamos que nos han sucedido. Otros dicen que no, sino que verdaderamente vamos en cuerpo y en ánima; y entrambas opiniones tengo para mí que son verdaderas, puesto que nosotras no sabemos cuándo vamos de una o de otra manera, porque todo lo que nos pasa en la fantasía es tan intensamente que no hay diferenciarlo de cuando vamos real y verdaderamente" (II, 339-40).   The implications of this last statement for the maker—and receptor—of fictions, faced with the task of judgment, should be obvious.

[34] As Cañizares so bluntly puts it, "rezo poco, y en público; murmuro mucho, y en secreto; vame mejor con ser hipócrita que con ser pecadora declarada: las apariencias de mis buenas obras presentes van borrando en la memoria de los que me conocen las malas obras pasadas. En efeto: la santidad fingida no hace daño a ningún tercero, sino al que la usa" (II, 340).

[35] We are reminded of the highly complex and deliberately ambiguous treatment of the old women, and of the female principle in general, in José Donoso's

upon this creation, Cañizares—through Berganza's eyes, Cervantes's words—we see many things. Yet we are quite liable to be tricked by the grotesqueness and the inconsistencies of what we see. In and through the body of Berganza's narration we have two portraits of Cañizares: a kind of complex moral self-portrait (in Cañizares's own, relayed, words) and a visual, physical representation, given by Berganza himself. In each case, there are mysteries and inconsistencies. As has often been noted, the woman is a complex, contradictory combination of a resolute loyalty to satanic evil and a sophisticated sense of common morality and Christian values.

The culminating moment of this episode, concretely visual and morally symbolic, is Cañizares's trance. The trance itself is quite ambiguous: smeared with her magic unguents, Cañizares (either) undergoes an authentic out-of-body experience or does little more than hallucinate. What is clear is that her naked, supine body lies on display for Berganza's and our own horrified yet absorbed contemplation. The description of the body, as rendered by the dog, is both precise and confusing. The passage itself demands quotation at length:

> Ella era larga de más de siete pies; toda era notomía de huesos, cubiertos con una piel negra, vellosa y curtida; con la barriga, que era de badana, se cubría las partes deshonestas, y aun le colgaba hasta la mitad de los muslos; las tetas semejaban dos vejigas de vaca secas y arrugadas; denegridos los labios, traspillados los dientes, la nariz corva y entablada, desencasados los ojos, la cabeza desgreñada, las mejillas chupadas, angosta la garganta y los pechos sumidos; finalmente, toda era flaca y endemoniada. (II, 344)

---

hallucinatory text, *El obsceno pájaro de la noche*. As one of Donoso's ambiguous voices puts it, "Las viejas como la Peta Ponce tienen el poder de plegar y confundir el tiempo, lo multiplican y lo dividen, los acontecimientos se refractan en sus manos verrugosas como en el prisma más brillante, cortan el suceder consecutivo en trozos que disponen en forma paralela, curvan esos trozos y los enroscan organizando estructuras que les sirven para que se cumplan sus designios" (222-23). Clearly, the line between the supernatural (witchcraft) and the all-too-natural (the art of telling, of manipulating time through narration, stories) is ambiguous and problematic.

The details of the description vacillate between the poles of a certain plausibility (a picture of what might be an aged and wasted body) and a surreal exaggeration of features that thus take on symbolic value. Physically Cañizares is simultaneously imposing and yet insubstantial. Berganza's own reaction is a combination of deep revulsion and sufficiently cool mastery of this same fear, such that he can drag the inert, unconscious body by the heel out into the patio: "Quise morderla, por ver si volvía en sí, y no hallé parte en toda ella que el asco no me lo estorbase; pero, con todo esto, la así de un carcaño y la saqué arrastrando al patio; mas ni por esto dio muestras de tener sentido" (II, 344). The fact that the dog can't bear to touch or be touched by the woman and yet can take her heel in his mouth, along with the fact that a presumably large human body can be dragged out of the room, like a nearly weightless rag, is significant. Weight and insubstantiality also mark the content and implications of this episode. It is hard not to sense that Berganza's dragging of Cañizares out into the light is not only an exposure of her evil but also an exposure of her questionable power and significance. The image itself is telling: with Berganza's dragging of this grotesque, huge yet small entity out into the light, it is as if Cervantes were dragging a massive fictional "red herring" across the trail of his deeper story. More than a few readers, it would seem, have been drawn off the track. The text itself gives little help: Cañizares is either an authentic witch (with all that this entails) or she is a "witch" only in her own mind, with nothing more special about it: no magic, no transformations. She is perhaps just a deranged old woman, aware of sin and evil, but making self-congratulatory claims to a power that exists more in her fantasy than in any real human or canine realm. Which is she? Cervantes forces the reader to speculate.[36]

---

[36] The confused aftermath of Cañizares's trance (II, 344-45) serves, yet again, to suspend the possibility of knowledge: did the witch "go" anywhere either in fantasy or through some magical, out-of-body mode? The fact that the curious crowd turns on Berganza, suspecting him of satanic involvements or possession as

No, the real climax of the *Coloquio* is not the powerful, hypnotically arresting moment of Cañizares's trance, the vision of her body, or the strange aftermath when she wakes up. The key moment comes a page or two later, with the end of Berganza's narration of this section and Cipión's sage dissection of what he has just heard. Cipión's skeptical view, his attitude and method of critique are not merely a distancing of himself from the unpleasant suggestion that he is a "son of a witch." They are also, and more crucially, the continuation of the ulterior process and mission, begun on yet another level of the larger text, the metafictional and critical game initiated by Campuzano. Cipión begins in critique ("Antes, Berganza, que pases adelante, es bien que reparemos en lo que te dijo la bruja y averigüemos si puede ser verdad la grande mentira a quien das crédito" [II, 346]) and ends in skepticism. His cold, clear-eyed consideration of Cañizares's tale of the two dogs' origin leads inexorably to rejection:

> Mira, Berganza, grandísimo disparate sería creer que la Camacha mudase los hombres en bestias. . . . Todas estas cosas y las semejantes son embelecos, mentiras o apariencias del demonio; y si a nosotros nos parece ahora que tenemos algún entendimiento y razón, pues hablamos siendo verdaderamente perros, o estando en su figura, ya hemos dicho que éste es caso portentoso y jamás visto, y que aunque le tocamos con las manos, no le habemos de dar crédito hasta tanto que el suceso dél nos muestre lo que conviene que creamos. (II, 346)

Or, if not outright rejection, it leads to a suspension of belief and acceptance so profound and subtle that we are brought back to the question of fiction, meaning, and authority once again. In other words, it is not Cañizares, her trance, and the grotesque yet questionable illusion of satanic evil, but rather the ongoing textual web being woven by Cervantes, through the agency of a patent absurdity, that defines the core of this *novela*. The most brilliant yet off-hand part of Cipión's seemingly too rational, almost pedestrian dismissal of

---

much as they suspect Cañizares, is both plausible and ironically appropriate: yet another deferral of conclusion.

Cañizares and what she represents brings the theme of "literature" and the act of telling once again back into sharp focus. As Cipión, very much the voice of reason, puts it, "Considera en cuán vanas cosas y en cuán tontos puntos dijo la Camacha que consistía nuestra restauración; y aquellas que a ti te deben parecer profecías no son sino palabras de consejas o cuentos de viejas, como aquellos del caballo sin cabeza y de la varilla de virtudes, con que se entretienen al fuego las dilatadas noches del invierno, . . . " (II, 346). Literally, yet another "Winter's Tale."

Cipión's final, rational rejection of Cañizares's prophecy is not just an act of reason but also a model of literary criticism.[37] As Cipión argues,

> Y si en esto [the fulfillment of the prophecy] consistiera volver nosotros a la forma que dices, ya lo hemos visto y lo vemos a cada paso; por do me doy a entender que no en el sentido alegórico, sino en el literal, se han de tomar los versos de la Camacha; ni tampoco en éste consiste nuestro remedio, pues muchas veces hemos visto lo que dicen y nos estamos tan perros como ves; así, que la Camacha fue burladora falsa, y la Cañizares embustera, y la Montiela tonta, maliciosa y bellaca, con perdón sea dicho, si acaso es nuestra madre, de entrambos o tuya, que yo no la quiero tener por madre. (II, 347)

It must be recalled that, on a first level of internal logic, Cipión is not talking about Cañizares and her story and prediction as if they were the kind of discourse clearly marked off and self-identified as "literature." Nonetheless, his act of sorting out literal fact from figurative implication mirrors our own activity as readers. In particular, it recalls the necessary posture of the first-order reader, Peralta. Cipión's final comment—giving yet another, deliberately playful spin to the notion of the exalted being abased and the abased

---

[37] Cipión continues with his critical reading of Berganza's story and brings into focus the sense of the different capacities and uses of language; he states, continuing the previously cited sentence, that "si no es que sus palabras se han de tomar en un sentido que he oído decir se llama al[e]górico, el cual sentido no quiere decir lo que la letra suena, sino otra cosa, que, aunque diferente, le haga semejanza, . . . " (II, 346).

exhalted—repeats his rejection of the validity of the prediction. But it also introduces an image and an idea that echoes the very opening of the *novelas*, Cervantes's "Prólogo": "Digo, pues, que el verdadero sentido es un juego de bolos, donde con presta diligencia derriban los que están en pie y vuelven a alzar los caídos, y esto por la mano de quien lo puede hacer" (II, 347). The "juego de bolos" is, of course, more fitting to the notion of rising and falling than is the Prologue's reference to the "mesa de trucos" (I, 52), where the motions are more horizontal, the balls tracing patterns of interaction, collision, and the transfer of energy in a way that reminds us a great deal of the journeys and clashes encountered throughout the *Novelas ejemplares*. The two allusions, however, share the principle of recreation and the idea of the game as a place and an activity set aside from, and yet within, society's routine and vital demands.

Cipión does not, of course, have the last word here. In a very real sense, in neither the *Coloquio* nor the *Casamiento* is there a "last word" in any way comparable to what can be found in the previous *novelas*. Cipión's rejection of the "truth" of what Cañizares has, through Berganza's reportage, said cannot totally remove the ambiguous possibility or suspicion that the dogs are men. Rather, what this moment of the text accomplishes is a return of the focus to the core problem of the nature of fiction and the aesthetic and ethical endeavor, or responsibility, of the reader. It might not be unwarranted to say that the ostensible centrality and impact of the Cañizares episode, followed by its rather more subtle de-authorization—thus creating a kind of false cadence (as we would call it in musical form)—is a serious and powerful reiteration of the imaginative challenge posed here and, by extension, in any confrontation of reader and text. The recreation and edification that Cervantes has proposed in his Prologue will not be cheaply purchased.

In terms of the narrative or dramatic shape of Berganza's life story, meanwhile, the conclusion of the scene with Cañizares is followed by a section shorter than that of the episodes that preceded this part. After fleeing Montilla, the witch, and the chaotic aftermath of her trance, Berganza deals, in turn and in each case quite briefly, with a group of gypsies, a *morisco*, poets, and people of the theater. He finally arrives in Valladolid and decides to offer his canine services to Mahudes at the Hospital de la Resurrección. Here he encounters the four convalescents—or what we might call the four madmen. The character of each of these concluding episodes tends toward detachment and brevity: Berganza is no longer a "player" (not even in his brief time with the theater troup, ended by an unfortunate injury, in the line of duty) in quite the same way that he was in the episodes prior to and including the encounter with Cañizares. There is, moreover, something more than a little chilling and harsh in Berganza's judgments about the gypsies and the *moriscos*, a view that reflects more the prejudices and official culture of the epoch than the more nuanced views that Cervantes himself has offered elsewhere (for example, the portrayal of the gypsies in *La gitanilla*; see Chapter One above). What appears to be happening in this closing section, after the more climactic moment of Cañizares's trance and Cipión's perspective-restoring analysis of it and its implications, is a brief return to an overview of society. This time, however, instead of the penetrating examination or unmaskings found in the first four epsisodes, Berganza observes with a certain cool detachment the situation of individuals and groups considered marginal or suspect.

The emphasis upon poets and those who work in the theater falls neatly into the familiar satiric tradition.[38] But the fact that, as the *Coloquio* ends with Berganza finally finding a home in the hospital, Cervantes returns his attention to alienated types is worth reconsideration. What we have here is, among other things, an unexpected number of persons who, however silly and satire-worthy they may seem, are connected to the endeavors of imagination, mind, and creation. The penultimate episode—something that is really more a *tableau* in the manner of Quevedo (e.g., *La hora de todos*) than an

---

[38] In this regard, we are reminded of Cervantes's treatment of poets in *El licenciado Vidriera*; see also Quevedo's satiric treatment of poets in the *Sueños* and in the *Buscón*.

episode containing meaningful action—involving the four convalesc-ing madmen embodies the playful duality of Cervantes's strategy throughout much of the *Casamiento* and *Coloquio*. His four madmen are simultaneously easy to dismiss and yet also revealing of deeper issues. One might even say that their appearance here, as persons who also are suffering, like Campuzano, from disease and who perhaps have been infected as well by the disease of telling, provides further resonance to the theme of the imagination and the problem of artistic authority in fiction. The four men are archetypal: a poet, an alchemist, a mathematician, and an *arbitrista*.[39]

The poet and his complaints add little to what has already been offered by the cases of the other poets in this text, or (for that matter) by the treatment of poets in *El licenciado Vidriera*. The scheme of the *arbitrista* is, if anything, touchingly ingenuous and rather more plausible than the plans ridiculed by Quevedo. The lunacy of the alchemist, meanwhile, is largely conventional. Unlike the alchemists and the alchemy often portrayed by Cervantes's contemporaries as the stuff of self-evident fraud, this alchemist suggests the sincere yet deluded desire to find the magical transformative object and to elevate base material to an essence of the highest level or value. Of the four men, I would suggest that the mathematician and his lament represent the most subtle yet elegantly telling conception. The mathematician is the third to speak, and replying to the poet and the alchemist, he describes his own frustrated search as follows:

> Veinte y dos años ha que ando tras de hallar el punto fijo, y aquí lo dejo y allí lo tomo, y pareciéndome que ya lo he hallado y que no se me puede escapar en ninguna manera, cuando no me cato, me hallo tan lejos dél, que me admiro. Lo mismo me acaece con la cuadratura del círculo: que he llegado tan al remate de hallarla, que no sé ni puedo pensar cómo no la tengo ya en la faldriquera; y así, es mi pena semejante a las de Tántalo, que está cerca del fruto y muere de hambre, y propincuo al agua, y perece de sed. Por momentos pienso dar en la conyuntura de la verdad, y por

---

[39] On the representation of the *arbitrista* in the *Coloquio* and in other key texts of the epoch, see J. Vilar Berrogain, *Literatura y economía: La figura satírica del arbitrista en el Siglo de Oro*.

minutos me hallo tan lejos della, que vuelvo a subir el monte que acabé de
bajar, con el canto de mi trabajo a cuestas, como otro nuevo Sísifo. (II, 356)

The wretched mathematician and his plight can be viewed in at least two ways. Given that the man is in the hospital, perhaps another syphilis sufferer and clearly deranged, he is a figure of derision and already in a sense disqualified, as being unworthy of respect and serious consideration. Yet at the same time, he and his quest are curiously suggestive and invite a more serious reading. His searches—for the fixed point and for a way to square the circle—are self-evidently symbolic of the search for the impossible, the unattainable. They are also, given the particular aura one tends to grant to things mathematical, resonant with a certain sense of the autonomously beautiful. In their abstraction, they belong to a sphere that while imaginable is frankly beyond normal, real-world experience and the supposed laws of nature. Yet for all this, his imaginings are no less beguiling.

The mathematician's rather rhetorical and formulaic references to Tantalus and Sisyphus serve to underscore the futility as well as the folly and pretentiousness of this man's project. But this image of frustration, of things just beyond one's reach and the simultaneous need and desire for attainment and satisfaction are not irrelevant to the situation of the artist or the writer, the person who seeks an unattainable perfection or who pursues the impossible. The mathematician and in fact all four of these madmen fit well into the pattern of isolation, mania, and alienation that El Saffar has proposed as one of the notable characteristics of the "novel" phase of Cervantes's fiction.[40] It is the all-too-male, overly intellectualized, abstract

---

[40] See *Novel to Romance*, especially 13-29; and speaking specifically about the vein of alienation that runs through the *Coloquio*, El Saffar suggests that "increasing alienation is expressed not only by a movement from the heart of society to its fringes and ultimately beyond its borders, but by a movement from physical work to intellectual activity that finally becomes so rarefied as to have no practical application whatever. The madmen in the hospital are seeking perfection in the abstract, while the pillars of society have sacrificed both perfection and abstraction to a corrupt concrete reality" (65).

dead end into which so many of Cervantes's characters wander. There is indeed a sense of pathos and sterility in the extremes and follies suggested by these four men. But at the same time, there is a sense of elegance. What the mathematician is after is, on the literal level, unattainable, and to persevere in the search is madness. But considered metaphorically, what he seeks is the contemplation of a perfection possible to the imagination. The creator of fictions is also the seeker of such paradoxical perfections.

The conclusion of the *Coloquio* returns us, ostensibly, to the level of the frame tale, the world of Campuzano and Peralta in the *Casamiento*. But first, Berganza offers two final anecdotes—one in which he tried, vainly, to "talk" with a Corregidor, to give advice about problems of public morals, but failed since all that came out was violent barking, and a second story in which a small, cowardly lap dog attacked him and got away with it, since the smaller dog was able to hide behind the protection of its mistress, "una señora principal." Cipión then offers his own opinion of the situations and makes a kind of summation, one that refers to the immediately mentioned cases but that is also a comment, both philosophical and laudatory, on Berganza's fortitude and ethical sense:

> La virtud y el buen entendimiento siempre es una y siempre es uno: desnudo o vestido, solo o acompañado. Bien es verdad que puede padecer acerca de la estimación de las gentes, mas no en la realidad verdadera de lo que merece y vale. Y con esto pongamos fin a esta plática, que la luz que entra por estos resquicios muestra que es muy entrado el día, y esta noche que viene, si no nos ha dejado este grande beneficio de la habla, será la mía, para contarte mi vida. (II, 359)

Berganza answers in brief agreement ("Sea ansí, y mira que acudas a este mismo puesto."), and a wider than usual white space on the page signals that the fiction of the text within a text has ended. The story, which is to say the transcript of the putative colloquy, ends abruptly and without the sort of comment, exemplum, or closure offered in all the other previous *novelas*. The dogs merely "disappear."

The transition back to the space and moment of the *Casamiento*, which is to say, back to Peralta's and Campuzano's world of reading and dreaming, also returns us to the essential theme and the insoluble conundrum of the text. We may perhaps have lost sight of the activity of our agent, Peralta, and of the dream of the questionable transcriber, Campuzano. But now we are reminded that our just finished reading has been, in effect, our insertion into their world. Or their insertion into ours:

> El acabar el *Coloquio* el Licenciado y el despertar el Alférez fue todo a un tiempo, y el Licenciado dijo:
> —Aunque este coloquio sea fingido y nunca haya pasado, paréceme que está tan bien compuesto que puede el señor Alférez pasar adelante con el segundo.
> —Con ese parecer —respondió el Alférez— me animaré y disporné a escribirle, sin ponerme más en disputas con vuesa merced si hablaron los perros o no. (II, 359)

Peralta's summation, needless to say, parallels and echoes the comments offered by Cipión concerning the validity of the story and prophecy told by Cañizares. But it is significantly, if slightly, different. Raising the critical discourse to a higher and yet more ambiguous level, Peralta concludes by not concluding. Couching his remarks in the suspension of the subjunctive ("Aunque este coloquio sea fingido y nunca haya pasado, . . ."), Peralta votes in favor of aesthetic value. The colloquy and in fact the story told on the first level by Campuzano himself (his unfortunate marriage) are clearly not without their serious socio-critical point. These stories have led us through a complex landscape of human corruption with brief glimpses of possible redemption and recuperation. But the entire edifice of these interwoven texts has also both questioned and enacted the elusive character of fiction and the art of telling, suggesting in the process not a set of programmatic solutions to society's ills, but the always beguiling promise of the healing properties of art.[41]

---

[41] As El Saffar has suggested, "Peralta and the reader alike are asked to choose

The image and allusion to disease with which the *Casamiento* began has brought us to the hospital of the dogs, and in fact, as M. Molho as reminded us, the *Coloquio* itself is defined by the points of two hospitals: beginning and ending at Mahudes's hospital in Valladolid after the mid point determined by Cañizares's hospital in Montilla.[42] Cervantes's examination of society—or at least those parts of it that he has illuminated through the foolish and self-damaging experience of a soldier and the necessarily lower-angled vision of a dog—has perhaps been the stuff of hospitals and illness. But if this vision and the urge to narrate can be seen as versions of disease, the enactment of art offers the possibility of recovery, of re-creation. The *licenciado* reiterates this suggestion, the *alférez* answers, and the text (as in the case of the dogs' colloquy) ends without the imposition of a narrative conclusion:

> —Señor Alférez, no volvamos más a esa disputa. Yo alcanzo el artificio
> del *Coloquio* y la invención, y basta. Vámonos al Espolón a recrear los ojos
> del cuerpo, pues ya he recreado los del entendimiento.
> —Vamos —dijo el Alférez.
> Y con esto, se fueron. (II, 359)

This elegantly simple ending underscores the core issue of the aesthetic and ethical imperatives of language and fiction. It reminds us that the obligations imposed are not just proper to the author or teller of the tale, but that they pertain as well to us as readers. The amazing conclusion of this text, which is a kind of subtle melting into thin air, suspends any and all authorial or narratorial intrusions or

---

between an image of art as entertainment like that provided by the drummer, and art as a mediator between the self and the deepest mysteries of life" (El casamiento engañoso *and* El coloquio de los perros, 68). I would propose that the real healing power of the arts of fiction, for Cervantes, lies within this ability to connect us and not just to divert or amuse.

[42] On the implications of this contrast of the two hospitals, see Molho, "Remarques," 66-67. The hospital of Montilla within which Cañizares works as a way of hiding her true self implies one type of disease of telling; the Hospital de la Resurrección, which heals Campuzano and which gives him (either) his overheard colloquy or the inspiration to create a fantasy that is also his "recovery," defines yet another possible way in which the urge to narrate can be both disease and recuperation.

judgments. We are left with a sense of anti-climax that, in this case, is unmistakably more resonant and significant than would have been a conclusive comment on (either) the *Casamiento/Coloquio* or on the *Novelas ejemplares* as a whole. The final *novela* leaves us with a consciousness of our own autonomy and responsibility. We are, in effect, craftily asked to re-read the entire collection, either in fact or in a foreshortened recollection. We are challenged to make new sense of that which we have, less than adequately, tried to understand.

In the course of the *Casamiento* and the *Coloquio*, the familiar themes of identity and social order have entered into the tapestry of the double *novela*. But this time, it has not been identity as a social foundation to be understood and regained; nor has social order been the unquestioned given, the ideal structure that must finally be restored. Rather, identity has been, in its acutely complex and shifting nature, a device for the exploring of larger questions. Social order, meanwhile, has been revealed as something other than the comforting, always renewed and renewable source of affirmation. The social order and institutions familiar to Campuzano and his milieu and penetrated by Berganza are the unromantic, anti-ideal possibilities, the "contingencies" that we sense to exist beyond art, but that we may come to deal with more adequately through the art and insights of stories, through the structures of self-aware critique that simultaneously unmask disease and also allow the hope of recuperation.

Conclusion: Closing the Circle

The conclusion of the *Casamiento* and *Coloquio* completes its implicit, ostensible mission: it tells the stories promised—and begged—by the diseased, chastened, but restored, and perhaps redeemed ensign, as well as the stories or portents intimated by the miraculous and absurd possibility of speech-endowed dogs. But, as I have suggested in the previous chapter, the larger implications of what seems to happen in the *Casamiento* and the *Coloquio* and, more pointedly, of how language is manipulated in this double text transcend the ostensible narrative purpose. The exploration of identity and the all but surgical analysis of society and its various institutions do take place in this *novela*. Yet while identity and social order seem necessary, these questions have about them a sense that they are essentially just preliminary concerns. The *Casamiento* and *Coloquio* is, more fundamentally, a lesson in the complex, exquisite, and troubling endeavor of narrating and reading.[1] To one degree or another, as I would insist, each of the ten previous *novelas* subtly questions its own illusions of imaginative wholeness or seamless autonomy. The other *novelas* also provide, each in its own way, peculiar "lessons in reading." But only the concluding text so deeply and obsessively keeps the issues of play, epistemological authority, and the aesthetic and ethical challenges of art so constantly and troublingly at the fore.

To the extent that the *Casamiento* and *Coloquio* achieves any sort of effective or meaningful reordering of our conception of reading, it is not only the creation of a new sensitivity appropriate to this final *novela*. Rather, what the last text accomplishes—and must accomplish—is an aesthetic and moral recapitulation of the total adventure, the entirety of the collection, through which we as readers have passed and from which we have just emerged. Appropriate too is

---

[1] In addition to the studies mentioned in Chapter Ten, in so many of which this issue is (inevitably) acknowledged and often dealt with quite sensitively, see N. Spadaccini and J. Talens, *Through the Shattering Glass: Cervantes and the Self-Made World*, especially 117-33.

the fact that this final and definitive lesson in reading underscores the picaresque sensitivity that we as readers have gradually had to acquire in our experience with Cervantes's subtly double narratives. The new and more ambiguous art of reading—taught to us by a text dominated by a syphilitic soldier, by talking dogs, and by a frank but mendacious witch—brings us back to the beginning of the collection. Whether or not we immediately re-read *La gitanilla* or any of the other *novelas*, we find ourselves changed, our assumptions modified and our putative but never really authentic innocence now quite undermined, if not completely taken away. We must go back to the beginning.[2]

The self-conscious, metafictional essence of the *Casamiento* and *Coloquio*, then, represents the closing of a larger, more complex circle. Ironically, what is clearly the most "open" narrative conclusion, or set of conclusions, effects the closing of a vast circle of expectation. The completion of the last *novela*, and in particular the closing image or gesture of the text—Peralta's suggestion: "Vámonos al Espolón a recrear los ojos del cuerpo, pues ya he recreado los del entendimiento."—returns us to the "Prólogo" and the subtle interplay of aesthetic, moral, and socially restorative motives presented there by Cervantes. As the author articulates it in this initiatory statement, "Mi intento ha sido poner en la plaza de nuestra república una mesa de trucos, donde cada uno pueda llegar a entretenerse, . . . " (I, 52). We now know that this particular game is far more serious and

---

[2] In her commentary on this text (*Cervantes:* El casamiento engañoso *and* El coloquio de los perros), El Saffar has noted in various passages, the subtle play of circularity; see for example 16-17. Near the conclusion of her monograph, El Saffar suggests that "Everything really ends when Campuzano entrusts his autobiography to Peralta. Then he must wait, like Berganza and Cipión, for another narrator, necessarily unknown, to rescue his conversation from oblivion and make it available to another reading public. And now we are back again to the milk-can image [mise en abyme] from which we started this discussion, and we suddenly have to acknowledge that we are also contained in the story. . . . Cervantes' acknowledgement of an external authority suggests yet another level beyond ourselves, with which we are, like the dogs and men inside the story, in dialectical relationship" (86).

demanding than we might have expected. The consequences of manipulations, the angles of collision, and the ricochets and interactions of Cervantes's billiard balls have been much more involved and significant than the notion of innocent recreation might have implied.

What gives this implicit return to the beginning its peculiarly forceful, subtly revolutionary character is the deeply critical, subversive nature of the *Casamiento/Coloquio*. It has been argued that this concluding *novela* constitutes a sort of meta-text, an act of criticism that supplements, among other things, Cervantes's other masterpiece, *Don Quijote*.[3] The notion that the *Casamiento/Coloquio* represents a reply to the *Quijote* may seem an overstatement. Something about the relative scope of each text—the differing degrees of inclusiveness of social and self-consciously literary worlds in the two works—makes such an assertion highly debatable. Yet there can be no doubt that, if the *Quijote* is (among many other things) about the question of reading and the imperatives of judgment, then the acute and all but obsessively reiterated concern for reading (or listening) and imaginative judgment present in this final *novela* complements Cervantes's most serious treatment of this question in the *Quijote*.

There is something uniquely challenging and disturbing about the shape and peculiar character of intellectual dissection present in the *Casamiento* and *Coloquio*. Despite its ostensible openness and its apparent dismissal of any solemn or far-reaching judgment, it clearly opens the door to another way of thinking about literature. As Edwin Williamson has asserted, the *Casamiento* and *Coloquio* poses a very modern, or postmodern, response to the problems of literary form and the kind of knowledge offered by the work of fiction:

> However, if Cervantes shares Thomas Mann's anxiety about "the ironic dissolution of form", this comes fully into the open not in *Don Quixote* but

---

[3] See in particular the essays contained in M. Nerlich and N. Spadaccini, *Cervantes's 'Exemplary Novels' and the Adventure of Writing*, and for a critical reaction to this notion of the meta-textuality of the *Coloquio*, see the "Afterword" by A. K. Forcione (331-52).

in a text which appeared in 1613, only a couple of years before the
publication of Part II. I refer to the interlocking stories of *The Deceitful
Marriage* and *The Colloquy of the Dogs* in which literary reflexivity is carried
to vertiginous heights of self-consciousness. In the double novella of the
Marriage/Colloquy meaning threatens to dissolve in a virtuoso display of
textual ironies that would be the envy of a contemporary post-modernist.
Thus, if Cervantes inaugurates the modern novel with *Don Quixote*, he
anticipated its possible death even before he had completed his masterpiece. And yet, at the centre of the currents of language swirling about in
this two-tier novella there is an intriguing quest for a spiritual or ethical
anchorage. Perhaps now that the modernists have come to the brink of
that vortex, this exemplary, "post-novelistic" novella of Cervantes
may—to borrow a phrase from Walter Benjamin—flash up as a memory
at the moment of danger.[4]

Williamson's judgment concerning the nature and implications of
Cervantes's concluding *novela* is convincing. The *Casamiento* and
Coloquio does indeed question the nature and possibilities of fiction,
of "novelizing," as Cervantes would have it. But it also forms a part
of the diverse yet now perceptibly unified collection. The contrary
worlds of the *Novelas ejemplares* present to us a vast array of questions: the possibility of harmonious reunion or the triumph of human
love, as well as the inescapable limits of human knowledge, the all
too familiar frustrations of illusory desire, and the complex inconsistencies and inequities of the same social orders that contain and
protect us. Perhaps the reading of Cervantes's *Novelas ejemplares* is,
for the late twentieth-century reader, not only an excursion through
exotic and irrecoverable worlds, but also the rearticulation of our
own imagination's questions and desires, a way to reread the world,
to reread and rediscover ourselves.

---

[4] This statement comes at the conclusion (8) of his Introduction to the collection of
essays *Cervantes and the Modernists*; the whole Introduction (1-8) is most pertinent
to the larger problem of reading and reflection at the heart of the *Novelas ejemplares*.

Bibliography

I.   Primary texts:

Cervantes, Miguel de. *El Ingenioso Hidalgo Don Quijote de la Mancha.*
    Ed. John J. Allen. 2 vols. Madrid: Cátedra, 1987.
——. *Novelas ejemplares.* Ed. Harry Sieber. 2 vols. Madrid: Cátedra,
    1984.
——. *Novelas ejemplares.* Ed. Juan Bautista Avalle-Arce. 3 vols.
    Madrid: Clásicos Castalia, 1982, 1987.

II.   Secondary sources:

Alcázar Ortega, Mercedes. "Palabras, memoria y aspiración literaria
    en *La española inglesa.*" *Cervantes* 15.1 (1995): 33-45.
Alsina, Jean. "Algunos esquemas narrativos y semánticos en *La*
    ilustre fregona." Bustos Tovar 199-206.
Alvarez Martínez, José Luis. "Berganza y la moza ventanera."
    Cervantes 12.2 (1992): 63-77.
Amezúa y Mayo, Agustín González de. *Cervantes, creador de la novela*
    corta española. 2 vols. Madrid: C.S.I.C., 1956, 1958. (2nd ed.,
    1982)
Avalle-Arce, Juan Bautista. "*El celoso extremeño* de Cervantes."
    Homenaje a Ana María Barrenechea. Eds. Lía Schwartz Lerner and
    Isaías Lerner. Madrid: Castalia, 1984. 199-205.
——. "Cervantes entre pícaros." *NRFH* 38 (1990): 591-603.
——. "*La gitanilla.*" *Cervantes* 1.1, 2 (1981): 9-17.
——. "*Novelas ejemplares*: Reality, Realism, Literary Tradition."
    Mimesis: From Mirror to Method, Augustine to Descartes. Eds. John
    D. Lyons and Stephen G. Nichols, Jr. Hanover: UP of New
    England for Dartmouth College, 1982. 197-214.
Avalle-Arce, Juan Bautista, and E. C. Riley, eds. *Suma Cervantina.*
    London: Támesis Books, 1973.

Aylward, Edward T. "The Device of Layered Critical Commentary in *Don Quixote* and *El coloquio de los perros.*" *Cervantes* 7.2 (1987): 57-69.

Bakhtin, Mikhail M. *The Dialogic Imagination: Four Essays.* Trans. Caryl Emerson and Michael Holquist. Ed. Michael Holquist. Austin: U of Texas P, 1982.

———. *Rabelais and His World.* Trans. Helene Iswolsky. Cambridge MA and London: The M.I.T. P, 1968.

———. *Speech Genres and Other Late Essays.* Trans. Vern W. McGee. Eds. Caryl Emerson and Michael Holquist. Austin: U of Texas P, 1986.

Bandera, Cesáreo. *Mímesis conflictiva: Ficción literaria y violencia en Cervantes y Calderón.* Madrid: Editorial Gredos, 1975.

Barrenechea, Ana María. "*La ilustre fregona* como ejemplo de estructura novelesca cervantina." *Actas del Primer Congreso Internacional de Hispanistas.* Oxford: Dolphin Book Co., 1964. 199-206.

Barthes, Roland. *S/Z.* Trans. Richard Miller. New York: Hill and Wang, 1974.

Beaupied, Aída M. "Ironía y los actos de comunicación en *Las dos doncellas.*" *Anales Cervantinos* 21 (1983): 165-76.

Beeching, Jack. *The Galleys at Lepanto.* New York: Charles Scribner's Sons, 1983.

Belic, Oldrich. "*La estructura de* El coloquio de los perros." *Análisis estructural de textos hispanos.* Madrid: Editorial Prensa Española, 1969. 61-90.

———. "Los principios de composición en la novela picaresca." *Análisis estructural de textos hispanos.* 19-60.

Bell-Villada, Gene, Antonio Giménez, and George Pistorius, eds. *From Dante to García Márquez: Studies in Romance Literatures and Linguistics Presented to Anson Conant Piper.* Williamstown, MA: Williams College, 1987.

Boyd, Stephen F. "The Mystery of Cervantes' *La gitanilla.*" *Forum for Modern Language Studies* (St. Andrews, Scotland) 17.4 (1981): 312-21.

——. "Sin and Grace in *El casamiento engañoso y El coloquio de los perros.*" *What's Past is Prologue: A Collection of Essays in Honour of L. J. Woodward.* Eds. Salvador Bacarisse, et al. Edinburgh: Scottish Academic Press, 1984. 1-9.

Bradbury, Gail. "Lope, Cervantes, a Marriage Trick and a Baby." *Hispanófila* 82 (1984): 11-19.

Braudel, Fernand. *The Mediterranean and the Mediterranean World in the Age of Philip II.* Trans. Sian Reynolds. 2 vols. New York, Evanston, San Francisco: Harper and Row, 1972.

Bravo Villasante, Carmen. *La mujer vestida de hombre en el teatro español (Siglos XVI-XVII).* 3rd ed. Madrid: Mayo de Oro, 1988.

Britt, Linda. "Teodosia's Dark Shadow? A Study of Women's Roles in Cervantes' *Las dos doncellas.*" *Cervantes* 8.1 (1988): 39-46.

Burón, Antonio L. "Proceso de semiosis en la picaresca cervantina." Criado de Val, *Cervantes* 125-35.

Bustos Tovar, José Jesús de, ed. *Lenguaje, ideología y organización textual en las* Novelas Ejemplares. Madrid and Toulouse: U Complutense and U de Toulouse-Le Mirail, 1983.

Buxó, José Pascual. "Algunas estructuras semiológicas en *El celoso extremeño.*" Criado de Val, *Cervantes* 389-96.

Calcraft, R. P. "Structure, Symbol and Meaning in Cervantes's *La fuerza de la sangre.*" *BHS* 58 (1981): 197-204.

Camamis, George. "The Concept of Venus-*Humanitas* in Cervantes and Botticelli." *Cervantes* 8.2 (1988): 183-223.

Carrasco, Félix. "*El coloquio de los perros*: Veridicción y modelo narrativo." *Criticón* 35 (1986): 119-33.

——. "*El coloquio de los perros* / v. / *El asno de oro*: Concordancias temáticas y sistemáticas." *Anales Cervantinos* 23 (1983): 177-200.

Casalduero, Joaquín. "Cervantes rechaza la pastoril y no acepta la picaresca." *BHS* 61 (1984): 283-85

——. *Sentido y forma de las* Novelas ejemplares. Madrid: Gredos, 1974.

Cascardi, Anthony J. *The Bounds of Reason: Cervantes, Dostoevsky, Flaubert.* New York: Columbia UP, 1986.

Castro, Américo. "La ejemplaridad de las novelas cervantinas." *Hacia Cervantes*. Madrid: Taurus, 1967. 451-74.

Chauchadis, Claude. "Los caballeros pícaros: contexto e intertexto en *La ilustre fregona*." Bustos Tovar 191-97.

Checa, Jorge. "El *romance* y su sombra: hibridación genérica en *La ilustre fregona*." *Revista de Estudios Hispánicos* 25 (1991): 29-47.

Clamurro, William H. "Identity, Discourse, and Social Order in *La ilustre fregona*." *Cervantes* 7.2 (1987): 39-56.

———. *Language and Ideology in the Prose of Quevedo*. Newark DE: Juan de la Cuesta, 1991.

———. "The *Quijote*, the 'Curioso,' and the Diseases of Telling." *Revista de Estudios Hispánicos* 28 (1994): 378-93.

———. "Value and Identity in *La gitanilla*." *Journal of Hispanic Philology* 14.1 (1989): 43-60.

Cluff, David. "The Structure and Theme of *La española inglesa*: A Reconsideration." *Revista de Estudios Hispánicos* 10 (1976): 261-81.

Coles, Paul. *The Ottoman Impact on Europe*. London: Harcourt, Brace and World, 1968.

Collins, Marsha S. "Transgression and Transformation in Cervantes's *La española inglesa*." *Cervantes* 16.1 (1996): 54-73.

Colomina, Beatriz. "The Split Wall: Domestic Voyeurism." *Sexuality and Space*. Ed. Beatriz Colomina. New York: Princeton Architectural P, 1992. 73-128.

Corral, Helia M. "La mujer en las *Novelas ejemplares* de Miguel de Cervantes Saavedra." Criado de Val, *Cervantes* 397-408.

Covarrubias Orozco, Sebastián de. *Tesoro de la Lengua Castellana o Española* [1611] Edición facsímil. Madrid and Mexico: Ediciones Turner, 1984.

Criado de Val, Manuel, ed. *Cervantes: su obra y su mundo. Actas del I Congreso Internacional sobre Cervantes*. Madrid: EDI-6, 1981.

———. *La picaresca: Orígenes, textos y estructuras. Actas del I Congreso Internacional sobre la picaresca organizada por el Patronato "Arcipreste de Hita"*. Madrid: Fundación Universitaria Española, 1979.

Cruz, Anne J., and Mary Elizabeth Perry, eds. *Culture and Control in Counter-Reformation Spain*. Minneapolis and Oxford: U of Minnesota P, 1992.

Cruz Camara, María A. "Cervantes como analista de la conducta humana: La inseguridad ontológica del protagonista de *El licenciado Vidriera*." *Explicación de Textos Literarios* 20.1 (1991-1992): 13-23.

Davis, Nina Cox. "The Tyranny of Love in *El amante liberal*." *Cervantes* 13.2 (1993): 105-24.

Débax, Michelle. "Ser y parecer." Bustos Tovar 163-70.

Deffis de Calvo, Emilia I. "El cronotopo de la novela española de peregrinación: Miguel de Cervantes." *Anales Cervantinos* 28 (1990): 99-108.

Díaz-Migoyo, Gonzalo. "Lectura protocolaria del realismo en *Rinconete y Cortadillo*." *Josep Solà-Solé: Homage, homenaje, homenatge: Miscelánea de estudios de amigos y discípulos*. Eds. Antonio Torres-Alcalá, et al. Barcelona: Puvill Libros, 1984. II: 55-64.

Diccionario de Autoridades. Edición facsímil. 6 vols. Madrid: Editorial Gredos, 1984.

Diez Taboada, J. M. "La estructura de las *Novelas ejemplares*." *Anales Cervantinos* 17 (1979-1980): 87-106.

Djaït, Hïchem. *Europe and Islam*. Berkeley, Los Angeles, London: U of California P, 1985. [First published in French as *L'Europe et L'Islam*. Paris: Editions du Seuil, 1978.]

Donoso, José. *El obsceno pájaro de la noche*. Barcelona: Seix Barral, 1972.

Doody, Margaret Anne. *The True Story of the Novel*. New Brunswick NJ: Rutgers UP, 1996.

Dunn, Peter N. "Cervantes De/Re-Constructs the Picaresque." *Cervantes* 2.2 (1982): 109-31

———. "Las *Novelas ejemplares*." *Suma cervantina*. Eds. J. B. Avalle-Arce and E. C. Riley. London: Támesis Books, 1973. 81-118.

Durán, Manuel. "Picaresque Elements in Cervantes's Works." Maiorino 226-47.

Elliott, J. H. *Imperial Spain 1469-1716*. Harmondsworth, England: Penguin, 1963.

——. *Spain and its World, 1500-1700: Selected Essays*. New Haven and London: Yale UP, 1989.

El Saffar, Ruth S. *Beyond Fiction: The Recovery of the Feminine in the Novels of Cervantes*. Berkeley, Los Angeles: U of California P, 1984.

——. *Cervantes:* El casamiento engañoso *and* El coloquio de los perros. London: Grant and Cutler, 1976.

——. "The 'I' of the Beholder: Self and Other in Some Golden Age Texts." *Cultural Authority in Golden Age Spain*. Eds. Marina S. Brownlee and Hans Ulrich Gumbrecht. Baltimore and London: The Johns Hopkins UP, 1995. 178-205.

——. *Novel to Romance: A Study of Cervantes's* Novelas ejemplares. Baltimore and London: The Johns Hopkins UP, 1974.

——. "On *Cervantes ou les incertitudes de désir*." *MLN* 97.2 (1982): 422-27.

Empson, William. *Some Versions of Pastoral*. New York: New Directions, 1960.

Ezquerro, Milagros. "Tres por dos son seis." Bustos Tovar 171-78.

Febres, Eleodoro J. "Forma y sentido de *El amante liberal*." *Anales Cervantinos* 19 (1981): 93-103.

Fernández, James D. "The Bonds of Patrimony: Cervantes and the New World." *PMLA* 109 (1994): 969-81.

Finch, Patricia S. "Rojas' Celestina and Cervantes' Cañizares." *Cervantes* 9.1 (1989): 55-62.

Finello, Dominick. *Pastoral Themes and Forms in Cervantes's Fiction*. Louisburg, PA: Bucknell UP, 1994.

Forcione, Alban K. *Cervantes and the Humanist Vision: A Study of Four Exemplary Novels*. Princeton: Princeton UP, 1982.

——. *Cervantes and the Mystery of Lawlessness*. Princeton: Princeton UP, 1984.

——. "El desposeimiento del ser en la literatura renacentista: Cervantes, Gracián y los desafíos de *Nemo*." *NRFH* 34 (1985-1986): 654-90.

Fox, Dian. "The Critical Attitude in *Rinconete y Cortadillo*." *Cervantes* 3.2 (1983): 135-47.

Friedman, Edward H. *The Antiheroine's Voice: Narrative Discourse and Transformations of the Picaresque*. Columbia: U of Missouri P, 1987.

——. "Trials of Discourse: Narrative Space in Quevedo's *Buscón*." Maiorino 183-225.

Friedman, Ellen G. *Spanish Captives in North Africa in the Early Modern Age*. Madison: U of Wisconsin P, 1983.

Frye, Northrop. *Anatomy of Criticism*. Princeton: Princeton UP, 1957.

——. *A Natural Perspective: The Development of Shakespearean Comedy and Romance*. New York: Harcourt, Brace and World, 1965.

——. *The Secular Scripture: A Study of the Structure of Romance*. Cambridge, MA and London: Harvard UP, 1976.

——. *Spiritus Mundi: Essays on Literature, Myth, and Society*. Bloomington: Indiana UP, 1976.

Garber, Marjorie. *Vested Interests: Cross-Dressing and Cultural Anxiety*. New York: HarperPerennial, 1993.

Gerli, E. Michael. "La picaresca y *El licenciado Vidriera*: Género y contragénero en Cervantes." Criado de Val, *La picaresca*: 577-87.

——. *Refiguring Authority: Reading, Writing, and Rewriting in Cervantes*. Lexington: The UP of Kentucky, 1995.

——. "Romance and Novel: Idealism and Irony in *La Gitanilla*." *Cervantes* 6.1 (1986): 29-38.

Girard, Albert. "Les étrangers dans la vie économique de l'Espagne aux XVIe et XVIIe siècles." *Annales d'Histoire Économique et Sociale* 24 (1933): 567-78.

Gitlitz, David M. "Symmetry and Lust in Cervantes' *La fuerza de la sangre*." *Studies in Honor of Everett W. Hesse*. Eds. William C. McCrary and José A Madrigal; John E. Keller, foreword. Lincoln, NE: Society of Spanish and Spanish-America Studies, 1981. 113-22.

Glannon, Walter. "The Psychology of Knowledge in *El licenciado Vidriera*." *Revista Hispánica Moderna* 40 (1978-79): 86-96.

Gómez-Reinoso, Manuel. "El mito recurrente en *El celoso extremeño*." *Festschrift José Cid Pérez*. Eds. Alberto Gutiérrez de la Solana and

Elio Alba Buffill. New York: Senda Nueva de Ediciones, 1981. 281-87.

Güntert, Georges. "*La gitanilla* y la poética de Cervantes." *Boletín de la Real Academia Española* 52 (1972): 107-34.

Hart, Thomas R. *Cervantes' Exemplary Fictions: A Study of the* Novelas ejemplares. Lexington: UP of Kentucky, 1994.

——. "La ejemplaridad de *El amante liberal*." *NRFH* 36.1 (1988): 303-18.

——. "Versions of Pastoral in Three *Novelas ejemplares*." *BHS* 58 (1981): 283-91.

Hayes, Aden W. "Narrative 'Errors' in *Rinconete y Cortadillo*." *BHS* 58 (1981):13-20.

Hegyi, Ottmar. *Cervantes and the Turks: Historical Reality versus Literary Fiction in* La Gran Sultana *and* El amante liberal. Newark, DE: Juan de la Cuesta, 1992.

Heiple, Daniel L. "Cervantes' Wise Fool: A Study of Wisdom and Fortune in *El licenciado Vidriera*." Diss. U of Texas at Austin, 1977.

——. "*El licenciado Vidriera* y el humor tradicional del loco." *Hispania* 66 (1983): 17-20.

Hermenegildo, Alfonso. "La marginación social de *Rinconete y Cortadillo*." Criado de Val, *La picaresca* 553-62.

Herrero, Javier. "Emerging Realism: Love and Cash in *La ilustre fregona*." Bell-Villada 47-59.

Hilty, Gerold. "Zur Struktur der *Novelas ejemplares* von Cervantes." *Typologia Litterarum: Festschrift für Max Wehrli*. Eds. Stefan Sonderegger, Alois M. Haas, Harald Burger. Zürich: Atlantis, 1969. 367-86.

Huerga, Alvaro. "El proceso inquisitorial contra *La Camacha*." Criado de Val, *Cervantes* 453-62.

Hutchinson, Steven. "Las brujas de Cervantes y la noción de la comunidad femenina." *Cervantes* 12.2 (1992): 127-36.

——. *Cervantine Journeys*. Madison: U of Wisconsin P, 1992.

——. "Counterfeit Chains of Discourse: A comparison of Citation in Cervantes' *Casamiento-Coloquio* and in Islamic *Hadith*." *Cervantes* 8.2 (1988): 141-58.

Inalcik, Halil. *The Ottoman Empire: The Classical Age 1300-1600*. Trans. Norman Itzkowitz and Colin Imber. New York and Washington: Praeger, 1973.

Iser, Wolfgang. *The Act of Reading: A Theory of Aesthetic Response*. Baltimore and London: The Johns Hopkins UP, 1978.

Jennings, Ronald C. *Christians and Muslims in Ottoman Cyprus and the Mediterranean World, 1571-1640*. New York and London: New York UP, 1993.

Johnson, Carroll B. "Catolicismo, familia y fecundidad: el caso de *La española inglesa*." *Actas del IX Congreso de la Asociación Internacional de Hispanistas*. Ed. Sebastian Neumeister. Frankfurt: Vervuert, 1989. I: 519-24.

——. "Defining the Picaresque: Authority and the Subject in *Guzmán de Alfarache*." Maiorino 159-82.

——. "*La española inglesa* and the Practice of Literary Production." *Viator* 19 (1988): 377-416.

——. "Of Witches and Bitches: Gender, Marginality and Discourse in *El casamiento engañoso y Coloquio de los perros*." *Cervantes* 11.2 (1991): 7-25.

——. "The Old Order Passeth, of Does it? Some Thoughts on Community, Commerce, and Alienation in *Rinconete y Cortadillo*." Parr, *On Cervantes* 85-104.

Johnston, R. M. "Picaresque and Pastoral in *La ilustre fregona*." *Cervantes and the Renaissance*. Ed. M. D. McGaha. Easton, PA: Juan de la Cuesta, 1980. 167-77.

Joly, Monique. "En torno a las antologías poéticas de *La gitanilla* y *La ilustre fregona*." *Cervantes* 13.2 (1993): 5-15.

——. "Para una reinterpretación de *La ilustre fregona*: Ensayo de tipología cervantina." *Aurem Saeculum Hispanum: Beiträge zu Texten des Siglo de Oro*. Eds. K. H. Körner and D. Briesemeister. Weisbaden: Steiner, 1983. 103-16.

Jones, Joseph R. "Cervantes y la virtud de la *eutrapelia*: la moralidad de la literatura de esparcimiento." *Anales Cervantinos* 23 (1985): 19-30.

Joset, Jacques. "Bipolarizaciones textuales y estructura especular en *El licenciado Vidriera*." Criado de Val, *Cervantes* 357-63.

Kagan, Richard L. *Students and Society in Early Modern Spain.* Baltimore and London: The Johns Hopkins UP, 1974.

Kamen, Henry. *La inquisición española.* Trans. Gabriela Zayas. Barcelona: Editorial Crítica, 1985.

——. *Spain 1469-1714: A Society of Conflict.* London & New York: Longman, 1983.

Kedar, Benjamin Z. *Crusade and Mission: European Approaches toward the Muslims.* Princeton: Princeton UP, 1984.

Keightley, Ronald G. "The Narrative Structure of *Rinconete y Cortadillo*." *Essays on Narrative Fiction in the Iberian Peninsula in Honour of Frank Pierce.* Ed. R. B. Tate. Oxford: The Dolphin Book Co., 1982. 39-54.

Lacadena y Calero, Esther. "*La señora Cornelia* y su técnica narrativa." *Anales Cervantinos* 15 (1976): 199-210.

Laffranque, Marie. "Encuentro y coexistencia de dos sociedades en el Siglo de Oro: *La gitanilla* de Miguel de Cervantes." *Actas del Quinto Congreso Internacional de Hispanistas* (1974). Eds. Maxime Chevalier, Francois López, Joseph Pérez, & Noël Salomon. Bordeaux: PU de Bordeaux, 1977. 549-61.

Lane-Poole, Stanley. *The Story of the Barbary Corsairs.* New York: G. P. Putnam's Sons and London: T. Fisher Unwin, 1890.

Lerner, Isaías. "Aspectos de la representación en *El amante liberal*." *Filología* 22 (1987): 37-48.

——. "Marginalidad en las Novelas ejemplares, I. *La gitanilla*." *Lexis* 4.1 (1980): 47-59.

Lewis-Smith, Paul. "The Two Versions of *El celoso extremeño*: On the Questions of Authorship and Intent." *Neophilologus* 76 (1992): 559-68.

Lipmann, Stephen H. "Revision and Exemplarity in Cervantes' *El celoso extremeño*." *Cervantes* 6.2 (1986): 113-21.

Lipson, Lesley. "'La palabra hecha nada': Mendacious Discourse in *La gitanilla*." *Cervantes* 9.1 (1989): 35-53.

Loomie, Albert J. *The Spanish Elizabethans: The English Exiles at the Court of Philip II*. New York: Fordham UP, 1963.

Lowe, Jennifer. *Cervantes: Two* Novelas Ejemplares: La gitanilla *and* La ilustre fregona. London: Grant and Cutler, 1971.

Maestro, Abraham Martín. "Conjunciones y disyunciones en *La ilustre fregona*." Bustos Tovar 69-79.

Maiorino, Giancarlo, ed. *The Picaresque: Tradition and Displacement*. Minneapolis and London: U of Minnesota P, 1996.

Mancini, Guido. "La 'morale' della 'Española inglesa'." *Aspetti e problemi delle letterature iberiche: Studi offerti a Franco Meregalli*. Ed. Giuseppe Bellini. Rome: Bulzoni, 1981. 219-36.

Maravall, José Antonio. *La cultura del Barroco*. Barcelona: Ariel, 1980. (3rd ed.)

——. *Poder, honor y élites en el siglo XVII*. Madrid: Siglo XXI, 1979.

Marcos, Balbino. "Un exponente ideal de exaltación femenina: *La gitanilla*." *Letras de Deusto* 15.33 (1985): 95-111.

Mariscal, George. *Contradictory Subjects: Quevedo, Cervantes and Seventeenth-Century Spanish Culture*. Ithaca and London: Cornell UP, 1991.

Mas, Albert. *Les Turcs dans la littérature espagnole du siècle d'or*. Paris: Centre de Recherches Hispaniques, 1967.

Mazzucco, Cecile. "The Doorways to the Maelstrom of Discourse in Cervantes's *El casamiento engañoso* and *El coloquio de los perros*." *Romance Languages Annual* 4 (1992): 516-20.

Molho, Maurice. "Antroponimia y cinonimia del *Casamiento engañoso* y *Coloquio de los perros*." Bustos Tovar 81-92.

——. "Aproximación al *Celoso extremeño*." *NRFH* 38 (1990): 743-92.

——. Remarques. *El casamiento engañoso y coloquio de los perros*. By Miguel de Cervantes. Ed. and trans. M. Molho. Paris: Aubier-Flammarion, 1970. 11-88.

Mota, Giselda. "A Sociedade espanhola, vista através de *La gitanilla* (1613)." *Revista de História* 95 (1973): 217-22.

Munguía García, Víctor Eduardo. *"El licenciado Vidriera* y don Quijote." *Anales Cervantinos* 30 (1992): 157-62.

Murillo, L. A. "Cervantes' *Coloquio de los perros*, A Novel-Dialogue." *Modern Philology* 58 (1961): 174-85.

——. "Narrative Structures in the *Novelas ejemplares*: An Outline." *Cervantes* 8.2 (1988): 231-53.

Nerlich, Michael, and Nicholas Spadaccini, eds. *Cervantes's 'Exemplary Novels' and the Adventure of Writing.* Minneapolis: The Prisma Institute, 1989.

Nimetz, Michael. "Genre and Creativity in *Rinconete y Cortadillo.*" *Cervantes* 10.2 (1990): 73-93.

Oliver, Antonio. "La filosofía cínica y el *Coloquio de los perros.*" *Anales Cervantinos* 3 (1953): 291-307.

Olsen, Michel. "Structures narratives et vision du monde dans les *Novelas exemplares* de Cervantes." *(Pré)Publications* 2 (1973): 3-20.

Pabón, Thomas. "Viajes de peregrinas: La búsqueda de la perfección en *El amante liberal.*" Criado de Val, *Cervantes* 371-75.

Pabst, Walter. *La novela corta en la teoría y en la creación literaria.* Trans. Rafael de la Vega. Madrid: Gredos, 1972.

Paglia, Camille. *Sexual Personae: Art and Decadence from Nefertiti to Emily Dickinson.* New Haven and London: Yale UP, 1990.

Parker Aronson, Stacey L. "La 'textualización' de Leocadia y su defensa en *La fuerza de la sangre.*" *Cervantes* 16.2 (1996): 71-88.

Parodi, Alicia. *"La española inglesa* de Miguel de Cervantes y la poética de las adversidades provechosas." *Filología* 22 (1987): 49-64.

Parr, James A., ed. *On Cervantes: Essays for L. A. Murillo.* Newark DE: Juan de la Cuesta, 1991.

Paulino, José. "El espacio narrativo en *La ilustre fregona.*" Bustos Tovar 93-108.

Paz, Octavio. *La llama doble: Amor y erotismo.* Mexico: Seix Barral, 1994.

Percas de Ponseti, Helena. "El 'misterio escondido' en *El Celoso Extremeño.*" *Cervantes* 14.2 (1994): 137-53.

Perry, Mary Elizabeth, and Anne J. Cruz, eds. *Cultural Encounters: The Impact of the Inquisition in Spain and the New World.* Berkeley, Los Angeles, Oxford: U of California P, 1991.

Phillips, Adam. *On Kissing, Tickling, and Being Bored: Psychoanalytic Essays on the Unexamined Life.* Cambridge, MA: Harvard UP, 1993.

Pierce, Frank. "Reality and Realism in the *Exemplary Novels.*" *BHS* 30 (1953): 134-42.

Pozuelo Yvancos, José María. "Enunciación y recepción en el *Casamiento-Coloquio.*" Criado de Val, *Cervantes* 423-35.

Price, R. M. "Cervantes and the Topic of the 'lost child found' in the *Novelas ejemplares.*" *Anales Cervantinos* 27 (1989): 203-14.

Quevedo, Francisco de. *Epistolario.* Mexico: Consejo Nacional para la Cultura y las Artes, 1989.

———. *Sueños y discursos.* Ed. James O. Crosby. Madrid: Editorial Castalia, 1993.

———. *La vida del Buscón llamado don Pablos.* Ed. Fernando Lázaro Carreter. Salamanca: C.S.I.C., 1965.

Ramond, Michèle. "'Yo soy la ilustre fregona' o la simbolización de un delirio." Bustos Tovar 179-90.

Redondo, Alicia, and Carlos Sáinz de la Maza. "*La ilustre fregona*: cuatro cuartos y una cola." Bustos Tovar 109-18.

Redondo, Augustin. "La folie du cervantin licencié de Verre (traditions, contexte historique et subversion)." *Visages de la folie (1500-1650).* Eds. Augustin Redondo and André Rochon. Paris: Publications de la Sorbonne, 1981. 33-44.

Reed, Helen H. "Américo Castro, Cervantes, y la picaresca: Breve historia de unas ideas." *Américo Castro: The Impact of His Thought.* Eds. Ronald E. Surtz, et al. Madison: Hispanic Seminary of Medieval Studies, 1988. 223-30.

———. "Theatricality in the Picaresque of Cervantes." *Cervantes* 7.2 (1987): 71-84.

Resina, Joan Ramon. "Cervantes's Confidence Games and the Refashioning of Totality." *MLN* 111.2 (1996): 218-53.

Ricapito, Joseph V. "Cervantes and the Italian *Novellistica*." *NEMLA Italian Studies, Selected Proceedings: Italian Section*, 18 (1994): 31-43.

——. *Cervantes's* Novelas Ejemplares: *Between History and Creativity*. West Lafayette, IN: Purdue UP, 1996.

Rodríguez-Luis, Julio. *Novedad y ejemplo de las Novelas de Cervantes*. 2 vols. Madrid: José Porrúa Turanzas, 1980.

Ruiz, Roberto. "Las 'tres locuras' del licenciado Vidriera." *NRFH* 43 (1985-86): 839-47.

Ruta, Maria Caterina. "*La española inglesa*: El desdoblamiento del héroe." *Anales Cervantinos* 25-26 (1987-1988): 371-82.

Sampayo Rodríguez, José Ramón. *Rasgos erasmistas de la locura del licenciado Vidriera de Miguel de Cervantes*. Kassel: Reichenberger, 1986.

Sánchez, Francisco J. *Lectura y representación: Análisis cultural de las* Novelas ejemplares *de Cervantes*. New York: Peter Lang, 1993.

Sánchez-Castañer, Francisco. "Un problema de estética novelística como comentario a *La española inglesa* de Cervantes." *Estudios dedicados a Menéndez Pidal*. Madrid: C.S.I.C., 1957. Tomo VII, vol. 1. 257-386.

Schleiner, Winfried. "The Glass Graduate and the Aphrodisiac That Went Wrong: New Light from Old Texts." *Forum for Modern Language Studies* 27 (1991): 370-81.

——. "Renaissance Exempla of Schizophrenia: The Cure by Charity in Luther and Cervantes." *Renaissance and Reformation* 9.3 (1985): 157-76.

Schmauser, Caroline. "Dynamism and Spatial Structure in *Las dos doncellas*." Nerlich, *Cervantes's 'Exemplary Novels' and the Adventure of Writing* 175-203.

Schwoebel, Robert. *The Shadow of the Crescent: The Renaissance Image of the Turk (1453-1517)*. New York: St. Martin's Press, 1967.

Sears, Theresa Anne. *A Marriage of Convenience: Ideal and Ideology in the* Novelas ejemplares. New York: Peter Lang, 1993.

Selig, Karl-Ludwig. "Cervantes' *Rinconete y Cortadillo* and the Two 'Libros de memoria'." *Revista Hispánica Moderna* 40.3-4 (1978-1979): 126-27.

——. "The Metamorphosis of the *Ilustre fregona.*" *Filología y crítica hispánica: Homenaje al Prof. Federico Sánchez Escribano.* Eds. Alberto Porqueras Mayo and Carlos Rojas. Madrid: Ediciones Alcalá and Atlanta: Emory UP, 1969. 115-20.

——. "Some Observations on Cervantes' *El amante liberal.*" *Revista Hispánica Moderna* 40.1-2 (1978-1979): 67-71.

Setton, Kenneth M. *Western Hostility to Islam and Prophecies of Turkish Doom.* Philadelphia: American Philosophical Society, 1992.

Sicroff, Albert A. *Les Controverses des Statuts de «Pureté de Sang» en Espagne du XVe au XVIIe Siècle.* Paris: Didier, 1960.

Sieber, Harry. Introducción. *Novelas ejemplares.* By Miguel de Cervantes. Madrid: Cátedra, 1989. I: 13-32.

Slaniceanu, Adriana. "The Calculating Woman in Cervantes' *La fuerza de la sangre.*" *BHS* 64 (1987): 101-10.

Smith, Paul Julian. *Writing in the Margin: Spanish Literature of the Golden Age.* Oxford: Oxford UP, 1988.

Soons, Alan. "Three *Novelas ejemplares* of Cervantes. Diptych Pattern and Spiritual Intention." *Orbis Litterarum* 26 (1971): 87-93.

Southern, R. W. *Western Views of Islam in the Middle Ages.* Cambridge, MA and London: Harvard UP, 1962.

Spadaccini, Nicholas, and Jenaro Talens. *Through the Shattering Glass: Cervantes and the Self-Made World.* Minneapolis and London: U of Minnesota P, 1993.

Speak, Gill. "*El licenciado Vidriera* and the Glass Men of Early Modern Europe." *MLR* 85 (1990): 850-65.

Spieker, Joseph B. "Preciosa y poesía (Sobre el concepto cervantino de la Poesía y la estructura de *La gitanilla*)." *Explicación de Textos Literarios* 4.2 (1975): 213-20.

Spitzer, Leo. "Das Gefüge einer cervantinischen Novelle: *El celoso estremeño.*" *Die Romanische Novelle.* Ed. Wolfgang Eitel. Darmstadt: Wissenschaftliche Buchgesellschaft, 1977. 175-213.

Stagg, Geoffrey. "The Composition and Revision of *La española inglesa.*" *Studies in Honor of Bruce W. Wardropper.* Eds. Dian Fox, Harry Sieber, and Robert ter Horst. Newark, DE: Juan de la Cuesta, 1989. 305-21.

Stallybrass, Peter, and Allon White. *The Politics and Poetics of Transgression*. Ithaca: Cornell UP, 1986.

Starkie, Walter. "Cervantes and the Gypsies." *The Huntington Library Quarterly* 26 (1963): 337-49.

Stern, Charlotte. "*El celoso extremeño*: Entre farsa y tragedia." *Estudios sobre el Siglo de Oro en homenaje a Raymond R. MacCurdy*. Eds. Angel González, et al. Albuquerque: U of New Mexico P, 1983; Madrid: Cátedra, 1983. 333-42.

Stern, Karl. *The Flight from Woman*. New York: Farrar, Straus and Giroux, 1965.

Sullivan, Henry W. *Grotesque Purgatory: A Study of Cervantes's Don Quixote, Part II*. University Park: The Pennsylvania State UP, 1996.

ter Horst, Robert. "Une Saison en enfer: *La gitanilla*." *Cervantes* 5.2 (1985): 87-127.

——. "The Sexual Economy of Miguel de Cervantes." *Bodies and Biases: Sexualities in Hispanic Cultures and Literatures*. Eds. David William Foster and Roberto Reis. Minneapolis and London: U of Minnesota P, 1996. 1-23.

Thompson, Jennifer, "The Structure of Cervantes' *Las dos doncellas*." *BHS* 40 (1963): 144-50.

Toro-Garland, Fernando de. "Aproximación a lo sexual en las *Novelas ejemplares*." Criado de Val, *Cervantes* 365-70.

Urbina, Eduardo. "Incesto en *El celoso extremeño* de Cervantes y en *L'école de femmes* de Molière." *Homenaje al Profesor Antonio Vilanova*. Ed. Marta Cristina Carbonell. 2 vols. Barcelona: U. de Barcelona, 1989. 2:709-21.

Vilar Berrogain, Jean. *Literatura y economía: La figura satírica del arbitrista en el Siglo de Oro*. Trans. Francisco Bustelo G. del Real. Madrid: Revista de Occidente, 1973.

Waley, Pamela. "The Unity of the *Casamiento engañoso* and the *Coloquio de los perros*." *BHS* 34 (1957): 201-12.

Wardropper, Bruce W. "La eutropelia en las *Novelas ejemplares* de Cervantes." *Actas del Séptimo Congreso de la Asociación Inter-*

nacional de Hispanistas celebrado en Venecia del 25 al 30 de agosto de 1980. 2 vols. Rome: Bulzoni, 1982. 1:153-69.

Weber, Alison. *"La ilustre fregona* and the Barriers of Caste." *Papers on Language and Literature* 15 (1979): 73-81.

———. "Pentimento: The Parodic Text of 'La gitanilla'." *Hispanic Review* 62.1 (1994): 59-75.

———. "Tragic Reparation in Cervantes' *El celoso extremeño.*" *Cervantes* 4.1 (1984): 35-51.

Weiger, John G. "A Clue to Cervantine Ambiguity: *Darse a entender.*" *Hispanic Journal* 3.2 (1982): 83-89.

Welles, Marcia L. "Violence Disguised: Representation of Rape in Cervantes' *La fuerza de la sangre.*" *Journal of Hispanic Philology* 13.3 (1989): 240-52.

Williamson, Edwin. "Introduction: The Question of Influence." *Cervantes and the Modernists: The Question of Influence.* Ed. Edwin Williamson. London and Madrid: Tamesis, 1994. 1-8.

———. "El 'misterio escondido' en *El celoso extremeño*: una aproximación al arte de Cervantes." *NRFH* 38 (1990): 793-815.

Wilson, Diana de Armas. *Allegories of Love: Cervantes's* Persiles and Sigismunda. Princeton: Princeton UP, 1991.

———. "Contesting the Custom of the Country: Cervantes and Fletcher." *Bell-Villada* 60-75.

Woodward, L. J. *"El casamiento engañoso y el coloquio de los perros."* *BHS* 36 (1959): 80-87.

———. *"La gitanilla."* Criado de Val, *Cervantes* 445-51.

Zimic, Stanislav. "El *Amadís* cervantino (apuntes sobre *La española inglesa*)." *Anales Cervantinos* 25-26 (1987-1988): 467-83.

———. "Demonios y mártires en *La fuerza de la sangre* de Cervantes." *Acta Neophilologica* (Ljubljana, Slovenia) 23 (1990): 7-26.

———. *"La señora Cornelia*, una excursión a la *novela* italiana." *Boletín de la Real Academia Española* 71 (1991): 101-20.

Index

STUDIES ON CERVANTES AND HIS TIMES

Eduardo Urbina, *General Editor*

As the creator of Don Quixote and the author of what is widely recognized as the first modern novel, Cervantes occupies a key place in the history of Hispanic and world literature. This series publishes manuscripts that make a significant contribution to the understanding of Cervantes' works and times. It is open to a variety of perspectives and critical methods that are linguistic, historical, bibliographical, and literary. We welcome monographic studies of individual works, studies analyzing Don Quixote from new perspectives or essaying new approaches, as well as comparative studies evaluating Cervantes' impact on other writers and national literatures.

For additional information about this series or for the submission of manuscripts, please contact:

Peter Lang Publishing, Inc.
Acquisitions Department
275 Seventh Avenue, 28th floor
New York, New York 10001